Infant Play Therapy

Infant Play Therapy is a groundbreaking resource for practitioners interested in the varied play therapy theories, models, and programs available for the unique developmental needs of infants and children under the age of three.

The impressive list of expert contributors in the fields of play therapy and infant mental health cover a wide range of early intervention play-based models and topics. Chapters explore areas including: neurobiology, developmental trauma, parent–infant attachment relationships, neurosensory play, affective touch, grief and loss, perinatal depression, adoption, autism, domestic violence, opioid crisis, sociocultural factors, and more. Chapter case studies highlight leading approaches and offer techniques to provide a comprehensive understanding of both play therapy and the ways we understand and recognize the therapeutic role of play with infants.

In these pages professionals and students alike will find valuable clinical resources to bring healing to family systems with young children.

Janet A. Courtney is founder of FirstPlay Therapy® and editor of *Touch in Child Counseling and Play Therapy: An Ethical and Clinical Guide*, and author of *Healing Child and Family Trauma through Expressive and Play Therapies: Art, Nature, Storytelling, Body & Mindfulness*. She is an internationally recognized author and trainer specializing in infant mental health, developmental trauma, therapeutic storytelling and expressive, nature and somatic play therapies.

"This fascinating and useful text expands the focus of play therapy to include children from birth to age three. It will help mental health practitioners expand their knowledge about how play influences the developing brain and about how to enhance the reciprocal parent-infant relationship. An important contribution to the growing field of infant mental health."

Nancy Boyd Webb, DSW, LICSW, RPT-S, university distinguished professor of social work emerita, Fordham University; author/editor, supervisor, speaker, consultant.

"The field of play therapy, and indeed, the entire field of infant and child psychotherapy have long been waiting for a book of this magnitude to come along! Dr. Courtney and her colleagues have weaved a coherent and comprehensive book detailing theory, practice, and the importance of play-based, attachment-informed interventions. This book truly is a gem and will inform readers for generations to come."

Clair Mellenthin, LCSW, RPT-S, director of child and adolescent services, Wasatch Family Therapy, Salt Lake City, UT and author of Attachment Centered Play Therapy.

"At a time when play is being understood for developmental mental health in all children, Janet Courtney has gathered together experts in several fields and captured the essence of play for infants, and how to incorporate play therapy into their lives as well. This is a book that should be on the shelves of all clinicians who see children of all ages."

Heidi Gerard Kaduson, Ph.D., RPT-S, director, The Play Therapy Training Institute, Inc.

Infant Play Therapy

Foundations, Models, Programs, and Practice

Edited by
Janet A. Courtney

Routledge
Taylor & Francis Group

NEW YORK AND LONDON

First published 2020
by Routledge
52 Vanderbilt Avenue, New York, NY 10017

and by Routledge
2 Park Square, Milton Park, Abingdon, Oxon OX14 4RN

Routledge is an imprint of the Taylor & Francis Group, an informa business

Library of Congress Cataloging-in-Publication Data
Names: Courtney, Janet A., editor.
Title: Infant play therapy : foundations, models, programs, and practice / edited by Janet A. Courtney.
Description: New York, NY : Routledge, 2020. |
Includes bibliographical references and index. |
Identifiers: LCCN 2019050737 (print) |
LCCN 2019050738 (ebook) |
Subjects: LCSH: Play therapy. | Child psychotherapy. |
Games--Therapeutic use.
Classification: LCC RJ505.P6 I54 2020 (print) |
LCC RJ505.P6 (ebook) |
DDC 618.92/891653--dc23
LC record available at https://lccn.loc.gov/2019050737
LC ebook record available at https://lccn.loc.gov/2019050738

ISBN: 978-1-138-61329-4 (hbk)
ISBN: 978-1-138-61330-0 (pbk)
ISBN: 978-0-429-45308-3 (ebk)

Typeset in Sabon
by Taylor & Francis Books

To my precious grandchildren, Sophia, Abigail, Jacob, and Ezra. For the playful and warmhearted hugs and love we share, and who make my heart melt at just the word, *Mimi*.

Contents

List of illustrations	x
Acknowledgments	xii
About the Editor	xiii
List of contributors	xiv
Foreword	xvii
Preface	xx

PART I
Foundations   I

1   Conceptualizing Infant Play Therapy in the Context of Infant
Mental Health   3
JANET A. COURTNEY

2   The Impact of Play on the Developing Social Brain: New
Insights from the Neurobiology of Touch   18
EMILY JACKSON AND FRANCIS MCGLONE

3   Neurosensory Play in the Infant–Parent Dyad: A Developmental
Perspective   37
KEN SCHWARTZENBERGER

PART II
Assessment with Young Children   51

4   Play Ability: Observing, Engaging, and Sequencing Play Skills
for Very Young Children   53
JUDI PARSON, KAREN STAGNITTI, BRIDGET DOOLEY AND KATE RENSHAW

5   Trauma-Informed Infant Mental Health Assessment   67
EVA NOWAKOWSKI-SIMS AND DANNA POWERS

PART III
**New and Adapted Theoretical Approaches and Models
to Infant Play Therapy**   81

6   FirstPlay® Therapy Strengthens the Attachment Relationship
    Between a Mother with Perinatal Depression and Her Infant   83
    KAREN BALDWIN, MEYLEEN VELASQUEZ AND JANET A. COURTNEY

7   Infant Filial Therapy – From Conception to Early Years:
    Clinical Considerations for Working with Whole Family
    Systems   101
    KATE RENSHAW AND JUDI PARSON

8   Intervening with Theraplay with a 13-Month-Old Diagnosed
    with Medical Complications   117
    HANNA LAMPI

PART IV
**Programmatic Infant Play and Play-Based Interventions
with Infant and Toddler Populations**   127

9   Baby Doll Circle Time: Strengthening Attunement, Attachment
    and Social Play   129
    BECKY A. BAILEY

10 DIR®/Floortime™: A Developmental/Relational Play Therapy
    Model in the Treatment of Infants and Toddlers Exhibiting the
    Early Signs of Autism Spectrum Disorder   141
    ESTHER HESS

11 Reflections of Love in the TEACUP Preemie Program®:
    Strengthening the Attachment Relationship through FirstPlay®
    Infant Story-Massage   157
    CHELSEA C. JOHNSON

PART V
**Evidence-Based Infant Mental Health Models that
Utilize Play Therapy Practices**   169

12 Using the Healing Power of Relationships to Support Change in
    Young Children Exposed to Trauma: Application of the Child–
    Parent Psychotherapy Model   171
    HARLEEN HUTCHINSON

13 Incorporating Play into Child–Parent Psychotherapy as an
Intervention with Infants Exposed to Domestic Violence 185
ALLISON GOLDEN AND VERONICA CASTRO

14 Trust-Based Relational Intervention with a Two-Year-Old: An
Adoption Case 198
MONTSERRAT CASADO-KEHOE, CASEY CALL, DAVID CROSS AND
HENRY MILTON

PART VI
**Applications to Specific Populations in Infant Play
Therapy** 213

15 Children Born Opioid-Addicted: Symptoms, Attachment and
Play Treatment 215
ATHENA A. DREWES

16 Hope After the Storm: Addressing the Impact of Perinatal grief
on Attachment with Rainbow Babies Through an Embodied
Grief Process 230
RENEE TURNER AND CHRISTINA VILLARREAL-DAVIS

17 Healing Reactive Attachment Disorder with Young Children
Through FirstPlay® Kinesthetic Storytelling 245
JANET A. COURTNEY, VIKTORIA BAKAI TOTH AND CARMEN JIMENEZ-PRIDE

Index 255

Illustrations

Figures

1.1	Infant mental health organizational framework	7
1.2	Joyful mother and baby playing together	8
2.1	Dendritic morphology of pyramidal neurons in somatosensory cortex in rat housed in (left) standard and (right) enriched environments. The enrichment significantly increases dendritic branching as well as the number of dendritic spines (cf. Johansson & Belichenko, 2001)	19
2.2	Brains at play: What do we know	20
2.3	Three perspectives on play seen from the child, the father and the mother	23
2.4	Levels of early life touch experience determine the adult's ability to cope with stress	26
6.1	FirstPlay® supporting theories and literature	84
6.2	Stephanie Crowley connects through the Rainbow Hug "calm and relax" imagery and then asks "permission" from five-month-old Ezra to begin telling the FirstPlay® "Baby Tree Hug" story-massage	89
6.3	Demonstration illustration from the *FirstPlay Parent Manual*	95
7.1	Humanistic play therapy skills	106
7.2	Sequence of filial therapy	108
11.1	Baby Serenyty was born 23 weeks into her mother's pregnancy, weighing barely a pound	158
12.1	Introducing Ariel to Child–Parent Psychotherapy	175
12.2	Keeping the baby's emotional well-being in mind	177
17.1	Facilitating a FirstPlay® Kinesthetic Storytelling session: Mother, Stephanie Crowley is getting ready to tell a "BACK Story" to three-year-old Sophia	247

Tables

4.1	Pretend play enjoyment – developmental checklist: Assessing play skills and descriptors	55
4.2	Program skills with descriptions	57
4.3	Extension program skills with descriptions	57
4.4	Pretend play enjoyment – developmental checklist (pre-intervention)	61
4.5	Pretend play enjoyment – developmental checklist (post-intervention)	63
7.1	Planning with parents	111
7.2	Toy considerations and playful interaction ideas	112
7.3	Integrating skills into family life	113
8.1	Theraplay dimensions	118
8.2	Suggested structure for Theraplay process	120
8.3	Plan for the second Theraplay session	122

Acknowledgments

This book is dedicated, in part, to the late Viola Brody, PhD, author of *The Dialogue of Touch*, who understood the importance of caring touch and first-play experiences to life-long healthy attachments. I am especially thankful to Dr. Susan W. Gray, my former Barry University Dissertation Chair, and Dr. Nancy Boyd Webb, a valuable member of my dissertation committee who are both inspiring role models to me. I am greatly appreciative to Dr. Phyllis Scott, Dean of the School of Work at Barry University, and to *all* the Barry faculty who share my commitment to improving the lives of children. I am thankful to Kathy Lebby, CEO of The Association for Play Therapy, who invited me to Chair the APT Practice and Ethics committee of which it was an honor to serve. And a heart full of gratitude to Drs Joyce Mills and Eliana Gil, who are role models to me, for all their support and encouragement.

To my dear loving husband, Bob Nolan, my best friend, for reminding me of the importance of balance in my life. Much love to my mother—a natural born play therapist, my brother, Allen and sister, Carol, my sons, Jesse and Austin, and daughter-in-law, Stephanie—for their love and support and being my cheerleaders through this process. My deepest heartfelt gratitude to Prem Rawat, founder of the Prem Rawat Foundation, for his vital humanitarian and peace education efforts throughout the world.

I want to thank Anna Moore at Routledge who immediately recognized the importance of this book. To my colleagues and dear friends, too many to mention, I give a heartfelt hug for your support and heartening words. My deep gratitude goes to all the authors of this book who shared their expertise so generously and to which my heart leaped with joy and excitement every time a new gift of a chapter landed in my inbox. Finally, I am indebted to all the courageous families and children (and the wee ones too!) I have had the honor to work with and help.

About the Editor

Janet A. Courtney, PhD, LCSW, RPT-S, is Founder of FirstPlay® Therapy and helped organize the APT Play Therapy Center at Barry University School of Social Work, Miami Shores, FL. She is a TEDx Speaker and former Chair of the Association for Play Therapy Practice and Ethics Committee from 2017 to 2019, and is past President of the Florida Association for Play Therapy. She is co-editor of the ground-breaking book, *Touch in Child Counseling and Play Therapy: An Ethical and Clinical Guide*, and author of *Healing Child and Family Trauma through Expressive and Play Therapies: Art, Nature, Storytelling, Body, and Mindfulness*.

Dr. Courtney's research into practitioner experiences of training in touch and Developmental Play Therapy is published in the *American Journal of Art Therapy* and the *International Journal of Play Therapy*, and she is a contributing author for the chapter "Touching Autism through Developmental Play Therapy" in the book *Play-based Interventions for Children and Adolescents with Autism Spectrum Disorders*. She offers a certification in FirstPlay® Therapy (including FirstPlay® Infant Storytelling-Massage) and provides training to professionals in the Ethical and Clinical Competencies of Touch, StoryPlay®, Expressive Therapies, and Nature-based Play Therapy. She has been invited to speak nationally and internationally, including in Bali, the Cayman Islands, England, Ireland, Morocco, Russia, and Ukraine. She is a provider through the Florida state boards of Mental Health and Massage Therapy, and an approved provider through the Association for Play Therapy. She specializes in Infant Play Therapy/Infant Mental Health, Attachment, and Trauma related issues. Dr. Courtney's new form of Kinesthetic Storytelling® can be found in her children's book, *The Magic Rainbow*. Website: www.FirstPlayTherapy.com

Contributors

Becky A. Bailey, PhD, is an award-winning author and internationally recognized expert in childhood education and developmental psychology. She is the creator of Conscious Discipline®, which has impacted an estimated 15.8 million children and has over 1.2 million of her top-selling books in circulation.

Viktoria Bakai Toth, LMHC, RPT, is a Licensed Mental Health Counselor, a Registered Play Therapist, a Certified FirstPlay® Supervisor and owner of From Seedling To Blossom LLC, a private psychotherapy practice in Venice, Florida.

Karen Baldwin, DSW, LCSW, RPT-S, received her doctorate from Florida Atlantic University School of Social Work in Boca Raton, Florida, where she conducted research in FirstPlay® Therapy with teenage mothers and their infants residing in shelter.

Casey Call, PhD, is the Assistant Director at the Karyn Purvis Institute of Child Development (KP ICD). She serves at the Purvis Institute including research, training, and outreach connected to Trust-Based Relational Intervention® (TBRI®).

Montserrat Casado-Kehoe, PhD, is a licensed marriage and family therapist (LMFT), registered play therapist (RPT), TBRI-trained and a TBRI Educator. She was an associate professor at Palm Beach Atlantic University and the University of Central Florida.

Veronica Castro, PsyD, is a clinical supervisor at the Institute for Child and Family Health, Miami, Florida and her PsyD in Clinical Psychology is from NOVA Southeastern University, Florida.

David Cross, PhD, is the Rees-Jones Director of the Karyn Purvis Institute of Child Development and a Professor in the TCU Department of Psychology.

Bridget Dooley, MCPT, BOccThy (Hons), APPTA RPT, is a Play Therapist, Pediatric Occupational Therapist and academic at Deakin University. She is a Lecturer in Play Therapy and is responsible for providing teaching, research and supervision in Play Therapy.

Athena A. Drewes, PsyD, RPT-S, is former Board of Directors of the Association for Play Therapy, Founder and President Emeritus of the NYAPT and lives in Ocala, Florida.

Allison Golden, PsyD, is a FL & NY Psychologist and Supervisor and is EAGALA Certified. She specializes in infant mental health and early childhood trauma, and is rostered in CPP. She provides training, supervision and therapy services nationwide.

Esther Hess, PhD, Executive Director, Center for the Developing Mind, is a developmental pediatric psychologist, working in the areas of Child, Adolescent & Family Therapy/Development Delays.

Edward F. Hudspeth, PhD, RPT-S, is Associate Dean of Counseling Programs at Southern New Hampshire University, Manchester, New Hampshire, and is Editor of the *International Journal of Play Therapy.*

Harleen Hutchinson, PsyD, is Director of The Journey Institute, Early Childhood Mental Health Program. Dr. Hutchinson is an adjunct professor with the Barry University School of Social Work, and Chair of the Broward Chapter of the Florida Association of Infant Mental Health.

Emily Jackson, is a MSc neuroscience student at Liverpool John Moores University with an interest in studying early affective touch experiences.

Carmen Jimenez-Pride, LCSW, RCYT, RYT, RPT-S is a Registered Play Therapist Supervisor. She is a certified FirstPlay® Infant and Kinesthetic Storytelling Therapist. She is currently in private psychotherapy practice in families in Augusta, Georgia.

Chelsea C. Johnson, MS, MT-BC, LMT, is a Board Certified Music Therapist and coordinates the TEACUP Preemie Program® at The Children's Healing Institute in West Palm Beach, Florida.

Hanna Lampi is an Occupational Therapist, Certified Theraplay Therapist-Supervisor/Trainer, Family therapist. She worked in Helsinki University Hospital (HUCH) in Children Psychiatric Clinic during 2002–2010 and started own therapy practice in 2010.

Francis McGlone, PhD, is the head of the Somatosensory & Affective Neuroscience Group at the School of Natural Sciences & Psychology, Liverpool JM University.

Henry Milton is a Training Specialist with the Karyn Purvis Institute of Child Development, currently working with the team to conduct trainings on Trust-Based Relational Intervention® (TBRI®) techniques.

Eva Nowakowski-Sims, PhD, is an Assistant Professor in the School of Social Work at Barry University, where she teaches research and human behavior courses in the MSW and PhD programs.

Judi Parson, PhD, RN, APPTA & BAPT RPT/S, is a Senior Lecturer and Course Director for the Master of Child Play Therapy, School of Health and Social Development, Deakin University, Australia.

Danna Powers, LMHC was an Infant Mental Health Developmental Specialist at the Child First program, and is currently working with families at the Veterans Health Administration in Palm Beach County, Florida.

Kate Renshaw, APPTA & BAPT RPT/S, is a Play Therapist-Supervisor registered with APPTA and BAPT and is a Lecturer in Play Therapy and a PhD candidate at Deakin University, Melbourne, Australia.

Ken Schwartzenberger, LCSW, RPT-S, is an Experiential Play Therapy Diplomat and was an Instructor in the Play Therapy Certification program at the University of California San Diego.

Karen Stagnitti, PhD, is Professor, Personal Chair at Deakin University, Australia and has taught and carried out research in occupational therapy and child play therapy.

Renee Turner, PhD, LPC-S, RPT-S, is an Assistant Professor at the University of Mary Hardin-Baylor. She specializes in Gestalt Play Therapy, body-centered approaches, expressive arts therapies, traumatic loss, and trauma across the lifespan.

Meyleen Velasquez, LCSW, PMH-C, RPT-S, is a Certified FirstPlay® Supervisor. She serves as the Chair of the Florida chapter of Postpartum Support International and owns an online perinatal mental health practice.

Christina Villarreal-Davis, PhD, LPC-S, NCC, RPT-S, is an Assistant Professor at Liberty University and the clinical director at Wellspring of Life Counseling & Play Therapy Center.

Foreword

When thinking about infant and early childhood mental health, a quote comes to mind. One stumbles across many memorable quotes in a lifetime; however, some stick with you more than others. As a play therapist and child advocate, who already sees childhood as invaluable, quotes that urge parents to resist falling into older teachings are even more notable. L. R. Knost, author of *"Two thousand Kisses a Day: Gentle Parenting through the Ages"* and *"Stages* and *Whispers through Time,"* wrote:

> New mothers are often told that once they've fed, burped, and changed their baby they should leave their baby alone to self-soothe if they cry because all of their needs have been met. One day I hope all new mothers will smile confidently and say, 'I gave birth to a baby, not just a digestive system. My baby has a brain that needs to learn trust and a heart that needs love. I will meet all of my baby's needs, emotional, mental, and physical, and I'll respond to every cry because crying is communication, not manipulation'.

In the quote above, the old teaching that I allude to is, "leave their baby alone to self-soothe if they cry because all of their needs have been met." When I see this, I think, "What if all of the needs are not met?" Often, how some approach child development is based on information derived during a time when child development research was in its infancy. As such, we now know that this early research failed to address (or did not know to address) many important infant mental health factors.

Unequivocally, by now (2019), we should realize that 100 years ago child development research understood very little about the developing brain, self, personality, or even the importance of attachment. In my play therapy career, which is approaching 20 years, the importance of attachment has jumped from what we learned from the seminal writings of John Bowlby and Mary Ainsworth, to the comprehensive and easily applicable works of Charles Zeanah, Allan Schore, and many more. In many ways, we have left the *Dark Ages of Child Development* and entered the *Age of Discovery and Exploration in Child Development.*

Yes, there are more needs than the physical or basic needs of survival. In simple terms, Maslow's Hierarchy of Needs notes categories for physiological, safety, love and belonging, esteem, and self-actualization. So, meeting the physiological needs of the child might lay the foundation, but much more is necessary to address the gestalt. To return to my question, "What if all of the needs are not met?," I can respond and say, "If all of the hierarchical needs are not met, then addressing all of these needs becomes paramount and what supports the development of healthy, resilient children." When some needs go unmet, we set children up for life-long difficulties.

In some situations, children's needs may be met, but their development is impacted by issues such as abuse, domestic violence, or substance use, within the home. Now, consider adding to this the inconsistencies of environments outside the home, and we further impact the developmental potential of children. In a nutshell, harm can be done by things that happen to a child as well as things that fail to happen. In essence, this begins to paint a picture of a much bigger issue: mental health.

It is difficult to think that an infant might have a mental health issue. As is, infancy is a period of dramatic change in which the body and brain grow rapidly, in many ways, to survive. In infancy, the brain overproduces neural connections so that the child might quickly make sense of his or her surroundings. An infant is vulnerable, just as we were vulnerable in our infancy.

Those of us who work with infants and young children have long since recognized the importance of early childhood mental health; however, only within the last decade or so has the remainder of the world begun to look deeper. When those outside the mental health world seek information on early childhood mental health, they often find disconnected bits and pieces. Often, this information is overly technical and lacks practical application. When parents look for similar information, their efforts frequently lead to resources that are based on opinion versus practical, universal evidence. It is in this place that we find the need for texts like *Infant Play Therapy: Foundations, Models, Programs and Practice.* One of the goals of this text may be to teach play therapists and child therapists about the importance of infant and early childhood mental health. While reading, one will also read about topics ranging from developmental issues to adoption to the impact of trauma or familial issues such as substance use.

I see many other benefits. The text becomes the foundation for teaching those outside our helper community. It becomes a blueprint for coaching parents, grandparents, and others that play a role in a child's life. It becomes a bridge and communication tool for consistency across members of an integrative health team. Without extending its usefulness, this text fills a void in the comprehensive resources needed to train play therapists who do, or have a desire to work with, infants and young children. It opens the door for more research and better applications of what we know benefits the health and mental health of infants and young children.

Edward F. Hudspeth, PhD, NCC, LPC-S, ACS, RPh, RPT-S, CPC
Associate Dean of Counseling Programs
Southern New Hampshire University
Editor, *International Journal of Play Therapy*

Preface

In the 1980s during my early years of professional practice I was an adoption and foster care worker—a fulfilling but often heartbreaking career. Many of the young children in the care of our agency were considered "special needs" adoptions who had suffered varied types of trauma. Some infants were born testing positive for cocaine, a crisis epidemic at the time. Other children were removed from their parent's homes because of abuse and neglect—and then there were the infants voluntarily placed by their parents for adoption. It was during this time that I began to learn about the world of infant mental health and the detrimental impact of trauma upon young children. But it was the following heartrending case that had a lasting impact on my on-going clinical work.

It was late in the afternoon on a sweltering hot mid-summer day in South Florida. My office was located on the second floor of an early 1920s building; a window air conditioning unit struggled to cool the space. I was alone and getting ready to leave for the day when Mary, the agency secretary, called me.

"Janet, come downstairs quick," Mary said in a strained voice.

"Mary, what, what's wrong?" I asked.

"Just get down here now, hurry," Mary demanded.

I flew down the stairs and when I opened the door, I immediately understood the urgency. Standing in the lobby was a young mother drenched in sweat holding an infant in her arms with a toddler standing beside her with his arms wrapped around her leg. "Hi, I'm Janet, the adoption worker here," I said walking closer to them. The mother replied in a weak and tired voice, "I'm here as I want to place my children up for adoption." My heart immediately sank, and I felt a deep sense of compassion, "Please come up to my office and we can talk more," I said calmly, trying to hide my concern. This was the first time this had happened during my two years with the agency and I was perplexed and a bit unnerved.

Once settled in my office, the mother explained that she was overwhelmed with the responsibilities of taking care of her children and that she was no longer able to care for them. I asked if there were any family members that could help her or who could care for her children. She replied that she had no family members who could help her. I also asked about the father of the children and she stated that he had "taken off" and she did not know where he was. They were not married. Her responses were terse and vague with eyes diverted, and I could hear the frightened pain in her voice. She looked much older than her stated age of 25 years, and it seemed as if she had lived a hard life. She appeared anxious to leave and did not want to answer too many questions. She quickly filled out the contact information sheet and signed the placement papers, and within 15 minutes she stood up to leave, promising to return in the morning to provide more detailed history and a medical background. She placed her baby on my lap and, without saying anything else to me or the children, she burst out the office door, down the steps, and out of the building.

I was now alone with the children, holding the baby girl in my lap, and the two-year-old boy was sitting next to me staring blankly at the floor. During my early days of training as a social worker we were taught the importance of the parental attachment relationship. However, the level of understanding about the impact of trauma on children was rarely acknowledged and there were virtually no trainings or literature available related to the topic. But there's one thing I will never forget about that day: When their mother left the office, the children did not cry. There was no protest toward her leaving the room and afterward no indications of searching and seeking behaviors or missing her absence. Instead, they sat still with long somber faces as if being left by their mother was a common occurrence. It was as if they had given up. I knew this was not normal. And, although I had no understanding of the impact of trauma at the time, I knew that these children were suffering emotionally and psychologically. [Later, I realized that their depressed state fit Bowlby's stages of loss identified as withdrawal and emotional detachment (Bowlby, 1969).] At that moment, those children became my responsibility and I immediately went to work to secure some food and drink and locate a foster home that could take the children for the evening. I grabbed two car seats from the closet and was on my way. Sadly, the mother didn't return the next day. During the next several months of diligent search for the mother and father, the children stayed with the same caring foster parents who took in the children that first night and eventually they were approved to adopt the children.

Over the years I specialized in working with infants, children, and families through extensive training in a wide range of play therapy approaches. However, it was my training in Developmental Play Therapy (DPT), developed by play therapy pioneer, Viola Brody, with its emphasis on the importance of healthy touch, that showed me how best to work with young traumatized children at the pre-symbolic level of play—relationship engaged play, without the use of toys. This understanding eventually led to my doctoral research into DPT and touch and eventually to the development of my own model of infant play therapy, called FirstPlay® Therapy. Over the years I became a member of the Association for Play Therapy, Zero to Three, Florida Association for Infant Mental Health, and the World Association for Infant Mental Health. In this, I straddled the two fields of play therapy *and* infant mental health, which has provided me with a unique perspective and knowledge base. Since the field of play therapy has traditionally geared therapies toward children three to four years old and up, there are few play therapy specific literature sources available that addresses infant populations. The purpose of this book, therefore, endeavors to address that gap in the literature and seeks to provide a beginning conceptualization of what is meant by the term "infant play therapy" in relationship to infant mental health (refer to Chapter 1).

The case examples and vignettes throughout this book represent a range of developmental stages for young children from birth to three years, diverse therapy settings, a range of theoretical approaches, and varied infant and family problems—accordingly, all case-identifying information has been masked to protect confidentiality. The chapter authors have applied their own clinical perspectives related to their theoretical expertise in the realms of: (a) child development and welfare, (b) years of clinical practice experience in infant and child counseling and play therapy, (c) teaching graduate and undergraduate level curriculums related to infants and children in marriage and family, social work, play therapy, psychology, and school counseling, (d) providing supervision in multidisciplinary settings, and (e) extensive research of the literature and other resources on the subject of play therapy and infant mental health.

The book is divided into six parts. Part I is titled "Foundations." The first chapter (Janet A. Courtney) provides a broad overview of the topic of infant play therapy (defined as birth to three years) in relationship to infant mental health and sets the stage for the chapters that follow. In Chapter 2, Emily Jackson and neuroscientist Francis McGlone enlighten us with an understanding of the neurobiology of touch related to the impact of play on the developing social brain. In Chapter 3, Ken Schwartzenberger provides us with a developmental perspective of neurosensory play within the infant-parent dyad. Part II, titled "Assessment with Young Children" provides two different chapters that highlight the importance of assessment with infants. In Chapter 4, Judi Parson, Karen Stagnitti, Bridget Dooley, and Kate Renshaw demonstrate a unique assessment sequencing play skills method for young children. And, in Chapter 5, Eva Nowakowski-Sims and Danna Powers discuss trauma informed assessment for infants. Part III, titled "New and Adapted Theoretical Approaches and Models to Infant Play Therapy," comprises three chapters related to new and adapted play therapy models for infants. Chapter 6 (Karen Baldwin, Meyleen Velasquez, and Janet A. Courtney) presents a new attachment-based infant play therapy model of intervention called FirstPlay® Infant Story-Massage. In Chapter 7, Kate

Renshaw and Judi Parson demonstrate how Filial Play Therapy can be adapted to infant populations, and in Chapter 8, Hanna Lampi discusses the use of Theraplay in working with infants and young children.

Part IV, titled "Programmatic Infant Play Therapy and Play-Based Interventions with Infant and Toddler Populations," highlights play-centered interventions: Chapter 9, Baby Doll Circle Time® by Becky Bailey, Chapter 10, "DIR/Floor Time: A Developmental/Relational Play Therapy Model for Infants and Toddlers" by Esther Hess, and Chapter 11, "Reflections of Love in the TEACUP Preemie Program®" by Chelsea Johnson. Part V, titled "Evidence-Based Infant Mental Health Models that Utilize Play Therapy Practices" comprises three chapters that are well-recognized evidence-based models in the field of infant mental health including two chapters that present Child–Parent Psychotherapy: Chapter 12, by Harleen Hutchinson, and Chapter 13, by Allison Golden and Veronica Castro. Trust Based Relational Intervention is presented in Chapter 14 (Montserrat Casado-Kehoe, Casey Call, David Cross and Henry Milton). The final section (Part VI), titled "Applications to Specific Populations in Infant Play Therapy," focuses on specific problem areas related to infants. In Chapter 15, Athena Drewes sheds light on infant trauma related to infants born testing positive to opioid exposure in utero. In Chapter 16, Renee Turner and Christina Villarreal-Davis address the sensitive issue of perinatal grief and its effects on the attachment relationship with "rainbow babies." Finally, in Chapter 17, Janet A. Courtney, Viktoria Bakai Toth, and Carmen Jimenez-Pride address healing reactive attachment disorder through FirstPlay® Kinesthetic Storytelling.

As you read through this book, note that the authors have shared their expertise and experiences with a deep respect for this most vulnerable of human populations—infants and toddlers. In doing so, they have dedicated many hours of thoughtful reflection—mulling over the multifaceted clinical, cultural and ethical challenges that impact this population, exploring the most recent neuroscience, taking risks of vulnerability in presenting their case examples, exhibiting creativity and flexibility of thought, and demonstrating how the power of play can impact the healing attachment relationship with very young children. I am deeply grateful to the authors for their dedication to the topics presented.

Reference

Bowlby, J. (1969). *Attachment and loss*, *Vol.*1. New York, NY: Basic Books.

Part 1

Foundations

Chapter 1

Conceptualizing Infant Play Therapy in the Context of Infant Mental Health

Janet A. Courtney

The field of infant mental health is growing exponentially, and many practitioners from a range of professional disciplines are desiring to grow their expertise to work with young children. Among these, many play therapists and child counselors who utilize the therapeutic powers of play (Schaefer & Drewes, 2014) as a central intervention are choosing to bring their skill set to this younger population. However, working with young children from birth to three years old requires specialized knowledge and training that is often not included in most child counseling, play therapy, or even graduate school curriculums. This chapter seeks to provide a brief overview of work with infants to include a discussion related to infant trauma, and an introduction to infant mental health and the importance of early intervention. It then puts infant play therapy into context in relationship to infant mental health, as well as highlighting a selection of prominent "shapers" of the field in infant mental health.

The Need for Infant Mental Health: Infants and Trauma

Infants do experience trauma. Unfortunately, as noted by Osofsky, Stepka, & King (2017), many perceive that infants are unaffected by traumatic experiences because they do not retain a conscious memory of the trauma. This societal myth of infancy has caused much harm as we have overlooked the crucial needs of this population. We now understand that those trauma experiences are part of the implicit memory (Cozolino, 2014; Osofsky & Lieberman, 2011; Schore, 2012, 2019; Siegel, 2012). Fortunately, the old myths that humans in utero and as infants do not experience the effects of early life trauma are now being challenged and dispelled. This is particularly credited to the neuroscience revelations of the 1990s, to the rise of the infant mental health field, and to rigorous research studies such as the Adverse Childhood Experiences carried out at Kaiser Permanente or what is commonly known as the ACE study (Felitti et al., 1998). This study included 18,000 participants and was instrumental in providing evidence that early life trauma can have a detrimental effect throughout childhood and into adulthood. In brief, the

ACE study revealed strong correlations between the number of risk factors an infant was exposed to in relationship to later life stress and dysfunction within families. The United States Centers for Disease Control and Prevention website listed the following child maltreatment reports (note: this is only for the United States and does not represent numbers globally—refer to the World Health Organization, https://www.who.int/):

- There were 676,000 victims of child abuse and neglect reported to child protective services (CPS) in 2016.
- It is estimated that 1 in 4 children experience some form of child abuse or neglect in their lifetimes and 1 in 7 children have experienced abuse or neglect in the last year.
- About 1,750 children died from abuse or neglect in 2016.

(Source: https://www.cdc.gov/violenceprevention/
childabuseandneglect/index.html)

Infants are our most vulnerable population, and unlike children, adolescents, adults, or the elderly, if someone is harming an infant, they have no ability to run or move away, or block a slap or punch, and they certainly are not able to tell someone else if they have been harmed (Courtney, Velasquez, & Bakai Toth, 2017). Child (infant) maltreatment is recognized as any risk of physical or emotional harm including physical and emotional abuse, sexual abuse, neglect, and exposure to domestic violence. We also recognize the detrimental effects that those traumas have on young children (Gil, 2017). In Terr's landmark book, *Too Scared to Cry* (1990), she discussed observing withdrawn infant personalities due to abuse and neglect. In the following heartbreaking account, she described how she tried to help an abused infant in a hospital setting:

> One eight-month-old Cleveland girl, whom I tried to help at the university hospital there, had been ignored and occasionally beaten by her severely depressed mother. In her hospital crib, the infant lay on her back with her little hands clutched at midline. It was difficult to pry apart those tiny, fixed fingers. The baby ignored a brightly colored mobile that had been placed over her crib to keep her busy. She paid scant attention to Hospital procedures that would have brought shouts of protest from any ordinary child provoked hardly a complaint from this one. There was no brain damage. The damage resided only in the baby's still rudimentary, but benumbed, personality style.
>
> (Terr, 1990, p. 85)

Trauma is a whole body sensory-based experience and infants attune to what they see, hear, taste, touch, see, and smell. Their immature nervous systems are highly sensitive and can often be triggered into states of hyperarousal or hypoarousal, leaving infants vulnerable to a range of emotional states of fear, confusion, depression, withdrawal, and anger. Neuroscience literature over-whelmingly concludes that infant and childhood developmental trauma alters the brain and results in enduring problems related to executive functioning skills and emotional, behavioral, cognitive, social, and physical challenges (Badenoch, 2018; Cozolino, 2014; Hudspeth, 2016a; Humphreys & Zeanah, 2015; Perry, 2006; Porges, 2018; Schore, 1994, 2019; Siegel, 2012). Van der Kolk (2014) advised, "whatever happens to a baby contributes to the emotional and perceptual map of the world that its developing brain creates" (p. 56). This emotional map, *or internal working model*, as Bowlby (1988) described it, ori-ginates at the implicit level beginning in pregnancy. It is the responsibility of the caregivers to be the external regulators to stabilize arousal states, reduce suf-fering and ensure optimal emotional and physical safety and health.

Early Intervention—the Key to Healing Early Trauma Experiences

Play therapy pioneer, Virginia Axline (1969) saw the vital importance of healthy beginnings, from a Humanistic standpoint, in the following state-ment: "There seems to be a powerful force within each individual which strives continuously for complete self-realization. It goes on relentlessly to achieve consummation, but it needs good '*growing ground*' [italics added] to develop a well-balanced structure" (p. 10). The key words here are "growing ground" as Axline recognized that if given an optimal emotional and psy-chological foundation, then we (human beings) will naturally tap into our innate drive to reach our highest potential.

Understanding and screening for high risk factors can be a first step of early intervention. One glaring impediment to cognitive and language development revealed through extensive research is that children impacted by poverty often lag behind children noted from more affluent systems (Fernald, Marchman, & Weisleder, 2013; Hart & Risley, 2003; Piccolo & Noble, 2019; Votruba-Drzal, Miller, & Coley, 2016). Other identified risk factors growing in research and attention is maternal depression, substance abuse in parents of young children, pre-term infants, exposure to violence, and abuse and neglect (Boris, Renk, Lowell, & Kolomeyer, 2019; Murray, Halligan, & Cooper, 2019; Shah, Browne, & Poehlmann-Tynan, 2019).

What is clear is that early intervention and prevention with infants and families that are culturally sensitive, strength-based, and resiliency focused have been shown to be effective (Zeanah & Zeanah, 2019). Schaefer, Kelly-Zion, McCor-mick, & Ohnogi (2008) in their edited book, *Play Therapy for Very Young Chil-dren*, advocated, "It is never too soon to provide the appropriate play-based intervention to young children to help them adapt successfully to their environ-ment and family" (p. ix). Ideally, each infant and family system needs to be sized up to discern which model of therapy is best suited for that particular family or caregiver system. This "prescriptive" (Schaefer, 2003) or "integrative" (Gil, et al.,

2015) approach recognizes the uniqueness of each family system where practitioners must consider the presenting problem, the relevant research, and multicultural and diversity factors, to then choose the most appropriate treatment modalities that effect the highest potential for positive therapy outcomes.

Infant Play Therapy in Context

What is meant by Infant Play Therapy? The field of play therapy has traditionally been known to work with children ages four and older as the primary population of treatment (Schaefer, et al., 2008). The focus of most play therapy interventions is to work with children through the healing power of *symbolic* type play—with carefully planned playrooms to allow for a child's innate abilities to play out their worries, traumas, anger, and so forth. Some play therapy theoretical approaches work with children at the pre-symbolic level of play, including Developmental Play Therapy (DPT) (Brody, 1997; Courtney & Gray 2014) and Theraplay (Booth & Jernberg, 2010). However, these models, like the symbolic models, again have traditionally trained therapists to work with children primarily three to four years and older.

The concept of infant play therapy has emerged within recent years with the upsurge of demand by play therapists and other practitioners to find successful ways to provide therapy services to infant populations. The problem is that the traditional types of play therapy approaches, where the therapist may see the child for individual play therapy sessions without the parent in the room, becomes a ridiculous (and highly unethical) scenario if we were to imagine, say, seeing a five-month-old infant for therapy while the parent sits out in the office waiting room. Add to that absurd notion a therapist then telling a parent that what was going to happen in the play therapy room between the therapist and infant was "confidential." The practice wisdom is that all infant mental health interventions are relationally oriented and therefore must include the parents or caregivers within the therapy sessions. Zeanah & Zeanah (2019) wrote that the "relational framework of infant mental health distinguishes it from work with older children and adolescents" (p. 6). Therefore, if play therapists are generally seeking to bring their unique skill set to infant populations, then we can 1) adapt current known evidence-based play therapy modalities (e.g. Filial Play Therapy, Theraplay) to infant populations (e.g. Schaefer et al., 2008), or 2) new infant-based play therapy models can be developed (e.g. FirstPlay® Therapy), or 3) we can learn and receive training in the existing infant mental health models that utilize play principles (e.g. Child Parent Psychotherapy). These three different ways of envisioning infant play therapy within an infant mental health context are included in this book.

"Child mental health" can be envisioned as the overarching umbrella from which hundreds of child-based theories and interventions fall beneath. In like manner, we can imagine "infant mental health" to be an overarching umbrella term from which interventions that best assist infant populations

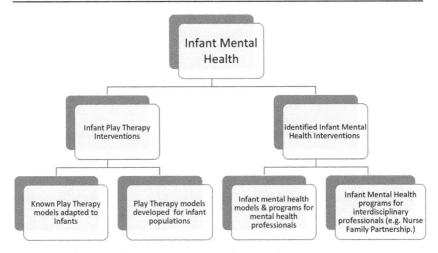

Figure 1.1 Infant mental health organizational framework.

fall. With this in mind, we can now think of infant play therapy as a secondary subset heading under which varied play therapy approaches fall (see Figure 1.1). As infant play therapy models are created and adapted, they must also integrate the vast literature and research established within the neuroscience and infant mental health fields. Additionally, new or adapted play therapy interventions must also set forth the rigor of qualitative and quantitative research designs to establish their overall effectiveness.

The question arises: What expertise does the field of play therapy bring to work with young children? The obvious answer is that play therapists' expertise is grounded in the understanding that play is intrinsically healing. They value that play is a child's natural language of communication and self-expression (Schaefer & Drewes, 2014). Play therapists also consider the latest research, including findings indicated in the field of neuroscience/neurobiology (Badenoch, 2018; Hudspeth, 2016a; Kestly, 2014). For the purposes of this book, and to offer a "working" definition of what is meant by the term infant play therapy, I offer the following: Infant play therapies are informed by the fields of neuroscience and infant mental health, are culturally sensitive, and utilize the therapeutic powers of play to effect positive change for the infant and parental (or caregiver) relational system and social environment.

Common Types of Young Children's Play

Children engage in different types of play throughout the developmental stages of their childhood, and play therapists advocate for relational and play-based interventions for birth to three (Schaefer & DiGeronimo, 2000; Schaefer, et al., 2008). Some common types of children's play that may be observed for the younger child include:

a   rough and tumble play (e.g., a toddler might bounce playfully on a father's back as they engage in active physical play interaction);

b   pre-symbolic play (e.g., joyful exciting engagement that happens between an infant and caregiver—without the use of toys—such as peek-a-boo, and sing-song kinesthetic play games);

c   parallel play (e.g., playing with an object along-side another infant, but not engaging the other in interactive play);

d   locomotor-active play (e.g., a toddler plays chase and running activities, hide and seek, etc.);

e   object play (e.g., playing individually with a toy such as a baby rattle);

f   exploratory play (e.g., infant crawls around to explore her environment);

g   imaginative or fantasy play (e.g., beginning about 18 months and older—child plays "mother" to a doll);

h   mastery play (e.g., stacking blocks).

Figure 1.2 Joyful mother and baby playing together.
Source: ©Canstockphoto.com/Flashon (2007337)

Because infant play therapy must consider the literature and research related to infant mental health, the following sections are presented to provide the reader with an introduction to infant mental health as well as a selected group of individuals and organizations of the shapers of the field.

The Infant Mental Health Landscape

"Infant" derives from the Latin words "in," meaning "not," and "fant," meaning "speaking." Thus, the word infant literally means "not speaking." Traditionally, infant mental health has been delineated to the developmental stages of birth to three. However, as Zeanah & Zeanah (2019) point out, the prenatal experience needs to be included in the infant mental health classification as we now understand the emotional and psychology landscape of the pregnant mother can influence the developing fetus and reach into early childhood. As well, some infant mental health practitioners extend the definition of infant mental health up to age five years. Hence the revised *Diagnostic Classification of Mental Health and Developmental Disorders of Infancy and Early Childhood* manual was updated from 0–3 to include 0–5 (Zero to Three, 2016). However, the chapters in this book pertain to ages birth to three years.

When it comes to professional involvement related to infants, the field is overwhelmingly "interdisciplinary" (Lillas & Turnbull, 2009; Zeanah & Zeanah, 2019). This means that, more than any other developmental stage of life, a wide range of professionals interface with the needs of infants, including pediatric nurses, physical and occupational therapists, speech and language therapists, pediatricians, obstetricians, certified birth doulas, and trauma specialists, as well as mental health professionals, such as social workers, mental health counselors, psychologists, marriage and family therapists, child life specialists, infant mental health specialists, play therapists, and university professors of varied schools and backgrounds who teach child developmental courses in the classroom.

The Zero to Three Infant Mental Health Steering Committee defined infant mental health as:

> the young child's capacity to experience, regulate, and express emotions, form close and secure relationships, and explore the environment and learn. All of these capacities will be best accomplished within the context of the caregiving environment that includes family, community, and cultural expectations for young children. Developing these capacities is synonymous with healthy social and emotional development.
>
> (Zero to Three, 2001, as cited in Zeanah & Zeanah, 2019, p. 6)

The Shapers of the Field of Infant Mental Health

Donald Winnicott, the British pediatrician and psychoanalyst, is often cited as the "father" of infant mental health, along with his most well-known quote,

"There is no such thing as an infant, meaning, of course, that whenever one finds an infant one finds maternal care, and without maternal care there would be no infant" (Winnicott, 1960, p. 587). Selma Fraiberg is known to have first coined the phrase "infant mental health" (Fraiberg, 1980) while also emphasizing the impact of intergenerational influence, with her concept of "ghosts in the nursery." [Note, some give credit that infant mental health was originally coined in Britain (Horton, 2016)]. The early work of Bowlby (1988), Brazelton (1973), Stern (1977), and others set forth a paradigm shift in our understanding of the infant–parent dyad, by studying not just how the parent's care impacts the infant's behaviors (the prevailing early century view), but also how infant responses can elicit and change the caregiver's behaviors and reactions—thus highlighting the evolving reciprocal parent–infant relationship. On another front, Escalona (1967) framed that it was not just about the nature versus nurture characteristics that impacted an infant's development, but rather the lens needed to be focused on the infant's life experiences in the context of relationships with others. Since the 1990s, many neuroscientists have proliferated our understanding of epigenetics and how early experiences and relationships sculpt the circuits of the developing brain (Cozolino, 2014; Dismukes, Shirtcliff, & Drury, 2019; Berens & Nelson, 2019; Porges, 2018; Schore, 2019; Siegel, 2012); including Allan Schore's 1994 landmark book, *Affect Regulation and the Origin of the Self: The Neurobiology of Emotional Development*.

In addition to those already mentioned, the following is a selection of some of the seminal leaders in the field of infant mental health including Charles Zeanah (2019) and his pivotal edited book, *Handbook of Infant Mental Health* (now in its fourth edition), first published in 1993. Renowned pediatrician T. Berry Brazelton developed the Neonatal Behavioral Assessment Scale and conceived a developmental model of intervention known as Touchpoints (Brazelton & Sparrow, 2006). Edward Tronick (2003), a developmental psychologist, is best known for his studies called "The Still Face Experiment." This (highly difficult to watch) experiment demonstrates that when connection between an infant and parent is disrupted, the infant makes an effect to re-engage the parent, and then when no response is provided, the infant can be observed as distressed and pulling back both physically and emotionally. Another prominent leading figure in infant mental health was Emmi Pikler, a Hungarian pediatrician, who was known for her revolutionary approach to infant and child care. In 1946, she founded a residential nursery in Budapest, Hungary, the Pikler® Institute, where the focus was to preserve the competence, autonomy, and integrity of the young child, ages birth to six years (refer to the Pikler website: https://pikler.org/?v=7516fd43adaa). Alicia Lieberman and Patricia Van Horn (2005) developed Child Parent Psychotherapy (CPP), a well-known evidence-based infant mental health treatment approach. Lieberman and Van Horn and colleagues observed that there are also "angels" in the nursery (Lieberman, Padron, Van Horn, & Harris, 2005).

Many universities are conducting cutting-edge research and offering advanced certificate curriculums in infant mental health. Joy Osofsky (Osofsky, Stepka, & King, 2017) was instrumental in the development of the Louisiana State University Health Sciences Center's Harris Center for the Infant Mental Health in the Department of Psychiatry (refer to: https://www.medschool. lsuhsc.edu/psychiatry/lsu-psychology-harris-program). The University of Massachusetts Boston offers a two-year internationally recognized parent–infant postgraduate certificate program offered through the psychology department (refer to: https://www.umb.edu/academics/cla/psychology/professional_devel opment/infant-parent-mental-health). The Center on the Developing Child Harvard University established in 2006, is an excellent resource for cutting edge research and policy advancements (refer to: https://developingchild.harvard. edu/about/). Since 1989, Florida State University (Tallahassee, FL) has supported the FSU Center for Prevention & Early Intervention focusing on research to impact infant mental health policies, research and training in communities (refer to: https://cpeip.fsu.edu/about.cfm).

Several organizations have also been leading the advancement of infant mental health. In 1977, the National Center for Infants, Toddlers, and Families was established (now known as Zero to Three). This organization has been a leader in the field of infant mental health with now over 160 employees and produces *Zero to Three Journal* and the *Diagnostic Classification of Mental Health and Developmental Disorders of Infancy and Early Childhood* (DC:0–5). (See the following link for an introduction to the current DC: 0–5: https://mi-aimh.org/wp-content/uploads/ 2017/11/2017-01-Zeanah-S.-intro-article.pdf.) In the 1970s, practitioners in Michigan, who were inspired by the work of Selma Fraiberg and colleagues, formed the Michigan Association for Infant Mental Health (MI-AIMH). They designed a service model to treat and identify mental health developmental and relationship disturbances in infancy and early parenthood and developed core competency guidelines to include reflective supervision. Many State infant mental health associations across the U.S. are adopting the MI-AIMH competency and endorsement standards. The World Association for Infant Mental Health (WAIMH) promotes research and education for professionals throughout the world and holds a yearly conference. The following is their mission statement found on the WAIMH website:

> WAIMH's mission promotes education, research and study of the effects of mental, emotional and social development during infancy on later normal and psychopathological development through international and interdisciplinary cooperation, publications, affiliate associations, and through regional and biennial congresses devoted to scientific, educational, and clinical work with infants and their caregivers.
>
> (https://waimh.org)

WAIMH—the Rights of Infants

Since the 1980s, the United Nations has worked to establish a universal set of principles recognizing the rights of children. The WAIMH organization determined that, in addition to the needs of children as set forth by the UN, the unique rights of infants had not fully been addressed. Consequently, WAIMH developed a list of basic principles of infant rights (see below), while also endorsing the child rights principles established by the UN Convention on the Rights of Children (as passed by the General Assembly of UN in 1989, and activated in Sept. 1990 with 54 Articles in total). Edwards, Parsons, & O'Brien (2016) advised that child practitioners need to be aware of how the UN Rights of the Child Articles translate into play therapy practice and advocate that training on child rights should be included within university curriculums. (Refer to the following link to read a "child friendly" version of the UNICEF Rights of the Child: https://www.unicef.org/southafrica/SAF_resources_crcchildfriendly.pdf.)

Basic Principles of Infant Rights (Birth to Three Years of Age) (WAIMH, 2016, p. 4, paraphrased):

1   Being absolutely dependent, infants must rely on others to safeguard their needs including when or where appropriate, the need for legal protection.
2   The infant has a right to healthy attachment and bonding relationships critical to secure development, and the continuity of a healthy attachment environment, especially in the event of separation or loss.
3   The infant has the right to be immediately incorporated as a valued member of a cohesive family regardless of gender or disability, and to be registered as a citizen.
4   The infant has a right to be loved and nurtured with adequate nutrition and sleep, and to have a safe environment.
5   The infant has a right to legal protection from neglect, physical and sexual abuse, and from infant trafficking.
6   The infant has a right to receive primary health care and to professional help for emotional and psychological trauma.
7   Infants with life-threatening conditions have the right to access palliative services based on the same standards that apply in the society for older children and adults.

Multi-cultural and Diversity Considerations

In infant mental health, multi-cultural and diversity factors are complex, and several contextual factors must be considered. Most important to the conversation with young children and families is recognizing the wide-range impact of multi-cultural and societal attitudes and values with attention to concerns of race, gender, prejudice, class, poverty (economic inequality), unequal distribution of power, concerns of social justice, reproductive justice, environmental and climate impact on families, refugees and the trauma of loss of homeland and entering unfamiliar societies, the imposing of one's cultural values and norms on another, diverse family systems, and intergenerational historical trauma (Hudspeth, 2016b; Michiko & Ippen, 2019; Piccolo & Noble, 2019; Zeanah & Zeanah, 2019). In this foregoing summary of multi-cultural and diversity factors, it is imperative that culturally appropriate assessment and screening tools be employed. Additionally, practitioners from all discipline backgrounds need to be aware of their own potential cultural and diversity biases and perceptions, and this can often be part of reflective supervision sessions (Tomlin, Weatherston, & Pavkov, 2014).

Summary

This chapter has examined infant play therapy within the context of an infant mental health framework and is meant to provide an introductory springboard for the chapters throughout this book. As the field of play therapy adapts its long-standing theoretical approaches or creates new infant play-based modalities to our most vulnerable of populations, we will need to invest in rigorous research designs to ethically establish sound and successful treatment practices and positive outcomes. Furthermore, the chapters within this book will set forth, through qualitative case studies, a beginning step forward to meet this goal. We now turn to Chapter 2, where we will discover the impact of touch and play related to an infant's developing social brain.

Discussion Questions

Together with a colleague, or in a small group, discuss the following questions:

1 Share your cultural and societal perceptions of infants related to experience and trauma. Do you think perceptions are changing and how do you think that might impact policies related to infant populations in the future?
2 Review the list of "Common Types of Young Children's Play" found in this chapter. Next, discuss for each one a recollection of when you might have observed a young child engaging in the different types of play. State how you felt and reacted when observing the play. Discuss how understanding young children's play might be relevant to your work with infant populations.
3 Review the UNICEF Rights of the Child. With the larger picture of the Rights of the Child in mind, read each of the WAIMH Principles of Infant Rights together and reflect on each point.

References

Axline, V. (1969). *Play therapy* (Rev. ed.). New York, NY: Ballantine Books.

Badenoch, B. (2018). Safety is the treatment. In S. W. Porges & D. Dana (Eds.), *Clinical applications of polyvagal theory: The emergence of polyvagal-informed therapies* (pp. 73–88). New York, NY: Norton.

Berens, A. E., & Nelson, C. A. (2019). Neurobiology of fetal and infant development: Implications for infant mental health. In C. H. Zeanah (Ed.), *Handbook of infant mental health* (4th ed., pp. 41–62). New York, NY: Guilford Press.

Booth, P. B., & Jernberg, A. M. (2010). *Theraplay®: Helping parents and children build better relationships through attachment-based play* (3rd ed.). San Francisco: Jossey-Bass.

Boris, N. W., Renk, K., Lowell, A., & Kolomeyer, E. (2019). Parental substance abuse. In C. H. Zeanah (Ed.), *Handbook of infant mental health* (4th ed., pp. 187–202). New York, NY: Guilford Press.

Bowlby, J. (1988). *A secure base: Parent-child attachment and healthy human development*. New York, NY: Basic Books.

Brazelton, T. B. (1973). *Neonatal behavioral assessment scale*. Clinics in Developmental Medicine, No. 50. London: Heinemann.

Brazelton, T. B., & Sparrow, J. D. (2006). *Touchpoints: Birth to three*, 2nd ed. Cambridge, MA: Da Capo Press.

Bowlby, J. (1958). The nature of the child's tie to his mother. *International Journal of Psycho-Analysis*, 39, 350–373.

Brody, V.A. (1997). *The dialogue of touch: Developmental play therapy* (2nd ed.). Northvale, NJ: Jason Aronson.

Courtney, J. A., & Gray, S. W. (2014). A phenomenological inquiry into practitioner experiences of developmental play therapy: implications for training in touch. *International Journal of Play Therapy*, 23(2), 114–129. http://dx.doi.org/10.1037/a0036366

Courtney, J. A., Velasquez, M., & Bakai Toth, V. (2017). FirstPlay® infant massage storytelling: Facilitating corrective touch experiences with a teenage mother and her abused infant. In J. A. Courtney & R. D. Nolan (Eds.), *Touch in child counseling and play therapy: An ethical and clinical guide* (pp. 48–62). New York, NY: Routledge.

Cozolino, L. (2014). *The neuroscience of human relationships: Attachment and the developing social brain*, 2nd ed. New York, NY: Norton.

Dismukes, A. R., Shirtcliff, E. A., & Drury, S. S. (2019). Genetic and epigenetic processes in infant mental health. In C. H. Zeanah (Ed.), *Handbook of infant mental health* (4th ed., pp. 63–94). New York, NY: Guilford Press.

Edwards, J., Parsons, J., & O'Brien, W. (2016). Child play therapists' understanding of the united nations convention on the rights of the child: A narrative analysis. *International Journal of Play Therapy*, 25(3), 133–145. http://dx.doi.org/10.1037/pla0000029

Escalona, S. (1967). Patterns of infantile experience and the developmental process. *Psychoanalytic Study of the Child*, 22, 197–244.

Felitti, V. J., Anda, R. F., Nordenberg, D., Williamson, D. F., Spitz, A. M., Edwards, V., Marks, J. S. (1998). Relationship of childhood abuse and household dysfunction to many of the leading causes of death in adults: The adverse childhood experiences (ACE) study. *American Journal of Preventive Medicine*, 14, 245–248. Retrieved 15 July, 2019 from: https://www.ncbi.nlm.nih.gov/pubmed/9635069

Fernald, A., Marchman, V. A., & Weisleder, A. (2013). SES difference in language processing skill and vocabulary are evident at 18 months. *Developmental Science*, 16, 234–258. doi: 10.1111/desc.12019.

Fraiberg, S. (1980). *Clinical studies in infant mental health: The first year of life*. New York, NY: Basic Books.

Gil, E. (2017). *Posttraumatic play in children: What clinicians need to know*. New York, NY: Guilford Press.

Gil, E., Konrath, E., Shaw, J., Goldin, M., & McTaggart Bryan, H. (2015). Integrative approach to play therapy. In D. A. Crenshaw & A. L. Stewart (Eds.), *Play therapy: A comprehensive guide to theory and practice* (pp. 99–113). New York, NY: Guilford Press.

Hart, B. B., & Risley, T. R. (2003). The early catastrophe: The 30 million word gap. *American Educator*, 27, 4–9. Retrieved 16 July, 2019 from: https://www.aft.org/sites/default/files/periodicals/TheEarlyCatastrophe.pdf

Horton, E. (2016). Counseling babies. *Counseling Today: A Publication of the American Counseling Association*. Retrieved July 31, 2019 from: https://ct.counseling.org/2016/07/counseling-babies/

Hudspeth, E. F. (2016a). Neuroscience influences in International Journal of Play Therapy articles. *International Journal of Play Therapy*, 25(1), 1–3. http://dx.doi.org/10.1037/pla0000021

Hudspeth, E. F. (2016b). Introduction: Play therapy applications with diverse cultures. *International Journal of Play Therapy*, 25(3), 113.

Humphreys, K. L., & Zeanah, C. H. (2015). Deviations from the expectable environment in early childhood and emerging psychotherapy. *Neuro-psychopharmacology*, 40, 154–170. Doi: 10.1038/npp.2014.165

Kestly, T. A. (2014). *The interpersonal neurobiology of play: Brain-building interventions for emotional well-being*. New York, NY: Norton.

Lieberman, A. F., Padron, E., Van Horn, P., & Harris, W. (2005). Angels in the nursery: The intergenerational transmission of benevolent parental influences. *Infant Mental Health Journal*, 26, 504–520. https://doi.org/10.1002/imhj.20071

Lieberman, A., & Van Horn, P. (2005) *Don't hit my mommy!: A manual for child-parent psychotherapy for young witnesses of family violence*. Washington, DC: Zero to Three Press.

Lillas, C. & Turnbull, J. (2009). *Infant/child mental health, early intervention, and relationship-based therapies: A neurorelational framework for interdisciplinary practice*. New York, NY: W. W. Norton & Co.

Michiko, C. & Ippen, G. (2019). Wounds from the past: Integrating historical trauma into a multicultural infant mental health framework. In C. H. Zeanah (Ed.), *Handbook of infant mental health* (4th ed., pp. 134–153). New York, NY: Guilford Press.

Murray, L., Halligan, S., & Cooper, P. (2019). Postnatal depression and young children's development. In C. H. Zeanah (Ed.), *Handbook of infant mental health* (4th ed., pp. 172–186). New York, NY: Guilford Press.

Osofsky, J., & Lieberman, A. (2011). A call for integrating a mental health perspective into systems of care for abused and neglected infants and young children. *American Psychologist*, 66(2), 120–128. DOI: 10.1037/a0021630 ·

Osofsky, J. D., Stepka, P. T., & King, L. S. (2017). *Treating infants and young children impacted by trauma: Interventions that promote healthy development*. Washington, DC: American Psychological Association.

Perry, B. D. (2006). Applying principles of neurodevelopment to clinical work with maltreated and traumatized children: The neurosequential model of therapeutics. In N. B. Webb (Ed.), *Working with traumatized youth in child welfare* (pp. 27–52). New York, NY: Guilford Press.

Piccolo, L. R., & Noble, K. G. (2019). Poverty, early experience, and brain development. In C. H. Zeanah (Ed.), *Handbook of infant mental health* (4th ed., pp. 157–171). New York, NY: Guilford Press.

Porges, S. (2018). Polyvagal theory: A primer. In S. W. Porges & D. Dana (Eds.), *Clinical applications of polyvagal theory: The emergence of polyvagal-informed therapies*, pp. 50–72. New York, NY: Norton.

Schaefer, C. E. (2003). Prescriptive play therapy. In C. E. Schaefer (Ed.), *Foundations of play therapy (pp. 306–320)*. Hoboken, NJ: Wiley.

Schaefer, C. E., & DiGeronimo, T. F. (2000). *Ages and stages: A parent's guide to normal childhood development*. New York, NY: John Wiley & Sons, Inc.

Schaefer, C. E., & Drewes, A. A. (2014). *The therapeutic powers of play: 20 core agents of change* (2nd ed.). Hoboken, NY: Wiley.

Schaefer, C., Kelly-Zion, S., McCormick, J., & Ohnogi, A. (2008). *Play therapy for very young children*. New York, NY: Jason Aronson.

Schore, A. N. (1994). *Affect regulation and the origin of the self: The neurobiology of emotional development*. Hillsdale, NJ: Lawrence Erlbaum Associates, Inc.

Schore, A. N. (2012). *The science of the art of psychotherapy*. New York, NY: Norton.

Schore, A. N. (2019). *Right brain psychotherapy*. New York, NY: W. W. Norton & Company.

Shah, P. E., Browne, J., & Poehlmann-Tynan, J. (2019). Prematurity: Identifying risks and promoting resilience. In C. H. Zeanah (Ed.), *Handbook of infant mental health* (4th ed., pp. 203–218). New York, NY: Guilford Press.

Siegel, D. J. (2012). *The developing mind: How relationships and the brain interact to shape who we are* (2nd ed.). New York, NY: Tarcher/Penguin.

Stern, D. N. (1977). *The first relationship*. Cambridge, MA: Harvard University Press.

Terr, L. (1990). *Too scared to cry: How trauma affects children and ultimately all of us*. New York, NY: Basic Books.

Tomlin, A. M., Weatherston, D. J., & Pavkov, T. (2014). Critical components of reflective supervision: Responses from expert supervisors in the field. *Infant Mental Health Journal*, 35(1), 70–80. DOI: 10.1002/imhj.21420

Tronick, E. Z. (2003). Of course all relationships are unique: How co-creative processes generate unique mother-infant and patient-therapist relationships and change other relationships. In *New Developments in Attachment Theory: Applications to Clinical Practice*, proceedings of conference at UCLA, Los Angeles, CA.

van der Kolk, B. (2014). *The body keeps the score*. New York, NY: Penguin Group.

Votruba-Drzal, E., Miller, P., & Coley, R. L. (2016). Poverty, urbanicity, and children's development of early academic skills. *Child Development Perspectives*, 10, 3–9. http://dx.doi.org/10.1111/cdep.12152

Winnicott, D. W. (1960). The theory of the parent infant relationship. *International Journal of Psycho-Analysis*, 41, 585–595. Retrieved 13 July 2019, from: http://icpla.edu/wp-content/uploads/2012/10/Winnicott-D.-The-Theory-of-the-Parent-Infant-Relationship-IJPA-Vol.-41-pps.-585-595.pdf

World Association for Infant Mental Health (2016). WAIMH Position Paper on the Rights of Infants, Edinburgh, 14–18 June, 2014. *Perspectives in Infant Mental*

Health (Winter-Spring), 1–5. Retrieved 14 July 2019 from: https://perspectives.wa imh.org/wp-content/uploads/sites/9/2017/05/PositionPaperRightsInfants_-May_13_ 2016_1-2_Perspectives_IMH_corr.pdf

Zeanah, C. H. (2019). *Handbook of infant mental health* (4th ed.). New York, NY: Guilford Press.

Zeanah, C. H., & Zeanah, P. D. (2019). Infant mental health: The clinical science of early experience. In C. H. Zeanah (Ed.), *Handbook of infant mental health* (4th ed., pp. 5–24). New York, NY: Guilford Press.

Zero to Three. (2001). *Definition of infant mental health.* Washington, DC: Zero to Three Infant Mental Health Steering Committee.

Zero to Three. (2016). *Diagnostic Classification of Mental Health and Developmental Disorders of Infancy and Early Childhood: DC:0–5.* Washington, DC: Author.

Chapter 2

The Impact of Play on the Developing Social Brain

New Insights from the Neurobiology of Touch

Emily Jackson and Francis McGlone

[I]t is reasonable to believe that a substantial amount of social motivation emerges from the pleasure of touch, and the pleasure of play is strongly dependent on the sensation of touch ... indeed it is possible that mammalian skin contains specialized receptors ... for detecting social contact.

(Panksepp, 2004, p. 271)

Introduction

Touch is the first sensory stimulus we all experience of the world around us, starting at about 12 weeks prenatally. Although it has long been recognized that touch is essential to children's physical, cognitive and emotional growth, from infancy to early childhood (and beyond) few have asked "why?" or "how?" In this chapter we report on recent advances in neurobiology that have identified a specific population of mechanosensory nerves in the skin of the body that respond preferentially to the types of touch experienced during close physical contact, such as nurture from the mother or play with peers. These recently discovered (in humans) nerves are called C-tactile afferents (CT) and when stimulated generate a rewarding sensation that promotes behaviors involving close physical contact. The key message in this report is that stimulation of CTs is not arbitrary, it is essential for the development of a healthy body and mind – and the science supporting this claim is indisputable.

Article 31 of the UN Convention on the Rights of the Child, an international treaty that sets out universally accepted rights for children, states: "every child has the right to rest and leisure, to engage in play and recreational activities appropriate to the age of the child and to participate freely in cultural life and the arts." Play is known to be of fundamental importance to the social and emotional well-being of children, and at a neural level impacts on developing cognitive functions (Tamis-LeMonda et al., 2004; Singer & Singer, 2009). It is known from animal studies that enriched environments where animals are reared in close proximity to their littermates promotes brain growth and development as measured by enhanced performance on a number of learning tasks (Figure 2.1).

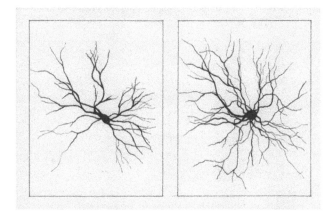

Figure 2.1 Dendritic morphology of pyramidal neurons in somatosensory cortex in rat housed in (left) standard and (right) enriched environments. The enrichment significantly increases dendritic branching as well as the number of dendritic spines (cf. Johansson & Belichenko, 2001).
Illustration courtesy of Francis McGlone.

Of particular interest here is that this enhanced performance is linked to biochemical and structural changes in the hippocampus (a brain area involved in memory and spatial navigation) such as an increased number of dendritic branches and spines, enlargement of synapses and enhanced circuit connectivity (Kuzumaki et al., 2011). Childhood play stimulates the brain to make connections between nerve cells. Extremely deprived children who do not have enough opportunities to play also experience impaired brain development and cognitive flexibility (Else, 2009; Johansen-Berg & Duzel, 2016). This is what helps a child develop both gross motor skills (walking, running, jumping, and coordination) and fine motor skills (writing, manipulating small tools, detailed hand work). Play during the teen years and into adulthood helps the brain develop even more connectivity, especially in the frontal lobe that is the centre for planning and making good decisions.

Background and Definitions

Jaak Panksepp was one of the first great neuroscientists to recognise the importance of play (or "social joy") in terms of its role in learning and development (Panksepp, 1991). The prescient opening quote of this chapter attests to Panksepp's recognition that there had to be a neurobiological basis for the play behaviors he observed, but the mechanism eluded him. By means of electrical stimulation, pharmacological challenges, and brain lesions of mostly mammalian vertebrates, Panksepp carved out seven primary

Figure 2.2 Brains at play: What do we know.
Illustration courtesy of Francis McGlone.

emotional systems; play being one, along with seeking, care, lust, fear, sadness, and anger. In his seminal book *Affective Neuroscience: The Foundations of Human and Animal Emotions*, the late Panksepp wrote:

> to play is also to learn ... play is fun for children, but it's much more than that – it's good for them, and it's necessary ... play gives children the opportunity to develop their intellect, emotions and imagination through encouraging reward seeking behaviour.
>
> (Panksepp, 2004, p. 280)

Panksepp recognised that play/social joy is a complex system which stimulates young animals to regularly engage in physical activities like wrestling, running, and chasing, helping them to bond socially and learn social limits. Several forms of play are recognised in the human and animal literature, including sensorimotor play, relational play, constructive play, symbolic play, games-with-rules play, and "rough-and-tumble" play – also called horseplay, rough-housing, or play fighting. It starts in the toddler years and becomes increasingly common until late elementary or middle school. This latter form of play is exhibited by non-human mammals and is seemingly the most fun of all; however, it has received little attention in human research. Here we describe the specialised receptors in the human skin he speculated would be responsible for his observations of play.

The Adaptive Nature of Play

The urge to play seems an intrinsic function of all animals, seemingly preserved in the brains of mammalian species. Rough-and-tumble type is the most basic form of play and the easiest to study in animal models; funnily enough, laboratory rats are one of the best species for systematic study of this behavior and the species on which Panksepp based the majority of his work. They provide a useful model for the systematic analysis of play mechanisms within the brain, as social-deprivation variables can be controlled and levels of playfulness can be effectively measured.

In most primates, early social isolation has a devastating effect on play instincts. After several days of isolation, young monkeys and chimps become despondent and depressed, exhibiting relatively little play when reunited. Juvenile rats, on the other hand, display the opposite reaction, with prior social isolation systematically increasing rough-housing play and social satiation reducing it. Rodents are better able to cope with social isolation compared to other mammals, likely because their social-bonding mechanisms are comparatively weak. Panksepp discovered that juvenile rats denied social interaction and prevented from engaging in play for up to 25 days demonstrated vigorous rough-and-tumble play behaviors as soon as they were given the opportunity. Rodent evidence shows that play reflects genetically ingrained impulses of the nervous system, and that the urge to engage in rough-and-tumble play is not created from past experiences.

The Purpose of Play – Why is it Fun?

Play is often observed between siblings, parents and peers, and involves vigorous physically active behaviors such as being bounced, swung, lifted, wrestled, tickled or chased – many of which we have fond childhood memories of. The precise nature varies widely across different mammalian species; however, the general flavor remains the same – a competitive yet joyful social exchange. As with other types of play, rough-and-tumble play is important for healthy child development and is observed cross-culturally in children from preschool age to early adolescence (Frost, 1998; Paquette et al., 2003; Paquette et al., 2006), making it an important adaptive behavior – play requires no learning, it is an evolved behavior instinctively built into our heritage.

During development, the brain is especially sensitive to social information, and it seems that a great deal of learning occurs during the course of rough-and-tumble play. It helps shape a range of social, emotional and cognitive behaviors (McArdle, 2001), teaching children about their own abilities in comparison with others and helping them to develop social skills such as compassion, self-control and social boundaries. In addition, it has been found to improve preschool children's attention during subsequent learning tasks (Holmes, Pellegrini & Schmidt, 2006). However, due to its boisterous nature, rough-and-tumble play is often viewed as disruptive and is mistaken for aggression or misbehavior; it was initially discouraged by the US National Association for the Education of Young Children (Bredekamp & Copple, 1997). It is still often discouraged by adults and schoolteachers (Tannock, 2008) with many holding the belief that it would escalate into real fighting. However, Scott and Panksepp (2003) found this to occur less than 1 per cent of the time, and evidence suggests that allowing children to engage in rough-and-tumble play enables them to better distinguish between real fighting and play fighting in later life – this is also true for children with learning disabilities (Nabuzoka & Smith, 1999). In addition, the global increase in screen time and technology use and the fact that children have increasingly less time and safe spaces to enjoy this form of social play is leading to its decline, threatening its existence in the play of current and future generations. Rough-and-tumble play provides opportunities for children to balance two opposing social skills; competition and cooperation (Paquette et al., 2003). Its decline may lead to a generation of children with too much of either trait, leading them to become socially isolated and unable to work with others, or unable to assert or defend themselves. For example, MacDonald (1987) found a direct correlation between preschool boys' popularity and their likelihood to engage in rough-and-tumble play, furthermore, Orobio et al. (2005) found that children who are less successful at grasping the concepts of play fighting in early childhood are more likely to be less socially skilled and more aggressive adolescents.

Along with the many beneficial effects for both brain and body, including the facilitation of certain kinds of learning and various physical skills, play also serves a range of social functions. It facilitates young animals to effectively integrate into the structures of their society by enabling them to identify those who rank higher and lower than them, which individuals they can develop cooperative relationships, and those whom they should avoid. Play likely allows animals to develop effective courting and parenting skills, as well as increase their effectiveness in hostile situations by instilling knowledge about how and when to accept defeat. It is seemingly a socially contagious process – when playful urges arise in one animal, they seem to spread to others via some type of sensory/perceptual influence. With all of these important functions, it is not surprising that play is so much fun – a behavior humans and animals need to experience in order to develop emotionally, physically and cognitively, and become well-rounded social beings.

Play and Parents

The full expression of play requires the right environment. In most mammals, play behaviors arise within their habitat/home environment (a secure base where parental support is available), and the most vigorous play occurs in the context of pre-existing social bonds. It is common in nature for infant–mother social bonds to be stronger than infant–father bonds, as fathers generally exhibit little-less enthusiasm for nurturing. Mother–offspring play is common throughout infancy, adolescence, and even adulthood, and the role of the mother in guiding play behaviors is evident in humans, chimpanzees and rats. However, even though fathers are less involved than mothers in most other aspects of child-rearing, physical play seems to be an exception (Bokony & Fortney, 2009).

Children benefit from play with both mother and father. In humans, fathers' play is typically more unpredictable and vigorous than the play of mothers, who are more likely to be cautious and engage in more pretend and object play (Paquette et al., 2003). The same study found that children experience more pleasure during rough-and-tumble play with fathers than mothers (Paquette et al., 2003), likely because male play tends to be more exciting and surprising. For example, fathers more often toss their children into the air or sneak up and grab them (Figure 2.3). For this reason, rough-housing with fathers seems to be

Figure 2.3 Three perspectives on play seen from the child, the father and the mother. Illustration courtesy of Francis McGlone.

especially important in promoting problem-solving by teaching children how to deal with unexpected events (Bokony & Fortney, 2009), and may be especially important in teaching boys how to regulate their emotions and behavior (Canfield, 2002). Roggman et al. (2002) found that father–toddler physical play enhanced toddlers' cognitive and language development, despite mothers typically using more language than fathers when engaging in play with their offspring.

Children's playfulness is related to their parent's responsiveness (Chiarello, Huntington & Huntington, 2006). Sensitive and competent fathers maintain a sense of safety and security while stimulating and challenging their children during play, avoiding frustrating their child or getting them over-excited (Paquette, 2004). McArdle (2001) found that securely attached children display more flexibility and complexity in their play than insecurely attached children. Adult support during childhood play promotes secure attachment, self-regulation and social skills, which allows children to develop skills that enable them to play cooperatively, solve conflicts and develop friendships. For example, parents of popular boys tend to be more sensitive and responsive to signs of over-stimulation and less controlling over their children's play (Chiarello, Huntington & Huntington, 2006).

Problems with Attachment Theory

A lot of research on the implications of early interactions for future development is viewed through the lens of Bowlby's Attachment Theory (Bowlby, 1973). Until recently the role of nurturing touch in the social development of infants has been overlooked, in part due to the dominance of Attachment Theory. Instead, the emphasis has been placed on the need for infants to develop "secure" attachments with their caregivers.

Harlow first discovered that infant monkeys removed from their mothers preferred an artificial surrogate made of cloth, which provided comfort, to one made of wire, which provided food (Harlow & Zimmermann, 1958; Harlow & Harlow, 1965). This innate desire for physical contact is thought to enable infants to form their first emotional bond, and an "internal working model" for understanding the world, self and others (Bowlby, 1973; Waters et al., 2000; Hazan & Shaver, 1987). According to Attachment Theory, internal schemas for emotion regulation and social relating are transferred from the infant–primary caregiver relationship to all other social relationships (Hazan & Shaver, 1987), and therefore individuals who receive insufficient maternal support adopt maladaptive schemas and become "insecure" (Hazan & Shaver, 1987). People tend to be given an insecure attachment phenotype in a non-revocable way even though researchers agree that attachment style can change over time and that an individual may be "secure" in one relationship/circumstance and "insecure" in another (Bowlby, 1973; Crowell et al., 2002; Fraley, 2002).

This deceptively simple theory has been adopted by many researchers over the years and has formed the basis of many subsequent theories of infant development. By recognizing the obvious importance of supportive maternal behaviors, Attachment Theory has been hailed a valuable tool for understanding and promoting children's well-being. Few people have questioned Attachment Theory, despite the fact that attachment classifications were not predicated on any scientific data. Instead, shared behaviors were clustered into a definition/diagnostic of "attachment style" resulting in a markedly reductionist compartmentalization.

Observations of attachment do have some veracity (as Harlow first noted), for example, individual differences in adult attachment have been found to influence psychosocial and somatic well-being, with a widely reported relationship between insecure attachment, and psychological adjustment problems, substance abuse and psychopathology (Brennan & Shaver, 1995; Griffin & Bartholomew, 1994; Mikulincer & Shaver, 2007). In addition, attachment relationships have been found to be important for establishing stress inhibition responses (Main, Kaplan & Cassidy, 1985; DeVries et al., 2003).

However, the original theory does not consider the importance of any neurobiological mechanisms, and in particular the role of touch, in the development of attachment phenotypes. This lack of recognition that the very nature of attachment relies upon an infant being "attached," i.e. that the physical touch between the mother and the infant is the critical stage in shaping the infant's psycho-social brain. Overall, the children who were more distressed as infants and did not receive as much physical contact had a molecular profile in their brain cells that indicated underdevelopment for their age. If touch is absent or compromised, as with Harlow's monkeys, all the criteria subsequently postrationalized by Attachment Theory are observed. Recent insights from the licking and grooming behavior (touch) of rat mums finds that a pup from a low-licking grooming mother grows up to be anxious, whereas those from a high-licking grooming mother grow up to be calm adults (Figure 2.4) (Weaver et al., 2004). This difference is explained by epigenetics – the science of gene × environment (G×E) – describing how the epigenetic code is sensitive to changing environmental conditions such as a socially enriched environment and play. The impact of childhood experiences on adult mental and physical health is not yet fully understood but these results bring to light the ways in which the simple act of a parent's touch or the opportunity to engage in peer-to-peer play has deep and potentially long-term consequences on gene expression.

The Role of Touch in the Genesis of "Attachment"

From the above it is clear that touch plays an important role in many forms of social communication and a number of theories have been proposed to explain observations and beliefs about the "power of touch." Research into

Figure 2.4 Levels of early life touch experience determine the adult's ability to cope
with stress.
Illustration courtesy of Francis McGlone.

the sense of touch in humans has largely concentrated on describing the
sensory and perceptual consequences of stimulation of low-threshold
mechanoreceptors (LTMs) and in a broader description the skin senses are
often described as encompassing the four submodalities of touch, temperature, itch and pain. Each of these channels is capable of generating distinct
sensory/perceptual qualities, processed by classes of stimulus-specific neurons
that project in defined anatomical pathways to the cerebral cortex. Here, we
propose that a recently discovered class of low-threshold unmyelinated
mechanosensitive C-fibres called C-tactile afferents (CT), that innervate the
hairy skin of the body, represent the neurobiological substrate for the affective
and rewarding properties of touch, as experienced during play behaviors. CTs
(or CLTMs in non-human mammals) have conduction velocities around 50
times slower than that of myelinated LTMs (Löken et al., 2009) and can
therefore not provide information of any immediate relevance. Using the
electrophysiological technique microneurography is has been found that CTs
are specifically tuned to respond to *affective touch* – gentle, caress-like stroking (Nordin, 1990; Essick et al., 1999; Vallbo et al. 1999; McGlone et al.,
2007; Löken et al., 2009; Ackerley et al., 2014; McGlone et al., 2014), making
them considerably different from the myelinated mechanosensitive afferents
responsible for discriminative touch. C-fibres, as a class of nerve fibre type,
constitute the majority of afferents in peripheral sensory nerves, around 70 per

cent (Willis & Coggeshall, 1978; Griffin et al., 2001) and evolved before the fast-conducting myelinated nerves. They have one key vital property – one of "protection." The significance of this is most clearly exemplified with the nociceptor (pain nerve) which plays a fundamental role in detecting potential or actual harmful stimulus or event occurring on or in the body, triggering defensive behavior. In the rare cases of children born with a congenital insensitivity to pain there is a lack in the ability to perceive physical pain (e.g. drinking a scalding hot beverage) and this lack of awareness often leads to health issues leading to the accumulation of multiple injuries and a reduced life expectancy. The CT performs an equally vital role in "protection," one that is only recently being recognized as we learn more about its functional role during development and throughout life. The Social Touch Hypothesis (Morrison et al., 2010) proposes that CTs code the hedonic and rewarding properties of touch and act as a peripheral pathway for pleasant tactile stimulation, encouraging interpersonal touch, attachment and affiliative behaviors, and perhaps mediating the emotional and rewarding properties of positive social touch. Unlike Attachment Theory, the Social Touch Hypothesis offers a mechanism highlighting the essential role of nurturing touch and linking its observations with a potential cause.

The Somatosensory Control of Play

Research investigating the importance of the senses in social play has selectively eliminated both vision and olfaction, as, at least in rats, vision is not essential in generating playfulness as blind animals play with the usual vigor, and removing a rat's sense of smell does not reduce the overall amount of rough-and-tumble play observed. The auditory system seems to contribute to play to some extent – during and prior to play, rats emit 50 kHz laughter-type chirps, and play in deafened animals is slightly less. However, touch is the leading sensory system for the provocation and maintenance of normal play. Anesthetisation of an animal's body surface diminishes their ability to perceive proximal play signals (measured by dorsal contacts), and research in this area suggests that certain areas of the body are seemingly more sensitive to play-instigation signals than others. Local anesthetisation of the skin of the dorsal neck and shoulder area of young rats is highly effective in reducing the level of playful behaviors; however, this is not accompanied by a decrease in play-solicitation behaviors (i.e. dorsal contacts), indicating that motivation/desire for play is not reduced. This suggests that the basic desire to play is an endogenous process, but that if the sensory feedback from the skin is not there then the behavior ceases. If local anaesthetic is applied to a rat's rump, a significantly smaller effect on playful behaviors is observed, and no effects are observed when it is applied to the ventral surface (i.e. the animal's belly). This suggests that rats have homologous "play/tickle skin" located on the dorsal body surface – where most (but not all) play solicitations are directed (i.e. dorsal contacts). Panksepp et al., (2003) speculated that there would be skin sites that were innervated by specialised receptors which would send particularly potent somatosensory inputs to specific play circuitry of the brain/ nervous system when they are touched in order to communicate playful intentions between animals. This is interesting, as rats' "play/tickle skin" areas correspond to those of humans (the back of the neck and around the rib cage) and areas where maternal grooming of rat pups is most commonly directed. The trunk, neck and head also happen to be the skin sites most densely innervated by CLTMs in rats (Liu et al., 2007) and the areas most finely tuned to slow gentle touch in humans (Walker, Trotter, Woods & McGlone, 2017). Understanding the neural processes underlying play systems may lie in analysis of the somatosensory stimulation of "play skin." The existence of cutaneous "neural play circuits" likely explains the phenomenon of tickling and helps answer the question of why we can't tickle ourselves (Blakemore, Wolpert & Frith, 2000). Therefore, the ability to identify and perceive play partners is a powerful, ingrained central nervous system concept (one that may have gone awry in autism).

The Neuroanatomy of Play: The Brain's Play Networks

The developmental time course of rough-and-tumble play in most species exhibits an inverted U-shape, with play increasing during the early child-hood, remaining stable throughout youth, and lessening during puberty. Although we can presume that this inverted U-shaped developmental func-tion is related to aspects of brain maturation, as well as neurochemical shifts that occur during development, we currently know essentially nothing about the neurobiological factors that regulate it. Understanding the brain mechanisms underlying play could provide important insights into certain childhood psychiatric problems such as autism and attention deficit dis-order. Within the last two decades, scientists have recognized that play is a primary emotional function of the mammalian brain, with a great deal of joy arising from the arousal of these play circuits. It recruits many brain abilities simultaneously, for example, most of the basic emotional systems are engaged at one time or another during play and therefore many neural circuits are expected to be involved. Neural systems that control movement such as the vestibular, cerebellar and basal ganglia are likely to play a fun-damental role in play; however, this is not currently supported by any con-vincing evidence since extensive damage to these areas compromises virtually all complex motor abilities. For example, bilateral damage to the caudate-putamen nuclei of infant rats abolishes play, but also appetite, curiosity and desire to move (Panksepp, 2004). Lesions in other areas, such as the cerebellum, temporal lobe/amygdala and lateral hypothalamus, also significantly reduce play; however, again, the overall conduct of the animal becomes so impaired that it prevents any meaningful interpretation with respect to specific play systems.

The symptoms of frontal lobe damage generally resemble Attention Deficit/Hyperactivity Disorder (ADHD), and right hemisphere frontal lobe lesions significantly increase playfulness in rats (Panksepp et al., 2003). Rodent models implicate frontal lobe deficits in ADHD and suggest that these brain areas contribute to the developmental processes which diminish play as animals mature. The authors suggested that one of the long-term functions of social play may be to promote maturation of various higher brain areas, including frontal cortical regions responsible for behavioral inhibition and the regulation of excessive play urges often reflected in impulsive behaviors characteristic of ADHD (Panksepp et al., 2003).

However, in animal models of neonatal decortication (surgical removal of the cortex) play motivation is not eliminated or play behaviors greatly affected in rats (Panksepp et al., 1994), suggesting that the primary process of play is deeply embedded in mammalian brains. Despite this, it seems clear that play has powerful effects on the cortex. C-fos expression is used as a marker for neuronal activity throughout the neuroaxis following peripheral stimulation; play elevates c-fos expression in medial thalamic areas such as the parafascicular and hippocampus, and in many higher brain areas, especially the somatosensory cortex. This evidence suggests a role of play in the development of various cortical functions. Smaller lesions are much more interpretable, and as of yet, specific play motivation effects have only been observed in the case of bilateral damage to the nonspecific reticular nuclei of the thalamus, such as the parafascicular complex and posterior thalamic nuclei. When the parafascicular region of the thalamus is lesioned in rats, play solicitation behaviors (i.e. pinning and dorsal contact) are reduced, indicating diminished play motivation compared to controls. However, other rather complex motivated behaviors, such as foraging, are not reduced (Siviy and Panksepp, 1985a, 1985b). This suggests that nonspecific reticular nuclei of the thalamus specifically mediate the urge to play.

The parafascicular thalamic nucleus is also thought to play a role in pain perception, as it contains neurons that respond to noxious stimuli such as pinpricks. However, it may be that these stimuli more closely resemble nipping or tickling than pain. This may explain why in humans, intense/prolonged tickling is almost unbearable. In addition, human laughter systems have also been associated with these primitive subcortical brain areas. For humans, the hallmark of play circuitry in action is laughter, which some have argued may emerge from play motivation. Amyotrophic lateral sclerosis (ALS) – a demyelination of motor neurons affecting the brain stem, along with gelastic epilepsy, are two neurological diseases accompanied by impulsive bouts of laughter in the absence of any positive affect. Interestingly, earlier phases of these diseases typically involve pathological crying, again in the absence of any sadness. This apparent relationship between laugher and crying suggests that they are intermediately related in the brain, with the ability to cry – a separation-distress, and social-bonding mechanism acting as a prerequisite for the evolution of laughter, and possibly play. This is supported by the fact that crying seems to emerge from lower levels of the neuroaxis.

The prevailing sensory system, which both provides comfort after separation and most readily provokes play, is touch. Therefore, in evolutionary terms the pleasure of affective touch may have established a neural framework for the emergence of play. If so, we might suppose that both play and laughter serve social-bonding functions – possibly helping us to discriminate friends and family from strangers.

The Neurochemistry of Play

According to Panksepp: "play is both a robust and a fragile phenomenon." Environmental manipulations aroused in a play context, which evoke negative emotional states such as fear, anger, and separation distress are surprisingly effective in reducing play. In addition, homeostatic imbalances such as hunger and bodily imbalances (i.e. illnesses) are powerful play inhibitors. Many of these negative factors have neurochemical underpinnings, and inhibiting play using drugs is remarkably easy; however, it is very difficult to determine whether these effects reflect specific changes in underlying play regulatory mechanisms or merely the generally disruptive psychological and behavioral effects of drugs. Despite this, there is currently considerable evidence that opioids specifically mediate play motivation, with low doses of opiate agonists increasing play behaviors, and opiate antagonists reducing them. For obvious reasons, to facilitate play, doses must be kept low, as opiate arousal over a certain point induces catatonia and inhibits the desire for all forms of social interaction including play. Indirect evidence from autoradiography studies suggests that during play there is a widespread release of opioids in the nervous system, especially in brain areas such as the medial preoptic area/anterior hypothalamus, where sexual and maternal behavior circuitries are situated. There is also a role for endogenous opioids in gentle touch behaviors – endorphins modulate pair bonding and attachment in primates and other mammals. Keverne et al. (1989) found that grooming duration related to changes in rhesus macaque's neural opioid systems, and Johnson and Johnson and Dunbar (2016) found that the density of human endorphin receptors corresponds with the size of an individuals' social network. CT-targeted touch has been found to activate similar neural pathways in humans to those that fire in rhesus macaques during grooming, triggering the same release of endorphins (serotonin & oxytocin) and endogenous opioids (Keverne et al., 1989; Walker et al. 2017).

When placed with controls and animals treated with low doses of morphine, animals treated with naloxone (an opioid antagonist) become submissive and lose during a wrestling match situation. However, when placed with a partner treated with scopolamine (a cholinergic blocking agent

making them totally non-reciprocating and non-threatening), animals treated with naloxone at doses that normally reduce play exhibit heightened
play solicitations, winning during wrestling matches. This is because naloxone-treated animals, when paired with scopolamine treated animals, and
morphine treated animals/controls, when paired with animals treated with
naloxone experience heightened social confidence and feelings of social
strength. Therefore, brain opioids may control social emotionality – which
may be why without them, an animal is more prone to experience negative
affect and feelings such as separation distress and reduced psychological
strength, and likely why we see a reduction in play solicitation following the
release of opiate antagonists. However, there are alternative explanations;
opiate receptor antagonists may reduce or eliminate the reinforcing pleasure
of social interaction, while opiate agonists enhance them. It is also possible
that morphine dulls the pain of playful scrapes, while opiate antagonists
make them more painful.

However, opioids cannot be the only factor modulating play, as it is not
possible to restore playfulness in older rats or play-satiated youngsters by
administering low doses of opiate agonists or antagonists. Many other neurochemical systems appear to have specific effects on play. For example, acetylcholine appears to promote play, as blocking cholinergic activity with
scopolamine markedly reduces play solicitation behaviors in rats. However, as
of yet, no one has been able to directly enhance play by activating the cholinergic system. Neurotransmitters serotonin and noradrenaline also reduce play,
while blocking their receptors can increase play to some degree. Conversely,
blocking dopamine receptors reduces play, and most dopamine agonists do the
same, indicating that play requires animals to have normal levels of synaptic
dopamine. A significant amount of research has been conducted on hormone
production in parents. In fathers specifically, active "rough-and-tumble" interactions have been positively correlated with oxytocin (Feldman et al., 2010) and
testosterone production (Rilling & Mascaro, 2017), whereas empathy-related
caring behavior would be negatively correlated with testosterone (Fleming et
al., 2002; Mascaro et al., 2014; Weisman et al., 2014).

Panksepp dedicated a lot of his time searching for a way to "turn on"
playfulness pharmacologically; however, all neurochemical systems participate
in the control of a large number of brain and behavioral processes, and virtually all of them must be administered directly into the brain's synapses.
Currently we don't know enough about play circuitry to accurately adminis-
ter these substances. The brain may contain highly specific play-promoting
neurochemicals; however, no such substance has yet been identified.

Conclusion

The basic desire to play is an endogenous impulse. The brain contains distinct neural systems for the generation of all types of play involving the

thalamus and cortex – midbrain somatosensory information processing centres. Modest brain opioid arousal promotes play, and ongoing play promotes opioid release, which may serve to gradually bring play episodes to an end. Since rough-and-tumble play arises from powerful neural activities which interact with many forms of learning, it is difficult to study comprehensively, and due to the complexity of the motor features of rough-and-tumble play, it is difficult to trace the source mechanisms in a systematic manner. Only when play can be "turned on" pharmacologically in animal models will we truly understand the neural underpinnings of playfulness, but even then its adaptive functions may be indefinite. Given the social significance of touch and the fact that the physical embodiment of attachment is touch, it's not unlikely that the CT-system represents an evolutionary mechanism responsible for promoting normative social development and the development of adaptive, "secure" attachment behaviors. It is also reasonable to hypothesise that the pleasure of touch may have established an evolved neural framework for the emergence of play.

Discussion Questions

1 What does the skin tell the brain?
2 Discuss the effects a lack of nurturing care had on Romanian orphanage infants.
3 Attachment has a nerve. Discuss the relevance of attachment in the light of recent evidence of C-tactile afferents.

References

Ackerley, R., Wasling, H., Liljencrantz, J., Olausson, H., Johnson, R. D., & Wessberg, J. (2014). Human C-tactile afferents are tuned to the temperature of a skin-stroking caress. *Journal Neuroscience*, 34(8), 2879–2883. doi:10.1523/JNEUROSCI.2847-13.2014

Blakemore, S, J., Wolpert, D., & Frith, C. (2000). Why can't you tickle yourself? *Neuroreport*, 3; 11(11), R11–16. Review. Retrieved September 2, 2019 from: https://stanford.edu/~knutson/ans/blakemore02.pdf

Bokony, P., Patrick, T., & Fortney, S. (2009). *What the experts say*. Retrieved September 2, 2019 from: https://ecep.uark.edu/_resources/pdf_other/pre-k_sel/wes-play.pdf

Bowlby, J. (1973). *Attachment and loss, Vol. II: Separation*. New York, NY: Basic Books.

Bredekamp, S., & Copple, C. (1997). *Developmentally appropriate practice in early childhood programs* (Revised Edition). Washington, DC: National Association for the Education of Young Children, 20036–21426.

Brennan, K. A., & Shaver, P. R. (1995). Dimensions of adult attachment, affect regulation, and romantic relationship functioning. *Personality and Social Psychology Bulletin*, 21, 267–283. https://doi.org/10.1177/0146167295213008

Canfield, K. (2002). *Horseplay advantages: Challenging ideas for action-oriented dads.* Missouri: National Center for Fathering.

Chiarello, L. A., Huntington, A., & Huntington, A. (2006). A comparison of motor behaviors, interaction, and playfulness during mother-child and father-child play with children with motor delay. *Physical & Occupational Therapy in Pediatrics,* 26(1–2), 129–151. https://doi.org/10.1080/J006v26n01_09

Crowell, J. A., Treboux, D., & Waters, E. (2002). Stability of attachment representations: The transition to marriage. *Developmental Psychology,* 38(4), 467–479. http://dx.doi.org/10.1037/0012-1649.38.4.467

DeVries, A. C., Glasper, E. R., & Detillion, C. E. (2003) Social modulation of stress responses, *Physiology & Behavior,* 79(3), 399–407. https://doi.org/10.1016/S0031-9384(03)00152–00155.

Else, P. (2009). *The value of play.* London: Continuum.

Essick, G. K., James, A., & McGlone, F. P. (1999). Psychophysical assessment of the affective components of non-painful touch. *NeuroReport: For Rapid Communication of Neuroscience Research,* 10(10), 2083–2087. http://dx.doi.org/10.1097/00001756-199907130-00017

Feldman, R., Gordon, I., Schneiderman, I., Weisman, I., & Zagoory-Sharon, O. (2010). Natural variations in maternal and paternal care are associated with systematic changes in oxytocin following parent–infant contact. *Psychoneuroendocrinology,* 35(8), 1133–1141. https://doi.org/10.1016/j.psyneuen.2010.01.013.

Fleming, A. S., Corter, C., Stallings, J., & Steiner, M. (2002). Testosterone and prolactin are associated with emotional responses to infant cries in new fathers. *Hormones and Behavior,* 42(4), 399–413. https://doi.org/10.1006/hbeh.2002.1840.

Fraley, C. R. (2002). Attachment stability from infancy to adulthood: Meta-analysis and dynamic modeling of developmental mechanisms. *Personality and Social Psychology Review,* 6(2), 123–151. https://doi.org/10.1207/S15327957PSPR0602_03

Frost, J. L. (1998). *Neuroscience, play, and child development.* Retrieved September 2, 2019 from: https://files.eric.ed.gov/fulltext/ED427845.pdf.

Griffin, D. W., & Bartholomew, K. (1994). The metaphysics of measurement: The case of adult attachment. In K. Bartholomew & D. Perlman (Eds.), *Advances in personal relationships,* Vol. 5. *Attachment processes in adulthood* (pp. 17–52). London: Jessica Kingsley Publishers.

Griffin, J.W., McArthur, J. C., & Michael, P. (2001). Assessment of cutaneous innervation by skin biopsies [Review]. *Current Opinion in Neurology,* 14(5), 655–659.

Harlow, H. F., & Harlow, M. K. (1965). The affectional systems. In A. M. Schrier, H. F. Harlow, & F. Stollnitz (Eds.), *Behavior of nonhuman primates,* Vol.2. New York, NY: Academic Press.

Harlow, H. F., & Zimmermann, R. R. (1958). The development of affectional responses in infant monkeys. *Proceedings of the American Philosophical Society,* 102(5), 501–509.

Hazan, C., & Shaver, P. R. (1987). Romantic love conceptualized as an attachment process. *Journal of Personality and Social Psychology,* 59, 511–524.

Holmes, R. M., Pellegrini, A. D., & Schmidt, S. L. (2006). The effects of different recess timing regimens on preschoolers' classroom attention. *Early Child Development and Care,* 176(7), 735–743.

Jarvis, P. (2006). "Rough and tumble" play: Lessons in life. *Evolutionary Psychology,* 4(1), 147470490600400128.

Johansen-Berg, H., & Duzel, E. (2016). Neuroplasticity: Effects of physical and cognitive activity on brain structure and function. *NeuroImage*, 131, 1.

Johansson, B. B., & Belichenko, P. V. (2001). Environmental influence on neuronal and dendritic spine plasticity after permanent focal brain ischemia. In *Maturation phenomenon in cerebral ischemia* IV, pp. 77–83. Berlin: Springer,

Johnson, K. V. A., & Dunbar, R. I. (2016). Pain tolerance predicts human social network size. *Scientific Reports*, 6, 25267.

Keverne, E. B., Martensz, N. D., & Tuite, B. (1989). Beta-endorphin concentrations in cerebrospinal fluid of monkeys are influenced by grooming relationships. *Psychoneuroendocrinology*, 14, 155–161.

Kuzumaki, N., Ikegami, D., Tamura, R., Hareyama, N., Imai, S., Narita, M., Torigoe, K., Niikura, K., Takeshima, H., Ando, T., Igarashi, K., Kanno, J., Ushijima, T., Suzuki, T., Narita, M., & Igarashi, K. (2011). Hippocampal epigenetic modification at the brain-derived neurotrophic factor gene induced by an enriched environment. *Hippocampus*, 21(2), 127–132.

Liu, Q., Vrontou, S., Rice, F. L., Zylka, M. J., Dong, X., & Anderson, D. J. (2007). Molecular genetic visualization of a rare subset of unmyelinated sensory neurons that may detect gentle touch. *Nature Neuroscience*, 10(8), 946.

Löken, J. L. S., Wessberg, J., Morrison, I., McGlone, F., & Olausson, H. (2009). Coding of pleasant touch by unmyelinated afferents in humans. *Nature Neuroscience*, 12(5), 547–548. Published online April 12, 2009. https://doi.org/10.1038/nn.2312.

MacDonald, K. (1987). Parent-child physical play with rejected, neglected, and popular boys. *Developmental Psychology*, 23(5), 705.

Main, M., Kaplan, N., & Cassidy, J. (1985). Security in infancy, childhood, and adulthood: A move to the level of representation. In I. Bretherton & E. Waters (Eds.), *Monographs of the society for research in child development*, 50 (1–2, Serial No. 209, pp. 66–106).

Martin, C. L., & Fabes, R. A. (2001). The stability and consequences of young children's same-sex peer interactions. *Developmental Psychology*, 37(3), 431.

Mascaro, J. S., Hackett, P. D. & Rilling, J. K. (2014). Differential neural responses to child and sexual stimuli in human fathers and non-fathers and their hormonal correlates. *Psychoneuroendocrinology*, 46, 153–163. https://doi.org/10.1016/j.psyneuen.2014.04.014.

McArdle, P. (2001). Children's play. *Child: Care, Health and Development*, 27(6), 509–514.

McGlone, F., Vallbo, A. B., Olausson, H., Loken, L., & Wessberg, J. (2007). Discriminative touch and emotional touch. *Can. J. Exp. Psychol.*, 61, 173–183.

McGlone, F., Olausson, H., Boyle, J. A., Jones-Gotman, M., Dancer, C., Guest, S., & Essick, G. (2012). Touching and feeling: differences in pleasant touch processing between glabrous and hairy skin in humans. *Eur. J. Neurosci.* 35, 1782–1788.

McGlone, F., Wessberg, J., & Olausson, H. (2014). Discriminative and affective touch: sensing and feeling. *Neuron*, 82, 737–755.

Mikulincer, M., & Shaver, P. R. (2007). *Attachment patterns in adulthood: Structure, dynamics, and change*. New York, NY: Guilford.

Morrison, I., Loken, L. S., & Olausson, H. (2010). The skin as a social organ. *Exp. Brain Res.*, 204, 305–314. http://dx.doi.org/10.1007/s00221–00009–2007–y. Epub Sep 22, 2009.

Nabuzoka, D., & Smith, P. K. (1999). Distinguishing serious and playful fighting by children with learning disabilities and nondisabled children. *The Journal of Child Psychology and Psychiatry and Allied Disciplines*, 40(6), 883–890.

Nordin, M. (1990). Low-threshold mechanoreceptive and nociceptive units with unmyelinated (C) fibres in the human supraorbital nerve. *J Physiol. (Lond.)*, 426, 229–240. [Published correction appears in *J. Physiol. (Lond.)* (1991), 444, 777.] http://dx.doi.org/10.1113/jphysiol.1990.sp018135

Orobio de Castro, B., Merk, W., Koops, W., Veerman, J. V., & Bosch, J. D. (2005). Emotions in social information processing and their relations with reactive and proactive aggression in referred aggressive boys. *Journal of Clinical Child & Adolescent Psychology*, 34(1), 105–116. http://dx.doi.org/10.1207/s15374424jccp3401_10

Panksepp, J. (1991). Affective neuroscience: A conceptual framework for the neuro-biological study of emotions. *International Review of Studies on Emotion*, 1(59–99), 57.

Panksepp, J. (2004). *Affective neuroscience: The foundations of human and animal emotions.* New York, NY: Oxford University Press.

Panksepp, J., Burgdorf, J., Turner, C., & Gordon, N. (2003). Modeling ADHD-type arousal with unilateral frontal cortex damage in rats and beneficial effects of play therapy. *Brain and Cognition*, 52(1), 97–105. https://doi.org/10.1016/S0278-2626 (03)00013-00017

Panksepp, J., Normansell, L., Cox, J. F., & Siviy, S. M. (1994). Effects of neonatal decortication on the social play of juvenile rats. *Physiology & Behavior*, 56(3), 429–443. http://dx.doi.org/10.1016/0031-9384(94)90285–90282

Paquette, D. (2004). Theorizing the father-child relationship: Mechanisms and developmental outcomes. *Human development*, 47(4), 193–219. http://dx.doi.org/10.1159/000078723

Paquette, D., Carbonneau, R., Dubeau, D., Bigras, M., & Tremblay, R. E. (2003). Prevalence of father-child rough-and-tumble play and physical aggression in pre-school children. *European Journal of Psychology of Education*, 18(2), 171–189. http://dx.doi.org/10.1007/BF03173483

Rilling, J. K., Mascaro, J. S. (2017) The neurobiology of fatherhood, *Current Opinion in Psychology*, 15, 26–32. https://doi.org/10.1016/j.copsyc.2017.02.013.

Roggman, L. A., Boyce, L., Cook, G. A., & Hart, A. D. (2002). Observational data on father play with infants: Challenging to get but valuable to have. Poster presented at a workshop at World Association of Infant Mental Health, Amsterdam, Netherlands.

Scott, E., & Panksepp, J. (2003). Rough-and-tumble play in human children. *Aggressive Behavior: Official Journal of the International Society for Research on Aggression*, 29(6), 539–551. https://doi.org/10.1002/ab.10062

Singer, D. G., & Singer, J. L. (2009). *Imagination and play in the electronic age.* Harvard University Press.

Siviy, S. M., & Panksepp, J. (1985a). Dorsomedial diencephalic involvement in the juvenile play of rats. *Behavioral Neuroscience*, 99(6), 1103.

Siviy, S. M., & Panksepp, J. (1985b). Energy balance and play in juvenile rats. *Physiology & Behavior*, 35(3), 435–441. https://doi.org/10.1016/0031-9384(85) 90320–90328

Tamis-LeMonda, C. S., Shannon, J. D., Cabrera, N. J., & Lamb, M. E. (2004). Fathers and mothers at play with their 2-and 3-year-olds: Contributions to language and cognitive development. *Child Development*, 75(6), 1806–1820.

Tannock, M. T. (2008). Rough and tumble play: An investigation of the perceptions of educators and young children. *Early Childhood Education Journal*, 35(4), 357–361.

Vallbo, A., Olausson, H., & Wessberg, J. (1999). Unmyelinated afferents constitute a second system coding tactile stimuli of the human hairy skin. *Journal of Neurophysiology*, 81, 2753–2763. https://www.physiology.org/doi/full/10.1152/jn.1999.81.6.2753

Walker, S. C., Trotter, P. D., Woods, A., & McGlone, F. (2017). Vicarious ratings of social touch reflect the anatomical distribution & velocity tuning of C-tactile afferents: A hedonic homunculus?. *Behavioural Brain Research*, 320, 91–96.

Waters, E., Merrick, S., Treboux, D., Crowell, J., & Albersheim, L. (2000). Attachment security in infancy and early adulthood: A twenty-year longitudinal study. *Child Development*, 71(3), 684–689.

Weaver, I.C.G, Cervoni, N., Champagne, F. A., D'Alessio, A.C., Sharma, S., Seckl, J. R., Dymov, S., Szyf, M., & Meaney, M. (2004). Epigenetic programming by maternal behavior. *Nature Neuroscience*, 7, 847–854. https://doi.org/10.1038/nn1276

Weisman, O., Zagoory-Sharon, O. & Feldman, R. (2014) Oxytocin administration, salivary testosterone, and father–infant social behavior, *Progress in Neuro-Psychopharmacology and Biological Psychiatry*, 49, 47–52. https://doi.org/10.1016/j.pnpbp.2013.11.006.

Willis, W. D., & Coggeshall, R. E. (2004). *Sensory Mechanisms of the Spinal Cord*. New York, NY: Springer. https://doi.org/10.1007/978-1-4757-1688-7

Neurosensory Play in the Infant–Parent Dyad

A Developmental Perspective

Ken Schwartzenberger

Preborn Neurosensory Development

Neuroscience and developmental psychology research has advanced our knowledge of early in utero experiences of preborn infants. The heart starts beating at six weeks and development of the brain begins during the first eight weeks of the embryonic period. The preborn infant's brain is organized and develops from the bottom up, starting with the brain stem, followed in sequence by the limbic brain and the neocortex brain systems. The brain is made up of specialized nerve cells (neurons) which communicate with one another via electrical and neurochemical signals and form new networks of connections and neural patterns every time the brain is stimulated (Perry, 2006).

The sensorimotor level of information processing, including sensation and movement, is initiated primarily in the brain stem. Sensory system receptors receive incoming stimuli via afferent nerves and send this information via efferent nerve pathways to the thalamus and across a synapse to the amygdala and the limbic brain system (Lillas & Turnbull, 2009). The structures of the limbic system are involved in emotion, motivation, learning, and memory. The physical and emotional needs of infants are dominated by the brain stem and the limbic brain systems (Lillas & Turnbull, 2009).

The neurological system is one of the first systems to develop in utero and consists of the central and sensory nervous systems. The central nervous system includes multiple branches that control intake and responses to sensory input. These neural circuits include the autonomic nervous system in the brain stem that regulates heart rate and breathing.

There are two branches of the autonomic nervous system, the sympathetic (activation) and the parasympathetic (inhibition) nervous systems. There are two branches of the parasympathetic nervous system, the ventral vagal (slow down) and dorsal vagal (shut down) nervous systems. The vagal nerve is central for the infant to sustain attention, regulate emotions, control heart rate variability, and engage in social emotional play interactions (Porges, 2011; Kestly, 2014).

The baseline for an infant's sensory nervous system development and capacities are set by genes and in utero sensory experiences. These sensory systems include touch (tactile), smell (olfactory), sound (auditory), sight (visual), taste (gustatory), balance (vestibular), body movements and position in space (proprioception), and emotional (visceral) senses. Seventy-five percent of the brain and nervous system development is genetic; however, the rest is the result of sensory experience (Lillas & Turnbull, 2009).

Preborn Infants

We now know in detail the physiological development of the preborn fetus from conception to birth. Research has evidenced that physical sensation in utero starts at around twenty-eight days; at six to eight weeks developmental movement begins, and preborns respond to touch. At twelve weeks they can smell, and at twenty-two weeks taste and hear (Nixon, 1983).

Preborns are attentive listeners and are constantly in tune with sounds inside and outside the uterus. They hear and sense rhythms of mother's heartbeat and breathing and the swooshing of blood rushing through the umbilical cord. Verny and Weintraub describe these sounds as a "symphony of music, a soothing and calming intrauterine lullaby" (Verny & Weintraub, 2014, p. 98).

Preborns experience continual tactile and kinesthetic stimulation in utero via mother's movement, talking, singing, and touch, and they respond with facial expressions, movement, turning, pushing, and kicking against the uterine wall. Sounds, touch, rhythmic movements, and other sensory stimulation are part of the experiences of prenatal life, and are imprinted on a preborn's brain (Chamberlain, 2013).

Starting around ten weeks, preborns develop rhythms of active and rest cycles and engage in spontaneous developmental movement and energetic play such as flexing and extending, stretching, yawning, kicking, turning, and doing somersaults in the amniotic fluid chamber that Chamberlain describes as a "prenatal ballet" (Chamberlain, 1998, p. 14).

Preborns express emotions through movement, and advanced ultrasound technology has allowed us to see a preborn's facial expressions and movements in utero, such as smiles and frowns, in the first eight to twelve weeks. Developmental movement carries emotional expression (Chamberlain, 2013).

Preborn Trauma

Studies show that early biological and psychological events experienced in utero shapes the architecture of the preborn infant's brain (Verny & Weintraub, 2014). Mothers share stress hormones, endorphins, sensory experiences, and emotional sensations with their preborns (Manrique et al., 1998). There are numerous sensory experiences in the intrauterine environment that are traumatic and adversely impact development for the newborn. These include exposure to chemical toxins, neurotoxins, noradrenaline, stress hormones passed through the umbilical cord and placenta, excessive cortisol levels, drugs, alcohol, cigarette smoke, domestic violence, inadequate nourishment, amniocentesis procedures, prenatal surgery, medical procedures, and mother's accidents, injuries, or illnesses (Emerson, 1995; Lillas & Turnbull, 2009; Chamberlain, 2013).

Prenatal and Neonatal Play Interventions

Early development of the sensory systems of the preborn makes it possible to begin using neurosensory play activities during the second trimester of pregnancy. At this stage the preborn's nervous and sensory systems are fully formed, developmental movement has started, and preborns respond to sensory stimulation.

In prenatal play interventions, parents are guided through a series of both structured and spontaneous interactive sensory stimulation play activities appropriate to each stage of development. Preborns are active participants in these playful sensory stimulating activities and interactions with parents. They cycle between alert and active periods with sleep and rest periods in utero and are most likely to engage in neurosensory play when they are alert and moving. The following neurosensory play interaction games are recommended in the second and third trimesters.

The Kick Game. This play interaction starts with the parent noticing the preborn kicking (quickening) and responds with an invitation to kick again by placing a hand over the abdomen or patting gently in the area of the kick, and saying "hello there," "kick, kick, kick." After every kick the parent gently pats back on the abdomen so the preborn feels the touch and the vibration and hears the parent say repeatedly "there you are," in a *game of tag.* Preborns learn to associate their movements with responses from parents and discover that their actions illicit a response, and the beginning of two-way communication in the preborn–parent dyad commences.

Music Games. Preborns hear music played at a low volume with the use of a headset or small speaker near the abdomen. Researchers have discovered that preborns respond to classical music such as Brahms's Lullaby. When played at lower decibels (40–50 dB) it reduces heart rate to sixty beats per minute and calms and soothes the preborn's developing nervous system (Van der Carr & Lehrer, 1997).

The Drum Beat Game. This game utilizes a small drum that is placed over the abdomen and the parent taps the drum to a simple beat and rhythm. Research suggests that repeatedly varying the beat and rhythm stimulates neuron connections that grow the brain (Van der Carr & Lehrer, 1997). The rhythm, cadence, and vibration from the drum beats and other musical sounds soothe and calm the preborn's developing nervous system overly sensitized by in utero trauma experiences.

Nurturing Touch Games. Parents use soft *caring touch* games by finding the flat surface of the preborn's back and gently rubbing the abdomen. saying "rub, rub, rub," or gently patting or tapping with one hand on the preborn's back and saying "tap, tap, tap." Movement, tactile, and vibration stimuli are activated with one hand by gently pushing on the side of the abdomen, quickly releasing it, saying "shake, shake, shake." Through these neurosensory play interactions the preborn begins to recognize and learn that repeated stimulus has pattern and meaning (Manrique et al., 1998; Van der Carr & Lehrer, 1997).

Parents balance stimulation play activities with rest periods by playing with the preborn for five to ten minutes at a time, two times per day, and limiting the frequency of the sensory activities to avoid over stimulation. Parents report that newborns are more easily calmed by touch, rocking, and singing. They sleep better, breast feed more easily, are alert and happy, and talk earlier as newborn infants (Manrique et al., 1998; Van der Carr & Lehrer, 1997). Research-based prenatal and neonatal neurosensory play interventions for expecting parents have proven to enhance emotional development and heighten attention and memory skills, facilitate acquisition of speech and language skills, and advance learning skills for the preborn infant (Manrique et al., 1998; Arenas, 1997; Van der Carr & Lehrer, 1997).

Newborn Neurosensory Development: Birth to Three Months

Newborn infants are thinking, feeling persons, always aware, conscious, and expressive (Vernallis, Landsberg, & Highsmith, 2001). They have a full range of emotions and sensory capacities with affective systems set before birth that are genetically prepared to respond to human interaction (Tronick, 2007; Van der Carr & Lehrer, 1997). Newborns clearly express emotions such as happy, sad, and surprise through facial expressions and developmental movement. As early as four weeks, researchers found newborns' emotional reactions to be a whole language (Klaus & Klaus, 1998; Stokes, 2002).

Infants are born with millions of nerve connections ready to chemically encode sensory stimuli. Their sensory systems are fully functional at birth and are capable of immediately responding to various stimuli, including sound, sight, taste, touch, and smell. They are extremely competent in perception, learning, and communication. As they develop, they transform from a sensate being, reacting to stimuli, to a sensory attuned being with mental alertness, consciousness, and early cognition (Verny & Weintraub, 2014).

Each infant has a unique sensory profile with identifiable sensory preferences and stressors (Lillas & Turnbull, 2009, Beil & Peske, 2005). They exhibit strong sensory preferences and can distinguish their own mother's voice, breast milk, and body odors (Klaus & Klaus, 1998). In the very first hours after birth, newborns have the ability to concentrate on visual stimulus and can track objects with their eyes and turn their heads toward mother's voice (Klaus & Klaus, 1998).

Newborns sleep twelve to sixteen hours per day, in and out of awake states on an average of six segments, in a twenty-four hour period. They exhibit six different behavior patterns, or states of consciousness: three awake states (quiet alert, active alert, and crying); two sleep states (quiet sleep and active sleep); and drowsiness, a transition between sleep and wakefulness (Klaus & Klaus, 1998).

The human face has a unique stimulus value for newborn infants. In the quiet alert state they will make eye-to-eye contact, fix gaze on faces, and reach out and touch their parent's face. This mutual gaze signals a readiness to engage in play and is the first form of visual dialogue (Klaus & Klaus, 1998; Verny & Weintraub, 2014). Newborns have a complex ability to imitate what they see and within the first thirty-six hours after birth they can imitate facial expressions, including smiles and frowns and protrusion of the tongue in what can be described as a developmental movement dialogue with parents (Winnicott, 1987; Klaus & Klaus, 1998; Verny & Weintraub, 2014).

Parents convey emotional messages via facial expressions and gestures and communicate with newborns through a visual language (Stokes, 2002). There is scientific evidence of intuitive sensory perception as preborns may be able to sense their parent's thoughts and feelings, including emotions of stress, anxiety, fear, anger, and joy (Verny & Weintraub, 2014).

Newborn Trauma

Trauma adversely affects the development of the newborn's brain and stress response systems and can interfere with attachment (Lillas & Turnbull, 2009). Newborns encounter multiple risks and trauma experiences that include labor and transition from the protective uterus, birth complications, cesarean birth, forceps- and vacuum-assisted birth, nuchal umbilical cord, umbilical cord prolapse, breach position, premature birth, incubation, IV sticks, monitoring lines, fetal scalp electrodes, heel sticks, needle injections, feeding tubes, temperature changes, use of suction devices to clear nasal passages, neonatal surgery, and medical procedures (Emerson, 1995; Lillas &Turnbull, 2009).

Newborns have limited ability to effectively soothe themselves when experiencing distress and trauma. They look away, averting gaze to modulate stimulation input, and reorient away from stressful stimuli or attempt to habituate to the stimuli. Researchers have observed a rhythmic, cyclic aspect of play interactions in an attention, then a non-attention pattern. These patterns are an infant's effort to control and modulate the intake of stimuli and are critical to maintaining engagement with parents during play interactions (Tronick, 2007).

Studies show that birth trauma memories are encoded in the body and brain as sensations and images (van der Kolk, 2014; Emerson, 1995). Neurosensory play with newborns shapes the stress response systems, calms and soothes the central nervous system impacted by trauma, provides neural activation for the formation of new neural patterns, and is the foundation for bonding and attachment (Schwartzenberger, 2011).

Newborn Neurosensory Play Interventions

Neurosensory play activates a newborn's ventral vagal nervous system and facilitates a state of social emotional engagement in the infant–parent dyad, shapes the neurochemistry of emotions throughout the newborn's nervous system and brain, and links the neural regulation of the heart to emotional expression (Porges, 2011). All sensory stimuli carry social and emotional connections and create memory circuits in the limbic brain and social learning centers (Graven & Browne, 2008). The following neurosensory play interactions and games are recommended in the first three months, the fourth trimester, stage of development.

Nurturing Caring Touch. A newborn's sense of touch is activated long before they are born and is critical to brain and nervous system development (Field, 2014). Caring touch is the essential component in the very first play interaction in the infant–parent dyad (Courtney & Nolan, 2017). It conveys emotional messages in a form of reciprocal communication that Brody has called the dialogue of touch (Brody, 1997, p. 13).

Parents instinctively touch, hold, carry, cuddle, rock, jiggle, swing, walk or play with their newborn to soothe and calm them. Infant massage and touch releases neurochemicals in the infant's brain including oxytocin, serotonin, and dopamine that lower the stress hormone cortisol and helps calm and soothe an infant's nervous system (Field, 2014; Perry, 2006).

Look at Me and Voice Games. In these games either the parent or the newborn initiates looking back and forth, mirroring and imitating each other's facial expressions, movements, and gestures to begin the play. A human voice is the newborn's favorite sound, and they listen with precision and hear subtle differences in parents' voices in pitch, tone, rhythms, cadence, and prosody. Newborns respond with purposeful movements, facial expressions, gestures, and vocalizations. They can be observed physically moving in rhythm and synchrony to parent's speech (Klaus & Klaus, 1998). Parents naturally mirror and imitate the infant's sounds and rhythmic movements such as cooing, babbling, tongue clicking, grunting, giggling, and laughing (Winnicott, 1987). Parents mimic infant sounds and wait for them to respond in *call out and respond games*, also known as *serve and return games* (Stokes, 2015, p. xxiv). Parents use a high-pitched voice to activate the sympathetic (activation) nervous system and get the infant's attention and a low-pitched voice to activate the parasympathetic nervous system and ventral vagal system (inhibition) to soothe and calm the infant (Porges, 2011).

Music and Movement. While holding their infant, parents sing songs and dance and move to the rhythm of music to provide auditory, vestibular, tactile, and movement stimulation that calms and soothes a distressed infant.

Infant Neurosensory Development: Four to Six Months

Mothers and fathers have most likely known what scientists are just discovering, namely that relationships between parents and infants are mutual and reciprocal, sometimes even magical (Pearce, 1977). Infants actively seek sensory stimulation and engage in neurosensory play interactions in a mutually synchronizing exchange in the infant–parent dyad. These interactions shape the neural rhythms of the infant and help regulate hormone levels, cardiovascular function, sleep rhythms, immune function, and the stress response system (Lillas & Turnbull 2009).

Although brain development is genetically predisposed to advance, neurobiologists point out that an infant's sensory experience shapes neural development. An infant's brain is shaped by interpersonal experience and develops as a reflection of thousands of infant–parent neurosensory interactions, a process described as interpersonal neurobiology (Schore, 1994; Seigel, 1999). Infant–parent play interactions build neural circuitry for social emotional engagement and secure attachment and the brain organizes in response to sensory stimuli in play. An infant has the capacity to express at least seven primary emotions, including joy, interest, sadness, anger, fear, surprise, and distress (Porges, 2011; Tronick, 2007; Kestly, 2014).

Infant Trauma

Trauma experiences during infancy impacts multiple areas of the brain and nervous system and can adversely affect development and attachment in the infant–parent dyad. These sensory-based trauma experiences can include medical procedures, circumcision, vaccinations, blood tests, illnesses, accidents, injuries, domestic violence, sensory deprivation, insufficient touch and tactile stimulation, parent's postpartum depression and mental illness, neglect and abuse (physical and emotional), malnutrition, parent's inability to read and react to the infant's signals and cues (lack of attunement), separation and loss of attachment figures. (Lillas & Turnbull, 2009, van der Kolk, 2014; Perry, 2006).

Infants become emotionally and behaviorally reactive to sensory triggers associated with trauma experiences. Key neurochemical systems such as cortisol levels and stress hormones become altered, and infants may stop smiling and avert gaze (Tronick, 2007). Their reactions can take the form of hypoalert (such as a blank stare), hyperalert (such as darting eyes), or flooded response (such as inconsolable crying), also referred to as "load conditions" (Lillas & Turnbull, 2009, p. 137).

The physiology of emotion is closely linked to the regulatory system and arousal of the nervous system. The ability to maintain a calm and alert state and recover back to the alert state following a stress response is referred to as "self-regulation" (Lillas & Turnbull, 2009). The ability to modulate and self-regulate affective states is shaped by repeated sensory soothing play interactions and mutual co-regulation in the infant–parent dyad (Stern, 1974). Traumatized infants may also present with mood dysregulation, fear, anxiety, restlessness, sleeping and feeding difficulties, stomach aches, immune disorders, startle responses, sensory processing problems, crying outbursts, difficulty calming and soothing, developmental delays, and attachment interference (Lillas & Turnbull, 2009).

Infant Neurosensory Play Interventions: Four to Six Months

At four to six months the infant's developmental movement repertoire is expanding and movement increases with spinal and head extension. They can roll over from front to back and remain at a side-lying position to play games and sustain attention in play for thirty seconds or longer. Playing in a side-lying position activates several key nervous and sensory systems. They can point with their index finger at toys and objects to communicate, the start of declarative pointing skills development. By directing attention to toys through pointing, reaching, and rolling over, they can initiate and lead play interactions.

Infants are self-directed learners motivated by emotions, able to formulate goals and problem-solving strategies in their play (Stokes, 2015). In the pre-locomotive stage they are ready to play in the prone position (on the tummy). They can begin to lift their head and learn to push and yield to achieve balance and body awareness. There is a heightened visual acuity along with stronger neck control to tilt and turn and track objects horizontally, side to side, and the best play position is lying on the back in a supine position.

The following neurosensory play interaction games are recommended in the four to six months stage. These games activate multiple sensory systems, including the visual, auditory, tactile, proprioceptive, and kinesthetic senses. Timing is important, as infants are most receptive to play when rested, dry, fed, and in a quiet or active alert state.

The Tummy Time Game. This game is played by placing the infant in a prone body position on the parent's tummy, looking face to face, and using a soft humming voice to provide vibration that can soothe and calm a distressed infant's nervous system (Stokes, 2015, p. 59).

Peek-A-Boo and Where's Baby Games. Parents start by hiding their face with their hands or behind a blanket and saying "where's baby, I can't see baby"; then uncovering their face saying "peek-a-boo, I see you, there's baby." To prevent over stimulation, parents modulate the level of stimulus from their facial and vocal responses in play.

Touching and Naming Games. A play interaction that is fun and sensory stimulating is the touching and naming game initiated by the parent lightly touching the infant and saying "here is your nose and your ears," "here is your hand and your fingers," "here is your foot and your toes." Parents are cautioned to limit tickling as it may result in overstimulation of the infant's nervous system (Brody, 1997).

Take a Bike Ride Game. The take a bike ride game is played with the infant in a supine position (on the back), where the parent gently moves the infant's legs as if they are pedaling a bicycle and says "here we go." Parents can improvise many different *developmental movement games* and initiate spontaneous play interactions with infants.

Infant Neurosensory Play Interaction Mismatch

An infant's nervous system depends on synchrony during the play interaction exchange for neurophysiologic stability, rhythm regulation, and mutual co-regulation of emotions (Lillas & Turnbull, 2009). Play interactions may start out synchronized and match with both infant and parent in sensory and emotional attunement with each other, then may shift and become out of sync. These mismatched interchanges occur when the infant and parent are not accurately reading each other's facial expressions, cues, gestures, and emotional messages and fail to accurately signal, decode, and respond in a way that keeps both engaged in the play (Stokes, 2002).

Observation studies of infants show that during play interactions the infant and parent are out of sync with a mismatch rate of about seventy percent of the time and are in attunement, matched, only thirty percent of the time. Adapting to the interactional mismatches is a key element in the infant developing self-regulation of emotions and behavior and requires playful repairs on the part of the parent. Interactive reparation ensures a transformation from negative to positive emotional experiences, which is also critical to developing secure attachment (Tronick, 2007; Stern, 1974).

Infant Neurosensory Play Interventions: Seven to Nine Months

At seven to nine months, infants add more patterns to their movement repertoire and can sit up on their own, lift their body up to crawl and creep on their hands and knees, repeatedly rock back and forth in this position, propel forward to reach the parent or objects, practice rhythmic coordination, and move on their own. They have increased symmetrical movement of arms and legs with midline orientation and the ability to bring both hands together. Eye–hand coordination skills and reaching and grabbing for toys and objects, as well as handling skills, are developing rapidly. Sitting upright is now a more functional play position, and they can sustain attention for one minute or longer. In the following neurosensory games, infants practice motivation, goal attainment, self-directed movement, and problem-solving skills.

Visual and Vocal Games. Each infant has a repertoire of unique signature expressions. Face-to-face vocal and visual games start with imitating the infant's facial expressions, sounds and movement, then pausing to allow the infant to take the lead. Parents closely observe and learn the meaning of the infant's sounds and expressions, what is being said in a visual language with the eyes, facial expressions, gestures, and movements.

Hand-Clapping Games. Infants can now bring their hands together at midline and clap their hands. They can practice movements in rhythm and synchronization in floor clapping games with the parent making rhythmic vocal sounds while they clap their hands together or slap their hands on the floor.

Toy Ring Games. Infants are capable of grasping, holding, shaking, and playing tugging-pulling games with toy rings, activating visual, tactile, and joint compression sensory systems. Remarkably, they can also differentiate the size, shape, texture, and color of the rings (Stokes, 2002).

One, Two, Three Drop It Games. They can pick up toys with their fingers, transfer toys from one hand to another hand, roll a ball and keep a firm grip and drop the toy on the floor or into containers. Handling toys and playing "one, two, three drop it" games are fun, enhancing visual and tactile sensory systems development, creating new neural patterns that shape the brain and are integrated into the nervous system.

Infant Neurosensory Play Interventions: Ten to Twelve Months

At ten to twelve months, infants can stand and walk, exhibit more developmental movement variations, and sustain attention in play for up to five minutes. They have an expanded repertoire of expressive movements to use in social play, initiate more play interactions with parents, and can engage in reciprocal communication that expresses rhythm and timing similar to adult language. The following neurosensory play interaction games are recommended in the ten to twelve months stage.

Matching Rhythm Game. Research shows that infants initiate and respond to rhythmic body messages. Infants like to play *slap the floor games* with their hands out flat and will imitate the parent or initiate and take the lead. In this game the parent responds to the feelings behind the infant's expressive rhythms by matching and reflecting the movements and facial expressions, and vocalizing the emotional excitement levels of the infant in play interactions.

Drumming and Action Songs Games. Sitting together on the kitchen floor, parents can play drumming on pots and pans games and add action songs that rhyme during the play interactions to stimulate tactile and auditory senses.

Finger- and Face-Painting Games. These games, using face paint or lotion, provide tactile stimulation to fingers and the face and colorful visual stimulation. They activate the infant's sympathetic nervous system and provide touch, tactile, kinesthetic, auditory, and proprioceptive sensory stimuli.

Slippery Hands Games. Parents use lotion to play *slippery hands and feet games* that provide tactile stimulation critical to brain development and attachment (Brody 1997). Playing *water games* with toys in the tub or sink and splashing and pouring water in and out of containers is fun and soothing for the infant.

Knock-'Em-Down Game. Stacking blocks and letting infants knock them down with their hand s or feet activates the visual and tactile senses and infants get excited when they see them all fall down.

Peek-A-Boo, Hiding, and All-Gone Games. Research shows that the prefrontal cortex, executive system, of an infant becomes more active at twelve months (Lillas & Turnbull 2009). Along with variations of the peek-a-boo game, parents can play hiding games. In the all-gone game the parent removes a toy from the sight of the infant and says "all gone," then brings the toy back in sight and in an excited voice says "here it is." The infant must hold the image of the hidden toy for five to ten seconds. This game entails a complex integration of action and thought, where the infant cannot see the parent or the toy, yet learns that it will reappear (object constancy), and marks the beginning of imaginary and symbolic play (Pearce, 1977; Winnicott, 1987).

Summary

Neurosensory play interactions with preborns, newborns, and infants are critical for brain and nervous and sensory systems development. Play interactions that are rich in sensory stimuli promote an infant's healthy physical and emotional development and strengthen attachment in the infant–parent dyad. Trauma care that includes neurosensory play activities that target the brain system provides stimuli to soothe and calm the central nervous system of the distressed infant and assist in self-regulation of affect and behavior (Lillas & Turnbull, 2009). Research shows that brain and neural systems negatively impacted by trauma can change with patterned, rhythmic, repetitive neurosensory activities that provide the lower brain area's neural activation necessary for reorganization and the formation of new neural systems (Perry, 2006).

Discussion Questions

---

1 Preborns' nervous systems develop very early in utero, and neuroscience has verified that their sensory systems, including touch, hearing, sight, smell and taste, begin to come on line starting at eight weeks' gestation. What are some biological and emotional explanations for such early development of the senses?

2 Newborns instinctively look at human faces and demonstrate the ability to imitate facial expressions, including smiles and frowns. D. W. Winnicott suggests that mothers are mirrors for their infants. Are infants expressing their own emotions or reflecting mother's feelings?

3 Infants actively seek sensory stimulation and engage in neurosensory play interactions in a mutually synchronizing exchange in the infant–parent dyad. What is the meaning of such spontaneous social play and how does it benefit both the infant and parent?

References

Arenas, C. (Producer). (1997). *Make way for baby: Talking your way through pregnancy while improving your baby's mind.* [DVD]. Available from Amphion Communications, Pompano Beach, FL. amphionweb.com. Phone: 954.782.8668. Email: sales@forimage.com

Beil, L. & Peske, N. (2005). *Raising a sensory smart child.* New York: Penguin Group.

Brody, V. A. (1997). *The dialogue of touch: Developmental play therapy* (2nd ed.). Northvale, NJ: Jason Aronson.

Chamberlain, D. (1998). *The mind of your newborn baby.* Berkeley, CA: North Atlantic Books.

Chamberlain, D. (2013). *Windows to the womb: Revealing the conscious baby from conception to birth.* Berkeley, CA: North Atlantic Books.

Courtney, J. A., & Nolan R. (2017). *Touch in child counseling and play therapy: An ethical and clinical guide.* New York, NY: Routledge.

Emerson, W. (1995). The vulnerable prenate. Paper presented to the APPPAH Congress, San Francisco. Available at http://karenmelton.com/articles-and-media/

Field, T. (2014). *Touch* (2nd ed.). Cambridge, MA: MIT Press.

Graven, S. & Browne, J. (2008). Sensory development in the fetus, neonate, and infant: Introduction and overview. *Newborn and Infant Nursing Reviews,* 8(4), 169–172. doi:10.1053/j.nainr.2008.10.007

Kestly, T. (2014). *The interpersonal biology of play: Brain-building interventions for emotional well-being.* New York, NY: W. W. Norton.

Klaus, M. & Klaus, P. (1998). *Your amazing newborn.* Cambridge, MA: Da Capo Press.

Lillas, C. & Turnbull, J. (2009). *Infant/child mental health, early intervention, and relationship-based therapies: A neurorelationship framework for interdisciplinary practice.* New York, NY: W. W. Norton.

Manrique, B., Contasti, M., Alvarado, M., Zypman, M., Palma, N., Ierrobino, M., Ramirez, I., & Carini, D. (1998). A controlled experiment in prenatal enrichment with 684 families in Caracas, Venezuela: Results to age six. *Journal of Prenatal and Perinatal Psychology and Health,* 12(3/4), 209–234. doi:1P3–1381123831/a-controlled-experiment-in-prenatal-enrichment-with-638-families-in-caracas-venezuela-results-to-age-6

Nixon, B. (Producer). (1983). *Miracle of life* [DVD]. Available from WGBH Educational Foundation, Boston, MA. https://www.wgbh.org

Pearce, J.C. (1977). *Magical child.* New York, NY: Plume/Penguin Books.

Perry, B. D. (2006). Applying principles of neurodevelopment to clinical work with maltreated and traumatized children: The neurosequential model of therapeutics. In: N. B. Webb (Ed.), *Working with traumatized youth in child welfare* (pp. 27–52). New York, NY: Guilford Press,.

Porges, S. W. (2011). *The polyvagal theory: Neurophysiological foundations of emotions, attachment, communication, self-regulation.* New York, NY: Norton.

Schore, A.N. (1994). *Affect regulation and the origin of the self: The neurobiology of emotional development.* Hillsdale, NJ: Erlbaum.

Schwartzenberger, K. (2011). Neurosensory play interactions and state regulation in play therapy. *California Association for Play Therapy Newsletter,* October.

Seigel, D. (1999). *The developing mind: How relationships and the brain interact to shape who we are.* New York, NY: Guilford Press.

Stern, D. (1974). Mother and infant at play: The dyadic interaction involving facial, vocal, and gaze behaviors. In Lewis, M., Rosenbloom, L., (Eds.). *The effect of the infant on its caregiver*. New York, NY: Wiley Publishing.

Stokes, B. (2002). *Amazing babies: Essential movement for your baby in the first year*. Toronto, ON: More Alive Media.

Stokes, B. (2015). *Your self-motivated baby: Enhance your baby's social and cognitive development in the first six months through movement*. Berkeley, CA: North Atlantic Books.

Tronick, E. (2007). *The neurobehavioral and social-emotional development of infants and children*. New York, NY: Norton.

Van de Carr, R. & Lehrer, M. (1997). *While you are expecting: Creating your own prenatal classroom*. Atlanta, GA: Humanics.

van der Kolk, B. (2014). *The body keeps score*. New York: Penguin Group.

Vernallis, M., Landsberg., & Highsmith, S. (2001). [DVD]. *Babies know: Seven principles of prenatal and perinatal psychology*. Santa Barbara Graduate Institute. Available from the Association for Pre- and Perinatal Psychology and Health (APPPAH). www.birthpsychology.com

Verny, T. & Weintraub, P. (2014). *Nurturing the unborn child: A nine-month program for soothing, stimulating, and communicating with your baby*. New York, NY: Open Road Integrated Media.

Winnicott, D.W. (1987). *Babies and their mothers*. Cambridge, MA: Perseus Publishing.

Part II

Assessment with Young Children

Play Ability

Observing, Engaging, and Sequencing Play Skills for Very Young Children

Judi Parson, Karen Stagnitti, Bridget Dooley and Kate Renshaw

Introduction

Play Therapy is a diverse field with a wide range of developmentally sensitive clinical practice approaches accommodating the various ages and stages across the lifespan, including very young children. A growing body of professional knowledge indicates that models of practice are being researched and scrutinized for efficacy. However, Winnicott (1971, p. 55) states "when a patient cannot play the therapist must attend to this major symptom before interpreting fragments of behavior." This quote indicates that not all children can self-initiate or engage in play and, therefore, some children need to "learn to play" so that they may fully access opportunities to enhance growth and development.

The Parent Learn to Play program is an emerging approach for working with children and families in order to develop a child's imaginative play skills. This program may be offered to very young children; however, special considerations include the need for observing, engaging, sequencing and scaffolding specific play skills. The key message is that assessment is essential for defining a targeted starting point for monitoring and scaffolding play skill development. Firstly, this chapter defines early play development and the assessment of pretend play. The Parent Learn to Play Program will then be outlined, with theoretical underpinnings and key terms defined, including the structure of the program outlined from start to finish. A case study will illustrate the application of using pretend play ability assessment to design an individualized therapeutic intervention.

Early Play Development

Pretend play is a type of play whereby children impose meaning on what they are playing. In some literature this is also referred to as fantasy or imaginative play. Pretend play begins to develop from the second year of life (Stagnitti, 1998); children can be observed beginning to engage in imitated single pretend actions, for example pretending to talk on the phone.

Due to the considerable amount of cognitive effort required to engage in this complex form of play, children who have acquired a brain injury find pretending in play challenging and particularly tiresome (Dooley, Stagnitti & Galvin 2019). They often have difficulties understanding symbolic representations in play and are limited in their ability to sequence thoughts and action to create narratives among other deficits which impact on their ability to engage socially with same-aged peers. For children experiencing these difficulties, an informed treatment plan is required. The first step in determining the specific therapeutic needs of the child is to complete a comprehensive intake and assessment.

Assessing Pretend Play Ability

In order to ameliorate or resolve a pretend play deficit, it is essential that play ability is evaluated. This ensures that the intervention begins within the child's zone of proximal development based on their current pretend play ability. In this case study, the Pretend Play Enjoyment – Developmental Checklist (PPE-DC) was used to gain a baseline measurement. The PPE-DC is a non-standardized, criterion-referenced assessment of a child's ability to pretend play. It provides a framework for observing the pretend play of children aged 12 months to 5 years developmental age. The PPE-DC is a developmental checklist that examines six skills, based upon the typical pretend play ability. The checklist also includes a rating scale for the child's enjoyment in play and self-representation in play. Table 4.1 outlines the skills measured in the PPE-DC. There are both therapist and parent rating booklets to record judgements based on the naturalistic play of the child.

The assessment is administered by inviting the child to play with a range of conventional imaginative and symbolic toys aimed at eliciting engagement in pretend play, for example, a tea set, animals, role-play props and unstructured items such as a box, cloth and sticks. The assessor maintains a passive yet attentive presence in order to observe what spontaneous pretend play skills the child demonstrates without adult instruction or guidance. The results of the assessment are then used as a baseline to design an intervention that will target ways to build the child's skills. If play activities are not appropriately pitched in their design or delivery in terms of complexity and speed, children can disengage from the process and enter non-play behavior and actions.

Parent Learn to Play Program

The Parent Learn to Play program is an extension of the Learn to Play program (Stagnitti, 1998, 2016), which focuses on building the spontaneous ability of children to engage in pretend play. Children with developmental difficulties or interruption often require specialized support to build and restore capacity to self-initiate play (Stagnitti & Pfeifer, 2017). Self-initiated

Table 4.1 Pretend play enjoyment – developmental checklist: Assessing play skills and descriptors

Play skill	Description
Play scripts	The topics of the stories that children play, e.g. doctors, going to the zoo, birthday party
Sequences of play actions	How many actions a child can make in a row in order to construct a play scene or narrative
Object substitution	Transforming an object to represent something else, e.g. box as car
Doll/teddy play	The way that children use decentration to act as if teddies/dolls/figures are alive
Role play	Embodying a character in play and pretending to be someone or something else
Social interaction	The level of social interaction and collaboration with peers in play
Enjoyment score	Refers to the level of joy and immersion the child experiences while playing
Self-representation in play	A description of the child's play behavior that gives insight into the child's self-representation and mental states

Note: Adapted from Stagnitti (2017b).

pretend play has been positively associated with increased social ability (Stagnitti, O'Connor & Sheppard, 2012) and the capacity to form and engage in narrative (Stagnitti, Bailey, Hudspeth-Stevenson, Reynolds & Kidd, 2016). In the Parent Learn to Play program (Stagnitti, 2014, 2017a), the therapist works with the parent and their child to provide psychoeducational knowledge about play and build the caregiver's capacity to optimize the child–parent relationship.

Axline (1969) first highlighted the importance of including parents in play therapy. Bernard and Louise Guerney extended this concept into the systemic practice known as Filial Therapy (Guerney, 2003). The Learn to Play program recognizes that the parental relationship with the child is fundamental to children's development and well-being (Stagnitti, 2014), and acknowledges the need to work systemically to achieve sustainable outcomes.

Theoretical Underpinnings

The theoretical underpinnings of the Parent Learn to Play program are based on the work of Carl Rogers. Virginia Axline (1969), as a student of Carl Rogers, drew on his person-centered approach and applied this stance to working with children. Axline's (1969) principles inform the approach of the therapist in the Parent Learn to Play program (Stagnitti, 2014). The Learn to Play program principles outline that the therapist:

1   develops a warm relationship with the parent and accepts the child and parent unconditionally;
2   creates a permissive atmosphere where the parent feels free to suggest play ideas and activities into the session when working with the therapist;
3   respects the parent's capacity to build knowledge of their child's play and supports their engagement with their child;
4   invites the parent to be part of the session and is responsive to both the parent and the child;
5   builds the knowledge of their child's play and how to engage their child in play;
6   redirects the parent to play activities that would be more appropriate in engaging their child.

As the Parent Learn to Play program focuses on building the parent's pretend play knowledge and capacity, the second theoretical influence is that of Vygotsky (1966, 1934/1986), a cognitive developmental play theorist, who believed that a child's mental capacity increases through play and more so when capable parents are available, thus increasing the child's play and optimizing development, "Hence, enhancing how a parent plays with their child who has a developmental difficulty should enrich their child's social context and development" (Stagnitti, 2014, p. 152).

To achieve flexibility in delivery, there are three different formats for implementing the Parent Learn to Play program: 1) information sessions, 2) small group training, and 3) individualized one-on-one interventions.

Parent Learn to Play Program – Information Session

In this format, parents attend two 3-hour parent-only information sessions without the child. The sessions introduce parents to seven skills and principles on how to engage their children in pretend play. The seven skills directly align with the items measured in the PPE-DC (see Table 4.2) as these are the areas of play ability that parents learn how to scaffold in order to improve their child's overall pretend play ability. Parents consolidate their skills by simulating play activities with time provided for discussion and questions. Table 4.2 outlines the seven program skills that constitute the teaching materials.

Parent Learn to Play Program – Small Groups

The second format is designed for small groups of parents (Stagnitti, 2017a). In the delivery of the small group course, parents may opt to bring their children or opt for the group to be solely for parents. The small group delivery of Parent Learn to Play is a 7- or 12-session short course, with the 12-week course being a more in-depth extension of the 7-session course.

Table 4.2 Program skills with descriptions

Program skills	Description
Attuning to the child	Learn to observe a child's emotional state, body language, energy and focus, and approach the child with a similar but considered stance.
Recognizing play sequences	Learn to observe how many actions a child can make in a row in order to construct a play scene or narrative.
Describing the play	Learn to observe and provide verbal descriptions of what is happening in the play while playing.
Recognizing object substitution	Learn to teach a child to transform an object to represent something else, e.g. box as car.
Recognizing decentration	Learn how to facilitate and observe when a child uses decentration, i.e. when a child acts as if the teddies/dolls/figures are alive.
Recognizing play scripts	Learn to observe and recall the topics of the stories a child is playing, e.g. doctors, going to the zoo, or a birthday party.
Joining the child in role play	Learn to embody a character in play by pretending to be someone or something else.

Note: Adapted from Stagnitti (2017a).

The 7-session course lays foundational skills knowledge that occur in pretend play. A short video, of their child engaged in a play activity, is taken by the parents in between each session and contributes to each group discussion. The 12-session Parent Learn to Play small group course includes an additional five sessions. These sessions cover an additional four skills and teaches parents to extend the complexity of the seven foundational skills. Table 4.3, outlines the four extension skills that constitute the teaching in the 12-session program.

Table 4.3 Extension program skills with descriptions

Extension program skills	Description
Attributing properties	Learn to facilitate and extend play by adding qualities or characteristics to toys and doll/teddy, (e.g. hungry, tired, hot)
Referring to absent objects	Learn to identify and extend play by referencing to invisible objects and spaces in play that aren't represented by a physical item.
Extending object substitution	Learn to extend play scenes by further incorporating unstructured objects to increase complexity of play.
Creating problems in the play	Learn to enhance the play by adding problems into the play scenes and narratives to promote problem solving.
Predicting what can happen next	Learn to facilitate thinking about what might happen next in play scenes and narratives.

Note: Adapted from Stagnitti (2017a).

Parent Learn to Play Program – Individual

The third format is an individualized one on one intervention with the parent, child and therapist. This format requires that the therapist meets the parents and child before the program begins to assess the developmental play level of the child and design a specific intervention targeted at extending the child's play ability. The child's current level of enjoyment in play is also noted and considered. The next paragraph outlines how the therapist works with the parent to increase their capacity to engage with their child.

Principles and Processes of Individualized Sessions

In individualized sessions, the therapist not only works to prescribe the targeted play skills intervention, but supports parents to act as co-therapist in the implementation of them. In addition, the therapist coaches the parents on how to tailor the therapeutic environment to optimize engagement in play. Additional clinical considerations include how to:

- Use only the number of toys or play materials needed.
- Be aware of not to overwhelm the child with too many toys, speed or complexity.
- Play beside and on the child's physical level to convey a sense of togetherness, acceptance, and safety.
- Engage in play themselves to model scaffolding of play.
- Playfully gain the child's focused attention.
- Welcome the child's ideas and integrate them into the pre-planned activities.
- Use developmentally appropriate language to talk about and describe the play.
- Meet the child in the positive emotional space, with fun and pleasure to amplify therapeutic change (Stagnitti & Casey, 2011).

The following case study illustrates a bespoke child–parent–therapist Parent Learn to Play therapeutic intervention.

Case Study

Following a referral from their medical doctor and initial intake, Austina, a two-and-a-half-year-old girl, was observed in a non-directive play session. The following case illustrates how the PPE-DC assessment was used to prescribe an individualized Parent Learn to Play intervention. Background information is provided to set the scene in relation to her family and the critical incident that led to this play therapy intervention.

Family Background

At the time of intake, Stacey was a sole parent of two children, Austina and Daniella (15 months of age). The family came from a middle class, Caucasian Australian heritage, living in a regional area of Victoria, Australia. The extended family included maternal grandmother and maternal grandfather, as well as Stacey's sister and paternal grandmother. The paternal grandfather, Austin, passed away just prior to the birth of Austina and is who she is named after. Before the accident, Austina had been progressing well in every developmental domain, including play. Stacey reported that they had strong family bonds and Austina was well loved and cared for.

Motor Vehicle Accident

Austina experienced significant trauma at 18 months of age, when her whole family were involved in a fatal motor vehicle accident. As a result of this accident, she sustained multiple traumatic injuries, including: traumatic Acquired Brain Injury (ABI); two fractured ribs; spiral fracture to left arm; fractures to both right and left tibia and fibula; and a fractured femur. She was hospitalized for four weeks.

Stacey, who was sitting in the front passenger side of the car, also suffered from a traumatic brain injury. This impacted her short-term memory and ability to care for Austina and Daniella. She was hospitalized for 6 months and required significant rehabilitation to coordinate and sequence her own activities of daily living. Ned, Stacey's husband and Austina's father, who was driving, was killed. Daniella, 3 months of age, was protected by the baby capsule and did not sustain any physical injuries.

Austina was cared for by Beth and Brian under a kinship care arrangement for 12 months while Stacey undertook medical rehabilitation. Twelve months after the car accident, she was able to be reunited with her children, and she understood that Austina would require an age-appropriate mental health service. Austina's psychosocial health and well-being required a scaffolded personalized therapeutic play intervention to recover regressed play ability by supporting Stacey to scaffold play. It was also hypothesized that because of disruption in caregiving and bereavement of her father, some attachment behaviors may need to be expressed.

As a result of the traumatic ABI sustained, Austina's play level was recorded at 12 months developmental play age, showing an 18-month deficit in her play skills when compared with expected play ability for her chronological age. At this time, she showed difficulty in initiating play sequences. The PPE-DC guided and informed the play therapist to structure Austina's play sessions and to teach Stacey the skills to facilitate home-based play sessions. Stacey was highly motivated and keen to support her daughter's developmental needs and re-establish their family structure and relationships.

Over a period of 2 months, Austina and Stacey attended 8 hours of Parent Learn to Play sessions with the support of Beth and Brian. The initial sessions were scheduled for only half an hour to accommodate the significant effort required of Austina to engage in play. The play sessions then progressed from half an hour to 45 minutes, to 1 hour. Austina was reassessed and showed a 2-year level of play which was evidenced by: logical sequential actions; play scripts (both in and out of the home); and the incorporation of characters within her play. These results showed (over a short period of time) a significant advancement in her play ability, restoring the deficit from 18 months to 6 months.

In addition, these sessions helped overcome an emotional and psychological trauma history and built their attachment relationship.

Assessment

Stacey and Austina were referred by their General Practitioner via an initial telephone call. Due to Stacie's ABI and memory loss, she was not able to fill out the Parent/Carer Pretend Play Enjoyment Developmental Checklist Scoring Booklet (Stagnitti, 2017b). Therefore, the first author completed the assessment using the Professional Scoring Booklet of the PPE-DC (Stagnitti, 2017b). The PPE-DC was completed both before and after the play therapy intervention. To ensure assessments were accurate, the first author carried out the pre-assessment and the second author carried out the post-assessment. It was important for the first author to carry out the pre-assessment for the Parent Learn to Play program as the therapist needs to understand the child's play level in order to begin the therapy.

The PPE-DC informed the bespoke Parent Learn to Play intervention. The PPE-DC was not only used to gain an understanding of Austina's play ability but was also used to monitor therapeutic change in Austina's play level over the 2-month period. The results of the PPE-DC assessment by the first author are detailed in Table 4.4.

Based on observations using the PPE-DC Professional Scoring Booklet, Austina had pre-pretend play ability. She was 18 months behind in her pretend play ability, did not enjoy play and her sense of self was low with lack of confidence and curiosity.

Brief Description of Setting for Therapy

In the Learn to Play program the play room is set up differently from traditional play therapy rooms. This is because children are sequentially scaffolded to learn how to play. The toys are hidden in a cupboard in the early sessions, as often children who have developmental difficulties may be overwhelmed with too many accessible toys. The therapist, after speaking with the parents at the intake and assessment, chooses play materials that are suitable for the child's developmental play age and interest. The toys are

Table 4.4 Pretend play enjoyment – developmental checklist (pre-intervention)

Play skill	Description of Austina's play ability
Play stories	There were no stories in Austina's play. She manipulated objects and repeated what she was doing (level A).
Sequences of play actions	She was highly repetitive. For example, she would put blocks in and out of a container (level A).
Object substitution	Austina manipulated and explored objects. She did not use them for any clear purpose (level A).
Doll/teddy play	Austina was not interested in characters such as teddy bears or puppets (level A).
Role play	Austina watched what the therapist did but only for short periods of time (level A).
Social interaction	Austina could wave goodbye. She liked peek-a-boo (level A).
Enjoyment score	2 (play was a task for Austina).
Description of behavior	Austina did not use personal pronouns, she was only fleetingly curious about toys. She did not anticipate events and became frustrated easily. She lacked confidence in doing things herself and often cried or seemed to give up. She could throw toys in frustration.

also bigger in size than play materials supplied in more traditional play therapies. For example, the dolls and teddies, vehicles and blocks are large. The types of toys used in early sessions for the Learn to Play program, for a child at Austina's play level would be: a tea-set, teddies, large dolls, wooden fruit, play doh, a shoe box, fabric cloth, a ball, bath, bed, and large blocks.

Treatment Plan

Twelve 1-hour sessions over a 3-month period were planned. However, this changed when Stacey was offered government-assisted housing closer to her family, which was over 100 kilometers from the play therapy center. Thus, Austina attended a total of 8 hours of therapy.

The sessions began with activities to emotionally engage Austina, such as the large doll catching a ball, and stacking large rubber blocks and knocking them down. The play activities were pitched at a 12–18-month level of pretend play, e.g. feeding the teddy, giving the teddy a drink, putting the doll to bed, cutting up fruit. These play activities reflected body-based play scripts such as eating, drinking and sleeping. As Austina was at a 12-month level of play, to begin with the play actions were single repeated actions. The therapist used repetition of sequences with variation so that Austina could practice her ability to play.

Initially, Stacey watched the therapist and Austina's play as she built her confidence to join in. If Austina added to the play ideas, the therapist would copy Austina, modelling to her mother how to engage Austina and extend her play. The therapist treated the dolls and teddies as if they were alive and enjoyed the play. The therapist also ensured that Stacey was engaged and enjoying playing with her daughter. The therapist responded to Austina and Stacy to ensure the therapy was emotionally engaging, pitched at the appropriate play level and including, when appropriate, play activities that were on a higher developmental level to extend her abilities. The therapist explained the play activities to Stacey and gave one-page handouts on each of the play skills. The handouts explained the play skills and why they were important.

Attention to the Stages of Therapy

In the Learn to Play program, therapy begins at the level of the child's play. For many children who cannot play, play is not of interest to them, so the first sessions aim to engage children emotionally in the enjoyment of playing. Emotional engagement has been noted to be important in increasing a child's engagement in wanting to play (Stagnitti & Casey, 2011). Once the child is beginning to emotionally engage in the play and the therapist understands what play activities catch the child's interest, the therapist then begins to slowly introduce other play activities at the same developmental level. At the early stages of the Learn to Play program with a child similar in presentation to Austina, five play activities need to be planned for each session.

When the therapist observes that the child begins to initiate their own play at that developmental level, the therapist then challenges the child by introducing play activities at a higher developmental level. All the while, the therapist is modelling play interaction beside the parent and explaining to the parent what play skill is being developed and why. The therapist is also cognizant of the range of play skills and plans for play activities that include scripts that the child can understand, appropriate number of play actions, object substitution, the inclusion of a character in the play, and the child carrying out a role in the play. Furthermore, the therapist is modelling to the parent how to socially engage the child in play through direct interaction with the child or through a doll, puppet or teddy.

When children understand how to use toys in play, initiate their own ideas in play, and begin to add spontaneous actions to the play, the therapist can reduce the number of pre-planned activities needed.

Post-assessment

Austina was reassessed by the second author after therapy. The second author had not been involved in the play sessions and was not aware of the progress in therapy. The PPE-DC Professional Scoring booklet was used to record Austina's play level. Her results are described in Table 4.5.

Table 4.5 Pretend play enjoyment – developmental checklist (post-intervention)

Play skill	Description of Austina's play ability
Play stories	Austina was showing play themes to a 2-year level with play scripts in and out of the home (doctors, eating, drinking, cutting cake).
Sequences of play actions	Austina showed simple, logical, sequential actions on a 2-year level. For example, she got the tea set, poured the tea, gave a cup of tea to mum, took cake from mum and gave to therapist, then ate some cake.
Object substitution	Austina showed ability to a 2-year level when she used the same object for two different things. For example, the box was a bed and a car.
Doll/teddy play	Doll/teddy play: Austina engaged in play where the snake was alive and "hurt." She attributed properties to the snake. At this age children play "as if" characters are alive and Austina showed evidence of this.
Role play	Role play at this age is very fleeting and is more about copying others. Austina showed ability in this area.
Social interaction	Austina moved between mum and first author, engaging both in play. She imitated actions in play as well as initiated actions in play. She was aware of play materials she needed for play scenes.
Enjoyment score	Austina's enjoyment was scored at 5, being an observable pleasure and enjoyment of play.
Description of behavior	Austina loved to come to the play sessions and would run into the room with anticipation of the pleasure to play. Her sense of self showed accomplishment of "I did it!" and a confidence and curiosity not previously seen.

Case Summary

In summary, Austina showed play ability at a 2-year level. This was a pleasing increase of 12 months in 8 hours of play sessions. Austina requires ongoing play therapy to extend her play further to bring her to her age equivalent abilities. We anticipate that Austina will meet age equivalent play skills after a further eight 1-hour sessions. Stacey has demonstrated her capacity to provide positive parenting. We expect that if Stacey continues to provide play sessions at home in a secure relationship, Austina will demonstrate further reduction in emotional dysregulation and related behaviors and display an increase in healthy emotional regulation through therapeutic limit setting, play and communication. In relation to communication, Austina has already shown a significant improvement in narrative language and play skills. Stacey needs further support to continue with the work she has already undertaken with Austina. Austina was referred to another play therapist with specialist knowledge of the Parent Learn to Play program and with clinical supervision from the initial therapist to continue supporting Stacey in developing Austina's play skills and psychosocial development.

Clinical Considerations

The use of assessments, such as the PPE-DC, may be used to enhance the identification for starting, scaffolding and tracking therapeutic play progress. It is important to access clinical supervision by a trained Learn to Play and Parent Learn to Play supervisor who is available to support the clinical reasoning before, during and after the therapeutic intervention. The toys were selected to enhance self-expression and increase pretend and imaginative play. Suggested toys and resources are included in the Learn to Play and Parent Learn to Play manuals (refer to the Recommended Resources list).

Conclusion

This chapter has provided the rationale to facilitate play development by utilizing the Parent Learn to Play program. This program is ideal to therapeutically meet the needs of children with developmental delays caused by traumatic ABI, neuro-atypical diagnosis and reduced neural growth, speech and language difficulties and other disabilities. The Parent Learn to Play program is recommended to expand the Learn to Play program in a systemically informed manner. The story of Austina has illustrated a Parent Learn to Play approach for a child with a traumatic ABI as an appropriate referral, as showcased by her rapid skill acquisition and progress over a 2-month period. It is important to respect the clinical considerations as part of a thoughtful case conceptualization that provides a highly individualized therapeutic intervention.

Recommended Resources

The Learn to Play Events website (https://www.learntoplayevents.com) provides several free resources. The following manuals and recommended assessment can also be purchased through the website:

- Learn to Play Manual
- Parent Learn to Play Manual
- Pretend Play Enjoyment – Developmental Checklist (PPE-DC)

Discussion Questions

---

1 Under what clinical circumstances do you think the use of play assessments will inform your prescriptive approach in working with children and families? Why?
2 Consider your current clinical caseload: Are there any children in your caseload with a play deficit that may suit this approach? Why might they be suitable? What might the long-term benefits to the child and family be?
3 Under what clinical presentations do you think that the Parent Learn to Play program would *not* be appropriate?

References

Axline, V. M. (1969). *Play therapy*. New York: Ballantine Books.

Dooley, B., Stagnitti, K., & Galvin, J. (2019). An investigation of the pretend play abilities of children with an acquired brain injury. *British Journal of Occupational Therapy*. https://doi.org/10.1177/0308022619836941

Guerney, L. (2003). The history, principles, and empirical basis of filial therapy. In R. VanFleet. & L. Guerney (Eds.), *Casebook of Filial Therapy*. Boiling Springs, PA: Play Therapy Press.

Stagnitti, K., & Pfeifer, L. (2017a). Methodological considerations for a directive play therapy approach for children with autism and related disorders. *International Play Therapy Journal*, 26(3), 160–171. http://dx.doi.org/10.1037/pla0000049

Stagnitti, K. (1998). *Learn to Play. A practical program to develop a child's imaginative play*. Melbourne, Australia: Co-ordinates Publications.

Stagnitti, K. (2014). The Parent Learn to Play program: Building relationships through play. In E. Prendiville & J. Howard (Eds.), *Play therapy today* (pp. 149–162). London: Routledge.

Stagnitti, K. (2016). Play therapy for school-age children with high functioning autism. In A. Drewes & C. Schaefer (Eds.), *Play therapy in middle childhood* (pp. 237–255). New York, NY: American Psychological Association.

Stagnitti, K. (2017a). *Parent Learn to Play facilitators manual and parent handbook*. Melbourne, Australia: Learn to Play.

Stagnitti, K. (2017b). *The Pretend Play Enjoyment Developmental Checklist. Manual and professional and parent/carer scoring forms*. Melbourne, Australia: Learn to Play.

Stagnitti, K. & Casey, S. (2011). Il programma Learn to Play con bambini con autismo: considerazioni pratiche e evidenze. *Autismo Oggi*, 20, 8–13. Retrieved July 29, 2019 from: http://www.fondazioneares.com/index.php?id=369

Stagnitti, K., Bailey, A., Hudspeth-Stevenson, E., Reynolds, R., & Kidd, E. (2016). An investigation into the effect of play-based instruction on the development of play skills and oral language: A 6-month longitudinal study. *Journal of Early Childhood Research*, 14(4), 389–406. http://dx.doi.org/10.1177/1476718X15579741

Stagnitti, K., O'Connor, C., & Sheppard, L. (2012). The impact of the Learn to Play program on play, social competence and language for children aged 5–8 years who attend a special school. *Australian Occupational Therapy Journal*, 59(4), 302–311. http://dx.doi.org/10.1111/j.1440-1630.2012.01018.x

Vygostsky, L. (1934/1986). *Thought and language* (trans. and edited by A. Kozulin). London: MIT Press.

Vygotsky, L. (1966). Play and its role in the mental development of the child. *Voprosy psikhologii*, 12, 62–76. Retrieved July 29, 2019from: https://files.eric.ed. gov/fulltext/EJ1138861.pdf

Winnicott, D. W. (1971). *Playing and reality*. London: Tavistock Publications.

Chapter 5

Trauma-Informed Infant Mental Health Assessment

Eva Nowakowski-Sims and Danna Powers

Introduction

Infants learn from the environment around them. We know that young infants have organized emotions and are able to react to the meanings of others' intentions and emotions (Brazelton, 1992; Reddy, 2008; Tronick, 2007). We also know that secure relationships in early childhood are critical for later emotional and mental wellness. Infancy, more than any other developmental period, is a time of heightened vulnerability to disruptions in secure relationships (Lyons-Ruth et al., 2017). Many factors can negatively affect children's social-emotional development, including psychosocial stressors (e.g., poverty, traumatic events, exposure to violence, and parental mental illness and/or substance abuse) and genetic and other physical health conditions (National Scientific Council on the Developing Child, 2012). Among children under 3 years of age, more than 1 million were the subject of abuse and neglect reports to U.S. child protection authorities in 2014 (U. S. Department of Health & Human Services, 2016). Exposure to traumatic events, like child abuse and neglect, affects developmental processes that have lifelong and even intergenerational consequences (Bowers & Yehuda, 2016). These challenges can lead to mental disorders in infancy.

The concept of mental disorders in infancy is not widely recognized. The lack of widespread recognition is particularly concerning due to the unique positioning of infancy at the beginning of the developmental process (Lyons-Ruth et al., 2017). Although the concept of mental disorders in infancy is not widely recognized, it is common. Epidemiological studies have revealed a 16–18% prevalence of mental disorders among children aged 1–5 years, with somewhat more than half (8–9%) being severely affected (von Klitzing, Döhnert, Kroll, & Grube, 2015). Among those young children who are identified as needing services, more than half do not receive them (National Survey of Children's Health, 2012).

Infant mental health is the developing capacity of the child (ages birth to 5 years of age) to form close and secure adult and peer relationships; to experience, manage, and express a full range of emotions; and to explore the environment and learn—all in the context of family, community, and culture (Osofsky & Thomas, 2012). Children grow into responsible well-adjusted adults when they have a secure beginning in life. A sound emotional base is the launching pad for the physical, motor and cognitive development that prepares children for school and for eventual success in life (Clinton, Feller, & Williams, 2016). However, some infants do not have such security during infancy, which results in mental health problems. Mental health problems in young children can cause distress, interfere with relationships, limit the child's or the family's participation in daily activities, and hinder developmental progress (Osofsky & Thomas, 2012). Understanding infant mental health is the key to preventing and treating such mental health problems.

An infant's mental health develops based on the connection between parent/caregiver and child. Loving, nurturing relationships enhance emotional development and mental health through attachment. Attachment theory, as proposed by John Bowlby (1969, 1988), sets forth that we need specific types of nurturing and joyful parent infant contact to support secure attachment relationships. Attachment theory recognizes that connections created during the earliest stages of life have the power to shape our lives. Schore and Schore (2012) proposed an expansion of Bowlby's attachment theory to include research on brain development. Modern attachment theory is informed by neuroscience in which "secure attachment relationships are essential for creating a right brain self that can regulate its own internal states and external relationships" (2012, p. 44). Caregiver and child attachment interactions are critical to the development of structural right brain neurobiological systems involved in processing of emotion, modulation of stress, self-regulation, and thereby the functional origins of the bodily based implicit self (Porges & Dana, 2018; Schore, 2009; Schore & Schore, 2012). Attachment theory, at its core, is about how the parent/caregiver helps the infant regulate emotion. These emotion-based parent–infant attachment communications are essential because they directly affect the development of the brain and lead to a background state of emotional wellbeing, and emotional wellbeing is critical to physical wellbeing (Schore & Schore, 2012). A number of controlled studies have confirmed that the quality of caregiver regulation in these formative years has widespread effects on the expression of genes that control aspects of brain growth and stress system function (Belsky & de Haan, 2011; Blair, 2010). Furthermore, these biological changes can lead to physical and mental health problems in adulthood, including alcoholism, substance abuse, depression, cardiovascular disease, obesity, and diabetes (Garner, 2013). Disturbances in caregiver–infant interaction are particularly important to infant mental health because developmental studies have consistently shown the importance of the caregivers' attentive regulation of infant stress for the infant's adequate health and development (Madigan, Brumariu, Villani, Atkinson, & Lyons-Ruth, 2016).

Disruptions in caregiver–infant interaction and subsequent developmental processes can have life-long effects. Experiencing trauma (i.e. physical or emotional abuse, chronic neglect, caregiver substance abuse or mental illness, exposure to violence, and/or economic hardship) without caregiver support creates toxic stress. Research has widely documented how toxic stress can contribute to developmental delays, emotional difficulties, and overall well-being (Carpenter & Stacks 2009; Lieberman 2004; Lieberman & Knorr 2007; Shonkoff et al., 2012). As the number of trauma experiences accumulate, the risk increases for medical, mental health, and behavioral problems later in life (Felitti et al., 1998). Toxic stress also contributes to parenting stress, where parents who report high levels of parenting stress are more likely to exhibit harsh discipline and less parental responsivity and warmth (Klawetter & Frankel, 2018) advancing an insecure attachment between caregiver and child.

Therapeutic interventions during infancy will have the strongest effects at correcting the damage from chronic experiences with trauma. There are a number of evidence-based interventions that are effective in treating infants with mental health problems and disrupted infant–caregiver relationships, utilizing trauma-informed interventions (Bernard et al., 2012; Cicchetti, Toth, Nielsen, & Manly, 2016; Tereno et al., 2017). Trauma-informed care (TIC) incorporates an understanding of the frequency and effects of early adversity on psychosocial functioning across the life span (Substance Abuse and Mental Health Services Administration [SAMHSA], 2014b). Trauma-informed workers rely on their knowledge about trauma to respond to clients in ways that convey respect and compassion, honor self-determination, and enable the rebuilding of healthy interpersonal skills and coping strategies (Levenson, 2017). Critical to successful infant mental health intervention is infant mental health assessment from a trauma-informed lens.

Trauma-Informed Assessment in Infant Mental Health

A comprehensive trauma-informed infant mental health assessment includes the infant, the parents and family, and the social and cultural context that contribute to the infant's overall health. A few things to consider:

1   **It is a family thing.** Infants should be assessed interacting with a parent or familiar caregiver. The infant mental health framework privileges the caregiver–child relationship rather than focusing solely on either the child or the caregiver, thus acknowledging the interdependence that exists between caregivers and their children (Klawetter & Frankel, 2018). Infants should not be separated from their family or trusted caregivers during the assessment. Additionally, caregivers' own mental health and life experiences influence how they respond to their child's needs. When a caregiver's ability to provide secure attachment is compromised due to a mental illness such as depression, the infant's mental health can be compromised as well.

2   **Developmental stage matters.** An important component of infant mental health assessment is observation and documentation of behaviors as it

applies to the infant's developmental milestones. Infant behavior changes frequently as they age and across different environments; thus it is important to remember that a single observation limits the mental health professional's ability to view the infant's overall behavior and functioning (Zero to Three, 2016).

3   **Collect information from multiple sources.** Infants are nonverbal. Therefore, it is crucial to collect observations from multiple sources and in different scenarios. A good assessment will collect information detailing the infant's behavior and their responses and the interaction between family members to understand the child's experience and their part in the current difficulties (Mares & Graeff-Martins, 2012).

Effective trauma-informed assessment strategies call on the trauma-informed principles of safety, trust, choice, collaboration, and empowerment (Fallot & Harris, 2009; SAMHSA, 2014a) to guide the assessment process. The principles, when infused into practice, minimize the likelihood of repeating dysfunctional dynamics in the helping relationship and capitalize on the opportunity to create a corrective experience for clients (Levenson, 2017). A trauma-informed assessment process begins with safety and trust.

Safety and Trust

The purpose of assessment is to identify and understand the problems facing the family, their strengths and vulnerabilities, in order to assist them in maximizing their parenting capacity and the developmental potential of their child (Mares & Graeff-Martins, 2012). To do this, infant mental health professionals must first establish trust to engage families in the assessment process. Safety, respect, compassion, and empathy are paramount to the creation of trust between the infant mental health professional and client (Porges & Dana, 2018). Warm and welcoming surroundings create a sense of safety for clients (Fallot & Harris, 2009). To create a safe emotional environment, the infant mental health professional can reassure the client they do not have to disclose information they are not ready to share (Levenson, 2017).

Choice and Collaboration

Trauma-informed services attempt to embolden client decision-making and a sense of control over one's recovery (Fallot & Harris, 2009). This is done best by asking families how to help achieve their goals, what is important to them, and how can we help make a difference (Child First, n.d.). Trauma-informed programming is based on shared power between the infant mental health professional and client so the relationship offers a true alliance in healing. When parents are involved in assessment process, they become equal partners in the process.

Trauma Screening and Assessment

Trauma-informed infant mental health assessment can prevent problems in the early stages from taking root and becoming more difficult to address as children grow (Ullrich, Cole, Gebhard, & Schmit, 2017). Standard, valid, and reliable assessment tools can help workers identify potential concerns and organize early intervention efforts. Both attachment theory and trauma research indicate that an infant's functioning should include an assessment of the child within the context of their primary attachment relationship. Current clinical practice guidelines promote evaluations that include both parent and child in order to provide a comprehensive picture of the young child's functioning (Dickson & Kronenberg, 2011). Special consideration should be given to the ethnic background and language of the family in selecting an appropriate assessment tool. An effective, culturally sensitive assessment, such as the DC: 0–5, can be an intervention in itself, because this gives a family an opportunity to give voice to their story, to prioritize their unique needs, and to recognize the infant as a participant in the relationship (Zeanah, Berlin, & Boris, 2011).

Infant mental health professionals use assessments and clinical observations to complete a clinical formulation and diagnosis. To assess children 0–5, a manual for disorders of infancy has been developed, termed the Diagnostic Classification: Zero to Five (DC:0–5) (Zero to Three, 2016). The DC:0–5 is a developmentally based system for diagnosing mental health and developmental disorders in infants and toddlers. It uses an axial system to identify diagnostics, including mental health, relationships, development, and medical issues. As part of the assessment it recommends that assessment be done in various appointment throughout the child's domains (school, home, foster placement), developmental screenings (for milestones, socio-emotional, and sensory), and the Crowell (which assesses attachment between parent and child).

Empowerment

The last TIC principle highlights client strengths as a powerful indicator of success. Both infant mental health and trauma-informed care offer a strengths-based perspective to assessing clients. A strengths-based assessment involves both the needs and strengths of the infant, their parent/caregiver, and the environment. During the assessment process, infant mental health professionals identify and emphasize the family's positive attributes and supports.

The Case of Thomas

The following case study describes the assessment process of Thomas and Carole through the Child First® program. Child First® is a national, evidence-based, two-generation model that works with very vulnerable young children and families, providing intensive, home-based services. Child First® develops nurturing, consistent, and responsive parent–child relationships by connecting families to needed community-based services to decrease toxic stress (Child First, n.d.). The program consists of clinicians and care coordinators who work to stabilize, assess, and provide parent–child relation-based therapy.

Thomas, age 1 month, was referred to the Child First® program through a liaison officer who noted the mother's lack of self-care and life-threatening medical concerns. Thomas was sent home from the hospital with a family friend for the first few days of life, as Carole underwent a surgery that left her unable to care for her newborn alone. Due to these unexpected circumstances, Carole was unable to bond with Thomas during this critical period. The Child First® team was able to connect with the mother the day she was discharged from the hospital, and conduct an infant mental health assessment.

Background Information

Thomas lives with his mother, his two-year-old sibling, and maternal grandmother. The mother, Carole, presents as intellectually impaired with poor adaptive functioning. Carole's father tragically died while Carole's mother was pregnant with her, thus Carole never knew her father. Because of this, the maternal grandmother was unable to care for Carole. This missed opportunity for early attachment, along with other environmental factors, may have contributed to Carole's limited cognitive and emotional growth. The maternal grandmother continues to struggle with unresolved grief, depression, and physical health problems.

The family is experiencing economic, educational and social barriers. Thomas's father does not spend time with him, nor does he provide any financial support for the child. Carole indicated that the father has a history of substance abuse and estrangement with his own family. Carole is unable to work due to her health.

Thomas has a sibling, Sam, who is two-and-a-half years old and presents as globally delayed. Sam does not speak; he barks like a dog and eats whatever is on the floor, including non-comestibles. Carole routinely pushes Sam away when he seeks assistance or affection. These failed attempts to bond with his mother have created an insecure and disorganized attachment style as evidenced by Sam's ambivalence towards his mother (i.e. he runs up to her, then pulls away with a flat, emotionless affect). Sam was referred to an early intervention team. The early invention team has recommended a neurological evaluation of this child due to overt symptoms of autism. He is currently receiving early intervention services in the interim.

Presenting Problem

The initial referral for Thomas referenced the mother's lack of self-care and health concerns. During the assessment, the mother presented with limited parenting skills (i.e. Thomas was observed in the middle of the room in a bouncy chair unattended) and missed attachment opportunities (i.e. Carole appeared to be annoyed: Carole pushed the baby's chair with her foot and demanded that the grandmother feed him; the grandmother complained about having to feed him, while lifting him up and plopping the bottle into his mouth). The overriding concerns for Thomas was for his emotional and physical safety in this home environment.

Assessment

The home-based assessment protocol includes two home visits a week for four weeks. This assessment identifies the child's development in context of the child's health and development, the child's important relationships, and the multiple parental challenges that interfere with the parents' nurturing and supporting their child (Child First, n.d.). During these home visits with the family, a care coordinator and an infant mental health professional observed the family and collected a comprehensive home-based assessment. Child First's engagement process recognizes that change grows out of a relationship of trust between family and professional and that lasting change within the family comes from a collaborative, "family-driven" approach. This is achieved by respecting the wishes, values, culture, and strengths of the family. The respect and sensitivity shown to parents helps them to have a different experience of relationships, which in turn, will influence their relationships with their children (Child First, n.d.). Multiple assessment tools were used:

- *child development:* The Ages and Stages Questionnaire 3rd Edition (ASQ3) and the Modified Checklist for Autism in Toddlers Revised (MCHAT-R);
- *child mental health:* Brief Infant-Toddler Social and Emotional Assessment (BITSEA) or Ages and Stages Questionnaire Social Emotional (ASQSE);
- *parent–child relationships/attachment:* Child Caregiver Interaction Scale (CCIS) and Parenting Stress Index 4th Edition (PSI 4);
- *trauma:* Traumatic Event Screening Inventory Parent Report Revised (TESI PRR);
- *parent mental health:* Center for Epidemiologic Studies Depression Scale Revised (CESD-R);
- *parental challenges:* Life Stressor Checklist (LSCR); and
- *strengths:* clinical interview questions, HOPE spiritual assessment.

During the early part of the assessment period, Thomas was reaching out, cooing, and crying for his mother's attention. Carole would hold the baby as far away from her body as possible. In this position, Thomas' head would bobble uncontrollably. Even after gentle reminders about baby safety,

Carole seemed disinterested in Thomas' well-being. During one visit, Carole called Thomas a twerp using an annoyed tone of voice, after the team suggested that his wet shirt may indicate he needed a diaper change. Carole responded by asking her mother for help. The maternal grandmother said that she was tired and did not want to change the diaper and was annoyed that Carole had asked her. Both the mother and maternal grandmother shared their strategies to prevent Thomas from waking during the night. When they related that they were thickening the formula to reduce feedings, the clinician provided basic infant care instructions and referred the family to a new parent visiting nurse program to provide the caregivers with the basic care knowledge required for safety and health. Thomas seemed to be a source of stress, rather than joy, for the mother and maternal grandmother.

During the final week of the assessment period, the team noticed that Thomas was not reaching out for mom or crying anymore. His skin lacked color and was sagging, as if he had lost weight. Carole reported that Thomas was sleeping through the night and that he was not producing many wet diapers. The high child–caregiver interaction scale score, along with the clinical observations indicated that Thomas's attachment to his mother at six weeks of life was disorganized and insecure.

Thomas met the Diagnostic Classification of Mental Health and Developmental Disorders of Infancy and Early Childhood (DC:0–5) criteria for depression and, using a cross walk to the Diagnostic and Statistical Manual 5th Edition (DSM 5), a diagnosis for depression was conferred. This diagnosis was used to inform the development of an individualized child and family plan of care that included Carole, Thomas, the maternal grandmother, and the attachment between parent/caregiver and child. This plan of care was family-driven, and reflected the family's culture, priorities, and needs.

Case Summary

Thomas is experiencing toxic stress, which is affecting him physically (sagging skin and loss of weight) and emotionally (feelings of depression). Without intervention, this toxic stress can lead to identifiable mental health disorders and developmental delays. Thomas' attachment to his mother is disorganized and insecure. Research supports that infants whose needs are ignored, rejected, or responded to harshly develop an insecure working model, characterized by feelings of unworthiness and a sense that they cannot trust others to meet their needs (Leerkes & Zhou, 2018). This is also more likely when caregivers have their own history of trauma or mental illness, suggesting that compromised parenting was likely a key factor (Verhage et al., 2016). Carole and her mother are unable to respond in a nurturing way to Thomas' distress. Thomas' mother, Carole, is intellectually impaired with poor adaptive functioning. This likely impacted her ability to both understand and respond to Thomas' needs for connection.

Additionally, Carole and her mother have economic, educational, and social barriers. When families experience multiple stressors, and their basic needs are not met, it is difficult for them to focus on the emotional and developmental needs of their children (Child First, n.d.).

The above case example showed how infant mental health professionals conduct assessments using a trauma-informed lens. The Child First® infant mental health professional utilized the principles of trauma-informed care to decrease stress within the family, increase stability, and support the development of healthy, nurturing, protective relationships. First, the Child First® professional worked to build a trusting relationship by respecting, valuing, and listening to Carole and her mother without judgement. Never once did the professional tell Carole what she was doing wrong, but rather looked for teaching moments to share parenting skills with Carole and her mother. Next, the Child First® professional engaged the family in partnership by helping Carole and the maternal grandmother identify their own goals. The Child First® professional assessed Thomas' health and development, Thomas' relationships with his mother and grandmother, trauma and other stressors (e.g., absent father, poverty), and the multiple challenges experienced by Carole and the maternal grandmother (e.g., declining health, no employment, limited parenting knowledge). This assessment period concluded with a family-driven action plan of intervention goals, supports, and services. [Note, because of concerns for Thomas and his brother's physical and emotional safety, the case was eventually referred to a higher level of intervention.]

Implications and Recommendations

A comprehensive infant mental health assessment can identify infant emotional and developmental needs, help caregivers better understand difficult behaviors, and recommend interventions. Sharing information about infant mental health with parents/caregivers is a critical part of the assessment process. Child Trends (2016) has five things they want parents to know about emotional wellness in children 0–5 that can be shared with families at risk for abuse and neglect:

- Infants perceive and experience a range of emotions (the infant mental health professional can help Carole and the maternal grandmother understand how to read Thomas' cues and provide him with a nurturing response).
- Early positive interactions promote emotional wellness throughout the lifespan (Carole and the maternal grandmother can learn about the benefits of infant–caregiver attachment and practice playful interactive activities to strengthen the bond between infant and parent/caregiver).
- Having appropriate expectations of young children's development is important (the infant mental health professional can teach Carole and the maternal grandmother about normal developmental challenges and expectations).

- Parents and caregivers should be mindful of their own emotional well-being, seeking support if they need it (the infant mental health professional will assess the family member's mental health and stressors and refer for services when necessary).
- Young children are resilient and, if properly supported, can overcome potentially traumatic events (although Thomas is diagnosed with depression and an insecure attachment to his primary caregiver, sharing research with the family about the intervention success could enhance treatment outcomes).

Infant mental health is an interdisciplinary professional field of inquiry, practice, and policy that is concerned with enhancing the social and emotional competence of young children (Zeanah, Bailey, & Berry 2009). Supportive caregiving relationships during infancy are crucial for development. Parents/caregivers constitute the essence of the infant's world and are essential for the infant's capacity to regulate emotional and physiological states. Loving relationships provide young children with a sense of comfort, safety and confidence. They teach young children how to form friendships, communicate emotions and deal with challenges (Zero to Three, 2016). Assessment of attachment requires a focus on problems and strengths in the relationship between caregiver and child, rather than a focus on strengths of difficulties as existing within the individual child alone (Zeanah et al., 2011). Finally, utilizing a trauma-informed lens during an infant mental health assessment offers professionals a new way of conceptualizing the family dynamics by redirecting the age-old question of, "what's wrong with you to what happened to you."

Discussion Questions

---

1 What are the principles of trauma-informed care that are relevant in infant mental health assessment?
   a Do no harm
   b Validating the client
   c Safety, trust, choice, collaboration, trauma screening & assessment, & empowerment
   d Strengths perspective

2 Considering the screening and assessment tools in infant mental health, which of the following tools to assess trauma would be helpful?
   a Parenting stress index
   b Becks depression inventory
   c Traumatic Event Screening Inventory Parent Report Revised
   d ACES

3 With a partner, discuss why it would be helpful to assess children 0–5 using the DC:0–5 (the Diagnostic Classification Manual for early childhood).

References

Belsky, J., & de Haan, M. (2011). Annual research review: Parenting and children's brain development: The end of the beginning. *Journal of Child Psychology and Psychiatry*, 52(4), 409–428. https://doi.org/10.1111/j.1469-7610.2010.02281.x

Bernard, K., Dozier, M., Bick, J., Lewis-Morrarty, E., Lindhiem, O., & Carlson, E. (2012). Enhancing attachment organization among maltreated children: Results of a randomized clinical trial. *Child Development*, 83(2), 623–636. https://doi.org/10.1111/j.1467-8624.2011.01712.x

Blair, C. (2010). Stress and the development of self-regulation in context. *Child Development Perspectives*, 4(3), 181–188. https://doi.org/10.1111/j.1750-8606.2010.00145.x

Brazelton, T. B. (1992). *Touchpoints*. New York: Guilford Press.

Bowers, M. E., & Yehuda, R. (2016). Intergenerational transmission of stress in humans. *Neuropsychopharmacology*, 41(1), 232. https://doi.org/10.1038/npp.2015.247

Bowlby, J. (1969). *Attachment and loss: Vol. 1. Attachment*. New York, NY: Basic Books.

Bowlby, J. (1988). *A secure base: Parent-child attachment and healthy human development*. New York, NY: Basic Books.

Child First (n.d.). *Our work*. Retrieved from https://www.childfirst.org/our-work

Carpenter, G. L., & Stacks, A. M. (2009). Developmental effects of exposure to intimate partner violence in early childhood: A review of the literature. *Children and Youth Services Review*, 31(8), 831–839. https://doi.org/10.1016/j.childyouth.2009.03.005

Child Trends. (2016). *Child well-being: Constructs to measure child well-being and risk and protective factors that affect the development of young children*. Retrieved from https://www.childtrends.org/wp-content/uploads/2017/03/2016-61ConstructsMeasureChildWellbeing.pdf

Cicchetti, D., Toth, S. L., Nilsen, W. J., & Manly, J. T. (2016). What do we know and why does it matter? The dissemination of evidence-based interventions for child maltreatment. In *The Wiley handbook of developmental psychology in practice: Implementation and impact* (pp. 367–406). https://doi.org/10.1002/9781119095699.ch15

Clinton, J., Feller, A. F., & Williams, R. C. (2016). The importance of infant mental health. *Paediatrics & Child Health*, 21(5), 239. https://doi.org/10.1093/pch/21.5.239

Dickson, A., & Kronenberg, M. (2011). The importance of relationship-based evaluations for traumatized young children and their caregivers. In J. D. Osofsky & J. D. Osofsky (Eds.), *Clinical work with traumatized young children* (pp. 114–135). New York, NY: Guilford Press.

Fallot, R., & Harris, M. (2009). *Creating cultures of trauma-informed care (CCTIC): A self assessment and planning protocol*. Retrieved from https://www.healthcare.uiowa.edu/icmh/documents/CCTICSelf-AssessmentandPlanningProtocol0709.pdf

Felitti, V. J., Anda, R. F., Nordenberg, D., Williamson, D. F., Spitz, A. M., Edwards, V., & Marks, J. S. (1998). Relationship of childhood abuse and household dysfunction to many of the leading causes of death in adults: The Adverse Childhood Experiences (ACE) Study. *American Journal of Preventive Medicine*, 14(4), 245–258. https://doi.org/10.1016/S0749-3797(98)00017–00018

Garner, A. S. (2013). Home visiting and the biology of toxic stress: opportunities to address early childhood adversity. *Pediatrics*, 132(Supplement 2), S65–S73.

Klawetter, S., & Frankel, K. (2018). Infant mental health: a lens for maternal and child mental health disparities. *Journal of Human Behavior in the Social Environment*, 28(5), 557–569. https://doi.org/10.1080/10911359.2018.1437495

Leerkes, E. M., & Zhou, N. (2018). Maternal sensitivity to distress and attachment outcomes: Interactions with sensitivity to nondistress and infant temperament. *Journal of Family Psychology*, 32(6), 753–761. https://psycnet.apa.org/doi/10.1037/fam0000420

Levenson, J. (2017). Trauma-informed social work practice. *Social Work*, 62(2), 105–113. https://doi.org/10.1093/sw/swx001

Lieberman, A. F. (2004). Traumatic stress and quality of attachment: Reality and internalization in disorders of infant mental health. *Infant Mental Health Journal*, 25(4), 336–351. https://doi.org/10.1002/imhj.20009

Lieberman, A. F., & Knorr, K. (2007). The impact of trauma: A developmental framework for infancy and early childhood. *Pediatric Annals*, 36(4).

Lyons-Ruth, K., Todd Manly, J., von Klitzing, K., Tamminen, TT., Emde, R., Fitzgerarld, H., Paul, C., Keren, M., Berg, A., Foley, M. & Watanabe, H. (2017). The worldwide burden of infant mental and emotional disorder: report of the task force of the world association for infant mental health. *Infant Mental Health Journal*, 38(6), 695–705. https://doi.org/10.1002/imhj.21674

Madigan, S., Brumariu, L. E., Villani, V., Atkinson, L., & Lyons-Ruth, K. (2016). Representational and questionnaire measures of attachment: A meta-analysis of relations to child internalizing and externalizing problems. *Psychological Bulletin*, 142(4), 367–399. https://doi.org/10.1037/bul0000029

Mares, S., & Graeff-Martins, A. S. (2012). The clinical assessment of infants, preschoolers and their families. In *IACAPAP e-Textbook of child and adolescent mental health*. Geneva: International Association for Child and Adolescent Psychiatry and Allied Professions. Retrieved from: http://iacapap.org/wp-content/uploads/A.4-Infant-assessment-2017.pdf

National Scientific Council on the Developing Child. (2012). The science of neglect: The persistent absence of responsive care disrupts the developing brain. Working Paper 12. Harvard University Center on the Developing Child.

National Survey of Children's Health. (2012). 2011/2012 data query. Data Resource Center for Child and Adolescent Health. Retrieved from www.childhealthdata.org.

Osofsky, J. D. & Thomas, K. (2012). What is infant mental health? *Zero to Three*, 33(2), 9.

Reddy, V. (2008). *How infants know minds*. Cambridge, MA: Harvard University Press

Schore, A. N. (2009). Attachment trauma and the developing right brain: Origins of pathological dissociation. In *Dissociation and the dissociative disorders: DSM-V and beyond*, (pp. 107–141). Retrieved from http://www.allanschore.com/pdf/__SchoreDissociation09.pdf

Schore, A. N., & Schore, J. R. (2012). Modern attachment theory: The central role of affect regulation in development and treatment. In A. N. Schore (Ed.), *The science of the art of psychotherapy* (pp. 27–51). New York, NY: Norton.

Substance Abuse and Mental Health Services Administration. (2014a). SAMHSA's concept of trauma and guidance for a trauma-informed approach. Retrieved from http://store.samhsa.gov/shin/content//SMA14-4884/SMA14-4884.pdf

Substance Abuse and Mental Health Services Administration. (2014b). TIP 57: Trauma informed care in behavioral health services. Retrieved from http://store. samhsa.gov/shin/content//SMA14-4816/SMA14-4816.pdf

Tereno, S., Madigan, S., Lyons-Ruth, K., Plamondon, A., Atkinson, L., Guedeney, N., ... & Guedeney, A. (2017). Assessing a change mechanism in a randomized home-visiting trial: Reducing disrupted maternal communication decreases infant disorganization. *Development and Psychopathology*, 29(2), 637–649. https://doi. org/10.1017/S0954579417000232

Tronick, E.Z. (2007). *Neurobehavioral and Social Emotional Development of the Infant and Young Child*. New York, NY: Norton Press.

Ullrich, R., Cole, P., Gebhard, B., & Schmit, S. (2017). *Education and training programs: A critical support for infants, toddlers, and families. building strong foundations: Advancing comprehensive policies for infants, toddlers, and families.* Center for Law and Social Policy, Inc. (CLASP).

U.S. Department of Health & Human Services, Administration for Children and Families, Administration on Children, Youth and Families, Children's Bureau. (2016). *Child maltreatment 2014*. Available from http://www.acf.hhs.gov/program s/cb/research-data-technology/statistics-research/child-maltreatment

Verhage, M. L., Schuengel, C., Madigan, S., Fearon, R. M., Oosterman, M., Cassibba, R., ... & van Ijzendoorn, M. H. (2016). Narrowing the transmission gap: A synthesis of three decades of research on intergenerational transmission of attachment. *Psychological Bulletin*, 142(4), 337–361.

von Klitzing, K., Döhnert, M., Kroll, M., & Grube, M. (2015). Mental disorders in early childhood. *Deutsches Ärzteblatt International*, 112(21–22), 375–393. https:// doi.org/10.3238/arztebl.2015.0375

Zeanah, C. H., Berlin, L. J., & Boris, N. W. (2011). Practitioner review: Clinical applications of attachment theory and research for infants and young children. *Journal of Child Psychology and Psychiatry*, 52(8), 819–833. https://doi.org/10. 1111/j.1469-7610.2011.02399.x

Zeanah, P. D., Carter, A.Cohen, J. (2015). DC:0–3 to DC:0–3R, to DC:0–5[TM]; a new edition. *Zero to Three*, 35(3), 63–66.

Zeanah, P. D., Bailey, L. O., & Berry, S. (2009). Infant mental health and the "real world"-opportunities for interface and impact. *Child and Adolescent Psychiatric Clinics*, 18(3), 773–787.

Zero to Three. (2016). *DC:0–5 Diagnostic classification of mental health and developmental disorders of infancy and early childhood* (Rev. ed.). Washington, DC: Author.

Part III

New and Adapted Theoretical Approaches and Models to Infant Play Therapy

FirstPlay® Therapy Strengthens the Attachment Relationship Between a Mother with Perinatal Depression and Her Infant

Karen Baldwin, Meyleen Velasquez and Janet A. Courtney

FirstPlay® Infant Story-Massage

FirstPlay® Therapy is a new model that fosters healthy connections between infants and caregivers. FirstPlay® was developed by Dr. Janet Courtney after 30 years of clinical practice in the area of developmental play therapy, and training in Ericksonian-based storytelling (StoryPlay®). FirstPlay® Infant Story-Massage is an attachment-based, parent-infant resiliency *manualized* model for ages birth to two-years (Baldwin, 2020; Courtney, 2015a; Courtney & Gray, 2011, 2014; Courtney & Now-akowski-Sims, 2019; Courtney, Velasquez, & Bakai Toth, 2017). Its methods are designed to be implemented along with other forms of parent/infant interventions including preventative modalities. As an adjunctive model to other parenting interventions, FirstPlay® intervenes to support caregivers to provide attuned nurturing touch with their infants to include caring, respectful, attuned, and joyful activities to build trust and security in the infant and to increase secure attachments that will provide a lifelong impact on the social, emotional, and psychological wellness of that child. FirstPlay® comprises the following underlying theoretical foundations: attachment theory, developmental play therapy, filial therapy, family systems theory, Ericksonian-based storytelling (StoryPlay®), components of mindfulness, and research related to infant massage, touch and neuroscience (see Figure 6.1). [Note, FirstPlay® Therapy is also adapted for ages two years and up, known as FirstPlay Kinesthetic Storytelling®—see Chapter 17 in this book.]

Developmental Play Therapy

Developmental Play Therapy (DPT) is a therapeutic component crucial to FirstPlay® Therapy (Courtney & Gray, 2011, 2014; Courtney & Now-akowski-Sims, 2019; Courtney, Velasquez, & Bakai Toth, 2017). DPT was developed by Viola Brody in the 1960s. Brody (1997) believed that touch as a

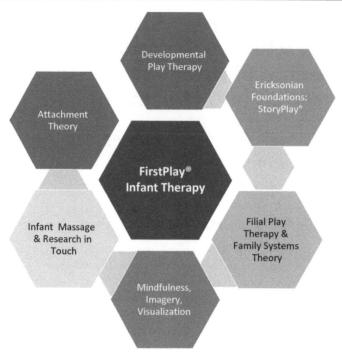

Figure 6.1 FirstPlay® supporting theories and literature.

therapeutic intervention was a core change-agent within the therapeutic relationship. She wrote, "The earliest self-experience is recognition of the body. This body awareness comes about through the physical contact and playful and loving attitudes the mother provides" (Brody, 1997, p. 3). Brody postulated that touch helps the child to produce the conditions necessary for the development of an inner self—a basic human need for healthy emotional growth. The influence of Brody's work is far reaching, and Theraplay co-founders, Jernberg & Booth (2001), acknowledged the impact of Austin Des Lauriers and her "model of healthy parent—infant interaction" to the development of Theraplay, as noted in the following: "Recognizing the work of Austin Des Lauriers and Viola Brody, an intuitively natural approach that could be understood...we adapted their methods [to Thera-play] to help children ... And it worked!" (p. 31).

Attachment Theory

FirstPlay® is grounded in attachment theory, which focuses on the quality of interactions between a parent (or a primary attachment figure) and the child and how that contributes to psychological, emotional, and social health or pathology. Attachment theory was conceptualized by John Bowlby (Bowlby, 1979). Bowlby believed that human infants needed a consistent and nurturing relationship with an attuned caregiver to develop healthy relationships, which is connected to the central nervous system. He also viewed the relationship between mother and infant as a biological necessity and the primary and essential influence in infant development (Fitton, 2012).

When an infant has repeated experiences of comfort in times of distress it creates a memory schema or an internal working model that lets the infant know they have a dependable caregiver in their environment (Bowlby, 1979). This internal working model helps the infant to formulate a positive representation of an available caregiver which in turn leads to a secure attachment and a foundation of trust. In infants where there is a caregiver that is unavailable or inconsistent, insecure attachments can develop (Hertenstein, 2002). Research has found that a lack of secure attachment can lead to long-term undesirable emotional states such as low self-esteem, lack of self-control, aggression and violence, lack of empathy, neediness, clinging behavior, and oppositional behaviors with parents or caregivers (Fearon, et al., 2010). This lack of secure attachment has also been correlated to high-risk behaviors in later development, such as teen pregnancy, substance abuse, or anti-social behavior (Karen, 1998).

Filial Therapy—Parents as "Change Agent"

Practitioners have recognized that adult–child relationships play an important role for both emotional difficulties and positive change for children (Ryan, 2007). Filial therapy was developed by Louise Guerney in the 1960s (Guerney & Guerney, 1989; Guerney, 2015). In filial therapy, the primary caretaker or parent is trained on how to become the "primary change agent" for their own children (VanFleet, 1994, p. 2). In FirstPlay® Therapy, the Certified FirstPlay® Practitioner instructs and guides the caregiver to provide touch-based activities by modeling on a baby-doll while they also supervise, model, and guide caregivers to practice with their infant (Courtney, 2015a; 2015b). This method of guided instruction allows the caregiver to become the primary "change agent" for their infant. Guerney (2015) wrote:

> The advantage to assigning a therapeutic role to the parents is that they become temporarily removed from the entanglements of the family dynamics. They learn new ways of relating to the child. They execute new concepts and perceptions of family relationships … parents become part of the solution instead of part of the problem.

(p. x)

Filial therapy's ultimate goal is to help families attain happiness and security through improved relationships by teaching caregivers healthier ways to interact with their infants and to develop positive interactions between the infant and the caregiver, thereby reducing possible future behavioral and or emotional issues (VanFleet & Topham, 2016). FirstPlay® adapts Filial Play Therapy concepts into practice with parents and infants.

Ericksonian-Based Storytelling and StoryPlay®

Making it uniquely different from other infant massage interventions, First-Play® Therapy incorporates Ericksonian-based therapeutic storytelling. Joyce Mills, PhD, adapted Milton Erickson's work to a play therapy model she founded, titled StoryPlay® (Mills and Crowley, 2014). Ericksonian storytelling uses indirect positive messages that are embedded within a story to "activate inherent healing processes that can reach a child at a deeper level of con-sciousness" (Courtney & Mills, 2016, p.19). The right brain hemisphere is activated in processing metaphorical types of storytelling, and clients can extract meanings that are relevant to them that can support new responses and ways of relating. Additionally, research in the area of literacy is showing that the more parents and caregivers speak directly to their infants (face to face, where the infant can visually see the parent speaking), and the more words spoken, the better they perform in school (Hillairet, Tift, Minar, & Lewko-wicz, 2017). In FirstPlay®, caregivers learn an original story, called *The Baby Tree Hug* (Courtney, 2015b), that includes story-massage and first-play activities that support the parent and infant bonding and attachment relationship.

Interpersonal Neuroscience

FirstPlay® is supported by the research in neurobiology. Studies in neuroscience have discovered the bio-chemical impact on early human brain development stimulated by the parent–child physical and emotional attachment interactions (Badenoch, 2018; Porges, 2018). Schore (2012) advocates that attachment theory should be updated to be known as *modern* attachment theory, which considers the most recent brain research. From this perspective, a nurturing and attuned relationship between the infant and primary caregiver are "The essential matrix for creating a right brain self that can regulate its own internal states and external relationships" (Schore & Schore, 2012, p. 44). Siqveland & Moe (2014) found that the quality between the infant and primary caregiver during the first year of life is vital for the child's brain development that impacts the social and emotional functioning of the infant. In another study, Bernier, Bell, & Calkins (2016) focused on children from inadequate environments, such as those where there was neglect, abuse or extreme relational deprivation, such as orphanages, and found that adverse conditions can impact normal brain development concluding that brain growth may be affected by extreme distress. Just the opposite is true for favorable environmental conditions that can influence a positive impact on healthy brain development. One of the most important influences of healthy brain development is the need for safety, which is an essential aspect related to the process of FirstPlay® implementation with parents. Porges (2018) informed that the social engagement system of safety emerges from a face–heart connection that coordinates the "…heart with the muscles of the face and head.' This further functions to regulate bodily states of growth and restoration and for face–heart connection … via facial expression and prosody" (p. 55–56).

Touch and Infant Massage

Since FirstPlay® incorporates techniques of infant massage imbedded within a metaphorical storytelling framework, the research and literature of infant massage and touch is foundational to this model (Courtney & Gray, 2011, 2014; Courtney & Nolan, 2017; Courtney & Siu, 2018). Touch is essential to human growth and development—without which, we may die (Field, 2014; Linden, 2015). When a child experiences touch from a caring caregiver, they begin to develop a sense of self, learn how to relate to others, and learn to modulate their affect and master their own environment (Brody, 1997; APT, 2019). Touch is a unique form of communication that is often experienced at an unconscious level. When touch is appropriately provided, it can promote healing and growth. When touch is misused, it can impede healthy development and cause harm. Fortunately, as Linden (2015) informed, in situations where infants have been neglected and deprived of touch, gentle massage can "reverse the deleterious effects of touch deprivation on infants" (p. 27). Infant massage promotes infant mental health, and research has revealed the qualitative and quantitative benefits of infant massage and touch, including enhancing the quality of the attachment relationship and promoting social, emotional, and physical well-being, and healthy brain development (Field, 2014; Hertenstein, 2002; Linden, 2015; O'Brien & Lynch, 2011). Infant massage initiates teaching babies about positive caring touch and respectful boundaries. It also stimulates the release of oxytocin, which is important for attachment and bonding, and calming (Courtney, Velasquez, & Bakai Toth, 2017; Field, 2014).

Mindfulness

Mindfulness is one way that caregivers can learn relaxation skill building before they begin the FirstPlay® infant story-massage (Courtney, 2020). For an infant to receive calming attuned presence, the parent must first come from their own place of calm and focus (Courtney, 2015a). When caregivers are unable to calm their own stress and anxiety, they may be challenged in helping their infants to calm and relax. From the perspective of co-regulation, we know that parents and infants can positively and negatively impact

each other's internal states of being (Schore, 2012). Therefore, a FirstPlay®
Practitioner not only guides parents to connect with their infant, but also
guides the parents to "calm, relax, and connect" before beginning the First-
Play® story-massage. This is done through a simple guided imagery called
the *Rainbow Hug*® (Courtney, 2015b) where parents place their hand on
their heart and the other hand is placed gently on the infant's chest (see
Figure 6.2 for a visual example).

Facilitating Attunement and Attachment in FirstPlay®

FirstPlay® utilizes the following techniques to model and support parental
attunement and attachment:

1   From a client-centered perspective, the practitioner supports following
    the infant's lead during the FirstPlay® implementation—the baby is
    considered to be in the "driver's seat."
2   "Speaking *for* the baby" is a therapeutic intervention that provides a way
    for practitioners to respectfully heighten a parent's awareness and empathy
    about the observed physical and emotional needs of the baby and is done
    as if the baby was speaking (Carter, Osofsky, & Hann, 1991).
3   "Speaking *to* the baby" is a way for practitioners to encourage parents
    to talk directly to their babies.
4   "Seeing and being seen," utilized by Brody (1997), is engaged by practi-
    tioners to highlight the evolving reciprocal back-and-forth (also known
    as, "serve and return") relationship.
5   Attuning to infant cues: FirstPlay® practitioners also assist parents to
    respond to the cues of their infant for readiness for touch and engage-
    ment and when they are not read.
6   Preparing infants for transitions: Practitioners support parents to pre-
    pare and talk to their infant when moving from one activity to the next.
7   "Baby breaks" recognizes that infants have short attention spans, and
    the practitioner is on the alert to observe the infant's ebb and flow of
    needs during a session, and when it may be time for a break.
8   "Calm, relax and connect": Attunement is also supported by guiding the
    parent to slow down and calm their own nervous systems prior to the
    beginning of the FirstPlay® session. At the same time, they are sup-
    ported to connect with their baby.
9   Modeling and guiding parent's to "ask permission" from their infant
    prior to beginning the FirstPlay® session supports respect for the infant.

Perinatal mental health

*(The following review is intended to support understanding for the case
study presenting problem presented in this chapter.)*

Figure 6.2 Stephanie Crowley connects through the Rainbow Hug "calm and relax" imagery and then asks "permission" from five-month-old Ezra to begin telling the FirstPlay® "Baby Tree Hug" story-massage.
Used with permission from Stephanie Crowley; photographer, Author, Janet A. Courtney

Perinatal mental health problems are the most common complication of the postpartum period, commonly identified from conception up to one year old (Postpartum Support International, 2010). Pregnancy and postpartum mental health difficulties occur in about 14–23% of all women (American College of Obstetricians and Gynecologists, 2018). These numbers are twice the rate of gestational diabetes and high blood pressure, for which women are routinely screened throughout their pregnancy (Kleiman, 2009). However, often parents are uninformed of the prevalence and may suffer mental health complications as symptoms begin to arise (Kleiman, 2009). The symptoms of postpartum depression can be severe and intense with a quick onset, placing the mother at high risk for suicide. Often less identified is that postnatal concerns for men can occur in one out of ten fathers, with the greatest risk factor being their partner's depression (Paulson & Bazemore, 2010; Goodman, 2004).

Parental mental illness can be a child's first ACE (Adverse Childhood Experience). If untreated, depression can affect the attachment relationship leading to changes in an infant's developing brain that may cause emotional, social, and/or physical delays. These effects on a young child's brain can be reversible with the right treatment, education and supportive environment. However, although postpartum depression is a treatable mental health condition, less than 15% of affected women receive treatment. These statistics leave a high number of women without receiving the services they need— potentially creating the foundation for an intergenerational pattern of disrupted attachment in infants (Center on the Developing Child at Harvard University, 2009).

When working with the infant population, clinicians should take into consideration that caregivers with postnatal mental health complications might be experiencing the most vulnerable period of their lives. As such, providers must use sound clinical judgment to discuss and provide services in a way that enhances the caregiver's capacity and self-esteem, as opposed to inadvertently increasing the caregiver's feelings of guilt, frustration, and incompetence. In addition, clinicians who are implementing infant play therapy in their work with perinatal parents should properly screen, treat, and/or refer parents for appropriate mental health services.

Case Study: Susana and Infant Karla, age 4 months

The following clinical case will demonstrate how the author (Velasquez), a perinatal mental health therapist and Certified FirstPlay® Supervisor, integrated FirstPlay® Infant Story-Massage into the treatment plan for a mother experiencing postpartum depression.

Presenting Problem and Family Background

Susana is a 26-year-old female, 4 months postpartum, referred for psychotherapeutic services following discharge from an involuntary inpatient mental health hospitalization. Susana and her husband attended an appointment with the baby's pediatrician where Susana disclosed feeling depressed and having difficulty bonding with her daughter. The pediatrician referred her to the local hospital's emergency room where she was consequently involuntarily hospitalized. Susana was born in El Salvador and reported being the youngest of ten siblings. She verbalized experiencing physical, emotional, and sexual abuse by her parents and grandmother. Her parents sent her to the United States when she was 16 to reside with her maternal aunt, where she remained until 19, when she married her husband. At the time of the intake, baby Karla was 4 months old.

Assessment and Beginning of Treatment

During the first session with her husband, Susana verbalized feeling scared to be alone with this clinician for fear she might be hospitalized again. The client completed a perinatal specific biopsychosocial assessment (originated by this author, Velasquez) and the Edinburg Postnatal Depression Scale (EPDS). Susana's results showed elevated EPDS scores, specifically for depression. The assessment indicated that Susana was experiencing postpartum depression as she relayed that the symptoms of depression began during pregnancy, as well as the tragic experience of two previous losses due to miscarriage. Further assessment, related to Susana's relationship with her infant, revealed the pain of her depressive state when she shared, "I don't think I was made for this" (when referring to her new role as a mother). She described Karla as "fussy" and often "crying when not being carried." Further, Karla was not sleeping through the night and Susana was constantly "checking the baby to make sure she was breathing." When asked about the quality of touch and playful activities, she stated, "I don't want to spoil her by giving her all my attention. I don't want to get her used to being in arms." Susana's husband, Juan, remained quiet for most of the assessment.

Initial Treatment Plan Following Assessment:

The following treatment goals were established:

(A) Decrease Susana's symptoms of depression using cognitive therapy and by utilizing her support network system.
(B) Discuss ways in which early childhood trauma can affect the postpartum period as well as her ability to bond with Karla, in addition to providing psychoeducation on developmentally appropriate infant expectations.
(C) Implement FirstPlay® Infant Storytelling Massage instruction to support mother–infant bonding and attachment.

Sessions Two to Six: Individual and Family (without infant present)

The focus of sessions two to six was on implementing cognitive therapy skills for individual therapy. Susana's symptoms were stabilizing, and her husband and mother had attended sessions to learn more about postpartum depression.

Session Seven (First Session with Infant Karla Present)

Susana attended the session with baby Karla, now 5 months old. It was noted that Susana placed the stroller at a distance from her as she sat down on the couch. Susana advised that Karla was not crying as often as she felt the "training" was working. (As stated in the assessment section, she believed that by not responding to Karla's cry it helped to train Karla to not be "spoiled" and expect to be held.) Attempts to provide brief psychoeducation throughout the first six sessions by this clinician were apparently not successful as Susana continued to believe that it was positive that she was not responding to Karla's signals of need. It was further observed that Karla was lying in the stroller with little body movement and minimal signaling to the mother during the session.

[*Side note:* It's important to note that current research indicates that mothers who experience depression can experience difficulty coping emotionally during times of stress and may demonstrate lower rates of sensitivity towards their infant's needs (Musser, Ablow, & Measelle, 2012). In addition, trouble with emotional regulation coupled with the intense desire to be a loving and protective caregiver can often lead mothers to experiencing intense feelings of guilt, anxiety, and shame (Kleiman, 2009).]

Rationale for Introducing FirstPlay® into Treatment with Susana

Although Susana was progressing in treatment, it was observed that Karla was experiencing a shut-down of her signaling response system which was concerning to this clinician, as it could indicate Karla was at risk for depression as well as for delays in her development (Zero to Three, 2016). FirstPlay® is a modality that increases the bond between a parent and infant as it provides a structured (and manualized) way for parents to learn loving and attuned methods to interact and connect with their baby. Treatments that focus solely on treating the mother's depression have not been shown to demonstrate an impact on the infant's development even after the mother's depression has ceased suggesting that effective treatment should focus both on the mother and the dyadic relationship (Center on the Developing Child at Harvard University, 2009). Although Susana's symptoms remained active, she expressed relief in the intensity of the depression and in knowing that postpartum depression was temporary. Due to the decrease in intensity of symptoms and the observations made by this clinician in the office, it was concluded that the dyad would benefit from introducing FirstPlay®.

FirstPlay® Sessions

Introduction

Susana and Juan were informed in the initial session that this clinician was trained in FirstPlay® Therapy. In the seventh session, this clinician introduced the modality and reviewed the introductory information found in the *FirstPlay® Parent Manual* with the mother. Psychoeducation on the importance of touch to the attachment relationship was highlighted and the modality was presented in a way that the parent can interact with her infant without concerns of "spoiling." The father was invited to the demonstration session on the following week.

FirstPlay® Implementation Session I

The family arrived to the appointment where the office area was comfortably set up with a blanket and pillows on the floor for the FirstPlay® Story-Massage session. This clinician noticed that the mother sat on the floor by the clinician while the father remained on the couch. The benefits of FirstPlay® were reviewed again and the father was encouraged to participate. He stated, "No, this is something for mothers to do." For the calm and relax portion of the therapy, the mother reported that she was not used to meditating and was concerned that she may not be able to do it correctly. This clinician normalized her feelings and assured her that the practice would be short and simple to follow. To engage the father in the relaxation, this clinician encouraged him to put his hand on his wife's back to help her ground. The father was receptive to this invitation and the clinician noted that he closed his eyes during the process. The next step in the preparation process was to model and guide the parents how to *ask the baby for permission to touch.*" The mother stated, "This is good for girls to know," as she made eye contact with Juan. This clinician then reinforced the importance of ways to teach children safe body boundaries beginning in infancy.

FirstPlay® Story-Massage utilizes a metaphorical story called the *Baby Tree Hug©*. With this story, the parent pretends that the baby is a tree, and the different body parts symbolize the branches and leaves, and so forth, of the "tree." The clinician demonstrates the story-massage on a baby-doll while the parents follow along with the techniques with their infant. The family chose for Karla to be a "mango" tree. As soon as Karla was placed on the blanket, she began to squirm and become fussy. The parents advised that she was experiencing acid reflux which caused constant crying. Karla was then placed on a wedge pillow, which appeared to help her feel more comfortable. Susana began following the lead of the clinician as she massaged the left leg. (The following is a selection of the session interactions.)

Therapist (reading out loud from the Baby Tree Hug story): "We can even climb those branches up, up, up and then again down, down, down."

Susana: "Look how she smiles (smiles back and then looks at Juan)."

Therapist: "She really likes interacting with you like this! I can see how happy you both get when she is smiling."

Juan: "We love her very much, but she can be a difficult baby."

Therapist: "It can be really hard dealing with an infant with acid reflux. Your family has been through a lot in the past months."

Susana: "And me with this depression, I don't help."

Therapist: "The depression is part of what your family has been through, it is not your fault. This is part of the journey to feeling like yourself again."

At this point, Karla became fussy and began crying. Susana picked her up and began rocking her as she stood up and walked around the office. Juan explained that when the baby starts crying, it helps when they move her around. When Karla was ready, we resumed the story moving through the legs, foot, toes and ankles. When it was time for the ankle, Karla pushed her feet against the mother.

Susana: "No, no, no mommy is being nice, we are doing a massage."

Therapist (noticing that mother misinterpreted the cue): "I wonder what happened?"

Susana: "She was trying to kick me!"

Therapist: "Hmm, you know babies have only so many ways that they can communicate with us and body movements is one of them. I wonder if there was anything else that she could have been trying to let us know?"

(Karla's face is turned to the side away from mother and she starts to cry.)

Juan: "Looks like she doesn't want any more."

Therapist (speaking for baby): "I just need a little break right now."

Karla became very upset, crying loudly as both her parents attempted to comfort her. Susana prepared her a bottle as she reported it was close to her feeding time. During this time, this clinician reflected with both parents on how hard they are working to meet their infant's needs and provided with positive reinforcement when they demonstrated attunement. Once Karla was calm, Susana asked about continuing. As the baby just ate and she experiences reflux, this clinician discussed the possibility of practicing on the right leg while Karla sat on the father's lap.

[*Side Note:* Sitting on her father's lap for the other leg is an adjustment to the FirstPlay® model that helps to engage the other parent in the activity. Due to the father's culture, he expressed that the massage was an activity reserved for mothers. It is crucial for therapists to take culture and beliefs into consideration when working with families and to find culturally appropriate ways to engage fathers in treatment.]

As the session time was over, this clinician encouraged the family to focus on practicing the leg story-massage as Karla was on the father's lap, and to return the next week for continuation.

FirstPlay® Implementation Session 2

Susana arrived alone to the session and stated that Karla was at home not feeling well. She reported having attempted to do FirstPlay® with Karla at home, but stated that Karla "did not want it." She continued, "She liked it when you were there, but she doesn't like it when I do it." Part of the session focused on understanding ways in which the depression was affecting her relationship with her daughter. The best time of the day for massages and infant cues were reviewed to ensure that Susana could pick up on Karla's *quiet alert* times. This clinician then asked Susana if she would like to practice the FirstPlay® techniques on a baby-doll, and she agreed. This clinician then demonstrated FirstPlay® on a baby-doll while Susana practiced on her own baby-doll. She appeared visibly relaxed as she practiced on the doll.

Figure 6.3 Demonstration illustration from the *FirstPlay Parent Manual.*
Source: Janet A. Courtney.

Therapist: "The good thing about this bonding moment is that it can be relaxing for mommy too."

Susana: "If only she would let me."

Therapist: "We are trying something new, sometimes babies need time to adjust. It can be hard when you are excited to play with your baby and she's not ready, but it just means she needs a little more time. The more we practice following her lead, the easier it becomes and the stronger your bond gets."

Susana: "I want to have a good relationship with her. I want her to trust me and come to me when she needs help."

Therapist: "Then we are on the right track. FirstPlay® can be part of the foundation for building that trust. The more she sees that 'you are listening to her' the more she will communicate with you."

FirstPlay® Implementation Session 3

For this session, Susana arrived at the office with Karla. When asked about how the FirstPlay® storytelling massage went at home, Susana mentioned that she had been able to practice with Karla a few times. This clinician positively reinforced her practicing with her daughter. Susana was asked about early FirstPlay® activities that she recalled as a child. She was able to identify different songs that are native to her country that she remembered hearing as a young child. Using Susana's inner resources, this clinician helped her to identify ways to add playful, caring, and respectful touch activities to go along with the songs. This practitioner demonstrated the techniques while Susana playfully practiced them with her baby.

FirstPlay® Implementation Session 4

A month later, Susana, Karla and Juan arrived for the last FirstPlay® session. This clinician encouraged the dyad to demonstrate what they had been working on during their at-home FirstPlay® sessions. Susana began by talking with Karla and playing a singsong game and clapping her legs together. The dyad then moved to the floor, and Susana began the FirstPlay® Story-Massage.

Susana (to Karla): "I'm going to give you a little story-massage."
(Karla looks intently at her mother and smiles.)
Therapist: "Look at the way she is smiling at you—looks like she is letting you know she's ready."

When Karla was ready for a baby break, Susana handed her to Juan. This clinician noticed that Karla became instantly calm as she sat on her father's lap.

Therapist: "Oh my goodness, I can see how much she loves being with you."

Juan: "She means everything to me," he said smiling.

Therapist: "You know, we can try to continue the massage in a different way if you're up for it. While she sits in your lap, so calmly, Susana, you can continue the arm story-massages, similar to how we did the first time, and see how she likes it."

(Susana begins the FirstPlay® story-massage.)

Therapist: "When you are all home together, this can be a nice way for everyone to participate in this bonding time. She can spend some special time with both mom and dad."

Summary

When empathy, attunement, and nurturing touch are present in the parent–infant relationship, the foundations for a healthy and secure attachment are set forth. This case demonstrated ways in which FirstPlay® storytelling-massage can be integrated in the treatment of mothers with perinatal depression, and highlighted the positive impact of including the infant in treatment. A therapeutic model that addressed the quality of the parent–infant relationship is needed when treating parents with perinatal depression. The practitioner's capacity to assess behaviors present in the infant and the dyadic relationship allowed for a focus on increasing maternal sensitivity. The safety established through providing a non-judgmental space and respecting for cultural differences created a therapeutic alliance with Susana and her husband, Juan.

FirstPlay® can enhance the caregiver–infant relationship by offering a structured way that caregivers can learn new methods of pleasant and tender physical contact that also teaches respect of the infant and develops empathy and increased connection. In turn, FirstPlay® provides caregivers opportunities to focus on the interpersonal experiences with their infants, which can help the infant to organize the development of brain structures early in life and ongoing throughout the lifespan (Siegel, 2012). These positive experiences can assist the infants' brains in developing regulation of their bodily states and emotions, the organization of memory, and the ability to communicate. Finally, FirstPlay® can expose caregivers to activities that they themselves may have never experienced as an infant, and they may be learning new ways of interrelating with their infants that can have a positive impact on future generations. FirstPlay® can teach caregivers how to utilize nurturing touch experiences with their infants to include caring, respectful, attuned, and joyful activities to build trust and security. These experiences will increase secure attachments that supports social, emotional, and psychological wellness beginning in infancy and throughout the lifespan.

Discussion Questions

1 Reflecting on the case study, discuss with a colleague any potential feelings or countertransference that may arise when working with a parent experiencing postpartum depression.
2 What are some circumstances that would make it clinically appropriate to include the infant in the mother's treatment of perinatal depression?
3 Discuss the potential effects of untreated parental depression on an infant's development and attachment system.
4. In what ways did the implementation of FirstPlay® with the family system make a difference in therapy outcomes? What did the clinician in this case do and say with the mother and father to support the attachment relationship with Karla?

References

American College of Obstetricians and Gynecologists. (2018). Depression and post-partum depression: resource overview. Retrieved on December 20, 2018 from http s://www.acog.org/Womens-Health/Depression-and-Postpartum-Depression   IsMo bileSet=false on

Association for Play Therapy (APT). (2019). *Paper on touch: Clinical, professional, & ethical issues.* Retrieved July 19, 2019from: https://cdn.ymaws.com/www.a4pt. org/resource/resmgr/publications/2019/Paper_on_Touch_2019_-_Final.pdf

Badenoch, B. (2018). *The heart of trauma.* New York, NY: Norton.

Baldwin, K. M. (2020). *An examination of adolescent maternal-infant attachment relationship outcomes following a FirstPlay® therapy infant storytelling-massage intervention: A pilot study* (IRB approved, doctoral dissertation). Boca Raton, FL: Florida Atlantic University.

Bernier, A., Bell, M.A., & Calkins, S. (2016). Longitudinal associations between the quality of mother-infant interactions and brain development across infancy . *Child Development,* 87(4), 1159–1174. https://dx.doi.org/10.1111/cdev.12518

Bowlby, J. (1979). *The making and breaking of affectional bonds.* New York, NY: Methuen.

Brody, V. A. (1997). *The Dialogue of Touch: Developmental play therapy* (2nd ed.). Northvale, NJ: Wiley.

Carter, S. L., Osofsky, J. D., & Hann, D. M. (1991). Speaking for the baby: A therapeutic intervention with adolescent mothers and their infants. *Infant Mental Health Journal,* 12(4), 291–301. https://doi.org/10.1002/1097-0355(199124)12:4% 3C291::AID-IMHJ2280120403%3E3.0.CO;2-3

Center on the Developing Child at Harvard University. (2009). Maternal depression can undermine the development of young children: Working Paper No. 8. Retrieved July 19, 2019 from: www.developingchild.harvard.edu

Courtney, J. A. (2015a). *FirstPlay practitioner manual.* Boynton Beach, FL: Devel-opmental Play & Attachment Therapies.

Courtney, J. A. (2015b). *FirstPlay parent manual.* Boynton Beach, FL: Developmental Play & Attachment Therapies.

Courtney, J. A. (2020). *Healing child and family trauma through expressive and play therapies: Art, nature, storytelling, body, and mindfulness.* New York, NY: Norton.

Courtney, J. A., & Gray, S.W. (2011). Perspectives of a child therapist as revealed through an image illustrated by the therapist. *Art Therapy: Journal of the American Art Therapy Association,* 8(23), 132–139. https://doi.org/10.1080/07421656.2011.599719

Courtney, J. A., & Gray, S. W. (2014). A phenomenological inquiry into practitioner experiences of developmental play therapy: Implications for training in touch. *International Journal of Play Therapy,* 23(2), 114–129. http://dx.doi.org/10.1037/a0036366

Courtney, J. A., & Mills, J. C. (2016). Utilizing the metaphor of nature as co-thera-pist In StoryPlay® Play Therapy. *Play Therapy,* 11(1), 18–21.

Courtney, J. A., & Nolan, R. D. (Eds.). (2017). *Touch in child counseling and play therapy: An ethical and clinical guide.* New York, NY: Routledge.

Courtney, J. A., & Nowakowski-Sims, E. (2019) Technology's impact on the parent-infant attachment relationship: Intervening through FirstPlay® therapy. *International Journal of Play Therapy.* 28(2), 57–68. http://dx.doi.org/10.1037/pla0000090

Courtney, J. A., & Siu, A. F. Y. (2018). Practitioner experiences of touch in working with children in play therapy. *International Journal of Play Therapy*, 27(2), 92–102. http://dx.doi.org/10.1037/pla0000064

Courtney, J. A., Velasquez, M., & Bakai Toth, V. (2017). FirstPlay® infant massage storytelling: Facilitating corrective touch experiences with a teenage mother and her abused infant. In J. A. Courtney & R. D. Nolan (Eds.), *Touch in child counseling and play therapy: An ethical and clinical guide* (pp. 48–62). New York, NY: Routledge.

Fearon, R. P., Bakermans-Kranenburg, M. J., van Ijzendoorn, M. H., Lapsley, A., & Roisman, G. I. (2010). The significance of insecure attachment and disorganization in the development of children's externalizing behavior: A meta-analytic study. *Child Development*, 81(2), 435–456. https://doi.org/10.1111/j.1467-8624.2009.01405.x

Field, T. (2014). *Touch* (2nd ed.). Cambridge, MA: MIT Press.

Fitton, V. (2012). Attachment theory: History, research and practice. *Psychoanalytic Social Work*, 19(1–2), 121–143. https://doi.org/10.1080/15228878.2012.666491

Goodman, J. (2004). Paternal postpartum depression, its relationship to maternal postpartum depression, and implications for family health. *Journal of Advanced Nursing*, 45(1), 26–36. Retrieved on December 20, 2018from: https://www.ncbi.nlm.nih.gov/pubmed/14675298

Guerney, L. F. (2015). Foreword. In E. Green, J. N. Baggerly, & A. C. Myrick (Eds.), *Counseling families: Play-based treatment*. Lanham, MD: Rowman & Littlefield.

Guerney, L. F., & Guerney, B. (1989). Child Relationship Enhancement: Family Therapy and Parent Education. *Person-Centered Review*, 4(3), 344–357.

Hertenstein, M. J. (2002). Touch: Its communicative functions in infancy. *Human Development*, 45(2), 70–94. http://dx.doi.org/10.1159/000048154

Hillairet, A., Tift, A., Minar, N., & Lewkowicz, D. J. (2017). Selective attention to a talker's mouth in infancy: role of audiovisual temporal synchrony and linguistic experience. *Developmental Science*, 20(3), e12381. https://doi.org/10.1111/desc.12381

Jernberg, A., & Booth , P. (2001). *TheraPlay: Helping parents and children build better relationships through attachment based play* (2nd ed.).San Francisco, CA: Jossey-Bass.

Karen, R. (1998). *Becoming attached*. New York, NY: Oxford University Press, pp. 281–286. doi:10.1542/peds.2005–0999

Kleiman, K. (2009). *Therapy and the postpartum woman: Notes on healing postpartum depression for clinicians and the women who seek their help*. New York, NY: Routledge.

Linden, D. J. (2015). *Touch. The science of hand, heart, and mind*. London: Penguin, Random House.

Mills, J. C., & Crowley, R. J. (2014). *Therapeutic metaphors for children and the child within* (2nd ed.). New York, NY: Routledge.

Musser, E. D., Ablow, J., & Measelle, J. R. (2012). Predicting maternal sensitivity: the roles of postnatal depression symptoms and parasympathetic dysregulation. *Infant Mental Health Journal*, 33(4), 350–359. https://doi.org/10.1002/imhj.21310

O'Brien, M., & Lynch, H. (2011). Exploring the role of touch in the first year of life: Mothers' perspectives of tactile interactions with their infants. *British Journal of Occupational Therapy*, 74(3), 129–136.

Paulson, F. J., & Bazemore, S. D. (2010). Prenatal and postpartum depression in fathers and its association with maternal depression: A meta-analysis. *Journal of the American Medical Association*, 303(19), 1961–1969. https://doi.org/10.1001/jama.2010.605

Porges, S. (2018). Polyvagal theory: A primer. In S. W. Porges& Dana, D. (Eds.), *Clinical applications of polyvagal theory: The emergence of polyvagal-informed therapies*, pp. 50–72. New York, NY: Norton.

Postpartum Support International. (2010). Depression during pregnancy and postpartum. Retrieved December 20, 2018from http://www.postpartum.net/learn-m ore/depression-during-pregnancy-postpartum

Ryan, V. (2007). Filial therapy: Helping children and new carers to form secure attachment relationships. *British Journal of Social Work*, 37, 643–657. https://doi. org/10.1093/bjsw/bch.331

Schore, A. N. (2012). *The science of the art of psychotherapy*. New York, NY: Norton.

Schore, A. N. & Schore, J. R. (2012). Modern attachment theory: The central role of affect regulation in development and treatment. In A. N. Schore (Ed.), *The science of the art of psychotherapy* (pp. 27–51). New York, NY: Norton.

Siegel, D. J. (2012). *The developing mind: How relationships and the brain interact to shape who we are* (2nd ed.). New York, NY: Guilford Press.

Siqveland, T. S., & Moe, V. (2014). Longitudinal development of mother-infant interaction during the first year of life among mothers of substance abuse and psychiatric problems and their infants. *Child Psychiatry Human Development*, 45, 408–421. Retrieved July 19, 2019 from: https://mijn.bsl.nl/longitudinal-developm ent-of-mother-infant-interaction-during-the/529624

VanFleet, R. (1994). *Filial therapy: Strengthening parent-child relationships through play*. Sarasota, FL: Professional Resource Press.

VanFleet, R., & Topham, G. L. (2016). Filial therapy. In K. J. O'Connor, C. E. Schaefer, & L. D. Braverman (Eds.), *Handbook of play therapy* (2nd ed., pp. 135–164). Hoboken, NJ: John Wiley & Sons.

Zero to Three. (2016). *DC: 0–5^{TM}: Diagnostic classification of mental health and developmental disorders of infancy and early childhood*. Washington, DC: Author.

Chapter 7

Infant Filial Therapy – From Conception to Early Years

Clinical Considerations for Working with Whole Family Systems

Kate Renshaw and Judi Parson

Introduction

Filial therapy is a long-established therapeutic intervention for working with children and families in Play Therapy (Guerney, 2000). Play Therapy meta-analyses have found Filial Therapy to be the most effective Play Therapy intervention for children and families (Bratton, Ray, Rhine & Jones, 2005; Lin & Bratton, 2015). Training parents in therapeutic play skills and supporting them to undertake their own special play times with their children can be applied to families with children of all ages. Typically, Filial Therapy publications have focused on target children referred between the ages of 3 and 10 (VanFleet, 2005). Some publications have focused on including adolescents in Filial Therapy, but few to date that consider infants. In their clinical experience, the authors have applied Filial Therapy from pre-birth to late adolescence. Trained Filial Therapists are well placed to adapt this approach to work with whole family systems. A whole family systems approach has led the authors to include family members ranging from conception to 3 years of age in Filial Therapy interventions. It is the authors' experiences that including this age group in Filial Therapy enables parents to incorporate therapeutic play skills from conception. Filial Therapy in pregnancy, infancy and the early years combines both relationship enhancement and the therapeutic powers of play to enhance attachment relationships and support neurobiological development.

This chapter outlines the clinical considerations for Filial Therapists when planning and delivering interventions with expectant parents, infants and very young children up to the age of 3 years. Important aspects covered include: how to plan with parents for the inclusion of infants in Filial Therapy; toy choice and playful interaction ideas; and how to support parents to transfer and integrate Filial Therapy skills into day-to-day parenting. A composite case example will illustrate a Filial Therapy intervention with a whole family system, including an infant. Finally, future implications for researching Filial Therapy from conception through to infancy will be explored.

Filial Therapy

Filial Therapy is a highly specialized parent–child therapeutic approach originally developed by Bernard and Louise Guerney in the 1960s (Guerney, 2003; Guerney & Ryan, 2013). Whilst there are various models of Filial Therapy available, such as Child–Parent Relationship Therapy and Group Filial Therapy (see Thomas, 2018), this chapter is based on the Filial Therapy as proposed by VanFleet (2005). VanFleet adapted traditional Group Filial Therapy for work with individual families (Thomas, 2018). The authors are both trained in and practice the VanFleet individual family model of Filial Therapy.

Filial Therapy is described as effective across a "variety of populations, family structures, and presenting concerns" (Cornett & Bratton, 2015, p. 128). Attractive features of Filial Therapy include being cost-effective, short term and preventative of future mental health difficulties (Bratton, Ray, Rhine, & Jones, 2005). In 2015, Cornett and Bratton reviewed the literature from the previous 50 years of Filial Therapy and concluded that:

> Parents can serve as therapeutic agents in the lives of their children, that parents and children can experience significant positive changes in filial therapy, and that changes in the parent-child relationship can serve as a potent initiator of that growth.
>
> (p. 129)

Ryan and Bratton (2008) argued for parental inclusion in therapeutic service provision for very young children. They also strongly recommend Filial Therapy as the most appropriate therapeutic modality for young children. Glazer (2008) has also reported therapeutic success when using a Filial Therapy approach with an infant. The American Academy of Pediatrics (AAP) recently published a clinical report offering guidance that details the power of play for enhancing a child's development with a special focus on child-led play and parental engagement in play (Yogman et al., 2018). Reports such as this will help to facilitate referrals for Filial Therapy for families where play may be therapeutically integrated.

Filial Therapy has been described as the most effective type of Play Therapy, with the strongest treatment effect size (Bratton, Ray, Rhine & Jones, 2005). The most recent meta-analysis of Play Therapy research reconfirmed the benefits of parents' involvement in the therapeutic process (Bratton & Lin, 2015). Parents' experiences of Filial Therapy were studied by Foley, Higdon & White (2006); they found that parental stress decreased, and the parent–child relationship became more enjoyable. Cornett & Bratton (2015) also described benefits to parents, such as improved attunement to children's feelings and needs and a decrease in parental stress.

While further research is required for the different filial models as well as diverse populations, the science of Filial Therapy also integrates clinical wisdom with other theoretical knowledge and philosophical points of view. For example, the recent neurobiological research combined with attachment theory forms the basis for modern attachment theory (Schore, 2017).

Neuro-bio-psycho-social Approach

The last several decades of neuroscience research have yielded rich information for researchers and clinicians working with children and families. Filial Therapy as practiced today by the authors is a neuro-bio-psycho-socially informed approach whereby the therapists draw on this holistic view of the individuals and the family to personalize optimal conditions (Ryan & Wilson, 1995). Growth and healing are activated and modulated by the Filial Therapist to enhance the therapeutic relationship through the therapeutic powers of play (Schaefer & Drewes, 2014).

Systemic Practice

From the early days of Play Therapy, Virginia Axline (1969) described parents included in the Play Therapy process as indirect participants, who although not directly involved in clinical sessions were a crucial part of the therapeutic process. Play Therapy and Filial Therapy have been informed by general systems theory, family systems theory, systemic psychology, family psychology, and social ecology theory (Ferguson & Evans, 2019; Fiese, Jones & Saltzman, 2019). Systemic thinking sits alongside the neuro-bio-psycho-social as well as ecological considerations within the practice (Hayes, O'Toole & Halpenny, 2017) of Play Therapists. This knowledge of systems thinking is the cornerstone for the inclusion of parents in Play Therapy as part of the therapeutic alliance and in Filial Therapy as the "primary change agents" (VanFleet, 2005, p. 1).

Case Study

The following case example comprises a family of four: mother Marion, father David, 3-year-old son Jack and 1-year-old daughter Emily. The family self-referred their son Jack to Play Therapy. After completing intake with Marion and David, the Play Therapist recommended Filial Therapy that would be inclusive of the whole family system. As outlined in the chapter's introduction, Filial Therapy follows a flexible sequence that can be tailored to each family system and can be adapted to be inclusive of all children within the family system from antenatal to adolescence inclusive. The case study is a composite case to ensure anonymity.

Demographics

Jack, a 3-year-old Caucasian Australian, was referred for Play Therapy by his mother after the death of his maternal auntie, which led to a range of bio-psycho-social difficulties arising. The difficulties included: sleep disturbances, emotional dysregulation, separation anxiety, and peer relationship problems. His parents reported that family life and time spent at daycare were increasingly stressful. At the time of the referral, Jack was experiencing ongoing difficulties both at home, with his extended family and at daycare. Due to a maternal family history of anxiety and depression, Jack's mother was worried about Jack's difficulties escalating into anxiety and/or depression. She had reported suffering from anxiety and depression in the past, but at the time of referral she had been under consistent psychological care since before the birth of both children and had suffered no symptoms for many years.

Clinical Setting

During this therapeutic intervention, the therapist predominantly had contact with the family in a private practice setting. The therapist did a home visit to initially meet the children and another home visit in preparation for Special Play Times to transfer from the clinical setting to the family home. At the initial meeting with parents, the therapist explained the various therapeutic approaches that she offered, including individual integrative humanistic play therapy and Filial Therapy. The parents were keen to engage in Filial Therapy; the therapist suggested an infant Filial Therapy approach as being a developmentally sensitive and appropriate therapeutic approach that would allow the whole family to engage.

Description of Jack

Jack was born full term and healthy after an uncomplicated pregnancy. He consistently met developmental milestones and presented as a 3-year-old in good physical health, alert, socially shy, yet engaged and energetic. His parents reported that prior to his auntie dying, Jack had demonstrated self-regulation and was able to both self-regulate and seek co-regulation when needed. Both Jack and Emily met the therapist during a home visit where the schedule of Filial Therapy was described to them and confidentiality was explained in a developmentally sensitive manner. During the assessment and clinic-based supervised filial sessions, both children presented as happy and confident to attend and engage with their parents. At times in the assessment session and early supervised filial sessions, Jack displayed on several occasions his difficulties regulating his own emotions.

Description of Emily

Emily was born full term and healthy after an uncomplicated pregnancy. She consistently met developmental milestones and presented as a 1-year-old in good physical health, alert and socially engaged. Emily presented as a curious baby that enjoyed being physically close to both her mother and father.

Bio-psycho-social Difficulties

Jack was extremely close with his maternal auntie, who had died over 6 months before the referral for Play Therapy. In the months following the bereavement, Jack began to struggle with sleep disturbances, emotional dysregulation, separation anxiety, and peer relationship problems. As these difficulties were not deemed severe, and were mainly in the context of familial relationships, evidence pointed towards Filial Therapy as a gentle, developmentally sensitive systemic approach. Filial Therapy is suitable for a wide range of presenting difficulties (VanFleet, 2005). This preventative approach to mental health can support children and families to provide optimal conditions for regrowth of healthy bio-psycho-social aspects as well as strengthening the parent–child relational bond (VanFleet, 2005).

Therapeutic Assessment

Before detailing the therapeutic assessment used with Jack and his family, it is important to outline the therapeutic assessment as a concept in more detail. Assessment as part of a Play Therapy or Filial Therapy intervention incorporates the use of therapeutic skills. The Latin origin for assessment, *assidere*, means to sit beside (Gschwend, 2000). The concept of the therapist sitting beside the family forms the foundation of therapeutic assessment (Ryan & Wilson, 2000. Employing Humanistic Play Therapy skills (see Figure 7.1) in all aspects of the intake and assessment process is pivotal when working with families and very young children. The therapeutic assessment for this case comprised the Family Play Observation (FPO) (VanFleet, 2005; Guerney & Ryan, 2012), thematic tracking (Ryan & Edge, 2012) and naturalistic observation (incorporating skills learned from the Tavistock Approach (Waddell, 2013)).

Family Play Observation

Observation of family interactions during play has been included in Play Therapy and Filial Therapy assessments for some time now and in many forms (Harvey, 1991; Stollak, 2003. One such form is the Family Play Observation (FPO) (VanFleet, 2005; Guerney & Ryan, 2012). The purpose of the FPO is to observe the family playing together in an informal, non-stressful, non-structured play environment for 20–30 minutes. FPO

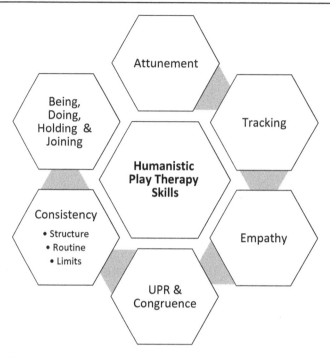

Figure 7.1 Humanistic play therapy skills.

allows the therapist to inconspicuously observe the child referred to Filial Therapy within the context of their family, as well as family interaction patterns. The FPO is immediately followed by a discussion between the therapist and the parents. This discussion is focused on the referred child's presentation within the family context, and if there are any similarities or differences with current their presentation at home and the family dynamics.

Naturalistic Observation

The Tavistock Approach to naturalistic infant observation develops key observational skills in pediatric mental health clinicians. The authors both undertook one year of infant observations, which was informed by the Tavistock Approach as part of their training to become Play Therapists. Naturalistic observation has since informed their approach to assessment in Play Therapy and Filial Therapy. In Filial Therapy, naturalistic observation across the course of the intervention can yield rich observational information of the child referred to Filial Therapy and the family system. This information can be incorporated into meetings with parents to "notice" aspects with them and track the process of therapy.

Thematic Tracking

Themes in Play Therapy are defined as "inferences made by play therapists about children's main emotional issues" (Ryan & Edge, 2012, p. 356). Theme co-construction takes place between the therapist and parent/s during parent–therapist meetings that take place after each supervised session. The therapist supports parents to notice and track themes over multiple sessions; this is referred to as thematic tracking.

Therapeutic Assessment with Jack and His Family

Throughout the course of the Filial Therapy intervention, naturalistic observation was utilized with Jack and his family. The FPO yielded rich information about Jack and his family. Jack's mother and father appeared to take it in turns to naturally flow between giving each child individual attention in the play observation; it was as if two dyads were spending time together yet separately. Jack's mother presented as relaxed and curious in the play but not fully immersed in the play with the children. Jack's father presented as very quiet and mainly used nonverbal communication to display his presence in the play. Jack was observed as being tentative and shy with the play resources and needed coaxing by his mother initially to begin to engage with her with the play resources. Jack appeared to dominate the attention of his parents, and at times Emily would have to compete for their attention. Jack was emotionally regulated at times throughout the observation; however, if anything did not go to his plan within the play, he became dysregulated quickly. He also became dysregulated when Emily attempted to share the attention of the parent Jack was playing with. Emily seemed to enjoy the individual focus of each parent and was comfortable exploring the play resources. Finally, thematic tracking enabled the therapist to co-construct themes with Jack's parents in the parent–therapist consultation time and facilitated the tracking of themes throughout the intervention.

Sequence of Filial Therapy

The sequence of Filial Therapy outlines the stages of the therapeutic process (VanFleet, 2005) (see Figure 7.2). This individual family model of Filial Therapy allows for flexibility with the timings of the stages and the flow of the therapeutic process (Thomas, 2018). Jack and his family progressed sequentially through Filial Therapy.

Case Presentation Outcomes

Jack and his family progressed through the Filial Therapy sequence over a 6-month period. Jack's parents learnt and practised the four filial skills of structuring, empathic listening, limit setting and imaginary play. Marion

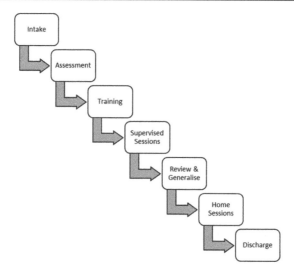

Figure 7.2 Sequence of filial therapy.

and David both reported starting to organically transfer the skills into everyday life ahead of formally working with the therapist to integrate the skills into their family life.

Jack's Filial Therapy

After observing Jack interact with a diverse range of play resources during the FPO, the toy selection was agreed on with his parents. With his parents in the role of therapeutic agents, Jack was able to explore and express many of his worries as well as navigating important developmentally appropriate aspects of bio-psycho-social growth and development. Jack's thematic shifts were tracked during the supervised sessions and by his parents during the home sessions. Initially, Jack focused heavily on exploring his sense of trust in self and in others through relational play. He was then able to move on to exploring a range of play resources across the filial sessions. Throughout the intervention, Jack expressed a range of emotions. Jack's parents were able to use empathic listening to attune to and validate Jack's feelings. As the intervention progressed, Jack showed decreased emotional dysregulation and increased greater emotional regulation in sessions. At the close of the intervention, Jack's bio-psycho-social difficulties were reviewed. Marion and David reported that his sleep disturbances were no longer problematic, his emotional regulation had recalibrated to previously developed levels of competence prior to his auntie's death and that he had increased his sense of joy and felt competence during peer play times.

Emily's Filial Therapy

Emily was observed during the FPO for suitability of play resources in alignment with her age and stage of development. Some of the play resources used for Jack were suitable for incorporation into Emily's sessions and resources were supplemented with other age-appropriate play materials such as stacking cups, shape sorter, etc. Emily eagerly engaged with both parents in her filial play sessions. They reported that Emily benefited from the individualized play time with each parent. They described feeling more attuned to her progressing through typical developmental milestones during the timespan of the intervention. Advanced psychological development (Schaefer & Drewes, 2014) began to be noted by both the therapist and parents. Marion and David felt that the filial sessions had supported Emily's psychosocial development to become more advanced than her peers in certain domains such as: developing her own interests, self-regulation, and developed peer-relational skills as observed with her brother and her daycare peer group.

Final Family Assessment

The Family Play Observation was repeated as a post-intervention assessment measure. After the final FPO, the discussion provided Marion and David with the space to reflect on the family's journey throughout the intervention. David reported increased confidence with engaging in imaginary play with his children; he also felt he was able to integrate all four filial skills into their everyday play and relational interactions. Marion felt she was aligned with David and able to reflect together on the process of Filial Therapy and the way they both incorporate the skills into their family life. From the final FPO the therapist had observed increased closeness in familial relationships, increased engagement of parents in imaginary play, increased emotional regulation of both children, and the sense of joy that was evident from the family playing together.

Clinical Considerations

There are a range of clinical considerations for Filial Therapists when planning and delivering interventions with expectant parents, infants and very young children. Accessing supervision by a trained Filial Supervisor is imperative; time within supervision is an essential component of preparing to deliver the therapeutic approach. Ongoing practitioner reflexivity is also essential to ensure an optimal intervention is delivered. Three key aspects of clinical planning will now be expanded on: planning with parents; toy considerations and playful interaction ideas; and transferring and integrating skills into family life.

Planning with Parents

In individual Play Therapy, the therapist considers and draws on information from the family and includes the child's system in case planning. In Filial Therapy, however, and especially when working with whole family systems that include infants, it is essential for parental involvement throughout the therapeutic process. Parental involvement in planning should occur at all points throughout the intervention. Table 7.1 outlines the stages of Filial Therapy with a key concept defined and clinical considerations for practitioners for each stage outlined.

The selection of toys and playful interaction ideas for Filial Therapy families with children during pregnancy, and the early years are informed by Play Therapy (Jennings, Gerhardt, & Ebooks Corporation, 2011). Practical suggestions for toy choices and playful ideas are summarized in Table 7.2, and extends on the Neuro-Dramatic-Play work of Jennings (Jennings, Gerhardt, & Ebooks Corporation, 2011).

Transferring and Integrating Skills into Family Life

The generalization stage of Filial Therapy is a critical point in whole family interventions. At this point in the intervention, families work with their therapist to reflect on the skills they've learnt, consider where these skills may have started to be transferred into daily life, and plan for how these skills can be even further integrated into their family life. Table 7.3 provides a brief overview of each filial skill and ideas for how they can be integrated into everyday family life.

Conclusion

Filial Therapy is a highly flexible model that can be tailored to the individual family's needs as well as the ages and stages of their children. Growing evidence suggests mental health and wellbeing considerations for optimal growth and development of children begins at conception. Filial Therapy is well placed to meet this need for therapeutic work with whole family systems, especially when children from conception to 3 years of age are included in the family system. Further research into this delivery mode of Filial Therapy is recommended to increase literature and resources for practitioners. Clinical considerations have highlighted three key areas for practitioners to focus on when planning a Filial Therapy intervention with a family system who are expecting a baby or have young children. Careful case planning in conjunction with Filial Therapy supervision is advised in order to work flexibly with individual family systems.

Table 7.1 Planning with parents

Stage	Key objectives	Clinical considerations
Intake	Establishing rapport and setting the scene for therapy	Careful and sensitive discussion during the intake phase should identify if there is a current pregnancy and the chronological and corrected ages as well as the birth history of all children in the family. Discuss targeted goals to include all members of the family.
Assessment	Demonstrating therapeutic presence. "Sitting with"	Drawing on intake information, the therapist proposes an assessment for the family. The family is consulted to ensure inclusion of all family members.
Training	Creating therapeutic alliance	Each filial skill is taught and practiced with each parent and child in the family system held in mind by the clinician. Parents are supported to practice each skill using role-modelling as if playing with each member of the family.
Supervised sessions	Scaffolding, observing and providing considered feedback	Reflect with the parent on parent–child play sessions. Consider each child's play experiences by supporting parents to use thematic tracking. Hone the parents' use of filial skills, individualized to each child's presentation and development.
Review and generalize	Reflecting on therapeutic process and future planning	The therapist and parents review together the entire intervention with a special focus on the therapeutic process for each child and any shifts made. Filial skills are discussed for use in everyday family life for each child. Playful moments are also explored for inclusion in day to day relational encounters.
Home sessions	Making time for family play	The therapist collaborates with parents to plan regular contact to review the home sessions. All children receive play sessions with both parents at home under the supervision of the therapist. Parents track play sessions, themes and shifts more independently with the support of the therapist.
Discharge	Saying goodbye as a therapeutic ending	The therapist and parents plan the ending together. Parents may choose to repeat assessments from the beginning of the intervention in order to track progress and reflect with their therapist. All children are included in ending the family's relationship with the therapist.

Table 7.2 Toy considerations and playful interaction ideas

Stage and age	Key objectives	Toy considerations	Playful interactions
Pregnancy: Conception–birth	Forming a relationship. A playful pregnancy, connection through play	Mother and father as a play resource. Music, books, voice, yoga, nature, swimming pool	Gentle stroking, listening to music, talking to baby, dancing, rhythmic movement, swimming, physical exercise, reading or telling stories, walking in nature, mentally holding the baby in mind and sending loving thoughts to them, daydreaming about the future with the baby.
Infancy: 0–1.5 years	"Being with." Connection, comfort and communication	Mother and father as play resources. Music, books, voice, nature, first toys, safe baby sensory toys and household found items such as: pots and pans, boxes, egg cartons and packaging	Physical touch, stroking, rocking, prosodic use of voice, humming, eye to eye contact interactions, use of facial expressions, holding and cuddling, laughter and giggles, voice echo play, baby massage, peek-a-boo, telling stories, reading books, singing, nursery rhythms, rhythmical interactions, dancing.
Early years: 1.5–3 years	"Joining with," "doing with" and "holding." Safe haven and co-regulator	Mother and father as play resources. Supervised sibling play. Music, books, voice, nature, introducing more sophisticated toys suitably safe for under 3 years of age	Attachment play interactions such as: peek-a-boo, hide and seek, rolling or catching ball to and from one another, mirroring/reciprocal play. Sensory play interactions such as: blowing bubbles, exploring various textured fabrics, ribbon or scarf play, exploring sensory toys (suitable for children under 3 years of age), musical instrument play, and mirror play.

Table 7.3 Integrating skills into family life

Filial skills	Integration into family life
Structuring	Structuring can be incorporated into everyday family life. Routines and consistency may support children of all ages and stages. Child can be scaffolded when transitioning through different points in their day by incorporating aspects of the structuring skill from Filial Therapy. An example of this would be when a child is given a 5-minute warning ready to prepare to walk to the park, then a 1-minute warning, and finally a "it's now time for us to walk to the park" completes the structuring sequence.
Empathic listening	Attunement to a child's needs, verbally tracking their play, moments and interactions and using empathic reflections together form empathic listening. Empathic listening can be utilized from conception through childhood within family life. An example of this would be a parent narrating the movement of the unborn baby as it moves and interacts: "Oh, kicking over here, now moving over here ... maybe feeling like you've got lots of energy right now!"
Limit setting	Often when structuring and empathic listening are utilized by parents the frequency of needing to set limits is reduced. Limit setting becoming clear, calm and matter of fact in family life with the inclusion of attunement and empathy into limit setting (as practised in Filial Therapy) supports parents to integrate gentle but clear limits into family life. A clear and consistent approach can be practiced by both parents in filial therapy and they can work together (with the support of their therapist) to find a method of delivering limits which is therapeutic. Therapeutic limits in everyday family life can support children across childhood.
Imaginary play	In Filial Therapy, parents accept a very special invitation to re-enter the kingdom of childhood. For some parents this can be harder than others. Appendix D – Play Time Exercise (Yasenik, Drewes, Gardner, & Mills, 2012, p. 231) can be a useful resource for gauging parent's own play experiences as they embark on creating play experiences with their children. Once a parent has developed imaginary play skills in Filial Therapy, ideas for transferring these skills can be easily discussed with the therapist. An example of a parent engaging in imaginary play can be clearly illustrated when instead of sitting at a park observing their children's play, a parent picks up a stick and has a wand with their children as they take turns to cast magic spells on each other.

Recommended Resources

- Family Play Observation Hypotheses Suggestions for Leaders (Guerney & Ryan, 2012, p. 365).
- Play Session Demonstration Notes (VanFleet, 2012, p. 47).
- Supervised Session Notes (VanFleet, 2005, p.31).
- Filial Play Session Notes (VanFleet, 2012, p. 48).
- Appendix D – Play Time Exercise (Yasenik, Drewes, Gardner, & Mills, 2012, p. 231).

Discussion Questions

1 Consider your current clinical caseload: Are there any families that you are currently working with that may suit this approach? Why might they be suitable? What might the benefits to the family be?
2 Imagine you are discussing with the family the potential to transition from your current method of therapeutic work with them into a Filial Therapy approach. How would you introduce this idea, the potential benefits, and how the infants in the family could be included in the intervention?
3 Under what clinical circumstances do you think working with families during pregnancy and infancy would *not* be appropriate for a Filial Therapy approach?

References

Axline, V. M. (1969). *Play therapy*. New York: Ballantine Books.
Bratton, S. C., & Lin, Y. (2015). A meta-analytic review of child-centered play therapy approaches. *Journal of Counseling & Development*, 93(1), 45–58. https://doi.org/10.1002/j.1556-6676.2015.00180.x
Bratton, S. C., Ray, D., Rhine, T., & Jones, L. (2005). The efficacy of play therapy with children: a meta-analytic review of treatment outcomes. *Professional Psychology, Research and Practice*, (4), 376. Retrieved July 31, 2019 from: http://search.ebscohost.com/login.aspx?direct=true&db=edsgao&AN=edsgcl.136075703&authtype=sso&custid=deakin&site=eds-live&scope=site
Cornett, N., & Bratton, S.C. (2015). A golden intervention: 50 years of research on filial therapy. *International Journal of Play Therapy*, 15(3), 119–133. https://doi.org/10.1037/a0039088
Ferguson, K. T., & Evans, G. W. (2019). Social ecological theory: Family systems and family psychology in bioecological and bioecocultural perspective. In *APA handbook of contemporary family psychology: Foundations, methods, and contemporary issues across the lifespan* (Vol. 1, pp. 143–161). Washington, DC: American Psychological Association. https://doi-org.ezproxy-b.deakin.edu.au/10.1037/0000099-009
Fiese, B. H., Jones, B. L., & Saltzman, J. A. (2019). Systems unify family psychology. In *APA handbook of contemporary family psychology: Foundations, methods, and contemporary issues across the lifespan* (Vol. 1, pp. 3–19). Washington, DC: American Psychological Association. https://doi-org.ezproxy-b.deakin.edu.au/10.1037/0000099-001

Foley, Y. C., Higdon, L., & White, J. A. F. (2006). A qualitative study of filial therapy: parents' voices. *International Journal of Play Therapy*, 15(1), 37–64. http s://doi.org/10.1037/h0088907

Glazer, H.R. (2008). Filial play therapy for infants and toddlers. In C. E. Schaefer., S. Kelly-Zion., J. McCormick., & A. Ohnogi (Eds.), *Play therapy for very young children* (pp. 67–84). Retrieved July 31, 2019 from: https://ebookcentral.proquest.com

Gschwend, L. (2000). Every student deserves an assessment tool that teaches. *Communication Teacher*, 14(3), 1–5. Retrieved July 31, 2019 from: http://search.ebsco host.com/login.aspx?direct=true&db=ufh&AN=31746500&authtype=sso& custid=deakin&site=eds-live&scope=site

Guerney, L. (2000). Filial therapy into the 21st century. *International Journal of Play Therapy*, 9(2), 1–17. https://doi.org/10.1037/h0089433

Guerney, L. (2003). The history, principles, and empirical basis of filial therapy. In R. VanFleet., & L. Guerney. (Eds.). *Casebook of filial therapy*. Boiling Springs, PA: Play Therapy Press.

Guerney, L. F., & Ryan, V. (2013). *Group filial therapy: the complete guide to teaching parents to play therapeutically with their children*. London; Philadelphia: Jessica Kingsley Publishers.

Harvey, S. (1991). Dynamic Play approached in the observation of family relationships. In K. Gitlin-Weiner., A. Sandgrund, & C. E. Schaefer. (Eds.), *Play diagnosis and assessment* (2nd ed). New York, NY: John Wiley &Sons.

Hayes, N., O'Toole, L., & Halpenny, A. M. (2017). *Introducing bronfenbrenner: A guide for practitioners and students in early years education*. Retrieved July 31, 2019 from: https://ebookcentral.proquest.com

Jennings, S., Gerhardt, C., & Ebooks Corporation. (2011). *Healthy attachments and neuro-dramatic-play*. London: Jessica Kingsley Publishers. Retrieved July 31, 2019 from: http://search.ebscohost.com/login.aspx?direct=true&db=nlebk&AN= 387928&authtype=sso&custid=deakin&site=eds-live&scope=site

Lin, Y., & Bratton, S. C. (2015). A meta-analytic review of child-centered play therapy approaches. *Journal of Counseling and Development*, 93(1), 45–58. https://doi. org/10.1002/j.1556-6676.2015.00180.x

Moore, T., Arefadib, N., Deery, A., Keyes, M., & West, S. (2017). The first thousand days: An evidence paper – summary. In *The first thousand days*. Melbourne: The Royal Children's Hospital, Centre for Community Child Health.

NSW Ministry of Health (2019). *First 2000 days framework*. Sydney: NSW Ministry of Health. Retrieved July 31, 2019 from: https://www1.health.nsw.gov.au/pds/ ActivePDSDocuments/PD2019_008.pdf

Ryan, V., & Bratton, S. (2008). Child-centered play therapy for very young children. In C.E. Schaefer., S. Kelly-Zion., J. McCormick., & A. Ohnogi (Eds.), *Play therapy for very young children*. Retrieved July 31, 2019 from: https://ebookcentral.proquest.com

Ryan, V., & Edge, A. (2012). The role of play themes in non-directive play therapy. *Clinical Child Psychology and Psychiatry*, 17(3), 354–369. https://doi.org/10.1177/ 1359104511414265

Ryan, V., & Wilson, K. (2000). *Case studies in non-directive play therapy*. London: Jessica Kingsley Publishers.

Ryan, V., & Wilson, K. (1995). Non-directive play therapy as a means of recreating optimal infant socialization patterns. *Early Development and Parenting*, 4(1), 29– 38. https://doi-org.ezproxy-b.deakin.edu.au/10.1002/edp.2430040105

Schaefer, C. E., & Drewes, A. A. (2014). *The therapeutic powers of play: 20 core agents of change*. Hoboken, NJ: John Wiley &Sons.

Schore, A. N. (2017). Modern attachment theory. In S. N. Gold (Ed.), *APA handbook of trauma psychology: Foundations in knowledge* (Vol. 1, pp. 389–406). Washington, DC: American Psychological Association.

Stollak, G. E. (2003). Family assessment. In J. J. Ponzetti (Ed.), *The International Encyclopedia of Marriage and Family Relationships*, 2nd ed. (Vol.2, pp. 562–568). New York, NY: Thompson/Gale.

Thomas, G. (2018). Filial therapy: Forming therapeutic partnerships with parents to achieve intrapsychic, interpersonal and neurobiological change for families. *British Journal of Play Therapy*, 13, 20–34.

VanFleet, R. (2005). *Filial therapy: strengthening parent-child relationships through play* (2nd ed.). Sarasota, FL: Professional Resource Press.

VanFleet, R. (2012). *A parent's handbook of filial therapy. Building strong families with play* (2nd ed.). Boiling Springs, PA: Play Therapy Press.

Waddell, M. (2013). Infant observation in Britain: A Tavistock approach. *Infant Observation*, 16(1), 4–22. https://doi.org/10.1080/13698036.2013.765659

Yasenik, L., Drewes, A. A., Gardner, K., & Mills, J. C. (2012). *Play therapy dimensions model: a decision-making guide for integrative play therapists*. London: Jessica Kingsley.

Yogman, M., Garner, A., Hutchinson, J., Hirsh-Pasek, K., Golinkoff, R. M., Baum, R., & Wissow, L. (2018). The power of play: A pediatric role in enhancing development in young children. *Pediatrics*, 142(3). Retrieved from https://pediatrics.aappublications.org/content/142/3/e20182058

Chapter 8

Intervening with Theraplay with a 13-Month-Old Diagnosed with Medical Complications

Hanna Lampi

Introduction to Theraplay History and Theoretical Background

Theraplay was first developed in the late 1960s by Ann Jernberg after she became the director of psychological services for the Head Start program in Chicago. There was a need for a program that would easily be achievable and effective. To the developers it made sense that the new approach would be an active playful way of interacting, where adults would help children to reach their full potential. Development of Theraplay was influenced by Austin DesLauries, Viola Brody and John Bowlby. It modeled healthy parent–child interactions and emphasized active engagement, direct physical contact and supporting a positive attitude (Booth 2010). The first edition of Theraplay was published in 1979. Since its early days, Theraplay has spread through the world and is now being used in over 36 countries.

Theraplay is a therapy for building and enhancing attachment and joyful engagement. It focuses on four dimensions in child–parent relationships (see Table 8.1). Theraplay sessions are preverbal, relying more on the unspoken interactions than discussing on a cognitive level and can be used from pregnancy and throughout the lifespan. The Theraplay process includes parents or primary caregivers in the sessions and there are both one-therapist and two-therapist models. The basic Theraplay process is around 20 sessions including the assessment and treatment. There can also be some follow-up sessions within a year from finishing the treatment. Theraplay is a flexible method where each treatment takes into account a family's circumstances, the age and developmental level of the child, and the severity of symptoms.

Theraplay is based on the thought that early parent–child interaction is vital for development of cognitive functions and socioemotional development and general well-being. In a healthy relationship between parent and child both have shared experiences in the following ways: a) love and play, b) attention and shared attention, c) cognition and differentiated emotions, d) communication and organization, e) the use of symbol and narrative, and f) internal safety and hope (Shanoon-Shanok, 1997). In early childhood

Table 8.1 Theraplay dimensions

Dimension	Key message to child	Activity examples
Engagement	In your eyes I see myself worthy	Peek-a-boo; beep and honk; checkups
Structure	World is safe and predictable	Measuring; bean bag game; soap bubbles
Nurture	I am loved and safe	Special songs; lotioning; slippery, slippery, slip; blanket swing
Challenge	I am competent and able to learn	Crawling race; feather blow; karate chop; wiggle in and out

research, social and emotional development shows that the overall quality of human relationships is an important predictor of later developmental outcomes. Theory about Emotional Availability (EA) as conceptualized by Biringen, postulates that this relationship quality is determined by the fit between a child's capabilities of signaling needs and the parents' experiences and emotional tone and availability throughout everyday life (Biringen & Easterbrooks, 2012). Noticing and interpreting social signals is mostly automatic for us, but we can also recognize when there is or isn't social synchrony (Feldman, 2007). Stern (1985) believed that these synchronous co-regulated patterns develop during infancy and can represent typical ways of being together.

Current Theraplay Research

Research in Theraplay has been growing in the past decades and Theraplay is now designated as an evidenced-based treatment accepted by the U.S. Substance abuse and Mental Health Services Administration for inclusion on the National Registry for Evidence-based Programs and Practices. Hiles Howard et al. (2018) studied the impact of Theraplay on children with autism spectrum disorder, and the results showed improvement in the post-intervention interactions where the parents showed more affect and were more responsive to their child. As well, children vocalized more, maintained closer proximity with their parents, and were more accepting of guidance post-intervention. Siu (2009) studied the effectiveness of Theraplay in reducing symptoms of internalizing problems. She found that there was a significant difference on CBCL-internalizing scores between the control group and Theraplay group, wherein the Theraplay group scores were lower than the scores of the control group. Salo (2011) conducted a pre- and post-pilot study on infant Theraplay among mothers with substance abuse disorder. The results showed that there was a statistically significant improvement in maternal sensitivity and creativity in play in mothers participating in Theraplay as compared to mothers who did not receive Theraplay.

MIM Assessment

In Theraplay, the Marschack Interaction method (MIM) is a recommended assessment tool as a beginning step of intervention. It is a structured technique for observing and assessing the relationship between individuals. It was developed my Maryanne Marschack (1960) to observe parent–child interaction. Since its development different applications have been developed, for example the Prenatal MIM (Jernberg, 1988).

Theraplay Dimensions

The following Theraplay dimensions in Table 8.1 are used to guide the treatment plan for clients.

Theraplay in Action

In Theraplay treatment, the therapist helps parents and children to be together with playful and developmentally appropriate activities in carefully planned and structured 30-minute sessions. The role of the therapist is very active and sensitively administered. Each session is videotaped both for the therapist to review her own work, and to use in video feedback sessions with the parents. The goal of Theraplay is to help both parent and child to find ways to co-regulate, feel safe and secure, and most of all enjoy each other's company. Theraplay is provided by certified Theraplay Practitioners or by practitioners who are in the certification practicum. Training is provided by The Theraplay Institute or its affiliates. Table 8.2 is a suggested structure for the Theraplay process.

Case Study. Asher: Theraplay with a 12-Month-Old Infant with Medical Complications

Reason for Referral

Asher's mother contacted me (the author) with concerns related to her son's social emotional development as he had some severe medical challenges. He was 12 months old and had been through a surgery, endoscopies, and several ultrasounds and scans. Soon after his birth he was diagnosed with a rare chronic metabolic disease and his overall development was delayed. He had a Gastrostomy Tube (GT) for medication and feeding. Mom had heard of Theraplay and thought that it could be a way to enhance their relationship.

Mom described Asher as a happy and content baby, but felt that he was not always easy to connect with and that he seemed at times more interested in objects rather than interaction. The mother had done a lot of reading about infant development and was worried that Asher was showing early signs of

Table 8.2 Suggested structure for Theraplay process

1	*Meeting with parents*
2	MIM observation
3	MIM observation 2
4	MIM discussion
5	Parent's own Theraplay session
6–8	Theraplay begins
9	Video feedback session with parents
10–12	Theraplay
13	Video feedback session with parents
14–16	Theraplay
17	Video feedback
18–20	Theraplay
21	Video feedback, reflection on the process
22–24	Theraplay
25	Theraplay party
26	Meeting with parents
27–29	Follow-ups within next 6–13 months

autism. Asher had continuous medication and his insulin levels were followed 24 hours a day. She was a single mother with a good supportive network including her father, sister, and sister's boyfriend and friends. Her mother had died when she was three years of age and she had started her own therapy as she felt that she had not really dealt with this loss previously.

I met with Asher and Mom at their home, and Asher was observed as a cute, curly haired baby who was crawling around and exploring his surroundings. I interviewed Mom in more detail about Asher's infancy and her concerns at the moment. During the first visit I administered the MIM. During the MIM the following tasks were chosen:

1 Take toy animals, give one to the child and make them play together.
2 Build a simple structure with blocks and ask the child to build the same with his blocks.
3 Tell a story of your child as a small baby, starting "when you were a little baby ..."
4 Teach your child something new.
5 Play a familiar game together.

(I chose not to include the feeding task, since at the time in addition to breastfeeding Asher was fed through gastrostomy tube.)

Observations from the MIM

Mom and Asher sit together on the floor and Mom reads the tasks one by one. Asher is sitting still but paying attention to other things in the room more than to Mom. Mom introduces the squeaky toys and Asher takes his time to carefully touch the piggy, making some babbling sounds and then squeaking the toy himself. Mom tries to keep the atmosphere joyful, but there is some hesitancy in her attempts to engage Asher and she does not get a lot of feedback from him. Mom is persistent, and it pays off in the end. She gets Asher to participate in building with the blocks and there is mutual joy—where Mom is praising Asher and he squeals with joy. Even though Asher is avoidant, he seeks some physical proximity. For example, when Mom turns him to a face-to-face position, he rests his forehead on Mom's cheek affectionately. He also follows Mom's movements when she is moving around the room, seemingly aware of her even when not directly looking at her. Mom is at times hurrying through the tasks and at the same time giving Asher a lot of space to explore and wander. She is very lively in her communication, but at times it appeared more as a type of self-talk, than actual communication directed to Asher.

Main points in the MIM observation:

- Asher's avoidance of direct face-to-face contact;
- Mom's anxiety leading to less structured interaction;
- Mom is overly tolerant in waiting for Asher to start or finish something, seeming to want to avoid moments when Asher may become frustrated.

Second Meeting: Theraplay Session with Asher and Mom

Theraplay was carried out in the home setting. Because these were infant Theraplay sessions, the parent meetings were included in each session (see Table 8.2). At the end of each meeting, Mom and I had a chance to talk about the session and other things happening in their life. In Table 8.3, the activities planned and implemented during the second session are highlighted.

Session 2

Welcome Activity

Asher and Mom greeted me at the door. Asher was crawling around and babbling. Mom and Asher sat on the sofa and I placed myself on the floor in front of them. Asher sat beside his Mom and I started the Theraplay session with a welcome song. I used a scarf to hide Asher from Mom and me and then bringing the scarf up in the end so that we could greet him. Asher listened to the song and made happy noises as the scarf was pulled up. As I was singing and holding the scarf, he paid a little more attention to me than

Table 8.3 Plan for the second Theraplay session

Activity	Dimensions	Goal
Welcome song	Engagement, structure	Create a shared experience and structure the beginning of the session
Checkup, measuring	Structure, engagement	Explore Asher's body and make connection/comparisons between Asher and Mom
Soap bubbles	Challenge, structure	Help Asher to join a shared attention and challenge him to explore new things
Lotion	Nurture	Give a nurturing experience for both Asher and Mom
Baby dance	Structure, challenge	Challenge Asher to participate in an adult-led structured activity in a fun way
Blanket swing	Nurture, structure	Create a calming and relaxing experience and structure the ending (same ending each time)

Mom. I then sang the song to Mom and hid her behind the scarf. Asher was then interested in the scarf again and shrieked with joy when Mom's face was found at the end of the song. We then played peek-a-boo for a while taking turns hiding Asher and Mom. As the game was repeated a few times, Asher tried to move away from the couch, but I gently guided him back and then helped him to find Mom under the scarf once more.

Checkup Activity

I took a measuring tape from my bag and started to measure Asher's foot. Asher was not interested in this activity as he was distracted by an open door next to the sofa until it was closed. After this was done, he sat next to Mom and shared attention was accomplished. We then continued measuring different parts of Asher, such as his fingers and toe and so forth. Then together with Asher we looked for similar lengths on Mom. After a few repetitions he got more interested in the activity and made small initiatives to continue measuring. He also got very interested of the length of the tape, so he took one end as I stretched the measuring tape to its full length. He was babbling and at times making high shrieks of joy.

Soap Bubbles Activity

The next activity was soap bubbles. These caught Asher's interest at once and he quickly picked up popping them as I sang a bubble song. When he was trying to get off the couch, I gently asked him to sit back down and he did, and we continued the game. He was now shrieking loudly and laughing. He had patience to wait as I failed to blow the bubbles, or the bubbles broke too soon.

Nurture

First, I applied lotion on Mom's hands and Asher was very interested in this. I also sang a song. Then Mom put lotion on Asher's hands and he was comfortable in Mom's lap and seemed to enjoy this. I wanted to show Mom the "slippery, slippery, slip" game with Asher. At first try I could see that he was a little cautious and on the second try he made it clear that he did not like the game by crawling closer to Mom and hiding his face from me. I expressed my observations out loud, "I notice that you did not like this game." And, I decided to change the activity.

Baby Dance

Baby dance is a simple activity where you repeat a simple choreography with hands and feet according to the song's lyrics "up and down, up and down, up and down and clap our hands etc." Asher picked up the game quickly and after each verse I paused for his reaction and when he made eye contact or otherwise signaled that he wanted more, I then continued with the song.

Swinging in a Blanket

We finished each session with the same activity where Mom and I swung Asher as he was laying on a blanket and we sang a special song for him. He enjoyed this a lot and it was a good way to end the session in a relaxing and calming manner.

Ongoing Sessions

The subsequent Theraplay sessions repeated mostly the same treatment plan, introducing some new activities at times. Asher was slow to warm up to new activities but remembered well the familiar ones and made initiatives showing something or trying to pick a specific item from my bag. At times he was tired or irritable but mostly he was in a good mood and participating in activities. He had a tendency to get distracted, but he was usually quite easy to guide back to the activities. He enjoyed face-to-face contact more each session but still had a tendency to turn away if I introduced something new or the interaction was prolonged. I was being very sensitive with him on not demanding to much too quickly. Mom was very reflective and used our time to talk about things on her mind and figuring out ways to engage Asher. For example, she helped him in difficult and potentially painful procedures that they still had to go through for his health. She was also changing her way of introducing solids to Asher, making the situation playful and letting him eat where he felt most comfortable, usually on the floor.

Outcomes

I met Asher and Mom regularly for the agreed period and also had a reflective discussion with Mom in between sessions. Mom felt that she had benefitted having someone to share observations of Asher and to have someone to share her worries with without being judged or dismissed. She also shared that being able to observe Asher interacting with someone else had been helpful and she had absorbed new ways of enticing interaction with Asher. Mom was very aware of her tendency to worry a lot but she felt that she had accomplished more of a relaxed attitude towards Asher's development. They had regular doctor checkups, and she was assured that although Asher was a little behind in some respects his development, he was still in normal variation and advancing well. Asher was now eating solid foods and the GT-tube was used only for medication. Reflective discussion with video feedback was something she felt that helped a lot in this process as she was able to see what I was talking about when watching the Theraplay session together. We agreed on continuing Theraplay with monthly intervals.

Follow-Up Session at 19 Months

Asher and Mom greeted me at the door, and I could see that Asher has started to walk by himself. As I praised him on this accomplishment he smiled, turned back and walked a triumphant extra circle in the foyer. He then took his Mom's and my hand and led us to the living room. I chatted with Mom for a while about the past month and Asher was at times taking part of the conversation by babbling or bringing toys to us. We then moved on the couch and started with a familiar welcome song. Asher was fully present from the beginning and remembered the pace of the session well. He enjoyed peek-a-boo and laughed out loud when he was found and also when he found Mom under the scarf that I was using for hiding. Mom put lotion on Asher's hands, and we played "slippery, slippery, slip" with him being on my lap facing Mom. Then I introduced a new game of "push me down, pull me up" which he was a little cautious in the beginning since it meant that I "fell" on the floor, but he started enjoying it after a few repetitions.

Soap bubble popping was always one of Asher's favorites and he enjoyed it, signaling for more when I was about to stop by pointing to the bubbles and wiggling up and down in Mom's lap. I took out a balloon which had previously scared Asher and blew some air in it. He remembered that he could touch the balloon and as he did, I slowly let the air out. He was a little hesitant but made gestures that Mom and I interpreted as wanting more. So, I repeated the game and he smiled slightly, and we went one more time. We did the familiar baby dance and Asher joined in the singing with his own babbling. He got a little restless in the end and Mom noted that he was getting tired. We then finished with the blanket swing and a special song.

Discussion Questions

1 Review Tables 8.1 and 8.3 in this chapter; discuss with a colleague your views on Theraplay's key concepts and their applications related to the therapy work with Asher and his mother.
2 When and where could you utilize MIM in your own practice?
3 Discuss in a group or with a colleague the possibilities of implementing Theraplay in your own practice. [Reviewing the Theraplay website will also lend insight to this discussion (https://theraplay.org).]

References

Biringen Z., & Easterbrooks, M. (2012). The integration of emotional availability into a developmental psychopathology framework: Reflections on the special section and future directions. *Development and Psychopathology*, 24(1), 137–142. https://doi-org.proxy.library.ju.se/10.1017/S0954579411000733

Booth, P., & Jernberg, A. (2010). *Theraplay – Helping parents and children build better relationships through attachment-based play* (3rd ed.). San Francisco, CA: Jossey-Bass.

Feldman R. (2007). Parent-infant synchrony and the construction of shared timing: Physiological precursors, developmental outcomes, and risk conditions. *Journal of Child Psychology and Psychiatry*, 48(3–4), 329–354. https://doi-org.proxy.library. ju.se/10.1111/j.1469-7610.2006.01701.x

Hiles Howard, A. R., Lindaman, S., Copeland, R., & Cross, D. R. (2018). Theraplay impact on parents and children with autism spectrum disorder: Improvements in affect, joint attention, and social cooperation. *International Journal of Play Therapy*, 27(1), 56–68. https://doi.org/10.1037/pla0000056

Jernberg, A. (1988). Promoting prenatal and perinatal mother-child bonding: A psychotherapeutic assessment of parental attitudes. In P. Fedor-Freybergh & M. Vogel (Eds.), *Prenatal and perinatal psychology and medicine: A comprehensive survey of research and practice*, pp. 253–266. London: Parthenon Publishing Group.

Marschak M. (1960). A method for evaluating child-parent interaction under controlled conditions. *Journal of Genetic Psychology*, 9, 3–22. https://doi.org/10.1080/00221325.1960.10534309

Salo, S. (2011). Does Theraplay increase emotional availability among substance-abusing mother-infant dyads? Live oral presentation, November 15, 2011, at European Child and Adolescent Psychiatry Conference (ESCAP), Helsinki, Finland.

Shanoon-Shanok, R. (1997). Giving back future's promise: Working resourcefully with parents of children who have severe disorders of relating and communicating. *Zero to Three*, 17(5), 37–48.

Siu, A. F. Y. (2009). Theraplay in the Chinese world: An intervention program for Hong Kong children with internalizing problems. *International Journal of Play Therapy*, 18(1), 1–12. https://doi.org/10.1037/a0013979

Stern, D. N. (1985). *The interpersonal world of the infant*. New York, NY: Basic Books.

Programmatic Infant Play and Play-Based Interventions with Infant and Toddler Populations

Baby Doll Circle Time

Strengthening Attunement, Attachment and Social Play

Becky A. Bailey

The brain develops through attuned interactions between caregiver and child. Research has suggested that in order to facilitate optimal emotional and brain development, 46% of a child's time awake must be spent in attuned, face-to-face interactions (Tronick et al., 1985). Since the 1980s, neuroscientists have concluded that the accelerated growth of brain structure during infancy is dependent on the social forces of attunement, mutual regulation and affect synchrony. Psychopathology is often attributed to abnormal early experiences of these social forces (Cirulli et al., 2002). One challenge facing families, educators and caregivers is how to ensure children can experience this vital connection time during group care.

Baby Doll Circle Time is an innovative approach that supports adults in providing the individual, intense social connections and attunement opportunities that build children's neural connections. Baby Doll Circle Time occurs in two phases. In phase one, therapists, teachers, caregivers and/or family members learn to engage children in one-on-one activities during times when touch and eye contact naturally occur (diapering, transitions, arrival, rest and play times). During these powerful moments, the adult and child achieve a playful, focused attunement that elicits the formation of synaptic pathways.

As a second phase, adults incorporate specific and focused doll play in the daily routine. During this group time, children experience similar neural firings as they re-enact the same play scenarios with the baby dolls. The children restore and relive the initial attuned experience with the adult, making it possible to meet the attunement needs of several children at one time. Shared joy and delight contribute to positive brain chemistry, and the children expand their repertoire of interactions through cognitive and relationship-building skills.

These two interventional phases, foundational information and the Baby Doll Circle Time activities themselves are presented in the curriculum workbook and accompanying instructional DVD titled *Baby Doll Circle Time: Strengthening Attunement, Attachment and Social Play* (Bailey, 2012).

The primary goal of Baby Doll Circle Time is to enhance the quality of the relationship between caregivers and children by strengthening attachment, attunement and social play.

During the first three years of life, we establish mental models we will utilize through adulthood. This includes our mental models for self, relationships, self-regulation, attention, motivation and stress management (Siegel, 1999). The attached, attuned, playful relationships encouraged by Baby Doll Circle Time help establish a healthy blueprint for all of these developmental components.

Additionally, Baby Doll Circle Time reduces the stress of childcare by creating healthy attachment, increases the positive affect between adults and children, and utilizes attachment, attunement and social play to wire the brain for optimal development.

Baby Doll Circle Time is particularly beneficial to children experiencing a lack of attunement, attachment or social engagement—challenges that apply to an increasing number of today's children (Huber, 2014). Children lacking in attuned encounters elsewhere can receive and remediate missed factors by engaging in loving, attuned behavior with the adult and the baby doll. Through Baby Doll Circle Time, children who struggle in a group care setting can form stronger bonds with in-school attachment figures, leading to increased resilience and reduced stress. Children who are resistant or who struggle with prosocial behaviors can expand their repertoire of noncognitive skills while reaping the benefits of connection in a way that feels safe.

The key to Baby Doll Circle Time's interventional power lies in the fostering of attachment through individual play with a loving adult that is then mirrored in group play with the dolls. In a childcare setting, the first step is often organizing children's care in a way that increases attachment. For example, in a center with two teachers and 10 toddlers, each teacher would be the designated attachment figure for five toddlers. The attachment figure would engage with these same five children for Baby Doll Circle Time's individual activities, while also serving as the child's primary source of care for personal functions like diapering, feeding and soothing during times of distress. The adult must commit to playing at least one individual Baby Doll Circle Time activity per day with each child for whom he or she is the in-school attachment figure. Without this daily attuned one-on-one play time, the group activities with the dolls lose their power.

Once the adult is regularly conducting the daily *individual* activities, he or she may begin conducting *group* Baby Doll Circle Time activities. The group activities involve a five-step process:

Step 1: Transition to Getting Your Baby
Baby Doll Circle Time always begins with the same song and the distribution of the baby dolls. The interventionist utilizes a transition song and gestures to indicate Baby Doll Circle Time is beginning.

Step 2: Beginning Awareness
This step involves group members holding the baby dolls in various positions and engaging the baby doll in different motor skill activities. These

activities incorporate spatial, visual, auditory and kinesthetic awareness, providing a manageable challenge within a safe and loving environment. An optimal learning environment requires exactly this type of high challenge with low stress (Squire et al., 2012).

Step 3: Connection

Connection is at the heart of Baby Doll Circle Time. Step 3 consists of interactive social games between the child and the baby doll. These are the activities the attachment figure is already playing individually with each child. Playing the games individually as well as in circle time enables children to relive moments of connection as they play with their baby dolls.

The connection activities support the shared joy and the brain state needed for optimal development. The lesson content is organized into six units that stimulate and enhance a child's development of skills like goal achievement, problem-solving, emotional regulation, impulse control and empathy:

1 *Peek-a-Boo:* Hide-and-seek games
2 *Body Parts:* Body awareness
3 *Booboos:* Healing the hurts
4 *I Love You Rituals:* Attachment games
5 *Stop and Go:* Impulse control and self-regulation
6 *Emotions:* Regulating emotions and naming feelings

Step 4: Cuddling and Soothing

The nurturing activities in this step provide a way to teach empathy, support the "gentle touch" learning process, and disengage stress. The disengaging stress function is particularly valuable because research shows that young children who are in group care for extended hours produce more stress hormones than those children who spend fewer hours in group care (Vermeer & van Ijzendoorn, 2006). These stress hormones inhibit the development of the frontal lobes and the executive skills (especially self-regulation) needed for school and life success. The cuddling and soothing activities in Baby Doll Circle Time can help counteract the stressful effects of extended group care.

Step 5: Ending and Transition to Next

The session always ends with the same calming song. As in Step 1, the interventionist will rely on pointing and nonverbal communications to reinforce the idea that the information children need is conveyed in the song.

Baby Doll Circle Time Sample Activity

Baby Doll Circle Time follows an easily accessible format that increases connection, emotional regulation and delight. As previously discussed, there are two components: individual play and group play. The adult must connect and attune with the child through individual, one-on-one play centered on the activity. Then during group play, the adult would revisit the same activity with the children and their dolls. The following is a reprint of Activity 4:4 of the Baby Doll Circle Time curriculum (Bailey, 2012), which features the "Round and Round the Garden" and "Here's the Bunny" I Love You Rituals (Bailey, 2000):

Individual Play:

First, conduct the I Love You Rituals during one-on-one time with the child.

Bear

Round and round the garden, goes the teddy bear. (Circle a finger around the child's belly.) One step, two steps, tickle under there. (Walk your fingers up the child's belly and tickle under the chin.) Round and round the garden, goes the teddy bear. (Repeat motions.)

One step, two steps, tickle under there! (Repeat motions.)

Bunny

Here's the bunny with the ears so funny. (Hold up two fingers on one hand for ears.)

Here's the hole in the ground. (Use your pointer finger on the other hand to trace a circle on the child's tummy.) When a noise she hears, she picks up her ears. (Make finger "ears" on the child.)

And jumps in the hole in the ground. (Gently jump the "ears" down to tickle the child's tummy.)

Group Play:

Next, conduct a group activity that complements the one-on-one time and follows the five steps discussed earlier in this chapter.

Step 1: Transition to Getting Your Baby

Sing to the tune of "Oh My Darlin'"
Get your baby, get your baby, get your baby, time to play.
Get your baby, get your baby, get your baby, time to play.

Step 2: Beginning Awareness

Sing to the tune of "The Farmer in the Dell"
My baby wants to play, (Pretend to play with the baby doll.)
My baby wants to play,
This is my baby,

My baby wants to play.
My baby wants to eat. (Pretend to feed the baby doll.)
My baby wants to eat.
This is my baby,
My baby wants to eat.
My baby's diaper is wet, (Pretend to change a diaper.)
My baby's diaper is wet,
This is my baby,
My baby's diaper is wet.
My baby's ready to play, (Place the baby doll face up in front of you.)
My baby's ready to play,
This is my baby,
My baby's ready to play.

Step 3: Connection

Based on the "Round and Round the Garden" and "Here's the Bunny" I Love You Rituals. Show a picture of a bear and a picture of a bunny. Have the child choose one, and then conduct the ritual that corresponds to that image.

Bear

Round and round the garden, goes the teddy bear. (Circle a finger around the baby doll's belly.) One step, two steps, tickle under there. (Walk your fingers up the baby doll's belly and tickle under the chin.) Round and round the garden, goes the teddy bear. (Repeat motions.)

One step, two steps, tickle under there! (Repeat motions.)

Bunny

Here's the bunny with the ears so funny. (Hold up two fingers on one hand for ears.)

Here's the hole in the ground. (Use your pointer finger to trace a circle on the baby doll's tummy.) When a noise she hears, she picks up her ears, (Make finger "ears" on the baby doll.)

And jumps in the hole in the ground. (Gently jump and tickle the baby doll's tummy.)

Step 4: Cuddling and Soothing

Sing to the tune of "The Farmer in the Dell"

My baby's calming down, (Take a deep breath in and then exhale with a "shhhhh" sound.)

My baby's calming down, (Take a deep breath in and then exhale with a "shhhhh" sound.)

This is my baby,

My baby's calming down, (Take a deep breath in and then exhale with a "shhhhh" sound.)

It's hard to stop the fun. (Pause and say, "You can do it!" to the baby doll.)
It's hard to stop the fun. (Pause and say, "You can do it!" to the baby doll.)
This is my baby,
Ready to take a rest.
My baby's going to rest.
My baby's going to rest.
Breathe in, (Take a deep breath in.)
Breathe out. (Exhale with a long "shhhhh.")
It's time for you to rest.

Step 5: Ending and Transition to Next

Sing to the tune of "Good Night Ladies"
Bye bye, baby.
Bye bye, baby.
Bye bye, baby,
We'll play again someday.

Case Studies

Baby Doll Circle Time is used extensively in Early Head Start, Head Start, preschools, home child care, therapeutic interventions, and both public and private kindergartens. The following case studies represent a small fraction of the kinds of interactions experienced nationwide. It may be important to note that Baby Doll Circle Time is often implemented within a Conscious Discipline framework that increases its effectiveness. Conscious Discipline is a social-emotional and classroom management methodology shown to decrease aggression, and improve social-emotional skills, school-readiness and school climate (Jones & Lesaux, 2013; Rain, 2014).

Nate (18 Months Old)

Elizabeth was working as an Infant/Toddler Developmental Specialist for the Early Steps program in Florida when she first met 18-month-old Nate. Her job was to teach interventions that build executive function and encourage the onset of new skills during home visits with families of children 0–3 years with developmental disabilities, speech and language delays, social-emotional issues and difficult behaviors. Baby Doll Circle Time is one of the core interventions Elizabeth utilized in the home. She said:

> The first time I met Nate, I was greeted kindly by his mother. But the moment I looked at Nate, he screamed and ran to his room. The only thing I could think of to say to his mom was, *"At some point, he will be overjoyed to see me, but today is not that day."*

As they began to work together, Elizabeth assessed that Nate was exhibiting early characteristics for the onset of Autism Spectrum Disorder, including no joint attention, no verbal communication, difficulty with connection and difficulty playing games with others. Elizabeth decided to introduce Baby Doll Circle Time as an intervention by bringing enough baby dolls for everyone in the house to join in the play. Her intent was to foster increased connection and communication, and the acquisition of new skills through Baby Doll Circle Time.

Nate was immediately fascinated with the dolls' faces and limbs that he could move. Dad joined in the first Baby Doll Circle Time session, so Elizabeth asked about games he likes to play with Nate, including any horse play-type games. Dad responded that "Rocket Ship" is Nate's favorite. Utilizing this information as an entrance point for Baby Doll Circle Time, Elizabeth asked Dad to demonstrate Rocket Ship with the baby doll. The moment Nate heard Dad initiate a countdown, he looked over. Nate laughed as Dad launched the baby doll up in the air. Elizabeth immediately followed with her own countdown and launch, receiving the same reaction from Nate. She said, "Nate's ability to generalize this experience with Dad and then with me using a baby doll showed huge progress in joint attention and connection. It also opened the door to additional interventions via the baby dolls."

After that session, Elizabeth would incorporate the Baby Doll Circle Time curriculum into every session with Nate. Nate started to imitate what Elizabeth and the other adults would model with the dolls, including I Love You Rituals that involve eye contact, touch, presence and playfulness. After they would do a Baby Doll Circle Time I Love You Ritual activity as a group with the dolls, Nate would become more willing to take part in the ritual himself. Nate also conducted the rituals in one-on-one time with a parent at various times during the week. "Round and Round the Garden" became a favorite ritual he enjoyed both in group time and in one-on-one time with Elizabeth or a parent.

Nate also spoke two of his first words during a session with the dolls. Elizabeth and the parents would each say "on" as they put a hat on their dolls and then say, "off" as they took the hats off. This was an activity that developed organically as an adaptation of the Peek-a-boo Baby Doll Circle Time script. The adults would model this on/off activity with a great deal of expression in a very playful way to pique Nate's interest. Ultimately, Nate spoke "on" and "off" while manipulating the hat in the same way.

Elizabeth, Nate and his family shared countless rounds of Baby Doll Circle Time over the course of their year together. As Elizabeth foretold at their first meeting, they did in fact share days when Nate was overjoyed to see her rather than running away in fear. His ability to engage socially improved greatly, as did his capacity for joint attention, his overall communication skills and his ability to connect one-on-one. "There is no doubt in my mind that Nate made the tremendous gains he did through the focused play that was made possible by Baby Doll Circle Time," Elizabeth said.

Eli (20 Months Old)

Eli arrived in the 2-year-old classroom at an Early Head Start program in urban New Jersey having spent the first two years of his life at home with his mother. Eli was very attached and had a difficult time separating from her during the school day. Both Eli and his mother often cried at drop off. For the first month, Eli continued to cry throughout the school day. His mother considered removing him from the school but Daniella, his Early Head Start Teacher, intervened. "When I say he cried the whole day, I mean he cried the *whole* day. I always had hope because he learned to follow the daily routine, but he cried the whole time he was doing it," Daniella said. She firmly believed Eli could be successful with time and assistance in regulating his emotions.

Eli's classroom had been practicing Baby Doll Circle Time two or three times per week upon his arrival. His teachers focused heavily on the deep belly breathing and emotional regulation strategies described in Baby Doll Circle Time and in Conscious Discipline, as the school was in its second year of Conscious Discipline implementation.

After about a month, Eli began to shift from constantly crying and asking, "Is Mama coming," to developing the ability to better manage the separation. Regular implementation of the Baby Doll Circle Time curriculum was an essential component in this shift. The Emotion unit is designed to assist with emotional regulation, while the I Love You Rituals provide a means for building healthy attachment at school and the independent use of the dolls enabled Eli to experience a degree of comfort whenever he needed it. Daniella said:

> He would stand at the window with his baby doll, breathing and doing the exercises we taught him. He would model with the doll just what I was modeling with him. It was like he was the caregiver and the doll was Eli. This is how he learned to calm himself.

Daniella says Baby Doll Circle Time gave her the tools she needed to help Eli learn to calm himself and adapt to a school setting. The activities and dolls provided a gateway for healing.

She said:

> It was hard for me and my coworkers. We had his family photo on our Friends and Family Board, and he would go to it and cry. My coworker wanted to remove it because it was upsetting him, but I knew he needed to see his family, to connect with them. He needed the time and the skills to relax and feel safe, not to avoid it.

By October, Eli was crying less and participating in classroom life more. He continued using the dolls to reproduce the calming, connecting and emotional regulation techniques his teachers taught during group Baby Doll Circle Time and one-on-one play throughout the day. As the school year continued, Eli transformed from crying all day, every day to thriving and becoming "the happiest kid in the classroom."

Without intervention, his teachers believe Eli's mother would have removed him from Early Head Start and his first school experience would have been a negative one. Instead, Eli learned to regulate his emotions in a compassionate school setting. According to Daniella, "We created a classroom where Eli felt secure enough to feel his emotions. He knew he was safe and that breathing like we practiced in Baby Doll Circle Time would help him." On a personal note, she says, "It really changed me because even though I had already been practicing Conscious Discipline and Baby Doll Circle Time for a while, seeing Eli struggle and succeed showed me that it really works."

Courtney (Lead Teacher, Toddler Classroom)

Courtney is the lead teacher in a toddler classroom in Richmond, Virginia. Her classroom participates in an intergenerational program in which the toddlers visit the residents in a retirement community's Memory Support Unit. Courtney recalls the first time she implemented Baby Doll Circle Time. She said:

> It was a new method of cognitive play that I had never thought of . . . My first time doing Baby Doll Circle Time was magical. The children were enthralled. They were listening to the songs and following along with the play. It was probably the first time I had walked away from a circle time feeling relaxed and overjoyed.

About a year after implementing Baby Doll Circle Time in her classroom, Courtney saw a resident holding a doll during one of the school's weekly trips to the Memory Support Unit. A lightbulb went off as she envisioned the connection potential and neural benefits Baby Doll Circle Time could bring to the intergenerational program. "I realized how valuable Baby Doll Circle Time could be in our interactions with the senior citizens," Courtney said. "Once I started implemention, play time became more meaningful and connections strengthened."

When doing Baby Doll Circle Time at the facility, Courtney says it is powerful to see children at the beginning of their cognitive development connect with residents who are beginning to lose their own to dementia. She says it's also powerful to see the way Baby Doll Circle Time helps her toddlers prepare for the whole spectrum of life transitions:

> My age group often is tasked with family changes like new siblings and pets passing away. When new siblings arrive and completely change their home life, for example, I can help prepare them by teaching body awareness and promoting gentle play through Baby Doll Circle Time. It makes it easier for the parents when they introduce the newborn.

One child in particular utilized Baby Doll Circle Time to heal a broken connection after one such life transition. 20-month-old Sara displayed typical toddler-age hesitancy when approaching new adults. During visits to the Memory Support Unit, she would cling to Courtney's lap and avoid attempts to engage. Sara's grandmother had recently left after an extended stay in Sara's home, and the toddler was feeling the loss of this beloved attachment figure. Courtney saw an opportunity to help Sara connect and heal through Baby Doll Circle Time, saying:

> At first, she was shy with the residents. She didn't want to leave my lap. I would sit with her next to a resident and do I Love You Rituals, but it was the baby dolls that seemed to make the greatest difference. She started engaging with a resident through the dolls.

Baby Doll Circle Time provided a medium through which Sara felt safe enough to connect with someone who could ease the transition of her grandmother leaving. Courtney said:

> Sara gravitated towards one certain resident. Instead of remaining glued to my lap, she would climb onto the resident's lap during Baby Doll Circle Time. I think she needed to connect with someone to help heal the void that was left when her grandmother went back home. Sitting on a resident's lap and playing peek-a-boo with the baby doll helped her to engage in similar play she was missing from her grandmother.

Sara's distress and hesitancy visibly lessened, and the resident (who had several children and grandchildren) was excited to connect with the little girl.

Courtney led 15-minute Baby Doll Circle Time sessions during each weekly visit to the Memory Support Unit. She says it is not only brain-enhancing, but also delightful to observe the residents and toddlers engaging with the dolls and each other. "It's the classic win-win situation." Courtney says. "We've seen a significant positive impact in children's behavior and development as they interact with the elderly. For the elderly, interacting with children helps them bring back memories and relieves stress."

The improved engagement and healing Sara experienced is one of many examples Courtney gives from her classroom. She also recounts a 17-month-old who used Baby Doll Circle Time to cope with weaning and learning to sleep in his own room. His teachers and parents played out the nightly routine of being cuddled and rocked to sleep using the baby dolls, and he did the same to help rehearse bedtime and soothe himself. Courtney also tells of a little girl who struggled with extreme emotional outbursts due in part to an unstable situation at home.

The toddler would often throw her baby across the room or tell it to "shut up" when Baby Doll Circle Time called for the doll to cry. During the group activities, Courtney would strategically place herself in front of the toddler in the circle so the little girl could see her playing and engaging lovingly with the doll. Gradually, the toddler became more willing to engage in Baby Doll Circle Time. Courtney was able to use the dolls to connect, establish herself as a safe attachment figure and guide the girl in calming strategies that would help her participate in classroom life more successfully and counteract some of the challenges her home life created.

Courtney says:

> Baby Doll Circle Time gives me a new way to explore play and helpful interventions with my students. I now have a chance to slow the chaos down, initiate the development of cognitive skills, and teach empathy, kindness and love.

Discussion Questions

1 Explore the idea of a primary attachment figure conducting a connecting intervention with a child, and then providing the child with a way to reproduce that activity with a doll or surrogate attachment figure. What benefits do you think this would provide for the child? For the surrogate? What challenges, if any, do you foresee?

2 Baby Doll Circle Time is widely practiced in Head Start, Early Head Start, preschool, Kindergarten and therapeutic home visit settings. What positive outcomes might you anticipate when implementing Baby Doll Circle Time your current work setting?

3 Identify a child or client you believe could benefit from Baby Doll Circle Time. How would you begin implementation? What gains would you expect the child to experience?

References

Bailey, B. (2000). *I love you rituals*. New York, NY: Harper Collins Publishers.

Bailey, B. (2012). *Baby doll circle time: Strengthening attunement, attachment and social play*. Oviedo, FL: Loving Guidance.

Cirulli, F., Berry, A., & Alleva, E. (2002). Early disruption of the mother-infant relationship: effects on brain plasticity and implications for psychopathology. *Neuroscience Biobehavior Review*, 27, 73–82.

Huber, R. (2014). Four in ten infants lack strong parental attachments. Princeton University. https://www.princeton.edu/news/2014/03/27/four-10-infants-lack-strong-parental-attachments

Jones, S., & Lesaux, N. (2013). *Supporting adults to support young children*. Harvard Graduate School of Education.

Rain, J. (2014). Conscious discipline research study research findings. Rain & Brehm Consulting. https://consciousdiscipline.com/conscious-discipline-improves-sel-school-climate-readiness-and-pro-social-behavior

Siegel, D. J., (1999) *The developing mind: Toward a neurobiology of interpersonal experience*. New York, NY: The Guilford Press.

Squire, L., Berg, D., Bloom, F., Dulac, S., Ghosh, A., & Spitzer, N. (2012). *Fundamental neuroscience* (4th ed.), pp. 3334–3336. Oxford: Academic Press.

Tronick, E., Krafchuk, E., Ricks, M., Cohn, J., & Winn, S., (1985). Mother-infant face-to-face interactions at 3, 6 and 9 months: Content and matching. Unpublished manuscript.

Vermeer, H.J., & van Ijzendoorn, M. H., (2006) Children's elevated cortisol levels at daycare: A review and meta-analysis. *Early Childhood Research Quarterly*, 21(3), 390–401.

Chapter 10

DIR®/Floortime™

A Developmental/Relational Play Therapy Model in the Treatment of Infants and Toddlers Exhibiting the Early Signs of Autism Spectrum Disorder

Esther Hess

The human infant is born immature compared with infants of other species, with substantial brain development occurring after birth. Infants are entirely dependent on parents to regulate sleep–wake rhythms, feeding cycles, and many social interactions. Play facilitates the progression from dependence to independence and from parental regulation to self-regulation. It promotes a sense of agency in the child. This evolution begins in the first 3 months of life, when parents interact reciprocally with their infants by reading their nonverbal cues in a responsive, contingent manner. Caregiver–infant inter-action is the earliest form of play, known as attunement, but it is quickly followed by other activities that also involve the taking of turns (Stern, 1980). These serve-and-return behaviors promote self-regulation and impulse control in children and form a strong foundation for understanding their interaction with adults. The back-and-forth episodes also feed into the development of language. However, children who are born with atypical sensory-modulation systems struggle with their caregivers to find these co-regulated moments. This can be a result of the central nervous system's inability to regulate its own activity in a way that is appropriately graded to incoming sensory stimuli (Reed, 2001). It is the irregularities, lack of sus-tainability, disruptions, and co-morbid incompatible affect states that not only signal the disruption of attuned and reciprocal play, but may also forewarn the first ominous signs of emerging autism spectrum disorder (Green et al., 2013; Pineda et al., 2015).

While there are several theoretical approaches to working with develop-mental delays like autism spectrum disorder, this chapter will focus exclu-sively on the developmental/relational perspective, DIR®/Floortime™. This developmental approach was founded on work first pioneered by major developmental theorists such as Piaget, Vygotsky, Erikson, and Kohlberg. This specific approach considers behavior and learning in the greater context of a developmental or changing process. In 1997, evidence first showed the promise of the DIR®/Floortime™ approach when Dr. Stanley Greenspan and his partner Dr. Serena Wieder reviewed 200 charts of children who were initially diagnosed with autistic spectrum disorder. The goal of the review was to reveal patterns in presenting symptoms, underlying processing difficulties, early development and response to intervention in order to generate hypotheses for future studies. The chart review suggested that a number of children with autistic spectrum diagnoses were, with appropriate intervention, capable of empathy, affective reciprocity, creative thinking, and healthy peer relationships (Greenspan & Wieder, 1997). The results of the 200-case series led Greenspan and Wieder to publish in 2000 the full description of the DIR®/Floortime™ Model (ICDL, 2000).

Developmental models emphasize individual processing differences and the need to tailor intervention to the unique biological profile of children as well as the characteristics of the relationship between parent and child. The subcomponents of this approach can be summarized by looking at the three major aspects of the DIR/® Floortime™ approach:

(A)   D – for **developmental** framework;
(B)   I – for the **individual**, underlying, neurological processing differences of a child;
(C)   R – for **relationship** and subsequent affective interactions.

D The Developmental Framework

Developmental approaches seek to measure changes in an individual's capacity for:

- shared attention;
- ability to form warm intimate and trusting relationships;
- the ability to initiate (rather than respond) using intentional actions and social engagement;
- spontaneous communication;
- the ability to participate in reciprocal (two-way, mutual) interactions while in a range of different emotional states;
- problem solving through a process of co-regulation, reading, responding and adapting to the feelings of others;
- creativity;
- thinking logically about motivations and perspective of others;
- developing an internal personal set of values.

I Individual, Underlying, Neurological Processing Differences

In 1979, occupational therapist Jean Ayres pioneered discoveries about the way in which a child's sensory processing capacities could impact the way children learned and integrated themselves into their worlds (Ayres, 1979). This revolutionary idea provided a new way of understanding the importance of movement and regulatory behaviors in children and began to offer explanations for some of the more worrisome behaviors impacting children with developmental concerns like autism spectrum disorders. Over the last 50 years, a large body of research has further illuminated the impact of biologically based differences in regards to both sensori-motor processing and its impact on emotional regulation (Pfeiffer et al., 2011). In addition, this work showed that these biological differences could be influenced and changed by specific therapeutic interventions.

Developmental models emphasize individual differences and the need to tailor intervention to the unique biological profile of the child and to the unique characteristics of the parent–child interaction. In 2001, the National Research Council of the National Academy of Sciences supported the first part of this statement when it published a report entitled *Educating Children with Autism*. In the report the council called for the tailoring of treatment approaches to fit the unique biological profile of the individual child (National Research Council, 2001). Lillas & Turnball (2009), added support to the second part of the statement as they described how all behavior is influenced by the sensory systems in the brain. They suggested that an infant's sensory capacities are genetically prepared to respond to human interaction and are in direct relationship to the caregiver's touch, facial, vocal, and movement expressions. The exchange that takes place during child–caregiver play interactions are an ongoing loop of sensori-motor transformations.

R Relationship and Affect

Developmental therapy models have evolved from many years of discovery in the field of infant mental health. Beginning in the 1950s, there was a new understanding of the importance of caregiver–child interaction (Bowlby, 1951). Building on these concepts, Drs Stanley Greenspan and Serena Wieder began their work studying the interaction of mother–infant dyads that were at high risk for attachment problems (National Center for Clinical Infant Programs, 2001). Subsequently, there have been numerous research studies confirming the importance of caregiver–child interaction and the value of intervention programs that focus on supporting the caregiver–child relationship, particularly in the areas of joint attention and emotional attunement (Mahoney & Perales, 2005). In 2006, Gernsbacher published a paper showing how intervention between a caregiver and child could change the way in which caregivers interact, in turn increasing reciprocity, and that these changes correlated to positive changes in the child's social engagement and language. Evidence continues to support caregiver-mediated intervention as effective for the treatment of children impacted by autism spectrum disorder (Cullinane, Gurry, & Solomon, 2017).

The Floortime™ Model

Floortime™ is a particular technique in which the play partner, usually the caregiver, is encouraged to get down on the floor and work with his or her child to master each of the child's developmental capacities. To represent this model fairly, you will need to think about Floortime™ in two ways (ICDL, 2000):

1 as a specific technique in which caregivers get down on the floor to play with their child for 20 or more minutes at a time;
2 a general philosophy guiding all of the caregiver's interactions with the child. All of the interactions have to incorporate the features and goals of Floortime™ including understanding the child's emotional, social, and intellectual differences in motor, sensory, and language functioning, as well as the existing caregiver, child, and family functioning and interaction patterns (Hess, 2012).

The definition of Floortime™ is split into two areas of emphasis; one is following the child's lead. The other is joining the child in their world and then pulling them into a shared world to help them master each of their functional, emotional, and developmental capacities (Greenspan & Weider, 2005). These emphases sometimes work together very easily and other times may appear to be at opposite ends of a continuum. Awareness of both of these polarities, tendencies, or dimensions of Floortime™ is critical because one element encourages the initial engagement of a child into the potential for a reciprocal relationship, while the other element encourages expansion and development of the initial "germ" of an idea into the potential for higher level learning and thought (Hess, 2016).

Following the Child's Lead

The most widely known aspect of Floortime™ is *following the child's lead*; that means harnessing the child's natural interests. But what exactly does that mean? Following a child's lead is taking the germ of that child's idea and making it the basis of the experience you are about to share with the child. Consequently, it encourages children to allow you into their emotional life. By attending to the child's interests; having an understanding of his or her natural desires, caregivers get a picture of what is enjoyable for the child. A child who feels understood and affirmed is a child who stays regulated and engaged longer and is able to learn within the experience and ultimately moves forward developmentally (Hess, 2016).

As mentioned, the focus of this chapter will be on the Floortime™ component that helps parents create a lifestyle with the potential for a reciprocal relationship with their infants and toddlers. For purposes of illustration, this chapter will also present the case study of Rebecca, a child who was initially diagnosed on the autism spectrum at age 18 months. The case will follow Rebecca and her parents during their first year in therapy. Additionally, throughout this chapter there will be an expansion on the implication of working from a developmental perspective with a special needs population.

Case Vignette: Rebecca's Story

The case presented in this chapter describes the treatment of an autistic toddler. The treatment process evolved out of the understanding of the whole family's therapeutic needs. Additionally, developmental information was offered as strategic suggestions that were explored for helping Rebecca form meaningful relationships. I incorporated the principles of DIR®/Floortime™ as a way to present new developmental tasks incrementally and sequentially in the context of learning through relationships. This developmental/relational informed play therapy approach permitted me to understand the additional influence of the parents' histories and personalities on their present relationship with their daughter.

Assessment

Rebecca's family was referred to our treatment facility, Center for the Developing Mind, for an assessment when their daughter was 18 months old. Since birth, Rebecca appeared to have a very sensitive constitution, particularly to touch and sound, but in the last 2 months, her parents reported that their daughter had been having staring spells (for which a seizure disorder had been ruled out) and often seemed extremely aloof, preoccupied, and difficult to connect with.

Additionally, in the past 2 months Rebecca had stopped using the majority of the 10–15 words she had acquired previously. In the course of the assessment, it became evident that both of Rebecca's parents were in crisis. They were continuing to reach out to their child, but with a sense of increased foreboding about their ability to get a response. Mom was unfailingly thoughtful if somewhat intellectualizing about her daughter and was obviously devoted to her child. Dad, on the other hand tended to take a rather passive role both in his family and in the sessions, but when he became active it was with notable warmth and spontaneity. He was a somewhat depressed man with major difficulties in his ability to modulate anger. In general, though, both parents were intelligent, thoughtful about Rebecca's behavior, and articulate in discussing their observations and feelings.

Rebecca was an only child, the product of an uncomplicated pregnancy and delivery. From birth, she was extremely sensitive and often irritable. She regularly cried inconsolably for long periods. She seemed to have particular trouble with the transition from sleep to waking and was unusually sensitive to touch, light, and noises. The parents' natural inclination was to make active attempts to soothe their baby through cuddling and talking to her, but the only approach that was even modestly successful was pushing Rebecca in a stroller or taking her for long car drives, where, after a period of severe agitation, she would eventually calm. In general, her parents felt that their daughter was most content when left alone. Rebecca's major developmental milestones were all within normal limits, although no true social smile had ever developed. After weaning, she insisted on feeding herself and refused any lumpy or rough-textured foods. The child also showed intolerance for shifts and changes in her routine or environment.

At the time of the assessment, Rebecca's affective and social functioning, her sensory integration, and her cognitive abilities were atypical. She never allowed prolonged eye contact or cuddling, and squirmed and arched her back in distress in her mother's lap. Her typical method of making contact was to direct the other person's hand like a tool in order to reach an object or facilitate its use.

There was evidence throughout the assessment that Rebecca had difficulties with sensory modulation and perceptual integration. She seemed easily overwhelmed by sensory input and gave evidence of unusual sensitivity to a variety of visual, auditory, olfactory, and tactile stimuli. When these stimuli were experienced as too intense, Rebecca completely withdrew and became preoccupied with self-stimulatory activity, most often rocking back and forth and on occasion, flapping her arms in an up and down motion.

In the area of symbolic functioning, she showed little evidence of early imitative abilities, and object permanence was as yet incompletely established. For Rebecca, the existence of objects was embedded in a visual gestalt, and she had no memory for things apart from the context with which she associated them. She showed no representational play and, in fact, had difficulty organizing her perceptions into meaningful representations of the world. Rebecca insisted that her world be ordered by rigid routines and the inflexible placement of objects. Her cognitive functioning was markedly uneven. She demonstrated precocious abilities on visual-motor tasks, but showed serious difficulties in language.

Her vocalizations included an unusual mixture of infantile sounds, squeals, and squeaks, and two or three words not used for communication. Rebecca's comprehension of language appeared limited to the recognition of a few key words and invariant phrases paired with a consistent gesture or visual cue. As mentioned, the possibility that this pattern of disturbance resulted from seizure disorder or hearing impairment was investigated and ruled out during the early part of the assessment. It became clear that Rebecca met all the DSM-5 criteria for the diagnosis of autism spectrum disorder (American Psychiatric Association, 2013). Much of her behavior was seen as a reflection of constitutional problems with perceptual organization and symbolic functioning. My working hypothesis was that Rebecca's social withdrawal was related to her innate inability to tolerate or modulate sensory stimulation or to process and organize perceptual input. Additionally, the difficulties in this child's relationship with her parents seemed to stem from an interaction between her own disabilities and her parents' reactions to her behavior.

First Year of Treatment

If we as a clinical community can uniformly agree that no child lives alone (Hess, 2012), then it becomes imperative when assessing a child impacted by autism spectrum disorder that the entire family is involved and needs support during the assessment/treatment. Rebecca's exceptional needs required a modification of the usual model of infant/parent psychotherapy, in which a single therapist meets weekly with all the family members. Rebecca's behavior during the assessment, where she would routinely wander off alone to a distant part of the playroom if attention was focused on anyone other than herself, necessitated that I work alongside an intern who initially filmed the sequence of treatment on the floor between me, the parents, and their daughter. Midway through the session the intern handed me the camera so that, after escorting the parents to an office adjacent to the playroom, I used the film as a teaching tool for the parents to become more aware of their interactions with their daughter while on the floor.

Rebecca

The immediate goal in the treatment was to discover a way to engage Rebecca in a relationship. I expected that, if I could "follow her lead" (Greenspan, 2010) and attune my affect and movements with her and supply her with continuous contingent gratification, I would draw her attention to me and gradually develop her interest in me as a person. I remained constantly available to Rebecca throughout each session. Whenever I had the opportunity, I playfully obstructed encouraging her to use me to open a latch, reach an object, or hand her a toy. I capitalized on these opportunities for contact by always handing her the object in our mutual line of vision so that she had to notice my face and hands simultaneously as I gratified her. I routinely wore artificial flowers in my hair to naturally encourage Rebecca to scan towards the upper regions of my face, so that she could not overlook the fact that this tool-like hand was part of the person who was responding to her wishes (Klin et al., 2015). In order to discover how to engage Rebecca in interaction and maintain her interest, I needed to incorporate the "I" of the DIR® model; to understand and accommodate to her underlying neurological differences; specifically, sensory sensitivities. I therefore experimented with a range of stimuli to explore how best to approach her. I carefully considered what inflection, speed, and intensity of my voice, combined with tactile stimulation and an optimal physical distance for eye contact could capture Rebecca's attention and decrease the likelihood of her withdrawal from contact. She initially tolerated and was then comforted by my using a monkey hand puppet (that she initially had shown interest in) that she allowed to gently rest on her shoulder. By combining the routine of a familiar toy with the offer of a light touch and eye contact at arm's length, she was provided the opportunity to integrate tactile contact with mutual gaze. Months later in the treatment, the integration of touch and vision evolved into a game of swinging and tossing the puppet back and forth, to eventually allowing her parents to swing her in the play. Eventually, she was prepared for a repertoire of highly interactive and pleasurable roughhouse games with her father (Elder et al., 2010). Once Rebecca became interested in the gratification available from human relatedness, the attention was turned to developing this child's interest in communication and reciprocal interaction. Rebecca's attention to speech was cultivated by minimizing the number of words directed to her, slowing the pace of speech, and exaggerating vocal inflection and facial expression. Efforts were made to ensure that Rebecca never experienced this clinician as intrusive. I did not use language to direct or disrupt her activity nor did I initiate any interaction. Instead, I followed the "D" (Development) segment of the DIR/® Floortime™ principles, where I focused less on Rebecca's chronological age and more on her current level of delayed development by providing an extremely simplified, slow-paced, repetitive monologue that described everything she was doing, as well as everything I was doing to interest her in relating to me. I was working on creating "a great date" (Hess, 2012), where this child would feel so emotionally validated by our relationship that she would want to spend as much time as possible engaged in this interaction. This method of relating was continually available for observation and discussion with Rebecca's parents, and soon they began to adopt these approaches to interaction in session and then later at home, adapting them to their own interpersonal styles.

After 3 months of treatment, Rebecca started to show some expectation that the people in her world would be helpful and gratifying, and she began to attend to interpersonal communication. Over the course of many sessions, I pursued a number of play activities with Rebecca that encouraged the potential for reciprocal interaction. We evolved a repertoire for exploring the "cooking area" of our Center's playroom. In the play kitchen section, kitchen cupboards have been placed to be both above and below eye level. While there are some pretend foodstuffs located in the lower cabinets, there are a variety of pots and pans located in the top cabinets that most children find interesting. Rebecca was very curious about wanting to explore the pots in the upper cabinets, but being out of reach, the situation created the opportunity for Rebecca to be dependent on myself and her parents for help. It also put us precisely at eye-to-eye level and, thus, facilitated eye contact. Rebecca's pleasure in her access to previously inaccessible territory allowed me to encourage small moves toward exploration without interfering with her familiar ritualized routines. I was also able to interpret Rebecca's interest in the kitchen as an interest in her parents, who were avid cooks. Over many weeks, Rebecca's exploration developed from a perseverative opening and closing of the toy kitchen's cupboard doors, expanding to an interest in exploring the interior of the cabinets, where a variety of foodstuffs were kept. This eventually led to tasting some unfamiliar foods. Gradually, Rebecca began to broaden her perspectives by trying these new foods during meals. The curriculum in the cupboards ultimately propelled us forward developmentally, encouraging Rebecca to name objects, pouring beans from one size container to another and finally to the beginnings of representational play – pretend cooking with playdough. Since both parents were excellent chefs, her interest in cooking enhanced her parents' gradually developing awareness of their importance to her. Food preparation became the arena for family activity; the parents began to include their daughter in all their baking, and even prepared home-made gluten-free playdough, in recognition of her sensitive sensory system.

Another of the reciprocal activities that Rebecca and I developed grew out of her parents' concern about some ritualistic behaviors. As mentioned, Rebecca engaged in an apparently pointless opening and closing of doors, which rapidly disintegrated into frenzied banging. Returning back to the basic principles of Floortime™, I explored the origins and details of the door-slamming activity during several sessions and was able to find the germ of meaning in her behavior (Hess, 2015). The opening and closing of the doors seemed to be a rough experimental attempt to find out where things were when behind a barrier. Once I discovered this explanation for the behavior, I was able to transform this ritual and expand the idea into a social game that would satisfy Rebecca's curiosity, promote her use of people as helpmates, and offer an active role to her parents. I suggested that her parents might substitute a large box discarded from an appliance purchase, for the door. Within a week, the box had become a focus of social and physical activity between Rebecca and Dad. The child's scurrying in and out of the box included opportunities for mutual gaze, vocal greetings, social smiles, and physical contact. On occasion, Dad moved too fast rather than following his daughter's lead. Rebecca could get easily overwhelmed if the play moved too rapidly. Her response was to arch her back and pull away, escaping her father's attempts to embrace. With support and guidance, Dad was able to understand that Rebecca's avoidant behavior was not a rejection of him, but an effort to protect herself from overwhelming sensory stimulation. Such explanations helped the father endure these rebuffs and carry on the game with the intensity of contact that Rebecca could manage (Elder et al., 2015). This experience underscored for the parents the importance of looking for the meaning in their daughter's behavior. It also demonstrated the possibility of transforming her rituals into playful interactions that addressed the developmental task that she was, however primitively, attempting to master (Hess, 2015).

Rebecca's gradual improvement in mental representation and her continuing interest in social interaction combined to lead naturally to a focus on developing her ability to use language for communication. In the first months of treatment, I had mirrored Rebecca's physical movements and vocalizations and encouraged her to imitate me. The first words that Rebecca imitated were those she had heard week after week, used in the same context each time, and offered as the descriptors of her activity with a person or an object. These initial words were highly communicative in intent, spoken to indicate something she wanted. Requests such as "open," "come," and "up" reflected her now well-founded expectation that she could have an effect on people (Pickles et al., 2016). Once Rebecca started to imitate words, she also began to babble conversationally and regularly inserted words that she had been able to pick up from her parents' conversations. The combination of her new interest in everything her parents said and the guidance about appropriate expectations for the course of Rebecca's language learning enabled the parents to anticipate enthusiastically in her development and prompt their daughter to extend her language use, just an increment beyond her current performance (Ingersoll & Meyer, 2015). Rebecca's verbalizations always took place in the context of her own activity; words and sounds never were rehearsed for their own sake. It was her actions upon objects that gave meaning to the words (Greenspan, 2001).

Rebecca's Parents

The work with Rebecca's parents had several foci. A central one was to help them express and explore their feelings about their daughter and themselves as parents. Both parents initially felt absolutely unimportant to their child and deeply rejected by her. They voiced their immense disappointment at Rebecca's distance from them. They both needed to discuss the frustration and anger they felt at Rebecca, as well. Their prolonged sense of rejection and helplessness was, of course, in part responsible for these feelings. Gradually, I came to see an additional source: Rebecca's irritability in her first year had led her parents to shape their lives in nearly unbearable ways so as not to precipitate her unhappiness. Due to her sensitivity to noise, she occupied the only bedroom in their apartment, the family's activities were limited to those she tolerated, and the parents' time together without their daughter was almost nonexistent. Dad, especially, needed to talk about his cumulative resentment and the anger he felt toward his wife, who seemed more willing to forgo her needs and wishes than he did. The parents also expressed their constant worry about Rebecca – not only about her immediate behavior and reactions, but about her future. Her early language regression had left them mistrustful that any positive changes could be secure and lasting, and they eventually spoke of how painful it was to hope while fearing disappointment. Their feelings of responsibility and guilt about Rebecca's difficulties were a topic in our discussions, as well.

In these exchanges, my role was largely facilitative and supportive. I appreciated the parents' pain, reflected the legitimacy of their anger and worry, and supported their need to have more pleasure in their own lives. At the same time, I was in a position to point out Rebecca's subtle approaches to them and evidence in her behavior that she was registering and responding to their feelings. This allowed the parents to risk more attempts to contact their daughter (Kasari et al., 2015). A second major focus of our early work involved exploring the ways in which the parents' reactive feelings had influenced their relationship with their daughter (Siller et al., 2014). Through experience they had learned not to disturb her, and they had become somewhat hesitant and tentative in trying to contact her. As the parents recognized this dynamic and its consequences, and as they began to glimpse some possibilities for interaction with their daughter, they became more able to reach out to engage her. The parents' concern about upsetting Rebecca also had led them to avoid making demands on her or setting limits. She had come to control their lives in a manner that only increased their resentment and stress and that was not helpful to her in structuring her world. The parents needed my support to acknowledge their own needs and right to impose limits on Rebecca, along with my reassurance that this new insistence would not harm her.

The third central issue in the early work with the parents involved helping them to understand the meaning of Rebecca's behavior (Greenspan, 2010). Both parents had many misconceptions, all of which required exploration and revision. For months, they had supposed that Rebecca was simply unwilling to relate or communicate. We spent many hours examining the details of problematic situations as the parents brought them up and as they occurred in our sessions. My task was to try to highlight the important elements, and with these in mind, raise questions about the meaning of the behaviors. Mom was certain, for example, that Rebecca "had" words; she was simply "withholding" and was purposefully resisting their wishes. Eventually, I was able to help focus the parents' attention on Rebecca's attempts at speech in our sessions. The effort that she put into language production gradually became apparent to the parents. We discussed the particular difficulties that Rebecca had in comprehending and producing speech as we observed the approaches used by Rebecca's speech and language therapist. (Speech and language support were added into Rebecca's treatment regimen approximately 4 months after the family began their daughter's Floortime™ intervention.) The parents then worked diligently to adopt these methods and suggestions in order to help their daughter understand language and learn to use words. This shift in their interpretation of Rebecca's motives and the consequent change in their own behavior were paralleled by an affective shift. Because both parents now could feel allied with their daughter, the tone of their interactions became one of empathy, concern, and support (Greenspan, 2001).

Other misunderstandings also were addressed. Both parents responded to Rebecca's social distance and physical withdrawal from people with a sense of rejection, shame, and irritation (Kogan et al., 2009). As we began to examine the situations that exacerbated Rebecca's retreating, however, it was possible to help the parents find the common element; the "I" of the DIR® model, Rebecca's extreme reaction to what her body interpreted as overstimulation. Eventually parents came to understand that their daughter's distancing was not a reflection on them, but, again, a misaligned response to an internal feeling. They readjusted their expectations, became able to anticipate situations that would cause her difficulty, and thought of various methods to help Rebecca feel more comfortable in the world. Once parents understood Rebecca's needs, they could introduce many effective alterations in her life, and they began to experience a sense of competence as parents (McConachie et al., 2005).

Discussion

The treatment model described in this case approaches autism spectrum disorder as a developmental disability that involves perceptual incapacities. These have debilitating effects on the infant/toddler's social and emotional development because they interfere with the child's ability to experience human relationships as gratifying. Because the autistic child is con- stitutionally poorly equipped to modulate and integrate stimulation, social contact may be experienced as overwhelming and unpleasant (Rogers et al., 2014). In the case of Rebecca, both her history and her behaviors gave evi- dence of perceptual difficulties that interfered with the development of social relationships. She showed hypersensitivity to stimulation and difficulty in modulating perceptual information. She experienced stimulation as over- whelming and distressing and felt repelled rather than enticed and gratified by her human partners, even when they attempted to soothe and comfort her. She fled from simultaneous vocalization, movement, touching, and changing facial displays and also from close physical contact and mutual gaze.

Another aspect of Rebecca's problem was her difficulty in organizing percepts. This incapacity left her unable to construct a meaningful repre- sentation of the world. Her experiences remained so fragmented that, at 18 months, she still seemed to lack a basic organized conception of her parents as whole beings and was aware of them only as fragmented body parts that performed various functions. It seemed likely that through this accumulation of distorted experiences, Rebecca failed to develop accurate expectations of both the social and nonsocial worlds. She frequently must have found sti- mulation unpredictable, so that people were associated with confusion as well as with overwhelming stimulation. She struggled to develop the expectation that other people were the source of social and emotional gratification.

Rebecca's perceptual sensitivities and faulty integration made it extraordinarily difficult for her parents to understand and meet her needs (Sealy & Glovinsky, 2016). Her requirements were atypical, and nothing in the parents' experience with ordinary children prepared them to recognize the ways in which she needed them to mediate her environment. Rebecca's behavior was difficult and confusing for them and lacked the predictability and clarity of signals that are a prime source of a parental sense of efficacy. Her failure to show the expected signs of their centrality for her left them feeling unimportant and incompetent as parents. This had a profound effect on both the parents' feelings toward her and on the ways in which they related to her. They felt increasingly alienated from their daughter and were without the usual parental attunement to their infant's affective state and level of arousal (Stern, 1980). Rebecca, in turn, never experienced the synchrony and pleasure associated with such human connection. Similarly, she did not develop the sense of effectiveness that comes from having signals interpreted correctly and needs met.

As in all child–parent psychotherapy cases, the primary goal was to develop the "R" element of the DIR®/Floortime™ model; the mutually satisfying relationships between the parents and their child. In this case, the parents' growing understanding of the meaning of Rebecca's behavior generated empathy for her struggle, which influenced the quality of their relationships with her. As they became able to adjust their behavior in order to engage her, Rebecca began to respond to them. These changes created an affective shift in the parents that led to their empathic effort to bring Rebecca into the world of human relationships. In this process, the mom and dad were able to sustain natural parental feelings and responses while they constantly were managing the environment in accordance with their child's needs. By the end of the first year of treatment, Rebecca's personality and behavior confirmed the parents' perceptions that they were finally beginning to establish the potential for a reciprocal relationship with their child (Siller, Hutman, & Sigman, 2013).

The case illustrates the development of relationships when an infant/toddler with autism spectrum disorder presents with underlying neurological differences that interfere with overall development and appropriate social interaction. It demonstrates the possibility of minimizing the impact of the autistic condition through integration of child–parent psychotherapy and DIR/® Floortime™ play therapy. As clinicians, we should take seriously any parents' concerns regarding their child's sociability. Additionally, practitioners can provide crucial early intervention by supporting the caregiver's increased understanding of the individual profile of their baby, helping parents gain empathy for their child's challenges, and helping parents learn how to draw their child into social play that is critical as a model for future developmental success.

Discussion Questions

1 What were some of Rebecca's perceptual difficulties and how did they interfere with the development of this child's social relationships?
2 Discuss the various difficulties that Rebecca's parents had in trying to understand and meet her social/emotional needs.
3 Describe the two areas of emphasis that define Floortime™.

References

American Psychiatric Association. (2013). *Diagnostic and statistical manual of mental disorders* (5th ed.). Washington, DC: American Psychiatric Association.

Ayres, J. A. (1979). *Sensory integration and the child.* Los Angeles: Western Psychological Services.

Bowlby, J. (1951). *Maternal care and mental health.* WHO, p. 51.

Cullinane, D. (2011). Evidence base for the DIR®/Floortime approach. Retrieved January 30, 2019 from: http://www.drhessautism.com/img/news/EvidenceBasefortheDIR®ModelCullinane0901.

Cullinane, D., Gurry, S., & Solomon, R. (2017). Research evidence re: developmental-relationship based interventions for autism. Retrieved January 30, 2019 from: http://www.drhessautism.com/img/news/ResearchEvidencereDevelopmental-RelationahipBasedInterventionforAutism0901.

Elder, J., O'Donaldson, S., Kairella, J., Valcante, G., Bendixon, R., Ferdig, R., Self, E., Walker, J., Palau, C., & Serrano, M. (2010). In-home training for fathers of children with autism: A follow up study evaluation of four individual training. *Journal of Child Family Study,* 20(3), 263–271. Retrieved January 30, 2019 from: http://issue.com/circlestretch/docs/evidence_base_for_dir_2015.

Gernsbacher, M. A. (2006). Toward a behavior of reciprocity. *Journal of Developmental Processes,* 1, 139–152. Retrieved January 30, 2019 from: http://www.gernsbacherlab.org/research/autism-research/papers.

Green, J., Wan, M. W., Gulsrud, J., Holsgrove, S., McNally, J., Slonims, V., Elsabbagh, M., Charman, T., Pickles, A., Johnson, M., & the BASIS Team. (2013). Intervention for infants at risk of developing autism: A case series. *Journal of Autism and Developmental Disorders,* 43, 2502–2514. Retrieved January 30, 2019 from: http://kidsattuned.com/recognizing-and-treating-early-signs-of-autism-the-unseen-half-of-the-story.

Greenspan, S. I. (2001). The affect diatheses hypothesis: the role of emotions in the core deficit. In autism and the development of intelligence and social skill. *Journal of Developmental and Learning Disorders,* 5, 1–46. Retrieved January 30, 2019 from: http://www.icdl.com/dir/affect-diathesis-hypothesis.

Greenspan, S. I. (2010). Floor Time™: What it really is, and what it isn't. Retrieved January 30, 2019 from: http://www.stanleygreenspan.com/portal/greenspan-floortime-what-it-really-is-and-what-it-isnt.

Greenspan, S. & Wieder, S. (1997). Developmental patterns and outcomes in infants and children with disorders in relating and communicating: A chart review of 200 cases of children with autistic spectrum diagnoses. *Journal of Developmental and*

Learning Disorders, 1, 87–141. Retrieved January 30, 2019 from: http:// www.cen terforthedevelopingmind.com/floor_time_emotional_approach.

Greenspan, S., & Wieder, S. (2005). Can children with autism master the core deficits and become empathetic, creative and reflective? A ten to fifteen-year follow-up of a subgroup of children with autism spectrum disorders (ASD) who received a comprehensive Developmental, Individual-Difference, Relationship-Based (DIR) approach. *Journal of Developmental and Learning Disorders*, 9, 43–46. Retrieved January 30, 2019 from: http://www.stanleygreenspan.com/resources/works-dr-greenspan.

Hess, E. B. (2012). DIR/Floor Time: A developmental-relational approach towards play therapy in children impacted by autism. In L. Gallo-Lopez, & L. Rubin (Eds.), *Play-based interventions for children and adolescents with autism spectrum disorders,* pp. 231–248. New York, NY: Routledge, Taylor and Francis Publishing.

Hess, E. B. (2015). The DIR/Floor Time model of parent training for young children with autism spectrum disorder. In H. Kaduson, & C. Schaefer (Eds.), *Short-Term Play Therapy for Children, 3rd ed.* New York, NY: The Guilford Press.

Hess, E. B. (2016). DIR/Floortime: A developmental/relational play therapy approach toward the treatment of children with developmental delays, including autism spectrum disorder (ASD) and sensory processing challenges. In K. J. O'Connor, C. E. Schaeffer, & L. D. Braverman (Eds.), *Handbook of play therapy* (2nd ed.). Hoboken, NY: Wiley Publishing.

Ingersoll, B. & Meyer, K. (2011). Examination of correlates of different imitative functions in young children with autism spectrum disorders. *Research in Autism Spectrum Disorders*, 5, 1078–1085.

Interdisciplinary Council on Developmental and Learning Disorders (2000). *ICDL clinical practice guidelines: Redefining the standards of care for infants, children and families with special needs.* Bethesda, MD: ICDL.

Kasari, C., Gulsrud, A., Paparella, T., Hellerman, G., & Barry K. (2015). Randomized comparative efficacy study of parent-mediated interventions for toddlers with autism. *Journal of Autism and Developmental Disorders*, 83(3), 554–563. Retrieved January 30, 2019 from: http://reference.medscape.com/medline/abstract/25822242.

Klin, A., Shultz, S., & Jones. W. (2015). Social visual engagement in infants and toddlers with autism: early developmental transitions and a model of pathogenesis. *Neuroscience and Behavioral Reviews*, 10, 189–203. Retrieved January 30, 2019 from: http://www.marcus.org/.../Summer-Symposium/Klin-Overview-of-ASD.pdf.

Kogan, M. D., Blumberg, S. J., Schieve, L. A., Boyle, C. A., Perrin, J. M., Ghandour, R. M., Singhi, G. K., Strickland, B. B., Trevathan, E., & van Dyck, P. C. (2009). Prevalence of parent-reported diagnosis of autism spectrum disorder among children in the US. *Pediatrics*, 10, 1522–1542. http://www.ncbi.nlm.nih.gov/pubmed/21606152.

Lillas, C., & Turnball, J. (2009). *Infant/child mental health, early intervention and relationship-based therapists: A neuro-relationship framework for interdisciplinary practice.* New York, NY: Norton & Company.

Mahoney, G. & Perales, F. (2005). Relationship focused early intervention with children with pervasive developmental disorders and other disabilities: A comparative study . *Journal of Developmental and Behavioral Pediatrics*, 26(2), 77–85. Retrieved January 30, 2019 from: http://journals.sagepub.com/doi/abs/10.1177/1362361310386502.

McConachie, H., Randle, V., Hammal, D., & Le Couteur, A. (2005). A controlled trial of a training course for parents of children with suspected autism spectrum disorder. *Journal of Pediatrics*, 147, 335–340. Retrieved January 30, 2019 from: http://www.ncbi.nlm.nih.gov/pmc/articles/PMC3825471.

National Center for Clinical Infant Programs. (1987). Infants in multi-risk families. Case studies in preventative intervention. In S. I. Greenspan, S. Weider, R. A. Nover, A. Lieberman, R. S. Lourie, & M. E. Robinson (Eds.), *Clinical infant reports*, Number 3. Madison, CT: International University Press.

National Research Council. 2001. *Educating children with autism*. Washington, DC: The National Academies Press. https://doi.org/10.17226/10017

Pfeiffer, B. A., Koenig, K., Kinnealey, M., Sheppard, M., & Henderson, L. (2011). Research Scholars Initiative—Effectiveness of sensory integration interventions in children with autism spectrum disorders: A pilot study. *American Journal of Occupational Therapy*, 65, 76–85. Retrieved January 30, 2019 from: http://ajot.aota.org/article.aspx?articleid=1853012.

Pickles, A., Le Couteur, A., Leadbitter, K., Salomone, E.*et al.* (2016) Parent-mediated social communication therapy for young children with autism (PACT): Long-term follow-up of a randomized controlled trial. *Lancet Psychiatry*, 6736(16), 31229–31226. Published online at http://www.thelancet.com/cms/attachment/2069571282/2067734889/mmc1.pdf.

Pineda, R., Melchior, K., Oberle, S., Inder, T., & Rogers, C. (2015). Assessment of autism symptoms during the neonatal period: Is there early evidence of autism risk? *American Journal of Occupational Therapy*, 69(4). Retrieved January 30, 2019 from: http://www.brown.edu/...projects/children-at-risk/nnns-publications.

Reed, K. L. (2001). Developmental disorders: Sensory integrative dysfunction. In K. L. Reed (Ed.), *Quick reference to occupational therapy* (2nd ed. pp. 139–174). Austin, TX: Pro-Ed.

Rogers, S. J., Vismara, L., Wagner, A. L., McCormick, C., Young, G., & Ozonoff, S. (2014). Autism treatment in the first year of life: a pilot study of Infant Start, a parent-implemented intervention for symptomatic infants. *Journal of Autism and Developmental Disorders* . doi:10.1007/s10803–10014–2202-y.

Sealy, J., & Glovinsky, I. P. (2016). Strengthening the reflective functioning capacities of parents who have a child with a neurodevelopmental disability through a brief, relationship-focused intervention. *Infant Mental Health Journal*, 37(2), 115–124. Retrieved January 30, 2019from: http://www.edgehill.ac.uk/education/dr-julie-sealy.

Siller, M., Hutman, T., & Sigman, M. (2013). A parent-mediated intervention to increase responsive parental behaviors and child communication in children with ASD: A randomized, clinical trial. *Journal of Autism and Developmental Disorders*, 43(3), 540–550. Retrieved January 30, 2019from: http://www.ncbi.nlm.nih.gov/pmc/articles/PMC4371529.

Siller, M., Swanson, M., Gerber, A., Hutman, T., & Sigman, M. (2014). A parent-mediated intervention that targets responsive parental behaviors increases attachment behaviors in children with ASD: Results from a randomized, clinical trial. *Journal of Autism and Developmental Disorders*, 44, 1720–1732. Retrieved January 30, 2019 from: http://www.marcus.org/Research/Meet-the-Team/Michael-Siller.

Stern, D. (1980). *The interpersonal world of the human infant: A view from psychoanalysis and developmental psychology*. New York, NY: Basic Books.

Chapter 11

Reflections of Love in the TEACUP Preemie Program®

Strengthening the Attachment Relationship through FirstPlay® Infant Story-Massage

Chelsea C. Johnson

The first time I (Author) entered a hospital Neonatal Intensive Care Unit (NICU), I was positively gobsmacked. Rows of isolettes, called "Giraffes" filled the room, along with a soft cacophony of monitor sounds, beeps, alarms, and whooshes. The baby I was there to see had been born at 24 weeks gestation—4 months too soon. She was about a foot long and weighed just over a pound. Her skin was beet red, shiny, and translucent. Her tiny hands and feet kicked and squirmed as the nurse repositioned a tiny eye-mask to protect her fragile eyes from the UV lights used to treat jaundice. She was the tiniest baby I had ever seen. It would be weeks before her mother would be able to hold her for the first time.

Introduction

The Children's Healing Institute, headquartered in West Palm Beach, Florida, partners with parents with the ultimate goal of keeping children healthy and safe in their homes. The mission of The Children's Healing Institute is to prevent child abuse by strengthening families facing crisis, challenge, and change (The Children's Healing Institute, 2019). Our vision is a happy, healthy, and safe childhood for every child, and we work side-by-side with parents in the home and other settings. We teach coping strategies and safe and gentle parenting practices, locate resources in the community, set and maintain goals, and ensure the wellbeing of children.

The Children's Healing Institute has an excellent reputation as a community leader in the field of child abuse prevention. Its acclaimed TEACUP Preemie Program® is well known among the infant mental health community, hospital NICUs, and lactation professionals for its caring support to families and expertise in preterm birth. Since 2008, the TEACUP Preemie Program® has helped parents cope with and navigate the struggles of parenting a preemie through free support groups, individual guidance, home visits, connection to community resources, and breast pump lending. TEACUP® has on-site services at several local hospitals, meeting parents in the NICUs to offer guidance and support through the harrowing journey of premature birth. The program continues after the baby is well enough to leave the hospital, providing encouragement, validation, community, and connection in the family home.

Epidemiology of Preterm Birth

According to the National Institute of Child Health and Human Development (NICHD, 2017, 9.9% of babies in the U.S. were born prematurely in 2017, a percentage that rises each year. A premature infant is a baby born at least 3 weeks too soon, before 37 completed weeks of gestation (WHO, 2017). Complications from preterm birth are the leading cause of death of children under the age of five years. Women have an elevated risk for preterm labor if they have abnormalities of the reproductive organs (i.e. short cervix) and other medical conditions such as high blood pressure and preeclampsia, or are carrying multiple babies. Other risk factors include ethnicity (African American mothers are more likely than Caucasian mothers to deliver prematurely), age (mothers less than 18 years of age and older than 35 are at a higher risk), lack of prenatal medical care, and substance use and abuse (Martin, Hamilton, & Osterman, 2018).

Preemie babies can face a multitude of medical complications at birth and during the first year of life compared to full-term babies, and the earlier they are born, the higher the risk (Linden, Paroli, & Doron, 2010). Preemies are more likely to have long-term intellectual and developmental disabilities, chronic lung disease and other breathing problems, vision and hearing loss, infections, and disorders of the intestines. These medical complications can lead to impaired long-term health and even death (March of Dimes, 2013).

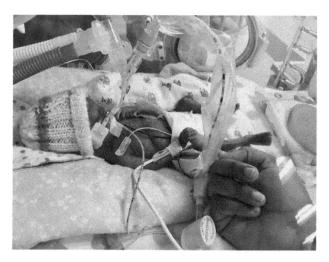

Figure 11.1 Baby Serenyty was born 23 weeks into her mother's pregnancy, weighing barely a pound.
Used with permission from Charity Walker, Serenyty's mother. Photo by Chelsea Johnson.

Emotional Impact of NICU and Attachment Risk

Although society tends to think of preemies as simply being born smaller than full-term babies, preemies enter the world with an uphill battle for their own health and survival. Their delicate organ systems are underdeveloped, their lungs often not strong enough to breathe without a ventilator, their skin far too delicate to withstand cuddles, strokes, and affection from their parents. They have a genuine fight for life, which poses a tremendous risk to the attachment relationship with the mother or father.

Beginning with a traumatic birth, premature infants come into the world at high risk for developing an insecure attachment to their mothers (Forcada-Guex et al., 2011). According to the tenets of attachment theory, infants have an inborn survival instinct to attach to another individual, and the hours and days immediately following birth are vital for the establishment of attachment and bonding between newborns and their parents (Hallin et al., 2011). A newborn preemie is quickly rushed to NICU, where they are connected to complicated medical equipment including ventilators, heart monitors, IVs, and feeding tubes, creating immediate separation from the mother during this crucial time of initial attachment and bonding. Days, or even weeks, can pass before a parent is able to hold her baby for the first time, and even longer before she gets a good look at her baby's face without tubes and tape obstructing her view. These complex events can jeopardize parents' ability to bond with their newborns.

Both moms and dads may experience depression, anxiety, and post-traumatic stress from the emotional rollercoaster of the NICU as their babies fight for life, which further disrupts secure attachment and bonding. According to Purdy, Craig, & Zeanah (2015), mothers of preterm infants have much higher rates of depression than those of full-term babies, and another study shows that 33% of fathers showed signs of Post-Traumatic Stress Disorder at 4 months after the birth (Cheng, Volk, & Marini, 2011). Unfortunately, a mother's mental health has a significant impact on a child's healthy development, regardless of term of birth. It is easy to see how all of these factors combine to weaken bonding and attachment between parent and child. The effects of an insecure attachment in infancy can be lifelong (Hallin et al., 2011; Schore, 2012). Without proper support and education, preemie parents are at risk of missing a vital step in their children's healthy cognitive and emotional development.

The complexities that stem from preterm birth can also compromise the achievement of major developmental outcomes. Research shows that children at the age of 10 who were born prematurely had more behavior problems, more attention deficit, and poorer performance in school than their full-term counterparts. This research further revealed that a poor attachment to the mother has a direct connection to these negative long-term outcomes of preterm birth (Hallin et al., 2011). By fostering preterm infants' loving and secure attachment to their caregivers, we strengthen the foundational steps to achieve major developmental outcomes from birth through adolescence.

Reclaiming Attachment

It is possible to reclaim essential attachment and bonding. The human brain has neuroplasticity, the ability to reorganize itself by forming new neural connections throughout life (Meyer, 2011). This neuroplasticity allows insecure or disorganized attachments to transform into healthy, loving bonds through positive, joyful interactions and experiences between parent and child.

During the NICU hospitalization, parents have the ability to engage in activities that encourage attachment and bonding to counteract the disorganizing effects of the NICU. They are often encouraged to participate in hands-on care with the baby as soon as they can safely do so, taking baby's temperature, changing diapers, and assisting with tube feedings. "Kangaroo Care" is a practice of close skin-to-skin contact between a newborn baby and parent, usually chest to chest (Jefferies, 2012). Kangaroo Care is widely embraced by NICUs worldwide for comfort, pain relief, stabilization of respiration, body temperature, and heart rate, and also as an effective encourager of breastfeeding. Recent research indicates Kangaroo Care's efficacy as a comfort and distraction during painful procedures, of which preemies have anywhere between 10 and 16 per day (Pagni, Kellar, & Rood, 2017). Perhaps the loving connection occurring between parent and baby during skin-to-skin contact has the greatest impact on continued attachment. According to Jefferies (2012), mothers who engaged in Kangaroo Care with their infants in the NICU reported an increase in parental confidence and a sense of their role as a mother and felt simply "needed."

Music therapy is often used in NICU settings to foster an emotional connection and attachment between mother and baby. An established health profession since the 1950s, music therapy involves the use of music-based experiences to achieve a therapeutic goal through the relationship between a patient and a properly credentialed board certified music therapist (AMTA, 2019). NICU music therapy includes the mother and father as active participants in the therapy session and fosters immense bonding that can be otherwise difficult to attain. In the NICU setting, music therapists have made breakthroughs in stabilizing vital signs, improving sleep, and assisting with sustained sucking patterns, which all lead to successful oral feeding (Loewy et al., 2013). Studies indicate that babies who received music therapy in the NICU left the hospital as much as 12 days sooner than babies who did not participate in music therapy (Standley, 2012).

With so many positive means for parents to establish attachment and bonding, it can be difficult to understand how some parents struggle to make up for lost time. However, many new parents lack the inner resources and knowledge to initiate this connection. Preemie parents need access to interventions that reinforce a loving attachment for their infant's short-term and long-term health. Fortunately, as the field of infant mental health expands, medical and mental health professionals are recognizing this necessity more frequently.

FirstPlay® Therapy

The TEACUP Preemie Program® has been offering FirstPlay® Infant Story-Massage to preemie families since 2017 through home visitation, and we have witnessed the efficacy of this model in action. FirstPlay Therapy® is a developmental play therapy model that incorporates interactive storytelling with playful infant massage. Developed by Janet A. Courtney, FirstPlay® is an attachment-based approach that promotes joyful interaction between parent and child (Courtney, Velasquez, & Bakai Toth, 2017). This highly effective approach has the ability to transform an insecure parental bond deficit into a secure one, potentially changing the course of health and wellness for preemies. FirstPlay® is rooted in Developmental Play Therapy, Attachment Theory, Filial Play Therapy, and therapeutic storytelling, as well as research pertaining to the neurobiology of touch, infant massage, and infant mental health (Courtney, Velasquez & Bakai Toth, 2017). It is a preventative, strengths-based model that teaches parents effective ways to connect with their babies through gentle touch with respect, love, and playful interactions.

The FirstPlay® model tells a story, *The Baby Tree Hug*©, while giving the baby a gentle massage (Courtney, 2015). The story keeps the baby engaged with the parent and brings a sense of joy and playfulness to the bonding experience. The Certified FirstPlay® Practitioner shows the parent how to perform the story-massage using a baby doll, while parents follow along with their baby. The practitioner exhibits engagement, gentle touch, and playful interaction with the baby-doll, while highlighting attunement and key moments when "the magic" is happening between the parent and child so that the parent begins to attune to those moments naturally.

Synthesis: FirstPlay® and TEACUP Preemie Program®

What began as a trial intervention for our program has become an anchor to TEACUP®'s scope of services, as the immediate and lasting effects of First-Play® have strong protective factors for infants. As FirstPlay® helps to establish healthy and loving attachment and bonding, it mitigates factors that can contribute to abuse and neglect. We now know that children exposed to adverse childhood experiences (ACEs) are at a higher risk for learning difficulties, emotional problems, developmental problems, and long-term health problems (Felitti et al., 1998). FirstPlay® Infant Story-Massage focuses on the relationship between parent and child, and teaches parents how to calm and center themselves when interacting with their child. The Certified FirstPlay® Practitioner offers gentle guidance and models positive interactions between parent and infant. The training also teaches parents how to connect to their infant through attunement, which involves listening and responding to their baby's cues. This attunement between parent and child poises them for open, positive communication as the child grows.

When practiced regularly, FirstPlay® also creates deeper sleep, increases oxygen and nutrient flow to the cells, and helps with digestion and elimination. Parents and babies engaged in the story-massage simultaneously experience the release of oxytocin, often called the "love hormone," along with a decrease in cortisol, a stress hormone (Feldman & Bakermans-Kranenburg, 2017). These calming and relaxing physiological changes help to create a fun, special time of intimacy each day between parents and their babies.

When we promote a healthy attachment in babies, the benefits are expansive. The same area of the brain associated with attachment also regulates empathy, fear, intuition, behavioral and emotional responses, flexibility, and morality (Meyer, 2011). We know that preemies often leave the hospital with a heightened sensitivity to touch, which is due to the lengthy NICU stay, isolation, and the unpleasant pokes, prods, and procedures that they face on a daily basis in NICU (Mantis and Stack, 2018). By offering FirstPlay®, we give parents and babies the opportunity to reframe their touch relationship in a joyful way that sets them up for secure bonding and attachment for life.

Case Vignettes

Following are case examples from The Children's Healing Institute's TEACUP Preemie Program®, in which FirstPlay® Infant Story-Massage served as a key intervention after the preterm infants' discharge from NICU to home.

Case of Penelope and Elena

Penelope was 34 years old and a first-time mom. I first met her when she gave birth to Elena, 26 weeks into her pregnancy. Baby Elena weighed less than 2 pounds at birth. Penelope sought emotional support from the TEACUP® Program when her baby was just a few days old, and received individual and group support through Elena's 90-day hospital NICU stay and after she went home.

Penelope's relationship with Elena's father Diego was contentious, at best, and emotionally abusive. He withheld everything from money to personal grooming items to nourishing food from Penelope. When she brought Elena home, Diego was not interested in a relationship with either of them, spending nearly all of his time out of the house, either at work or out with friends. I introduced the idea of FirstPlay® to her to give her and baby Elena a positive way to interact and temper the stressful environment of their home.

As FirstPlay® is a "manualized program," parents receive the *FirstPlay Parent Manual* at the first session, and the training closely follows the contents of the book (Courtney, 2015). In our first session, Penelope learned about the supporting literature and scientific backbone of FirstPlay® along with the benefits to both herself and her baby. Penelope remarked rather earnestly that it had never occurred to her to respect her baby. She loved her baby fiercely, but had not given thought to Elena's personhood. This moment was one of her first awakenings and an entry-point to a new level of relationship with her daughter.

Over the course of two in-home sessions, Penelope learned the story of the *Baby Tree Hug©* and the corresponding story-massage techniques. I sat with my baby-doll, in a dyad alongside hers with Elena. In the moments that she and Elena were engaged in FirstPlay®, it was as if the rest of the world fell away. The story and corresponding touch techniques came quite naturally to her. My role as instructor became a role as witness – she needed very little redirection, prompting, or guidance, although she was open to learning and making sure she was "doing it right." I amplified moments of attunement and connection between Penelope and Elena by simply stating my observations ("She's smiling and looking right into your eyes! Look Elena! Mommy is smiling right back at you!").

After learning the story-massage in the first session, the following visit is often a review of the whole process, with the mom and baby – instead of the practitioner – leading the story. Penelope was eager to show me how she and Elena had progressed, and their shared joy through the experience was palpable. Penelope remarked that when she and Elena were engaged in FirstPlay®, which she was using one to two times daily, the rest of life's stresses fell away and she saw herself as a confident and capable mother. This boost in self-confidence was no small feat, and ultimately helped her find the courage to leave her abusive partner and toxic home environment to start a healthy, loving life with her daughter.

Case of Ana, Dean, and Leo

Baby Leo was born 11 weeks early due to intrauterine growth restriction, a condition of pregnancy caused by placental insufficiency that results in a significant reduction in fetal growth for gestational age (Levine et al., 2014). Leo's growth had stopped 26 weeks into Ana's pregnancy and he only weighed 1 pound and 11 ounces at birth. Ana was distraught and inconsolable throughout Leo's 8-week NICU hospitalization, and she was worried about her tiny fragile Leo and hoped he could come home soon.

When Leo was finally discharged from NICU, I visited Ana and her husband Dean in their home. Baby Leo was resting in a "bouncer seat" close to his parents. I asked how he was adjusting to life at home, and Ana's tears began to flow. "I don't hold him often. He doesn't seem to like my touch." I paused for a moment and responded, "Let's reframe that. He is *learning* your touch. Up until now, he has had a very specific and limited relationship to touch from the NICU. We are going to change that." I told her about FirstPlay® and explained how it could help her and Leo redefine their touch relationship. She was open to trying it, so we scheduled a time the following week to get started.

After reviewing the preliminary didactic material, we began the FirstPlay® demonstration and instruction. Dean was reluctant to participate at first, saying that he was "leaving the nurturing stuff to mom," so we carried on without him, but left the invitation open for him to come join us. As I demonstrated the story and corresponding massage steps, Ana mirrored me with Leo. Her first touch brought a smile to his face and he locked eyes with her. In that moment, their beautiful dance began. Ana became more confident with every stroke, and every lyrical line of the story. There were many opportunities for me to bring to her awareness little Leo's fixed attunement with her, and her sheer delight in the exchange happening between the two of them.

Not long after we began, Dean came into the room to observe. I encouraged him to come closer and see how Leo was responding. He was immediately drawn into the beautiful moment with Ana and Leo. Ana showed him how she was handling one arm, and invited him to try it with the other. As the session progressed, Dean and Ana began naturally taking turns telling the story to Leo and using the massage techniques. Dean seemed to enjoy being part of this joyful and nurturing moment with his son and wife.

The following week, I returned for a follow-up visit. Ana met me at the door, wearing a baby sling with Leo snuggled close to her chest. When I mentioned her "babywearing," she smiled and remarked that she had kept him close to her all week. She shared that they were practicing FirstPlay® every day and having so much tender fun with it. In our review, she led the entire story with very few questions or prompts from me. Leo was relaxed to the point of dozing off by the end of the story, and Ana shared that they had been doing FirstPlay® right after his bath before bedtime. As this has become their routine, it was obvious that Leo was beginning to make the connection between FirstPlay® and readying for sleep.

When I brought up other FirstPlay® activities such as "This Little Piggy" and "Patty Cake," that she could build upon with what she has learned, she looked puzzled. Brazil is Ana's homeland, and English her second language. She stated, "These are not my songs." I encouraged her to use songs and games that she had learned as a child, in her native Portuguese. It was an important reminder to me that culture plays an important role in childhood songs, games, and FirstPlay® activities.

FirstPlay® helped Ana redefine her touch relationship with Leo. She was frightened of hurting him, and he was accustomed to not only the confines of the NICU isolette, but the daily needle sticks, painful and uncomfortable procedures, and minimal physical contact compared to what a healthy full-term newborn would receive. FirstPlay® gave Ana permission to have fun with Leo and enjoy loving and playful moments with him. The gentle massage helped Leo form new neurological connections in relation to touch, and Dean learned that dads can be part of the nurturing relationship just as much as moms can. Dean and Ana credit FirstPlay® with helping them reach a new level of confidence as new parents, and for establishing a foundation for a beautiful touch relationship as a family.

Closing Comments

The TEACUP Preemie Program® offers FirstPlay® to every family enrolled in the program, which has led to an increase in families' sustained engagement with the program. In 2018, 31% of families remained enrolled in our program after their babies' discharge from NICU compared to only 18% before we began to offer FirstPlay®. It offers gentle guidance and models positive interactions between parent and infant, teaching them how to connect through attunement and poising them for open, positive communication for years to come. Fostering preemies' secure attachment to their parents creates a foundation for positive developmental outcomes from birth through adolescence. By fostering a healthy and loving attachment and bonding through FirstPlay®, the TEACUP Preemie Program® continually champions our ultimate mission of eradicating child abuse and neglect.

Discussion Questions

---

1 Discuss with a colleague the various factors that can complicate the development of a healthy, secure attachment in preterm infants.
2 In the case of Penelope, why do you imagine it had never occurred to her to respect her baby? Discuss how Penelope's insight may influence her parenting style and her relationship with Elena.
3 Discuss your thoughts on FirstPlay® as it relates to maternal mental health. How might this modality affect a preemie-mother's mental wellness, particularly after a traumatic birth and the NICU experience?

References

American Music Therapy Association (AMTA). (2019). Retrieved July 17, 2019, from http://www.musictherapy.orgCheng, C. D., Volk, A. A., & Marini, Z. A. (2011). Supporting fathering through infant massage. *The Journal of Perinatal Education*, 20(4), 200–209. doi:10.1891/1058-243.doi:20.4.200

Courtney, J. A. (2015). *FirstPlay parent manual*. Boynton Beach, FL: Developmental Play & Attachment Therapies.

Courtney, J. A., Velasquez, M., & Bakai Toth, V. (2017). FirstPlay® infant massage storytelling: Facilitating corrective touch experiences with a teenage mother and her abused infant. In J. A. Courtney & R. D. Nolan (Eds.), *Touch in child counseling and play therapy: An ethical and clinical guide* (pp. 48–62). New York, NY: Routledge.

Feldman, R., & Bakermans-Kranenburg, M. J. (2017). Oxytocin: a parenting hormone. *Current Opinion in Psychology*, 15, 13–18. https://doi.org/10.1016/j.copsyc.2017.02.011

Felitti, V. J., Anda, R. F., Nordenberg, D., Williamson, D. F., Spitz, A. M., Edwards, V., Marks, J. S. (1998). Relationship of childhood abuse and household dysfunction to many of the leading causes of death in adults: The adverse childhood experiences (ACE) study. *American Journal of Preventive Medicine*, 14, 245–248. Retrieved July 18, 2019from: https://www.ncbi.nlm.nih.gov/pubmed/9635069

Forcada-Guex, M., Borghini, A., Pierrehumbert, B., Ansermet, F., & Muller-Nix, C. (2011). Prematurity, maternal posttraumatic stress and consequences on the mother–infant relationship. *Early Human Development*, 87(1), 21–26. doi:10.1016/j.earlhumdev.2010. 09. 006

Hallin, A., Bengtsson, H., Frostell, A. S., & Stjernqvist, K. (2011). The effect of extremely preterm birth on attachment organization in late adolescence. *Child: Care, Health and Development*, 38(2), 196–203. doi:10.1111/j.1365-2214.2011.01236.x

Jefferies, A. (2012). Kangaroo care for the preterm infant and family. *Paediatrics & Child Health*, 17(3), 141–143. doi:10.1093/pch/17. 3. 141

Levine, T. A., Grunau, R. E., Mcauliffe, F. M., Pinnamaneni, R., Foran, A., & Alderdice, F. A. (2014). Early childhood neurodevelopment after intrauterine growth restriction: A systematic review. *Pediatrics*, 135(1), 126–141. doi:10.1542/peds.2014-1143

Linden, D.W., Paroli, E.T., & Doron, M.W. (2010). *Preemies* (2nd ed.). New York, NY: Gallery Books.

Loewy, J., Stewart, K., Dassler, A., Telsey, A., & Homel, P. (2013). The effects of music therapy on vital signs, feeding, and sleep in premature infants. *Pediatrics*, 131(5), 902–918. doi:10.1542/peds.2012–1367d

Mantis, I., & Stack, D. M. (2018). The functions of mutual touch in full-term and very low-birthweight/preterm infant-mother dyads: Associations with infant affect and emotional availability during face-to-face interactions. *International Journal of Comparative Psychology*, 31. Retrieved July 27, 2019 from: https://escholarship.org/content/qt62x2k310/qt62x2k310.pdf?t=piy33l&nosplash=33ea8d7c6a5daad3c48f613ed26b14d6

March of Dimes. (2013, October). Long-term health effects of premature birth. Retrieved July 17, 2019, from http://www.marchofdimes.org/complications/long-term-health-effects-of-premature-birth.aspx

Martin, J. A., Hamilton, B. E., & Osterman, M. J. (2018, August). *Births in the United States, 2017* [PDF]. Hyattsville: U.S. Department of Health and Human Services.

Meyer, D. (2011). Neuroplasticity as an explanation for the attachment process in the therapeutic relationship. Retrieved from http://counselingoutfitters.com/vistas/vistas11/Article_52.pdf

National Institute of Child Health and Human Development (NICHD). (2017, January 31). What are the risk factors for preterm labor and birth? Retrieved July 17, 2019, from http://www.nichd.nih.gov/health/topics/preterm/conditioninfo/who_risk

Pagni, A. M., Kellar, S., & Rood, M. (2017). Effects of kangaroo care on procedural pain in preterm infants: A systemic review. *Honors Research Projects*, 441, 1–39. Retrieved from http://ideaexchange.uakron.edu/honors_research_projects/441

Purdy, I. B., Craig, J. W., & Zeanah, P. (2015). NICU discharge planning and beyond: Recommendations for parent psychosocial support. *Journal of Perinatology*, 35(S1). doi:10.1038/jp.2015.146

Schore, A. N. (2012). *The science of the art of psychotherapy*. New York, NY: Norton.

Standley, J. (2012). Music therapy research in the NICU: An updated meta-analysis. *Neonatal Network*, 31(5), 311–316. doi:10.1891/0730-0832. 31. 5. 311

The Children's Healing Institute (2019). Retrieved July 18, 2019, from http://www.childrenshealinginstitute.org

World Health Organization (2017, November 17). What is a preterm baby? Retrieved July 17, 2019, from https://www.who.int/features/qa/preterm_babies/en/

Part V

Evidence-Based Infant Mental Health Models that Utilize Play Therapy Practices

Using the Healing Power of Relationships to Support Change in Young Children Exposed to Trauma

Application of the Child–Parent Psychotherapy Model

Harleen Hutchinson

Introduction

Winnicott says it best when he stated that "there is no such thing as a baby ... if you set out to describe a baby, you will find you are describing a baby and someone" (Winnicott, 1964). This means that a baby does not function as a blank slate, but in context of relationships with others. Therefore, when these relationships become strained due to trauma or toxic stress that impacts young children's lives, these relational bonds are severed, creating a rupture in the parent–child relationship (Schore, 2001). Osofsky (2011) contends that "The ghosts of childhood that remain with adult women as they enter into relationships with their own infants must be called forth from the unconscious and invited into the treatment context to facilitate healing and change" (p. 215). When addressing the impact of intergenerational transmission of trauma, it is important to treat the parent–child relationship in order to strengthen the attachment bond, while providing a healthy and safe environment for parents to heal and become a "good-enough mother."

Overview of Child–Parent Psychotherapy

Child–Parent Psychotherapy (CPP) (Lieberman & Van Horn, 2008), is an evidence-based relationship intervention to help young children, birth to five years old, and their caregivers after exposure to trauma (Lieberman, Ghosh Ippen, & Van Horn, 2015). CPP is based on the premise that young children function within the context of caregiving relationships. According to Winnicott (1964):

> Having reached the child, we try to look at his world with him, and to help him sort out his feelings about it, to face the painful things and

discover the good things. Then we try to consolidate the positive things in the child and in his world, and to help him make the most of his life.

(pp. 46–57)

During these dyadic sessions, play is used as a modality to help parents understand how their children internalize feelings and unconscious emotions are expressed. Piaget (1951) describes this as "A way of bridging the gap between child's inner world and the reality of the world outside" (p. 147). CPP is divided into two phases: (1) the Assessment and Engagement Phase; and (2) the Intervention and Termination Phase.

Assessment and Engagement Phase

During the assessment and engagement phase, the clinician works closely in establishing a trusting relationship with the caregiver to gather information that will be the driving force of the treatment process. This process also helps the clinician gain insights in helping the parents develop an awareness and understanding into how the trauma has affected the child. In doing so, the clinician utilizes the *Life Stressor Checklist Index-Revised* (Wolfe et al., 1996) which is an intensive trauma instrument that focuses on trauma from a developmental life span perspective. This instrument helps the clinician gain insights into the intergenerational aspect of the caregiver's trauma in order to help the caregiver understand its impact on the child's level of functioning. Another important tool that is employed is the *Working Model of the Child Interview* (Zeanah, Benoit, & Barton, 1986). This tool is a semi-structured interview that includes a series of questions and probes that allows the clinician to help parents reflect on their own upbringing and how it has impacted their perception of parenting and their view of the child. This tool also allows the clinician to employ two interventions that are important to the process: "Ghosts in the Nursery" and "Angels in the Nursery" (Fraiberg, Adelson, & Shapiro, 1975; Lieberman, Padron, Van Horn, & Harris, 2005).

In gathering information from the child's perspective, several instruments are utilized to capture both developmental concerns and issues relating to the child's exposure to trauma that have affected the attachment relationship. These instruments are the *Traumatic Events Screening Inventory-Parent Report Revised* (Ghosh Ippen et al., 2002), which assesses trauma exposure in the child and its impact on the child's behavior; *The Ages and Stages Questionnaire* (ASQ:SE and ASQ:3) (Squires, Twombly, Bricker, & Potter, 2009) are both developmental screening tools that are also utilized to capture developmental risk factors that may have impacted the child as a result of the child's trauma exposure. The child is also observed in the natural environment, home, or preschool, to address the level of functioning. Additionally, *The Crowell Assessment* (Crowell & Feldman, 1988; Heller et al., 1998) is utilized to assess the parent–child relationship and is an important observation tool that was developed to be used to assess parental interactions during playful and stressful times in order to determine the quality of the attachment relationship between the child and the caregiver. In this procedure, parents are provided with a series of instructions and the dyad interaction is observed behind a two-way mirror. The observation consists of play, structured tasks, and a brief separation and reunion phase. This procedure helps set the foundation for the feedback session, which often provides information to the caregiver regarding their affect and attunement towards the child during the tasks provided. During this process, reflective questions are asked to help the parents wonder as they try to keep the baby in mind (Fonagy et al., 1991). Viewing of video clips during the feedback session helps parents understand the child's perspective, as well as helping them view the child through a different lens, based on the impact of the traumatic experience (Schecter et al., 2006).

Intervention and Termination Phase

During the intervention and treatment phase, the goal of CPP is to the help the child build a relationship with his or her caregivers. Play is utilized as a modality to address various issues such as helping the child to engage in developmentally appropriate play activities with caregivers, helping the parents prioritize safety within the relationship with their child, increasing the parent's understanding of their child's behavior and/or functioning when they become triggered by trauma reminders, and helping the parent and child improve affect regulation. In the termination phase of CPP, the clinician helps prepare the parent and child for termination through planning, discussing their progress throughout the treatment process, and in helping the parents prepare for their transition from therapy by identifying positive ways of building on strengths learned throughout the experience.

Case of Ariel

The following case study will illustrate how CPP was used in treating the parent–child relationship. The case study highlights the importance of the parent–child relationship to repair the rupture that has affected the relationship. All identifying information has been changed to protect confidentiality.

Presenting Problem

Athena is a 38-year-old Portuguese female, of Cuban descent, and her daughter, Ariel, is 12 months old. They were referred by the Early Childhood Court, through her dependency case manager, for CPP, as Ariel was removed from her care due to exposure to domestic violence. Ariel was first placed in foster care and then placed with her maternal grandmother. CPP was recommended to help Athena address her extensive trauma background and to aid in the reunification process with Ariel.

Family and Background Information

Athena described a long trauma history from the age of five years to 21. She was sexually abused around the age of five by a family friend till she was 11 years. She described witnessing the separation of her stepfather leaving her mother when she was 12 years old, and indicated that during his departure from the home, he often visited with her siblings, but neglected her during those visits. The abandonment and rejection she experienced led to her involvement with alcohol. Her continued negative life experiences resulted in her use of opioids, which led to her addiction. In her early twenties, she described giving birth to her first child, even though she continued to struggle with substances. Shortly after, she gave birth to a second child. Her two children were eventually removed from her care and placed in the custody of her mother. She described numbing the pain by resorting to drugs. During these challenges, she entered eight substance abuse treatment facilities but continued to struggle with drugs, resulting in her being arrested 38 times. While incarcerated, she discovered that she was pregnant with her fourth child, in addition to being diagnosed with breast cancer. These painful experiences became difficult for Athena to accept but she was determined not to lose her last child to the system. After her release from jail, she was placed in residential treatment, as her daughter was placed in the custody of her mother. In the midst of her treatment, she was given a great opportunity to heal the intergenerational cycle of her trauma by participating in the Early Childhood Court. This court is a problem-solving program that helps parents to heal the intergenerational cycle of their trauma by addressing its impact on the attachment relationship with their child.

Setting

At the time of the initial treatment, Athena was residing in a residential substance abuse facility, due to her extensive substance abuse history. Ariel was not residing with her at that time, although Athena was able to maintain weekly supervised visitation on weekends. These visits were supervised by her dependency case manager. During this period, CPP weekly sessions began in an outpatient clinic setting.

Intervention and Treatment Phase

Treatment goals were discussed with Athena during the feedback stage of the assessment to help her recognize areas in the attachment relationship that she felt had caused a rupture (Slade, 2007). In helping Athena view the video observation during the feedback session, it was the intention that it will would provide her with insights into her own struggles with substances, and her trauma issues that had affected her overall ability to become emotionally available in the relationship with Ariel (Schecter et al., 2006). In doing so, the clinician utilized the "triangle" (see Figure 12.1) to help name and identify those things that were traumatic to Ariel, such as her mother's departing and returning, and her parents' constant loud and angry voices, and to link those events to her behaviors and fears, in order to help heal the trauma that Ariel experienced (Lieberman, Ghosh Ippen, & Van Horn, 2015). Excerpts from the recorded interactions were discussed, utilizing a reflective stance, to help Athena recognize her strength during the interaction, as well as areas that were challenging to her as a parent (Stern, 1995).

Initial Phase (Sessions 1–6)

Ariel initially presented as a very quiet and shy infant, she rarely smiled, even when modeling was provided by the clinician. Her mother was encouraged to practice modeling those behaviors to her to increase affect regulation. During the first session, the clinician utilized the triangle model (Lieberman, Ghosh Ippen, & Van Horn, 2015) as a springboard to explaining the trauma narrative to the mother and the child (see Figure 12.1).

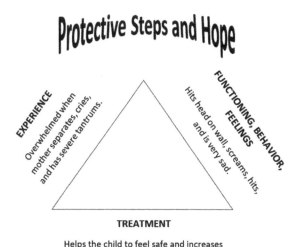

Figure 12.1 Introducing Ariel to Child–Parent Psychotherapy.
Used with permission from the authors, Lieberman, Ghosh Ippen, & Van Horn (2015).

Below is an excerpt from the first session with Athena and Ariel:

Therapist: I am so glad that you both are here today, how are you doing today Ariel?

(*Ariel stares at therapist, then looks at mom.*)

Therapist: Mom, how about you, how are you doing today since we last met at the feedback session?

Athena: I am a little nervous, the feedback session has allowed me to see how my baby is functioning as a result of what she has been exposed to. I feel so bad that I put her through this, I can't believe it. I didn't realize that they are seeing, hearing and taking in things that we do. I am willing to help my baby but I really don't think I have any trauma issues right now, even though the judge keeps telling me that I have to address my trauma issues before the healing process starts in order to get my baby back.

Therapist: That sounds very scary and overwhelming for you and I am glad that you are sharing your honest feelings. My job here is to help Ariel and you work through those underlying feelings that may have affected the relationship to ensure that you both are able to rebuild trust, and safety in your relationship.

Athena: I just don't see how we are going to do that.

Therapist: I certainly understand your concerns, it's a long process and I will be guiding you throughout your journey. One of the first thing that we need to do is validate Ariel's thoughts and emotions based on what she has been exposed to, so she knows that you understand and will try your best to always keep her safe. Are you okay to begin?

Athena: Yes, I am a little nervous.

Therapist: It is okay to be nervous; I am here for you and Ariel. Ariel, your mommy told me that you have heard and seen some really bad things that daddy said and did that she is concerned about, because when daddy yells at her and hits her it has made you sad—made you cry and become scared. All little kids who have seen and heard really bad things happen to their mommies get scared and afraid. It is my job to help you and your mommy work through the bad things that you saw and heard, so you will not be scared anymore, and mommy will keep you safe.

Athena: And I love you so much that I will not allow anyone to hurt you or mommy.

(*Ariel looks at mom, looks at therapist, and turns to play with toys.*)

(*Mom reaches for Ariel to comfort her.*)

(*Ariel walks towards the wall and begins to bang her head on the wall.*)

Athena: I wonder why she is doing that, she does the same thing at home.

Therapist: Sometimes, that is babies' way of communicating their pain through their behavior. What is it like for you when you see her doing that at home?

Athena: I get scared and I feel helpless because I don't know what she is thinking, so I actually yell at her and tell her not to bang her head on the wall.

(*Ariel looks at mom, then returns to banging her head on the wall.*)

Therapist: As we continue the sessions, we will begin to make meaning of what she is trying to tell us. One question that I have is, has she ever been directly exposed to the act of her father hitting you?

Athena: No, she was always in the other room.

Therapist: Sometimes when we think babies are not hearing and seeing us, they are, it's just that they do not have the language to communicate their needs and wants.

Athena: I am pretty sure that she did not see anything.

Therapist: Mom, I liked the way you comforted Ariel today, it tells her that you do care about her and will always do your best to keep her safe.

Middle Phase (Sessions 7–13)

As the therapy progressed, Ariel began to demonstrate an increased level of comfort in the therapy room. She continued to maintain close proximity to her mother, but at times would go outside the play and return to her mother, as if seeking validation (Ainsworth, Blehar, Waters, & Wall, 1978).

Figure 12.2 Keeping the baby's emotional well-being in mind.
Source: ©Istockphoto.com/Atikinka2

Athena tried hard in learning how to read Ariel's cues and helped her to verbalize her thoughts more openly. When Ariel became dysregulated during difficult times as Athena began to share her painful story, Athena demonstrated an increased level of awareness as she provided Ariel with comfort to help regulate her emotions (Van der Kolk, 2003). This type of comfort became so familiar to Ariel that she began asking for a hug when she felt dysregulated (Bowlby, 1969). Athena continued to be provided with a consistent level of praise during her response to Ariel. Athena appeared to be better able to keep Ariel's thoughts and feelings in mind, and help Ariel reflect on those feelings.

Advanced Phases of Treatment (Sessions 14–20)

By the 14th session, Ariel continued to demonstrate the behavior of hitting her head on the wall. Athena's level of concern began to increase to worrisome feelings as she discussed how these behaviors often trigger her. The clinician asked Athena what about Ariel's behavior that triggers her. Athena spoke about her own pain of receiving punches in her head from Ariel's father. During the session, as Ariel proceeded towards the wall to bang her head, the clinician used this opportunity as a port of entry with Ariel and Athena. As I wondered with Athena what Ariel might be telling us, Athena became more concerned. The clinician used the intervention, "speaking for the baby" (Carter, Osofsky, & Hann, 1991) and replied to Athena, "I feel no pain when I bang my head on the wall mommy because when I saw daddy hitting you, it made me angry as I watched." Athena began to cry, then reached over to Ariel and gave her a hug. They both began to cry as Athena consoled Ariel and told her how sorry she was for not protecting her and allowing daddy to hit her in her head (Tronick et al., 1978). As this critical moment transpired, the clinician reached for Athena's feelings to explore how she felt about what had just occurred (Fonagy et al., 1991). Athena cried and shared her feelings of shame and embarrassment as she spoke about not knowing how much young children are absorbing and internalizing their emotions in the absence of their parents not knowing (Bowlby, 1969). As the session progressed, it became clear that Ariel felt that her pain was acknowledged and understood by her mother. Ariel discontinued banging her head during the sessions, moving on from session 16 forward. This excerpt demonstrates how rupture in the parent–child relationship, due to trauma, can impede progress, unless the rupture is recognized and acknowledged.

Final Phase (Sessions 20–38)

The therapist and Athena worked very hard in improving the attachment relationship with Ariel by first helping Athena establish a consistent level of trust and safety in their relationship. Play therapy continued to be utilized to help Athena and her mother facilitate verbal communication. Athena was better able to recognize and identify the various developmental progression that Ariel experienced.

Treatment Completion

Athena and Ariel completed treatment successfully after 38 sessions of CPP intervention, over the course of 10 months. Throughout the course of treatment, Athena was able to reflect on her overall traumatic experiences and their connection and impact on the parent–child relationship with Ariel. She became more empowered in prioritizing safety within the relationship with Ariel, in addition to recognizing her own trauma triggers. Athena was better able to develop a new level of independence as she was able to obtain her own apartment, and with Ariel she rekindled the strained relationships with her two other children, who were ages 10 and 12 years at that time. Athena's work has allowed her to reflect on those important relationship within her family that had been ruptured. One relationship that became important for Athena was her relationship with her own biological mother. Athena's relationship had ruptured with her mother for nine years due to Athena's substance use, which led to lack of contact. Due to her efforts in treatment, she was able to work through the trauma of those painful relationship and make amends (Lyons-Ruth, Bronfman, & Alwood, 1999). At the time of the case, Athena was enrolled in a local community College as a paralegal, obtaining grades of "A's", while she held a part-time job cleaning houses.

During a discussion with Athena to help her reflect on her progress, she conveyed the following in this excerpt from the final session:

> Therapist: You have worked so hard to repair your relationship with Ariel and other important persons in your life. I have watched you grow throughout this journey and seen the many thorns that you had to work through. Tell me what has that journey been like for you?
>
> Athena: It has been a very rocky, scary and lonely road to travel. I had given up hope of a future but when I came in the system this time around, Ariel gave me the motivation to fight harder. But even though she gave me that motivation, I still was not at that place where I needed to be until I was able to come face to face with my demons, that demon who took a whole of me.
>
> Therapist: As I hear you share your thoughts, I can sense the very essence of the pain that you endured, and it sounds as if those demons have allowed you to reflect on your past trauma to fully understand the healing process, moving forward. What has that been like for you?
>
> Athena: My reality became real when I came face-to-face with my "pimp" on the city bus. He approached me and tried to convince me to work but it struck me real hard because for the very first time I was

sober and able to clearly see the kind of men that I chose over my kids. I tried hard to tell him that I don't do those things no more but he didn't believe me and tried to offer me a huge sum of money. As the bus approached my stop, I ran, and I cried. For the very first time, I realized that I needed to work through my pain and past trauma to fully heal. He made me realize that after all these years, that I have been putting a band aid on my pain. I have been arrested thirty-eight times and I have been in residential care for at least eight times, but I had never addressed my past trauma. I thank God for that day because it made me realize how deep my pain was. All those years, I have been avoiding addressing my trauma, but I did not realize how using substances have allowed me to put a band-aid on my life. Each time I became high, I was not available emotionally to meet Ariel's needs. Now, as I reflect on my progress, I am better able to understand her emotions and read her cues more readily. Had I had this therapy when my two girls were removed from my care, and my rights terminated, life would have been completely different. I just thank God for this opportunity. Every substance abusing mother should be given this opportunity to experience this therapy.

Therapist: And I thank you so much for allowing me to create that holding environment, that safe and honest place, where you felt safe doing the work. I know that this work is difficult and that you really worked hard in giving it your best, and in sharing those ghosts, but in spite of those ghosts, I am so proud that you were able to see the hope of a brighter future.

Athena: I thank you so much for being patient with me and not giving up on me, especially my judge, she saw something in me that I never saw. I have learned to be fully present when I am with Ariel now. I am better able to read her cues.

(*Ariel walks over and gives mom a hug.*)

Athena: I love you baby and I will always keep you safe.

During the termination of treatment, Athena was encouraged to maintain a consistent level of positive familial support system, utilize her sponsor, and reach out when help is needed. She was praised for her overall efforts and risk in sharing those sacred moments that contributed to her treatment progress.

Reflective Supervision: Presence and the Therapeutic Use of Self

During CPP with parents, one of the core components of this treatment is reflective supervision. Reflective supervision is a distinct field from clinical supervision, in that it helps the clinician to give credence to the various relationships, such as the one between the clinician and the supervisor, between the clinician and the parent, and between the parent and the child, to gain a deeper understanding into how these relationships affect one another (Weatherston, Weigand, & Weigand, 2010). In order for the reflective process to be successful, the relationship formed must be trusting, predictable, consistent, and regular. During these encounters, clinicians examine their own thoughts and feelings while exploring the parallel process. When working with a reflective supervisor, the supervisor can provide a holding environment for the supervisee to help contain and reflect on a wide range of emotions that the child and parent present.

The clinician is faced with many emotions that often become overwhelming at times due to the complexities of the parent's trauma, substance histories, and its impact on the child. However, when the clinician, with the help of the supervisor, is able to listen, wonder along with the client, remain in the present and create a safe holding environment, the clinician is able to recognize and reflect on emotions and thoughts that help to facilitate gradual healing (Parlakian, 2001). This also helps the clinician to make meaning of the family's story and its impact on the parent–child relationship (Watson, Harrison, Hennes, & Harris, 2016). The supervisor's keen sense of perception helps the clinician to recognize the role that her own thoughts and feelings play within the therapeutic relationship. In doing so, it is important for the clinician to recognize how to keep the baby in mind, while trying to balance the perspectives of the relationship. Therefore, a critical component in doing this work is to ensure that reflective supervision is part of the healing process which helps to prevent losing perspective of the relationship.

Reflective supervision during this case has allowed the clinician to ponder along with Athena in trying to understand her perspectives, while holding her thoughts and feelings as it relates to her need to be a "good enough mother" (Pawl, 1995). It was during those difficult moments of reflective supervision that clinicians can wander along the path along with a parent to fully understand the journey, hold the story and most importantly, keep the child's story in mind.

Closing Comment

This case demonstrates the link between the past and the present throughout the course of treatment with a mother, and her extensive ghosts. The Infant Mental Health clinician helped the mother to make meaning of her memories to better understand how her past experiences have impacted her relationship with Ariel. In therapeutic work with families,

> the ghosts, we know, represent the repetition of the past in the present. We are also the beneficiaries of the method Freud developed for recovering the events of the past and undoing the morbid effects of the past in the present.
>
> (Fraiberg, 1980, p. 166)

At the close of treatment, Ariel and Athena were securely bonded and Athena demonstrated delight and pleasure in her daughter. They both finally understood each other. Athena was able to engage in a new-found dance with Ariel, giving new meaning to her role as a "good enough mother" and accepting what this all means to her. This experience has allowed Athena to reparent herself to see Ariel through a different lens, one that she had not experienced with her prior children. Although residues of her past (ghosts) (Fraiberg, Adelson, & Shapiro, 1975) remain, she is able to recognize those triggers and disown aspects of the baggage they have placed on her and Ariel, while embracing those angels (Lieberman, Padron, Van Horn, & Harris, 2005) in the present as part of her continued journey through healing. This work reminds clinicians that change is possible when a safe, nurturing, non-judgmental, culturally sensitive and caring approach to relationship-based interventions is employed.

Discussion Questions

1 Describe the core components of Child–Parent Psychotherapy and its impact on the attachment relationship.
2 Discuss the importance of creating a safe, nurturing, and holding environment when addressing trauma within the parent–child relationship.
3 Discuss the importance of reflective supervision when working with clients with complex trauma challenges.

References

Ainsworth, M. D. S., Blehar, M. C., Waters, E., & Wall, S. (1978). *Patterns of attachment: A psychological study of the strange situation.* Hillsdale, NJ: Erlbaum.

Bowlby, J. (1969). *Attachment and loss*: Vol. 1. *Attachment.* New York: Basic Books.

Carter, S., L., Osofsky, J.D., & Hann, D. M. (1991). Speaking for the baby: A therapeutic intervention with adolescent mothers and their infants . *Infant Mental Health Journal*, 12(4), 291–301. Retrieved November 2018 from: https://doi.org/10.1002/1097-355(199124)12:4%3C291:AID-IMHJ2280120403%3E3.0.CO;2-3

Crowell, J. A., & Feldman, S.S. (19). Mothers internal model of relationships and children's behavioral and developmental status: A study of the mother child interaction . *Child Development*, 59, 1273–1285. doi:10.2307/1130490.

Fonagy, P., Steele, M., Steele, H., Moran, G.S., & Higgitt, A. (1991). The capacity for understanding mental states. The reflective self in parent and child and its significance for security of attachment. *Infant Mental Health Journal*, 12(3), 201–218. Retrieved November 2018 from https://doi.org/10.1002/1097-0355(199123)12:3%3C201:AID-IMHJ2280120307%3E3.0.CO;2-7

Fraiberg, S., (1980). *Clinical studies in infant mental health.* New York: Basic Books.

Fraiberg, S., Adelson, E., & Shapiro, V. (1975). Ghosts in the nursery: A psychoanalytic approach to the problems of impaired infant-mother relationships . *Journal of the American Academy of Child Psychiatry*, 14, 387–421. Retrieved November 2018 from https://doi.org/10.1016/S0002-7138(09)61442–61444

Ghosh Ippen, C., Ford, L.Racusin, R., Acker, M., Bosquet, M., Rogers, K.*et al.* (2002). *Traumatic Events Screening Inventory-Parent Report Revised*. San Francisco: University of California, San Francisco Early Trauma Network. Retrieved from https://www.ptsd.va.gov/professional/assessment/child/tesi.asp

Lieberman, A. F., Ghosh Ippen, C., & Van Horn, P. (2015). *Don't hit my mommy! A manual for child-parent psychotherapy with young children exposed to violence and other trauma* (2nd ed.). Washington DC: Zero to Three Press. Retrieved November 15, 2018 from https://www.zerotothree.org/resources/356-don-t-hit-my-mommy

Liberman, A. F., & Van Horn, P. (2008). *Psychotherapy with infants and young children: Repairing the effects of stress and trauma on early attachment*. New York, NY: Guilford Press.

Lieberman, A. F., Padron, E., Van Horn, P., & Harris, W. W. (2005). Angels in the nursery: The intergenerational transmission of benevolent parental influences, *Infant Mental Health Journal*, 26, 504–520. Retrieved November 2018 from https://www.researchgate.net/publication/2753541 Angels_in_the_nursery-The_intergenerational_transmisison_of_benevolent_Parental_influences

Osofsky, J. D. (2011). *Clinical work with traumatized young children*. New York, NY: Guilford Press.

Lyons-Ruth, K., Bronfman, E., & Alwood, G. (1999). A relational diathesis model of hostile-helpless states of mind: Expressions in mother-infant interaction. In J. Solomon & C. George (Eds.), *Attachment disorganization* (pp. 33–70). New York: Guilford Press. Retrieved November 2018 from: https://www.researchgate.net/publiction/309042835_A_relational_diathesis_model_of_hostile-helpless_states_of-mind_Expressions_in_mother-infant_interaction.

Parlakian, R. (2001). *Look, listen and learn: Reflective supervision and relationship-based work*. Washington, DC: Zero to Three Press. Retrieved November 2018 from: https://www.researchgate.net/publication/234626878_Look_Listen_and_Learn_Reflective_Supervision_and_Relationship-Based-Work.

Pawl, J. (1995). The therapeutic relationship as human connectedness: Being held in another's mind. *Zero to Three Journal*, 15(4), 3–5. https://files.eric.ed.gov/fulltext/ED385364.pdf

Pawl, J. & St. John, M. (1998). How you are is as important as what you do in making a Positive difference for infants, toddlers and their families. *Zero to Three Journal*, 18(16), 34.

Piaget, J. (1951). *Play, dreams and imitation in childhood*, London: Routledge and Kegan Paul.

Schecter, D. S., Myers, M. M., Brunelli, S. A., Coates, S.W., Zeanah, C. H., Liebowitz, M. R. (2006). Traumatized mothers can change their minds about their toddlers: Understanding how a novel use of videofeedback supports positive change of maternal attributions. *Infant Mental Health Journal*, 27(5), 429–447. doi:10.1002/imhj.20101.

Schore, A. (2001). Effects of a secure attachment relationship on right brain development, affect regulation, and infant mental health. *Infant Mental Health Journal*, 22(1–2), 7–66. Retrieved from http://citeseerx.ist.psu.edu/viewdoc/summary?doi=10.1.1.324.5612

Slade, A. (2007). Reflective parenting programs: Theory and development. *Psychoanalytic Inquiry*, 26(4), 640–657. Retrieved November 15, 2018 from http://reflectivecommunities.org/wp-content/Uploads/2015/03/Reflective_Parenting_Programs1.pdf

Squires, J., Twombly, E., Bricker, D., & Potter, L. (2009). *Ages and stages questionnaires*, (3rd ed.). Baltimore, MD: Paul Brookes Publishing.

Tronick, E., Als, H., Adamson, L., Wise, S., & Brazelton, T. B. (1978). Infant's response to entrapment between contradictory messages in face-to-face interaction. *Journal of the American Academy of Child and Adolescent Psychiatry*, 17, 1–13. Retrieved November 15, 2018 from: https://doi.org/10.1016/S0002-7138(09)62273–62271

Van der Kolk, B. A. (2003). Neurobiology of childhood trauma and abuse. *Child and Adolescent Psychiatric Clinics of North America*, 12(2), 293–317. Retrieved November 2018 from: https://doi.org/10.1016/S1056-4993(03)00003–00008

Watson, C., Harrison, M., Hennes, J., & Harris, M. (2016). Revealing "the space between." Creating an observation scale to understand infant mental health reflective supervision. *Zero to Three Journal*, 37(2), 14–21. Retrieved November 15, 2018 from: https://eric.ed.gov/?id=EJ1123774

Weatherston, D., Weigand, R., & Weigand, B. (2010). Reflective supervision: Supporting reflection as a cornerstone for competency. *Zero to Three Journal*, 31(2), 22–31. https://eric.ed.gov/?redir=http%3a%2f/2fmain.zerotothree.org%fsite%2fPageServer

Winnicott, D. W. (1964). *The child, the family, and the outside world*. London: Penguin.

Wolfe, J., Kimerling, R., Brown, P. J., Chrestman, K. R., & Levin, K. (1996). *Psychometric review of the life stressor checklist-revised*. Lutherville, MD: Sidran Press.

Zeanah, C., Benoit, D., & Barton, M. (1986). Working model of the child interview coding manual. *Child and Adolescent Psychiatric Clinics of North America*. doi:10.1037/t47439-000.

Chapter 13

Incorporating Play into Child–Parent Psychotherapy as an Intervention with Infants Exposed to Domestic Violence

Allison Golden and Veronica Castro

Introduction

It has been said that "the emotional quality of our earliest attachment experience is perhaps the single most important influence on human development" (Sroufe & Siegel, 2011). The relationship between an infant (children ages 0–3) and their parent (refers to infant's primary caregiver) shapes the internal and external experiences of that infant's life, from birth through adulthood. According to the Center on the Developing Child at Harvard University (2017), through serve-and-return interactions via timely, responsive, sensitive caregiving, an infant's brain begins to build neural pathways that set the stage for the infant's capacities to regulate emotion and behavior, engage in social relationships, learn, and develop. One of the most important mechanisms for serve-and-return interactions between parent and infant is play.

Early Childhood Trauma

Early childhood trauma can last a lifetime. When an infant experiences trauma, particularly when it is interpersonal in nature, it impacts the infant's developing brain; understanding of self, others and the world; academic success; and adult mental and physical health (Ludy-Dobson & Perry, 2010; Lieberman & Van Horn, 2008; Romano, Babchishin, Marquis, & Fréchette, 2015; Felitti, 2010). Neuroplasticity, the brain's capacity to reorganize in response to internal factors and the external environment (Shaffer, 2016), in the first few years of life, highlights the importance of early intervention to interrupt the negative impacts of trauma, and change the trajectory of an infant's current and future functioning.

John Bowlby (1982) recognized that the infant engages in heightened attachment behaviors toward the mother, such as seeking proximity, clinging, and crying, during times of stress or fear. When their mother is not present, either physically or emotionally, to provide the comfort and protection the infant is seeking, the infant is left to utilize whatever minimal coping skills they possess. This often results in aggression, withdrawal and/

or emotional dysregulation, all behaviors which may elicit negative reactions from the mother, further damaging the sense of trust the infant feels in the mother's ability to provide comfort and protection. As the parent–infant attachment is the foundation for brain development, infanthood mental health and long-term well-being, it follows that it is the focus of attention in the treatment of early childhood trauma.

Child–Parent Psychotherapy (CPP)

Child–Parent Psychotherapy is an approach that incorporates multiple the-oretical approaches including psychoanalytic, attachment, developmental and trauma theories, as well as techniques from cognitive behavioral and social learning therapies (Lieberman & Van Horn, 2008). This approach recognizes the attachment relationship between parent and infant as the basis for which infants create internal representations of themselves and others. It helps them to understand danger and safety and feel able to explore the world around them in order to develop capacities required for all areas of childhood development (Lieberman & Van Horn, 2008). Thus, CPP identifies the parent–infant relationship as the agent of change and the "client" in the therapeutic environment. This dyadic therapy focuses on repairing the negative impact of trauma on the parent–infant relationship, and the resulting behavioral and mental health difficulties of young children. It strives to strengthen the parent–infant relationship by renewing a sense of safety and trust in their attachment relationship.

Treatment utilizing CPP is completed in three phases: assessment and engagement; core intervention; and recapitulation and termination. The purpose of the assessment and engagement phase is to gain a better under-standing into the parent–infant relationship, presenting symptoms, and trauma history of both the infant and the parent. Additionally, goals during this phase are to determine sources of danger, promote safety and instill hope, and to create a treatment plan with the parent in which the trauma will be addressed through the parent–infant sessions. The core intervention in this phase is the creation of a "trauma frame" in which the parent begins to link the infant's symptoms and challenges with their traumatic experiences. And to create an environment that feels safe enough for the parent and infant to "speak the unspeakable" and tolerate difficult emotions in order to allow for relational repair (Lieberman, Ghosh Ippen, & Van Horn, 2015). During the core intervention phase, the trauma frame is introduced to the parent and the purpose for therapy is explained. Then through the words, behaviors, and experiences of the parent and infant individually, and the spontaneous inter-actions that present between them, the therapist looks for opportunities to intervene. These opportunities are known as "ports of entries" (Lieberman et al., 2015) where therapists utilize a variety of strategies in an effort to make ther-apeutic progress toward one of the CPP goals. The last phase of recapitulation and termination is focused on supporting the parent and infant to recognize the changes that occurred throughout sessions, helping the dyad prepare for and process the impending termination of services, as well as addressing how to maintain the gains made and manage challenges in the future.

As Child–Parent Psychotherapy is rooted in Infant–Parent Psychotherapy, one of the unique characteristics of this dyadic model is its acknowledgement and attention to the impact of intergenerational pathology, or as Fraiberg, Adelson, & Shapiro (1975) referred to it, as the parent's "ghosts in the nursery." Parent's experiences of childhood trauma may interfere with their ability to recognize or appropriately respond to their infant's need for care and protection (Lieberman et al., 2015), and often the infant's resulting traumatic stress behaviors act as triggers to the parent's repressed feelings of fear and helplessness (Fraiberg et al., 1975); thus initiating their own protective mechanisms. These protective mechanisms often result in parental behaviors of criticism, aggression, and withdrawal, furthering the infant's view of the parent as non-protective, and even dangerous. During parent–infant sessions, the CPP therapist is attuned to ways in which the parent's own history may be affecting their behaviors toward the infant, and may engage the parent in individual sessions to explore this further (Lieberman et al., 2015). CPP also recognizes the importance of the parent's "angels in the nursery" (Lieberman, Padron, Van Horn, & Harris, 2005); the experiences of love, safety, and security in the parent's childhood relationships. This expands the parent's ability to view their childhood experiences as a whole, and in turn, experience increases in self-esteem and hope for the future (Lieberman et al., 2015), thus promoting their use of similar positive parental behaviors toward their infant.

CPP has exhibited efficacy in both randomized controlled studies and longitudinal studies (Ciccehtti, Rogosch, & Toth, 2006; Toth, Rogosch, Manly, & Cicchetti, 2006; Lieberman et al., 2005; Lavi, Gard, Hagen, Van Horn, & Lieberman, 2015; Lieberman, Weston, & Pawl, 1991; Toth, Maughan, Manly, Spagnola, & Cicchetti, 2002) and is considered a research supported intervention for children ages 0–5 who have experienced trauma (The California Evidence-Based Clearinghouse for Child Welfare, 2006–2019).

Benefits of Parent–Infant Play in Infant Development

Play has been described as the "leading source of development" for children (Vygotsky, 2016/1966) and has been linked to increased brain development and executive functions, self-regulation, cognitive learning, literacy and language skills, physical health, social skills, and reduced behavioral challenges in children (Brown & Eberle, 2018; Milteer et al., 2012; Whitebread, 2010; Schore, 2012). Play in the parent–infant relationship not only produces benefits in a multitude of areas in children's development; it also strengthens the parent–infant relationship itself (Ginsberg et al., 2007). Receiving a parent's full attention and interest, provides infants with the message that they are important, loved, and accepted for who they are, which increases their self-esteem, competence, and their sense of relational safety. In times of breaks in attunement, play can assist in strengthening a repair, allowing the parent and infant opportunities to understand each other's experiences and connect through shared enjoyment (Olff et al., 2013). This process of repair is vital to the infant's understanding that the relationship can manage difficulties, which increases a sense of safety (Rees, 2007). Furthermore, parent–infant play, in which mothers provide affection and fathers provide stimulation, has neurobiological benefits for parents, increasing brain levels of oxytocin, which produces feelings of connectedness and stress reduction (Feldman, Gordon, Schneiderman, Weisman, & Zagoory-Sharon, 2010; Olff et al., 2013).

The Utilization of Play in CPP

Virgina Axline (1974) described play as an infant's "natural medium" and acknowledged the use of non-directive play therapy to provide an infant with opportunities to utilize play as a way to express feelings, so they may be brought out in the open in order to be released, understood and managed. Axline stated that infants need to feel free to express themselves fully and test out ideas, and require the adult participant to be accepting, understanding, and reflective in their observations, in order to allow the infant to better understand their experiences.

CPP also recognizes that infant's communication is most unrestricted through play, and therefore utilizes play as the primary modality during parent–infant sessions. Play is viewed as a vehicle for infants to tell their stories, experiment with realities, and express feelings freely. Play not only offers the opportunity for infants to describe their internal experiences, but allows for the infant to organize traumatic experiences and repair them by trying out different endings and gaining a sense of control over situations that once produced feelings of helplessness (Reyes & Lieberman, 2012). While the infant is playing, therapists work to support parents in witnessing their infants play and tolerating the stories that unfold. Play provides a port of entry for the therapist to act as a mediator, making meaning of an infant's symbolic expressions, so that the parents may better understand the impact of trauma on the infant and have an opportunity to offer acknowledgement, attunement, and empathy. One of the goals of CPP is for the parent to join the infant in play in an effort to co-construct a different, healthier meaning of the trauma. The therapist supports this endeavor, and then promotes the parent–infant relationship's capacity to move from enacting, to reflection and meaning making, to enjoyment in developmentally appropriate activities (Lieberman et al., 2015).

Domestic Violence in Early Childhood

Young children are exposed to domestic violence (DV) in a disproportionate number compared to older children (U.S. Department of Health and Human Services, 2010; Fantuzzo & Fusco, 2007, as cited in Lieberman et al., 2015). Such children are at a higher risk of experiencing physical abuse (Dong et al., 2004), internalizing and externalizing difficulties (Lewis et al., 2010) including Post-Traumatic Stress Disorder (Levendosky, Huth-Bocks, Semel, & Shapiro, 2002), poorer intellectual functioning (Huth-Bocks, Levendosky, & Semel, 2001), developmental regression (Gilbert, Bauer, Carroll, & Down, 2013), difficulties in forming adult relationships (Osofsky, 2003) and physical health complications (Graham-Berman & Seng, 2005).

In instances of domestic violence, the infant's parent is often either a victim or a perpetrator, leaving the infant to experience fear in isolation, as their need to seek protection is unmet, since the sources of protection become the sources of fear. Often, this leads to the infant wavering between approach toward and avoidance of the parent, torn between a desperate need for comfort and a simultaneous attempt to avoid danger (Lieberman, 2004). Young children exposed to DV often lose trust in their caregiver as a reliable presence, and in their ability to meet their needs, especially those related to safety (Lieberman et al., 2015). As a sense of safety is the bedrock of the parent–infant attachment, it follows that DV disrupts such a relationship. Furthermore, it has been suggested that internalizing and externalizing behavioral challenges exhibited by children who have been exposed to DV are mediated by parental stress (Huth-Bocks & Hughes, 2008). DV's impact on the parent–child attachment, and in turn, the child's functioning, make it imperative that it is a focus of intervention.

Although CPP has shown benefits for young children who've experienced multiple forms of early childhood trauma, it was initially designed as an intervention for young children exposed to DV, as it is considered an especially harmful form of trauma. In DV cases, the parent and infant unconsciously take on the alternating roles of the two parents involved in domestic violence, responding as both victim and perpetrator at varying times in their relationship, thus acting as triggers for each other's reactions to trauma, as they anticipate either aggression or victimization. When parents view their children's behavior from this standpoint, they often ascribe negative attributions to their infant, which may be internalized and impact their infant's understanding of themselves. The use of play in CPP offers parents and children exposed to DV an opportunity to explore danger/safety themes and co-construct a different understanding of the trauma, thus altering the distorted internal depiction that each have of the other, enhancing the parent's self-efficacy and capacity for protection of self and infant, and restoring the infant's trust in the parent as a protective figure (Lieberman et al., 2015).

and Veronica Castro

rianna

lem and Family Background

8-month old who was born in the United States and was the on-married parents in their early twenties of Hispanic descent. Her mother stated that Brianna met all her developmental milestones on time, but expressed concerns related to potential stressors that were impacting Brianna's functioning. Reportedly, Brianna witnessed verbal and physical altercations between her parents, and she often cried when near male figures, and became fussy during feeding and sleep routines.

Assessment and Engagement Phase

Brianna's trauma history revealed that during her time in utero, her parents often engaged in verbal arguments. Mother reported feeling depressed, stating that she cried often throughout pregnancy and felt "disconnected from the baby," missing the joy that often accompanies pregnancy. The arguments between her parents continued through to the start of treatment. Brianna's father frequently punched walls and threw objects, at times directed toward the mother. Mother's own trauma history showed that mother had witnessed domestic violence between her parents during her childhood. She also disclosed that her mother was verbally abusive and controlling.

When Brianna was approximately 7 months old, while being held in her mother's arms, her parents engaged in an argument, during which her father shoved her mother against the wall and chased Brianna and her mother outside the house, while throwing objects at them. A report was filed with the police and child welfare departments. Brianna had not seen her father since that incident.

Mother recognized Brianna's trauma, and expressed concern about what she had experienced. She stated that part of her reason for participating in therapy was an effort to seek assurance that her baby "would be alright." During observations, mother appeared to be very attentive to Brianna's needs, as she engaged with her in feeding, diaper changing, playing, and mutual smiling and laughter. However, when mother talked about negative emotions, such as when reflecting on her relationships with her own mother and Brianna's father, she became angry and agitated, and Brianna would cry. Mother appeared unaware of the impact of her affect on Brianna's behavior, and gave Brianna a pacifier when she cried. During the Working Model Interview, mother described Brianna as manipulative, demanding, loud, persistent, and frustrating. Despite these descriptions, their interactions did not portray a negative relationship.

During the feedback session, the structure of CPP and treatment goals were discussed. The therapist and mother connected Brianna's symptoms to her

trauma history. Mother displayed insight in relating Brianna'
male figures and raised voices as her anticipating a scary
acknowledged the importance of choosing non-violent partners
that supervised visits with Brianna's father were appropriate at the
agreed to allow the therapist to contact Brianna's father and invite
apy. Mother had entered the assessment phase with most of the afoi
insight, but formally discussing them appeared to help regulate her. Additionally,
mother recognized her own history and how it had shaped her view of relationships, and expressed fear that she would repeat her "mother's sins." Mother
agreed to engage in individual sessions with the therapist in order to openly
discuss these "ghosts in the nursery" with the therapist, as needed.

The therapist and mother discussed introducing the trauma narrative to
Brianna. Mother agreed that although Brianna was an infant, the trauma
would still be introduced, in the first dyadic session. Mother understood
that Brianna could pick up on tone, facial expression, and emotions in the
room while doing the introduction, and therefore agreed that mother would
communicate if she became overwhelmed, and a break would be given.

Treatment Goals

- Safety
- Introducing CPP to child and acknowledging the trauma
- Normalizing and understanding the symptoms of trauma
- Processing the impact of DV on a child
- Processing history to current relationships; furthering insight.

Post-Assessment Intervention Phase

During the first session, while Brianna was on her mother's lap, the therapist talked directly to her about how she had scary moments when her parents fought, but that things were different now and mommy wanted to keep
her safe. Mother appeared nervous, as evidenced by her restless body
movement and nervous smile, but after this introduction, she held Brianna
and hugged and kissed her. Brianna appeared regulated during this session.

During sessions, when speaking about Brianna's father and her mother,
mother would become agitated and Brianna would cry and appear irritable.
The therapist used "speaking for baby" and made statements about how
scary it was for Brianna for her mother to seem upset, since in the past
when mother was upset, big fights happened, and the importance of helping
Brianna understand that mother was just talking now, and she is safe.
Mother would regulate her tone and hold Brianna until she was calm.
Brianna would then smile and begin playing.

Mother entered the second session distressed and angry, stating that she
could only study at night while Brianna was sleeping, and Brianna continued

⌐⌐ be sleepless. As she shared her frustration, Brianna cried irritably on her blanket. The therapist normalized mother's frustration, stating, "You are trying so hard to study to benefit you and Brianna and it feels like the timing is never right with Brianna's needs, which can be frustrating and stressful." Mother stated, "Yes! Brianna is manipulative. I play all day with her and give her everything she needs and the moment I need something, like to study, she cries on purpose!" The therapist validated her feelings. Mother's breathing slowed, and her anger came down, and Brianna became regulated and began exploring toys.

The therapist commented on how prepared mother was with making sure Brianna had her blanket and toys to play with. Mother smiled but then quickly stated, "I don't always feel I am doing everything right." When the therapist inquired, mother mentioned the sleeping issue again. The therapist validated her efforts again, recognizing that mother appeared to need reassurance about her parenting capacity, as the feelings of not being good enough from her past experiences appeared to be present in her relationship with Brianna. Session ended with a game of peek-a-boo that seemed to recharge and energize the dyad as they both appeared to enjoy it, and the therapist hoped that it helped to change the distorted view mother had of herself as a parent.

Core Phase

Due to Brianna's age, many of the play interactions took place during daily interactions such as diaper change and bath time. This was important as much of Brianna's irritability happened during her daily routine, when mom yelled, or she heard a male voice. These instances reflected her past experience as Brianna interpreted these moments as dangerous.

During play, Brianna often used a toy phone, putting it to her face. The therapist would say, "mom, would you like to talk to Brianna on the phone?" Mother would get another toy phone and pretend to talk on it, while looking at Brianna. Brianna would laugh and initiate more, by looking at mother and mother would follow along. The therapist used this as a "port of entry" to encourage mother to talk to Brianna and share affectionate words. Mother would do so, and Brianna would smile and look at mother. Mother commented that Brianna was really listening to her. The therapist responded that Brianna, like mother, wants to be heard and talked to.

Another frequent play game was peek-a-boo with a blanket. It was simple and fun, and the therapist used it to highlight Brianna's desire to be near her mother and their enjoyment of each other, and to show Brianna that mother is always on the other side. This helped the mother to understand that Brianna was not manipulative, but desired to be with mother and emulate her.

As treatment progressed, mother became better able to regulate her emotions and in turn, Brianna's. Much of the focus was on helping mother connect her decisions and behaviors to the impact they had on Brianna.

Mother explored many of her past "ghosts" and was able to recognize how many of her fears for Brianna stemmed from her own experiences. She expressed fear that she is already down the same path as her mother, and Brianna will have the same life she did. The therapist used a lot of reframing, encouragement, empathy, and establishment of hope to support mother's progress. She also used her relationship with mother as the agent of change. When the mother felt heard, she was better able to hear Brianna.

Mother continued to worry that she was not a good enough mother and would repeat her mother's history. This worry arose when she began dating a new partner. The therapist and mother discussed the differences between herself and her own mother, and her desire to protect Brianna by not introducing her to any new partners unless the relationship became serious; something her mother did not shield her from. During this discussion, the therapist noted that mother continued to check in on Brianna, and she paused her discussions if Brianna needed attention. She became more conscious of her tone during times of aggravation. The therapist acknowledged the striking difference in her parenting of Brianna to what she had received. Though the therapist observed an improved demeanor in mother after this discussion, she continued to appear to struggle greatly with this, so the therapist encouraged her to seek her own individual therapy to openly discuss these topics.

Termination Phase

During this phase, the focus was on progress made and preparedness in the possible resurgence of symptoms during termination. The parent–child relationship had made many significant improvements, as mother became aware of Brianna's needs and no longer interpreted typical behaviors with negative attributions. The mother continued to have healthy boundaries with Brianna's father, and did not engage in maladaptive behaviors with him or his family. Though dad was invited several times to sessions, he never came. At the point of termination, the father had unsupervised visits with Brianna. The mother stated it was going well and trust was being rebuilt with regards to co-parenting, and she appeared very empowered with the acceptance of a new job and beginning school full time. However, she continued to struggle with the idea of being a good enough mother, but she never sought individual therapy, despite the therapist's continued recommendation.

Closing Comments

Brianna participated in 19 sessions over a 6-month period. Throughout treatment, Brianna's mother exhibited improved insight, and a desire to care for Brianna in a manner she never received, but she struggled at times due to fears of becoming like her own mother. Brianna had warranted fears around men and yelling, as her experiences of these things were related to danger and unpredictability. Though the mother could make this connection, she struggled to connect how her own dysregulation related to her difficult relationships (i.e. Brianna's father and her mother) impacted Brianna. The therapist focused on co-regulating with the mother so she could then co-regulate with Brianna. The therapist listened to the mother without judgement and empathized with her so she could feel heard, understood, and soothed. When the mother was regulated, the therapist could then highlight strengths and gently redirect her to Brianna's, using play process. The use of the phone in play was symbolic as it represented communication, and Brianna's desire to feel heard and important, the same way mother needed this. Brianna had lived through scary moments and she needed to be acknowledged and then assured that she was safe and loved. The game of peek-a-boo was also symbolic in many ways with Brianna. It reminded the therapist of both elements of fun and anxiety and was used to show Brianna that mother was always there, even during times of fear.

Discussion Questions

1 Often when clinicians work with families in CPP, they experience their own countertransference toward the parent for their role in the trauma experience, or toward the dyad as a whole. What reactions did you have toward the parent, child and/or the relationship as you were reading the case study? How might these reactions impact your work with this family and what would you need to do to prevent your reactions from interfering in the therapeutic process?

2 In CPP the client is considered the relationship between the parent and child, and the clinician's relationship with the dyad is the agent of change. Reflect back on the vignette and discuss how this parallel process helped evoke change in the relationship between Brianna and her mom.

3 In the first phase of treatment, the clinician and the mother created a trauma narrative and then at the start of the second treatment phase, that narrative was shared with Brianna. Though Brianna was a pre-verbal baby, what do you think was the importance of stating the narrative in this manner? If you were the clinician in this case, how would you feel about this and what would your process be?

4 Reflect on the use of play as a modality in CPP throughout the case study. What meaning did Brianna's play reflect about her history and her relationship with her mom? How was play used to bridge Brianna and her mom's experiences and perception of each other?

References

Axline, V. M. (1974). *Play therapy*. New York, NY: Ballantine Books.

Bowlby, J. (1982). *Attachment and loss: Vol. 1* (2nd ed.). New York, NY: Basic Books.

Brown, S., & Eberle, M. (2018). A closer look at play. In T. Marks-Tarlow, M. Solomon, & D. J. Siegel, *Play & creativity in psychotherapy* (pp. 21–38). New York, NY: Norton. https://www.cebc4cw.org/topic/infant-and-toddler-mental-health-0-3/

Center on the Developing Child at Harvard University (2017). https://developing child.harvard.edu/science/key-concepts/serve-and-return

Cicchetti, D., Rogosch, F. A., & Toth, S. L. (2006). Fostering secure attachment in infants in maltreating families through preventative interventions. *Development and Psychopathology*, 18, 623–649. doi:10.10170S0954579406060329

Dong, M., Anda, R. F., Felitti, V. J., Dube, S. R., Williamson, D. F., Thompson, T. J., Loo, C. M., & Giles, W. H. (2004). The interrelatedness of multiple forms of child abuse, neglect, and household dysfunction. *Child Abuse & Neglect*, 28, 771–784.

Fantuzzo, J., & Fusco, R. (2007). Children's direct exposure to types of domestic violence crime: A population-based investigation. *Journal of Family Violence*, 22, 543–552.

Feldman, R., Gordon, I., Schneiderman, I., Weisman, O., & Zagoory-Sharon, O. (2010). Natural variations in maternal and paternal care are associated with systematic changes in oxytocin following parent–infant contact. *Psychoneuroendocrinology*, 35, 1133–1141. doi:10.1016/j.psyneuen.2010. 01. 013

Felitti, V. (2010). Foreword. In A. Lanius, E. Vermetten & C. Pain (Eds.), *The impact of early life trauma on health and disease: The hidden epidemic*. Cambridge: Cambridge University Press.

Fraiberg, S., Adelson, E., & Shapiro, V. (1975). Ghosts in the nursery: A psychoanalytic approach to the problems of impaired infant-mother relationships. *Journal of the American Academy of Child & Adolescent Psychiatry*, 14(3), 387–421. doi:10.1016/S0002-7138(09)61442–61444

Gilbert, A. L., Bauer, N. S., Carroll, A. E., & Down, S. M. (2013). Child exposure to parental violence and psychological distress associated with delayed milestones. *Pediatrics*, 132(6), e1577–e1583. Retrieved from: https://www.ncbi.nlm.nih.gov/pmc/articles/PMC3838530/pdf/peds.2013-1020.pdf

Ginsburg, K. R., the American Academy of Pediatrics Committee on Communications, & the American Academy of Pediatrics Committee on Psychological Aspects of Child and Family Health (2007). The importance of play in promoting healthy child development and maintaining strong parent-child bonds. *Pediatrics*, 119, 182–191. doi:10.1542/peds.2006–2697

Graham-Bermann, S. A., & Seng, J. (2005). Violence exposure and traumatic stress symptoms as additional predictors of health problems in high-risk children. *Journal of Pediatrics*, 146(3), 349–354. doi:10.1016/j.jpeds.2004.10.065

Huth-Bocks, A. C., & Hughes, H. M. (2008). Parenting stress, parenting behavior, and children's adjustment in families experiencing intimate partner violence. *Journal of Family Violence*, 23, 243–251. doi:10.1007/s10896–10007–9148–9141

Huth-Bocks, A. C., Levendosky, A. A., & Semel, M. A. (2001). The direct and indirect effects of domestic violence on young children's intellectual functioning. *Journal of Family Violence*, 16(3), 269–290. doi:10.1023/A:1011138332712

Lavi, I., Gard, A. M., Hagen, M. J., Van Horn, P., & Lieberman, A. F. (2015). Child-parent psychotherapy examined in a perinatal sample: depression, posttraumatic stress symptoms and child-rearing attitudes. *Journal of Social and Clinical Psychology*, 34(1), 64–82. doi:10.1521/jscp.2015.34.1.64

Levendosky, A. A., Huth-Bocks, A. C., Semel, M. A., & Shapiro, D. L. (2002). Trauma symptoms in preschool-age children exposed to domestic violence. *Journal of Interpersonal Violence*, 17(2), 150–164. doi:10.1177/0886260502017002003

Lewis, T., Kotch, J., Thompson, R., Litrownik, A. J., English, D. J., Proctor, L. J., Runyan, D. K., & Dubowitz, H. (2010). Witnessed violence and youth behavior problems: A multi–informant study. *American Journal of Orthopsychiatry*, 80(4), 443–450. doi:10.1111/j.1939–0025.2010.01047.x

Lieberman, A. F. (2004). Traumatic stress and quality of attachment: Reality and internalization in disorders of infant mental health. *Infant Mental Health Journal*, 25(4), 336–351. doi:10.1002/imhj.20009

Lieberman, A., & Van Horn, P. (2008). *Psychotherapy with infants and young children: Repairing the effects of stress and trauma on early attachment.* New York, NY: The Guilford Press.

Lieberman, A. F., Ghosh-Ippen, C., & Van Horn, P. (2015). *Don't hit my mommy! A manual for Child-Parent Psychotherapy with young children exposed to violence and other trauma* (2nd ed.). Washington, DC: Zero to Three.

Lieberman, A. F., Padron, E., Van Horn, P., & Harris, W.W. (2005). Angels in the nursery: The intergenerational transmission of benevolent parental influences. *Infant Mental Health Journal,* 26(6), 504–520. doi:10.1002/imhj.20071

Lieberman, A. F., Van Horn, P., & Gosh Ippen, C. (2005). Toward evidence-based treatment: Child-parent psychotherapy with preschoolers exposed to marital violence. *Journal of the American Academy of Child & Adolescent Psychiatry*, 44 (12), 1241–1248.

Lieberman, A. F., Weston, D. R., & Pawl, J. H. (1991). Preventive intervention and outcome with anxiously attached dyads. *Child Development,* 62(1), 199–209. doi:10.2307/1130715

Ludy-Dobson, C. R., & Perry, B. D. (2010). The role of healthy relational interactions in buffering the impact of childhood trauma. In Gil, E. (Ed.), *Working with Children to Heal Interpersonal Trauma: The power of play* (pp. 26–43). New York, NY: The Guilford Press.

Milteer, R. M., Ginsburg, K. R., the American Academy of Pediatrics Council on Communication and Media, & the American Academy of Pediatrics Committee on Psychosocial Aspects of Child and Family Health. (2012). The importance of play in promoting healthy child development and maintaining strong parent-child bond: Focus on children in poverty. *Pediatrics*, 129(1), e204–213. doi:10.1542/peds.2011–2953

Olff, M., Frijling, J. L., Kubzansky, L. D., Bradley, B., Ellenbogen, M. A., Cardoso, C., Bartz, J. A., Yee, J. R., & Van Zuiden, M. (2013). The role of oxytocin in social bonding, stress regulation and mental health: An update on the moderating effects of context and inter-individual differences. *Psychoneuroendocrinology*, 38 (9), 1883–1894. doi:10.1016/j.psyneuen.2013.06.019

Osofsky, J. D. (2003). Prevalence of children's exposure to domestic violence and child maltreatment: Implications for prevention and intervention. *Clinical Child and Family Psychology Review*, 6(3), 161–170. Retrieved from: https://www.researchgate.net/profile/Joy_Osofsky/publication/9005364_Prevalence_of_Children%27s_Exposure_to_Domestic_Violence_and_Child_Maltreatment_Implications_for_Prevention_and_Intervention/links/00b495250bf5f716b8000000.pdf

Rees, C. (2007). Childhood attachment. *British Journal of General Practice*, 57(544), 920–922. Retrieved from: https://bjgp.org/content/57/544/920/tab-pdf

Reyes, V., & Lieberman, A. (2012). Child-parent psychotherapy and traumatic exposure to violence. *Zero to Three (J)*, 32(6), 20–25. Retrieved from: https://email.zerotothree.org/acton/attachment/18223/f-0233/1/-/-/-/-/Child-Parent%20Psychotherapy%20and%20Traumatic%20Exposure%20to%20Violence.pdf

Romano, E., Babchishin, L., Marquis, R., & Fréchette, S. (2015). Childhood maltreatment and educational outcomes. *Trauma, Violence, & Abuse*, 16(4), 418–437. doi:10.1177/1524838014537908

Schore, A. N. (2012). *The science of the art of psychotherapy*. New York, NY: Norton.

Shaffer, J. (2016). Neuroplasticity and clinical practice: Building brain power for health. *Frontiers in Psychology*, 7(1118). doi:10.3389/fpsyg.2016.01118

Sroufe, A., & Siegel, D. J. (2011). The verdict is in: The case for attachment theory. *Psychotherapy Networker*, March–April. Retrieved from: http://www2.psy chotherapynetworker.org/magazine/recentissues/1271-the-verdict-is-in

The California Evidence-Based Clearinghouse for Child Welfare. (2006–2019). www. cebc4cw.org

Toth, S. L., Maughan, A., Manly, J. T., Spagnola, M., & Cicchetti, D. (2002). The relative efficacy of two interventions in altering maltreated preschool children's representational models: Implications for attachment theory. *Development and Psychopathology*, 14, 877–908. doi:10.1017.S095457940200411X

Toth, S. L., Rogosch, F. A., Manly, J. T., & Cicchetti, D. (2006). The efficacy of toddler–parent psychotherapy to reorganize attachment in the young offspring of mothers with major depressive disorder: A randomized preventive trial. *Journal of Consulting and Clinical Psychology*, 74(6), 1006–1016. doi:10.1037/0022–006X.74.6.1006

U.S. Department of Health and Human Services, Administration on Children, Youth and Families. (2011). *Child maltreatment 2010*. Washington, DC: U.S. Government Printing Office.

Vygotsky, L. (2016). Play and its role in the mental development of the child (trans. N. Veresov & M. Barrs). *International Research in Early Childhood Education*, 7 (2), 3–25. (Original work published 1966.) Retrieved from: https://files.eric.ed.gov/fulltext/EJ1138861.pdf

Whitebread, D. (2010). Play, metacognition and self-regulation. In P. Broadhead, J. Howard & E. Wood (Eds.), *Play and learning in the early years* (pp. 161–172). London: Sage.

Chapter 14

Trust-Based Relational Intervention with a Two-Year-Old

An Adoption Case

Montserrat Casado-Kehoe, Casey Call, David Cross and Henry Milton

Introduction

Dr. Karyn Purvis, Dr. David Cross, and the team of professionals at the Karyn Purvis Institute of Child Development at Texas Christian University developed Trust-Based Relational Intervention (TBRI) as a model to be used with children from hard places initially, although the model today has been successfully used with children from all walks of life and is used as an evidence-based model in some schools. For foster or adoptive caregivers, TBRI presents a trauma-informed model that teaches caregivers about the effects of maltreatment, abuse, neglect, multiple home placements, and exposure to violence on children's brains (Purvis, Cross, Dansereau & Parris, 2013). TBRI's focus on Connecting, Empowering, and Correcting principles offers tangible tools that parents can apply to help children heal and develop competence in their world.

Like Infant Mental Health, TBRI is an attachment model that emphasizes the importance of our first social relationship with parents, foster parents or caregivers in terms of brain growth, social, emotional, and physical development in the first years of life. Young children's brains grow fast, and it is early interventions that provide most healing when integrating parent–child relations in play therapy. This model has been implemented with parents and babies as young as three months old in some of the TBRI family camps. Parents were learning the principles, strategies, and skills and meeting the attachment needs of their infants and young children (C. Call, personal communication, August 1, 2019). TBRI is a model that works for all age children but transitions easier for younger ones and their parents.

Trust-Based Relational Intervention (TBRI)

TBRI is an attachment-based, evidence-based, trauma-informed intervention that is designed to meet the complex needs of vulnerable children. TBRI is composed of three sets of holistic principles: (1) Connecting Principles which are based upon attachment theory and are designed to meet the attachment needs of the child, (2) Empowering Principles which are designed to meet the physical and ecological needs of the child, and (3) Correcting Principles which are designed to disarm fear and meet the behavioral needs of the child.

The Connecting Principles consist of two sets of strategies:

1   Engagement Strategies lists specific ways to facilitate connection with children. There are five specific strategies:

   a   Eye Contact: Looking into the eyes of a child sends the message to them that they are seen and that they are precious. Asking a child to look into your eyes is helpful in getting their full attention. Never force eye contact, just encourage it.

   b   Voice: Using the appropriate tone, cadence, and volume when speaking with a child can convey a very specific message, such as I am a safe person, let's have fun, or I mean business. Using a playful, melodic voice can disarm fear and help a child feel safe. The voice is a powerful tool for connecting.

   c   Healthy Touch: Touching a child in a safe and healthy manner such as a side hug or high-five can help build connection and model appropriate behavior. Never force touch, just encourage it.

   d   Behavioral Matching: Attuning with a child by sitting next to them instead of towering over them, or choosing the same color of an item as a child, can help build connection by identifying similarities between the two of you.

   e   Playful Engagement: Communicating with a child in a playful manner sends the message that the child is safe and that you like to be with them. Play disarms fear and allows the child to learn new skills and behaviors in a non-threatening manner. Playful Interaction in TBRI is based on the use of Theraplay where parents or caregivers are encouraged to use playful activities that foster attachment, build self-esteem, and teach social skills and competencies for life (Purvis & Cross, 2015).

2   Mindfulness Strategies are designed for the caregiver and the child. The caregiver should remain mindful concerning what they are bringing to the interaction based upon their personal history, as well as what the child is bringing to the interaction based upon their own history.

   a   Self-awareness: Caregivers should be proactive in increasing their self-awareness by identifying their own personal triggers. Some common triggers are aggressive or disrespectful behaviors such as ignoring instructions, hitting, kicking, cussing. After identifying triggers, caregivers should identify and practice ways to remain calm when triggered. Some caregivers find it helpful to take deep breaths, go for a walk, meditate, pray or journal.

b   Awareness of Child: Caregivers should be proactive in helping children to identify their own triggers and calming techniques, as well. Ask children to pay attention to their bodies when they begin to feel sad or mad and help them to identify the cause behind the feeling. Children can be triggered in many ways, a few examples include a smell, a noise, a month, the weather, a location, a facial expression, a season, a particular food, a color. Helping children to identify their triggers can be a difficult task, but it is worth the effort.

c   Flexible Responding and Creative Problem Solving: When caregivers are able to remain present and calm in the middle of distress, they are able to think of creative solutions to behavioral challenges, as well as be more flexible in their responses. Caregivers have clearer thinking when they remain calm, they also serve as a role model for the child.

The Empowering Principles consist of two sets of strategies:

1   Ecological Strategies are designed to set-up a child's environment for success. Caregivers should pay close attention to setting a predictable schedule, structuring transitions, both daily and life, and implementing routines and rituals.

2   Physiological Strategies are designed to set-up a child's body for success. Caregivers should assist children in keeping their blood sugar steady by eating meals and snacks about every two hours, staying hydrated, meeting sensory needs, getting adequate sleep, and participating in physical activity on a regular basis.

The Correcting Principles consist of two sets of strategies:

1   Proactive Strategies are designed to teach children appropriate behaviors during calm, alert times:

a   Life Value Terms are short phrases that can be used to remind a child of an expected behavior. Examples of Life Value Terms include Gentle and Kind, Use Your Words, and With Respect.

b   Behavioral Scripts are respectful ways to help both caregivers and children to negotiate their needs. Examples of Behavioral Scripts include offering or asking for a redo, choices, and compromises.

2   Responsive Strategies are designed to assist caregivers in responding during times of challenging behaviors:

a   IDEAL Response is a method for responding to children's behaviors:

I Immediate: respond to behavior within three seconds.

D Direct: respond to child directly, e.g., ask for hands and eyes.

E Efficient: respond to child with the least possible structure and lowest level (see Levels of Response).

A Action-Based: have child perform desired behavior, e.g., practice the correct behavior.

L Leveled at Behavior not Child: respond to child's behavior, not their character, e.g., "You made a bad choice," instead of "You are a bad child."

b   Levels of Response:

Level 1: Playful Engagement

    i   Use with low-level behaviors such as telling instead of asking and sassy tone of voice.

    ii   Caregiver's response is playful, e.g., "Are you asking or telling?" or "Whoa, I can't believe my ears!"

    iii   Child is calm and alert.

Level 2: Structured Engagement

    i   Use when playful engagement doesn't work and/or when it is appropriate to offer choices, redos, or compromises.

    ii   Caregiver response is calm, their voice is a little slower and deeper, e.g., "You have two choices. You can either have a snack first then sweep the floors or sweep the floors and then have a snack. Which do you choose?" Or "Try that again with respect." Or "Are you asking for a compromise?"

    iii   Child is calm and alert.

Level 3: Calming Engagement

    i   Use with child when they are beginning to dysregulate.

    ii   Assist child with regulation, e.g., deep breathing, walking, listening to music.

    iii   When child is calm, return to either Level 1 or 2.

Level 4: Structured Engagement

    i   Use when child is a danger to themselves or others.

    ii   Seek further training (i.e. Crisis Prevention Intervention (CPI), Satori Alternatives to Managing Aggression (SAMA).

    iii   When child is calm, return to either Level 1 or 2.

Clinical Case Example and TBRI Interventions in Play Therapy with a Young Child

The following example of a composite case will demonstrate how a marriage and family play therapist integrates the use of TBRI in working with a two-year-old and his parents. (This case was implemented by the chapter author Casado-Kehoe.)

Family Background and Medical/Mental Health

The Brown family (Maggie and Tim) contacted the office seeking help with their two-year-old adopted son, Anson, as they were really struggling with the toddler's behavior. Mom reported that he had demonstrated developmental delays (specifically speech and walking), issues calming down and being held, aggressive meltdowns, interrupted sleep, and recently diagnosed food allergies. The pediatrician had put a halt to vaccinations due to concerns of adverse reactions to previous vaccinations. The child was experiencing severe eczema all over his legs and had also demonstrated a seizure following the last vaccine. His pediatrician referred them to an allergy specialist and also recommended dietary modifications of holding all dairy and gluten prior to the referral appointment. Parents were at a loss as to how to handle his aggressive episodes. They had tried some behavioral modification with time outs, but he would become even more aggressive with this form of discipline. His inability to verbalize his feelings also made matters worse. Their pediatrician recommended play therapy, hoping it would help the parents sort out what the child's emotional needs were at this time.

Anson had started to participate in a five half-day per week daycare program, and the teacher reported him being inattentive, easily frustrated, and occasionally aggressive towards other kids. However, he was by all accounts a social child who generally did enjoy being around other children and did report that he liked his teachers. Parents also reported him struggling with major meltdowns any time they would go to a crowded park where he would experience a high degree of stimulation and responded negatively to the word "no." Sleep issues were a major concern, too. Despite the fact that he was a very active child, at night he struggled falling asleep, requiring one or both parents to help him, and he would wake several times throughout the night. He experienced high anxiety about being alone.

Processing the First Session

During the initial session with both parents alone, I (Montserrat) asked many questions to determine if Anson had experienced any early risk factors prior to the adoption. Some of the initial risk factors identified include the following: A difficult pregnancy with high levels of stress and trauma for the birthmother, suspicion of alcohol use and drugs, exposure to multiple partners, and domestic violence. The birthmother did not carry the baby to term, which led to premature birth of the baby; this required some assistance with a breathing machine for a couple of days because of his lungs. For the first couple of weeks, Anson went home with his birthmother, but was hospitalized at four weeks for abuse and neglect and an upper respiratory infection which developed into pneumonia. At that point, the birthmother consented to place Anson for adoption, and the Brown family was chosen as the adoptive family.

As a play therapist using TBRI, I explained to the parents the role of trauma and risk factors in terms of brain growth and development, neurotransmitter function, attachment, and affect dysregulation. I wanted them to understand that little Anson had had a very rough beginning from the time he was in utero and that his brain had been impacted deeply with such traumatic history; but, with their love, commitment, and dedication as parents he would be able to experience healing. I wanted to convey a message of hope, considering all we know about the neuroplasticity of the brain. I told them I would give them more information in future sessions, but that there could be developmental delays in Anson that we needed to address in play therapy. This marriage and family/play therapist operates from the belief that the more education the parents have about how to help their child, the more they can help their child heal and grow. The parents were given a copy of *The Connected Child: Bring Hope and Healing to Your Adoptive Family* (Purvis, Cross, & Lyons Sunshine,, 2007) to familiarize themselves with TBRI as a therapeutic intervention with adoptive families.

After the first initial consult with both parents, I scheduled a session with the whole family (parents and Anson). I wanted to evaluate the child as well as observing the parent–child interactions and Anson's attachment to each of his parents. Initially, Anson seemed a bit shy and hid behind Mom's leg. During the session, I asked the parents to leave me alone with Anson for a couple of minutes to evaluate the separation from his parents. Anson started crying the minute his parents left the room and he kept returning to the door looking for them. When the parents returned, he seemed relieved and happy to see them back and immediately tried to seek proximity with both of his parents.

After this exercise, I asked Mom and Dad if they would take turns reading a book to him. The book I chose was *Snuggle Puppy! A little Love Song* by Sandra Boynton (2002). I encouraged the parents to hold Anson and take breaks and look him in the eyes, repeating the message in the book. Mom picked up Anson right away and while holding him in her arms started to read him the book. Since the book reinforces how special the little puppy is, Dad picked up on the theme and started echoing the words to Anson, "… how 'specially FINE You are!" Mom started getting closer, showing the book to Anson and giving him some kisses as they read the book. At one point, I demonstrated that she could use touch and look him in the eyes to encourage attachment and help Anson feel more connected. Touch can play a critical role in terms of attachment, calming the nervous system (the fear response) and helping the brain heal. However, it was obvious that Anson was struggling with the use of touch, perhaps related to undiagnosed sensory issues. With this book, I also wanted to emphasize the idea of how "precious" Anson was. One of the primary tenets of TBRI is to convey the message of preciousness to each child which we see so clearly expressed in secure attachment.

Before leaving, I asked the parents if they normally read books to Anson at bedtime or at nap time. Mom and Dad said they did not. Mom also shared that after adopting Anson, she had been able to breastfeed him thanks to her doctor's help. I commended her for doing that and reinforced how helpful that had been for Anson in terms of attachment and "rewiring" his brain. Maggie and Tim gave me a puzzled look as I was explaining. I further explained that not only did breastfeeding positively impact his oxytocin levels creating "happy hormones," but it also helped his body produce natural immunoglobins to help fight viruses and develop a healthy immune system. Additionally, breastfeeding helped form new neural pathways in the brain as Mom and baby attached and bonded (gazing at each other's eyes, developing empathy and sensitivity towards baby), reducing stress, anxiety, and fear. I highlighted that her breastfeeding had created brain changes forever—new neuropathways repairing the brain. At this point, both parents looked at me with tears in their eyes while holding hands. I reinforced again what a gift they had given Anson impacting his brain forever. I asked if she was still breastfeeding him and she said she had stopped when he was 18 months. Now their routine was to put him down and wait in his room for him to fall asleep, but that they did not have a book routine. We discussed how the use of a book routine could help all of them with bonding, maybe Dad and Mom could take turns each night and perhaps even read to him while rocking him before putting him down in his crib.

Before they left the first session I gave them a couple of recommendations for an occupational therapy evaluation and also asked them if they would come for a follow up session to do an attachment inventory. I also recommended that they read *How We Love Our Kids: The 5 Love Styles of Parenting* (Yerkovich & Yerkovich, 1995). My goal in them reading this book was that they would become more familiar with their individual attachment style as parents and develop more awareness as to how to foster secure attachment for Anson. Attachment plays a critical role in adoption and parents are often unaware of the attachment styles they bring into parenting (typically their parents attachment styles). I also went over a handout of the TBRI Connecting Principles (Mindfulness Strategies and Engagement Strategies) and asked if they could focus on engagement strategies such as a bedtime book reading and play as part of their bedtime routine at home until our next session. I highlighted that the use of *touch, eye contact, voice quality, behavior matching, and playful interaction* were all TBRI Engagement Strategies to promote secure attachment.

Session 2 with Anson

TBRI Empowering Principles tell us that it is critical that we tend to Physiological Strategies (body/internal) to calm down children's bodies. As a TBRI practitioner, I look at blood sugar regulation and pay attention to sensory processing since many children who come from hard places have difficulties processing sensory input. Therefore, in working with children, I have healthy and allergen-friendly snacks and healthy water available at the beginning of a session. It is difficult for young children to focus in therapy when they are hungry, have low blood sugar, or are dehydrated. I also recommend parents to be mindful that young children often need a snack every two hours to avoid blood sugar dysregulation, which certainly has an effect on behavior.

After this feeding activity, we moved to the reading corner to do some play activities. I asked Mom and Dad if they would invite Anson to go there to read him a storybook called *The Magic Rainbow Hug* (Courtney, 2013). This book focuses on building attachment through the use of caring and respectful touch. The whole family sat on the floor in the reading corner. Dad started reading the book facing Anson and making eye contact with him, while mom sat behind Anson, gently embracing him and working on his back through the use of touch. Anson seemed to be engaged in this story and enjoyed the interactive relaxing activity with both parents.

Session 3 with the Parents

In this session with the parents, we worked on understanding the role of Empowering Principles and Physiological Strategies (food, hydration, and sensory needs) and developed a routine to follow with Anson throughout the day. The parents had great ideas of healthy snacks to give him and we brainstormed to add more to the list. Mom realized that at times Anson may have been hungry and this may have contributed to his emotional meltdowns. We discussed what happens to all of us when we are hungry and dehydrated and how it affects brain regulation.

Since sensory needs/issues also affect behavior, it is important to understand sensory regulation and dysregulation for each child. Anson had started Occupational Therapy (OT) outside play therapy following my recommendation for an OT evaluation. So, I asked the parents in this session, "What are the sensory needs of your child? What regulates him (calms him down) and what dysregulates him (sets them off)." In terms of sensory needs, we discussed a variety of play activities they could do at home that would help with sensory input including the following: A sensory tray (sand, beans, balls), animal walks with sounds (frog, giraffe, bear, etc.), singing "row-row your boat," a sandwich body game, sofa pillows, a jumping game, an obstacle course, making slime, making edible playdoh, making garden soup, making stress balls, face painting, and a water tray. TBRI encourages parents to be detectives and find ways to empower their kids.

Session 4 with Anson

Maggie, Tim, and Anson came to the session together. Anson was holding Dad's hand and seemed a bit tired. I asked both parents if I could offer Anson a snack and water. I had brought a variety of fruit snacks and asked the parents if they would feed Anson, and to also ask him if he wanted to feed them, too. The idea was to build on "giving and receiving care" while building attachment. After their snack, Anson moved to the car play area. I asked Dad if he would watch me interact with Anson for a couple of minutes and then take over. During my time playing cars with Anson, I reflected on what he was doing and asked if there was a car that was his favorite. He brought a fancy sports blue car to me and told me, "Shiny car. Like shiny car." I started describing the car and highlighting positives about the car. Then I asked Mom and Dad if they could point out positives about the car. After playing with the cars, Anson moved to the puppet theatre area and grabbed a mirror. I asked him if he could look into it and tell Mom and Dad what he saw in the mirror. At this point, I had asked the parents to move closer to Anson and focus on giving eye contact and, when appropriate, use touch to emphasize eye contact. Mom got really close to Anson and held the mirror for him and said, "Wow, look at that strong handsome boy." Anson smiled. Dad stayed close and said, "Wow, what did mom say?" Anson smiled again and repeated, "Boy handsome" with a grin from ear to ear.

Along with that mirror play activity to help Anson see his "preciousness" and feel connected with Mom and Dad, we also worked on a variation of a family drawing. I gave Anson a couple of baskets with different sets of animal families (Momma bear, Papa bear, Baby bear, etc.) and asked him to create a picture with them to represent his family. However, being that Anson was two, using family toys more representative of his age seemed more helpful. As a therapist, I do pay attention to what animal they choose and if they mix the various animals. Animals have a lot of meaning and I can gather more information about the animal from the child's perspective (not mine). I may even ask questions such as, "What does the tiger do to be safe?" "Can you show your mom and dad what the baby tiger needs to be safe?" It is always amazing the information that kids (even young ones) reveal through play— often these are very magical moments.

Session 5 with Parents

Maggie and Tim came to therapy upset. They had had a difficult week with Anson. I encouraged them to keep a behavioral journal and to log the times that Anson had more behavioral difficulties and then reflect on what happened prior to the meltdown. I reminded them that TBRI sees parents as detectives of their children's behaviors. In this session, we focused on helping parents learn how to use Mindfulness Strategies. Being mindful means focusing on the present moment—one's body, feelings, thoughts, and breathing. Parents learn how to breathe while also helping the child to breathe and calm down. Talking is not as important as finding ways to calm the child. Parents can also reflect about how the child and situation trigger previous experiences and what it means for this relationship with their child.

While using specific toys from the playroom, we discussed creating a "Calming Corner" for Anson at home. This would be a place he could go to when feeling dysregulated and upset. Mom and Dad could take him there and start showing him specific techniques that would help him calm down and self-soothe. In this corner, Anson could have a box or tote with some calming toys. I asked the parents if they could name some things that they thought could help Anson calm down. I also reminded the parents that this was not a punishing corner, but a place Anson could learn to self-regulate by himself or with their help. Many parents think that children need to be isolated after acting out. However, most children actually need more connection than ever and a loving adult who conveys the message: "I am here for you and together I am going to help you figure out how to regain a sense of calmness." It is important to remember that parents are their kids' emotional regulators. A child may need a hug to help him calm down rather than the parents getting upset about him throwing a tantrum. Learning how to self-regulate is a major skill that parents can provide children. Not only do children need to learn how to self-regulate, so do parents. It is often that parents become dysregulated when their child has a meltdown, modeling the very thing they do not want children to learn—dysregulation. In therapy, parents learn that self-regulation impacts brain development and encourages connection.

Parents tend to have the misconception that when their kid is upset and having a meltdown that somehow, if they lecture him or talk to the kid about what is happening, that the behavior will self-correct. The problem is that when a child is upset, his/her cognitive brain ("upstairs brain") is shut off as they are operating out of their amygdala ("downstairs brain") and reasoning is offline (Siegel & Bryson, 2012; Purvis, Cross & Sunshine, 2007). When we use TBRI in play therapy, we teach parents how to use short sentences, ways of connecting and de-escalating with the intent to correct behavior. We provide children with self-calming techniques and teach parents how to use those at home to help with dysregulation, connection, and behavioral changes. TBRI teaches parents to connect while correcting behavior. The 3 R's for handling a meltdown that parents learn are:

1 Regulate yourself (put your own mask on first before helping your child).
2 Regulate your child by using self-regulation strategies (parents are emotional regulators).
3 Reconnect in relationship (reconnecting is the path for healing).

Connection calms the child's brain down so he can be ready for behavioral changes and can practice new behaviors. Part of my work with this family was to teach them about "Time-In" versus "Time-out," ways to get Anson to be closer rather than sending him away physically and emotionally, focusing on solutions, teaching him how to problem-solve at his developmental stage, and helping the child see how precious he is despite all of the times that things do not work out right. A great way to help children feel connected and precious is through playful engagement. Children, and specifically very young children, communicate through play. Play is to kids what words are to adults. Meaning is expressed in play activities, but also parents can deepen connections through what TBRI calls "Playful Engagement."

Child–Parent Psychotherapy Assessments

Recommendations were made for parents to do an Adult Attachment Interview (AAI). When working with children, and specifically with adoptive families, it is important to understand the attachment history of parents since that will impact how they parent and attach to their kids. In this case, since Anson came from an adoption background and started life with insecure attachment, the goal was to help parents develop a secure attachment with Anson. We know that attachment-based activities have the potential to teach children self-regulating skills while also providing much healing and connection to the family. In therapy, with the guidance of a play therapist well-versed in TBRI, parents have the ability to be healing agents for their child.

Parents were also encouraged to do neurotransmitter testing with Anson and themselves. Understanding how Anson and the parents were doing in terms of brain health would be important since it can explain why kids may struggle with specific behavioral issues. When parents look at the neurotransmitter profile of a child, they can see the various elements that impact aggression, anxiety or depression, impulsivity, etc. In this way, they are more able and likely to see their child in the context of what is going on in their child's brain rather than looking at their child and thinking "my child is bad." In therapy, we looked at how previous trauma most likely impacted his neurotransmitter function and health. Finally, the Adverse Childhood Experiences Survey was conducted with the parents for themselves regarding Anson from the parents' perspective. The Adverse Childhood Experiences Survey can be helpful in terms of the parents having an understanding of trauma and adverse experiences and how those experiences could impact the future health of the person or child (Nakazawa, 2015).

Post-Assessment Considerations

Although the primary reason that Maggie and Tim came to therapy was to address Anson's behavior, it was clear that both parents benefitted from looking at their attachment styles and reconsidering new ways to connect and correct behavior with Anson. This is a fairly common issue in play therapy where parents are focused on how the child is acting out and are often unaware of the role that they themselves are playing that contributes to these behaviors. Thus, including parents in play therapy sessions and providing them with TBRI skills they can use at home has much promise for change.

In therapy, we processed Anson's neurotransmitter testing which showed that there was a lot of dysregulation going on in his brain, most likely the result of his trauma history. His serotonin levels were low, and epinephrine and glutamate levels were fairly high, for example. These factors contribute to anxiety, poor sleep, and aggression. I asked the parents to pay attention to foods that were high in glutamate and talk to their pediatrician for further dietary recommendations. The neurotransmitter lab had some recommendations for them as well.

Sensory Issues and Interventions in Play Therapy

During the play therapy sessions, a variety of sensory activities were integrated to help with transitions and meltdowns including the following activities: In order to help Anson through the play therapy session, we started using a ritual to assist him when transitioning into session. The first part of the ritual involved connecting with Anson, by holding his hands and gaining eye contact, letting him know he was safe and loved, and announcing (playfully) it was time to begin the session. Finally, Anson was then able to select a sensory toy from a nearby bin, specially geared towards meeting Anson's sensory needs. Selecting a sensory toy took time at first, but after a couple of sessions, Anson was able to make his choice a lot easier. The therapist reflected on this play process. During the activities, a variety of toys were available: kinetic sand, edible playdoh, weighted items (stuffed animals, socks). All of these were helpful to support any excessive fidgeting or sensory-seeking behavior.

We also created a visual for time so that Anson understood the time frame he had during sessions. We changed around the analog clock in the room so that pictures (with numbers still included) would represent the next activity during the play therapy session or when the session would end. If Anson required more support with staying in therapy or handling his dysregulation, the therapist taught the parents more ways to co-regulate with Anson so he could self-regulate. One example was the pillow sandwich, which is a sensory integration technique used by many occupational therapists to provide deep pressure. Another sensory technique was music that helped to calm Anson's arousal levels so he could best perform in sessions. We used "Up Goes the Castle—Sesame Street" to help with breathing and calming before the next activity. Finally, Anson did well in a room that was less distracting, and everything was within his reach for him to explore and touch. We made sure that the room was balanced sensory wise for Anson—with the lights dimmed, and sensory items and toys used in the session were organized to prevent overstimulation. To end the session, Anson was asked to place the sensory toy in the bin for next time, and given a hug or high five (if he said yes).

Case Presentation Outcomes

More sessions followed the five primary sessions where the main principles of TBRI were covered with this family. They remained in therapy for four months, averaging a weekly meeting. During that time Anson also participated in occupational therapy. At the end of therapy, the family showed signs of improvement with a more well-regulated child and the parents were more equipped to deal with the many challenges that toddlers, with a history of trauma, may bring into a family. Without a doubt, Anson showed developmental improvements in play therapy as well as in occupational therapy. The initial behavioral challenges that had brought this family to therapy had been greatly reduced.

Conclusion

In working with young children, and specifically toddlers, play is a critical component of helping the child communicate, connect, attach, and resolve previous behavioral issues. Trust Based Relational Intervention helps parents gain an understanding of their child's history and the impact of trauma, their attachment style, sensory issues behind maladaptive behavior and new ways to connect and correct. In the play sessions described above, the parents learned how to playfully engage with their child while being mindful of physiological needs and environmental factors that may impact the child's behavior. Through the use of touch and focus on connection, the child's brain can start to heal, and parents can begin to feel more aware of their own responses and ways to correct behavior without triggering a fight–flight response. Through education and coaching, parents learn the role of trauma in the brain and how to create new neuropathways that bring healing to the child and family. Furthermore, the use of TBRI in play therapy allows for trust and bonding to be restored. As exemplified in this chapter, TBRI is an evidence-based model that can be integrated in play therapy and bring great hope to adoptive parents.

Discussion Questions

1 Describe Trust-Based Relational Intervention, its theoretical roots, and how it is used as a therapeutic modality in play therapy.
2 How would you address sensory issues in play therapy while using TBRI?
3 In this case, discuss with a colleague why it is important to understand the effects of trauma on brain development.

References

Boynton, S. (2002). *Snuggle puppy! A little love song*. New York, NY: Workman Publishing.

Courtney, J. A. (2013). *The magic rainbow hug: A story to help children overcome fear and anxiety through playful relaxation and caring touch*. Boynton Beach, FL: Developmental Play & Attachment Therapies.

Nakazawa, D. J. (2015). *Childhood disrupted: How your biography becomes your biology, and how you can heal*. New York, NY: Atria Paperback.

Purvis, K., & Cross, D (2015, May 29). Karyn Purvis Institute of Child Development: Playful interaction. Retrieved August 2, 2019 from: https://child.tcu.edu/store/healing-families-dvds/playful-interaction/#sthash.Oh5qyK9s.Yrjb2lUE.dpbs

Purvis, K., Cross, D., & Lyons Sunshine, W. (2007). *The connected child: Bring hope and healing to your adoptive family*. New York, NY: McGraw Hill.

Purvis, K. B., Cross, D. R., Dansereau, D. F., & Parris, S. R. (2013). Trust-based relational intervention (TBRI): A systemic approach to complex developmental trauma. *Child & Youth Services, 34*, 360–386.

Siegel, D., & Bryson, T. P. (2012). *The whole brain child: 12 Revolutionary strategies to nurture your child's developing mind*. New York, NY: Random House.

Yerkovich, M., & Yerkovich, M. (1995). *How we love our kids: The 5 love styles of parenting. One small change in you, one big change in your kids*. Colorado Springs, CO: WaterBrook Press.

Part VI

Applications to Specific Populations in Infant Play Therapy

Children Born Opioid-Addicted

Symptoms, Attachment and Play Treatment

Athena A. Drewes

The Centers for Disease Control and Prevention (CDC) have identified opioid abuse as an epidemic, affecting all communities and ages (CDC, 2016). US use of opioids resurged from the 1980s, a 21% increase in 2015–2016, with 50,000 people overdosing per year. Over 2 million people are addicted to opioids, with approximately 28,000 adolescents reporting in 2014 having used heroin within the past year and 18,000 adolescents having a heroin use disorder. This epidemic is most significantly impacting infants and children, with not only a sharp increase in infants opioid-addicted, but also placed in foster care (Patrick et al., 2012).

Opioid is a catch-all term for a class of drugs that work on the central nervous system (CNS) to relieve pain. They include natural opioids such as heroin, morphine, manmade pain prescription drugs (i.e. codeine) and more recently oxycodone and hydrocodone. The synthetic fentanyl has been recently developed, produced both legally and on the black market. This drug is 50–100 times more powerful than morphine (Stahl, 2000). All opioids are addictive. Not only do they relieve pain, they also activate the brain's pleasure receptors. Opioids can cause low blood pressure, slowed breathing and potential for breathing to stop, or a coma (Stahl, 2000).

The CDC (2016) reports 4.5% of pregnant women use illegal drugs. From 2002 to 2012, treatment admissions for pregnant women with an opioid use disorder increased by 124% due to increase in use and misuse of opioid pain relievers (Patrick et al., 2012). After dropping sharply between 2005 and 2012, over 427,900 children are in foster care, a three-year increase, due in large part to worsening substance abuse by parents. At least 32% of 2015 foster care cases were due to parental substance abuse of opioids and methamphetamine. The largest increases in foster care placement were in Florida, Georgia, Indiana, Arizona and Minnesota (Patrick et al., 2015).

Neonatal Abstinence Syndrome

The number of babies suffering from opiate-related addictions and symptoms has tripled since 2008. Incidence of US babies born with Neonatal

Abstinence Syndrome (NAS) was estimated to be over 21,732, a rate of one infant every 25 minutes, in 2012 (National Institute on Drug Abuse, 2015). Costs associated with NAS births were estimated at $53,400 per birth in 2009, compared with $9,500 for other births (Patrick et al., 2012).

These opiate-addicted babies suffer from NAS, which is a treatable condition after chronic exposure to primarily opioids, while in utero. Repeated exposure to benzodiazepines, barbiturates and alcohol has also been linked to infant withdrawal symptoms, with chronic opioid use the most common source of NAS (Hudak et al., 2012). NAS results in a constellation of signs and symptoms of infant neurobehavioral dysregulation that occurs in the immediate neonatal period, resulting in central and autonomic nervous system regulatory dysfunction (Hudak et al., 2012). Further, in addition to NAS, untreated heroin dependence during pregnancy may increase the risk of fetal growth restriction, premature separation of the placenta, preterm labor and fetal death (ACOG & ASAM, 2012). Compounding the opioid problem is that abrupt withdrawal of a woman from opioid medications is not recommended given serious risks of inducing preterm labor, fetal distress, or miscarriage (ACOG & ASAM, 2012). And yet, medically supervised withdrawal is also not recommended given high rates of relapse (ACOG & ASAM, 2012).

NAS affects nearly eleven babies in every 1,000 births due to sudden withdrawal of opioids from the mother when the umbilical cord is cut and there is an increased production of neurotransmitters. Opioids are mu-receptor agonists in the autonomic nervous system and they result in disruption of the nervous system and overstimulation of bodily functions. NAS varies from child to child and is variable both in expression and intensity (Jansson et al., 2010). Prescription and nonprescription use later in pregnancy increases the chances of NAS. Use of methadone or other anti-addiction medications during pregnancy can also cause NAS in the infant. Often opioid exposed infants are actually poly-drug exposed, with contributory affects from maternal use of alcohol and nicotine all of which adds to the variability and severity of NAS. Interestingly, the dose of methadone shows no correlation with severity of NAS (Burgos & Burke, 2009).

The degree of withdrawal varies from infant to infant. Symptoms usually appear within 48–72 hours of birth and can last for months. Onset of NAS depends on which opioid was used during pregnancy: heroin-use NAS shows within 24 hours; methadone-use NAS shows within 48 hours of birth; and benzodiazepines or barbiturates NAS shows later than 48 hours. NAS creates disruptions in the nervous system that can be severe and last up to six months after birth (Logan, Brown & Hayes, 2013).

Signs and Symptoms

Symptoms include: hyperirritability and overstimulation of the CNS; tremors, difficulties with tone, movement, jitteriness, hyperactive deep tendon reflexes, tight muscles, seizures, restlessness, increased wakefulness/insomnia, anxiety, high-pitched crying, respiratory problems, and sleep apnea. There may also be neurodevelopmental problems: short attention span, hyperactivity, sleep disturbances at 12–24 months, behavioral impairments rather than physical birth defects (Lester & Lagasse, 2010; Logan, Brown & Hayes, 2013).

There can also be gastrointestinal symptoms: uncoordinated and/or excessive constant sucking, poor feeding, vomiting, loose stools, and dehydration. These symptoms lead to difficulties in feeding, weight loss or failure to thrive. Autonomic signs include: increased sweating, high temperature, frequent yawning and sneezing, increased heart rate/blood pressure, nasal congestion, gagging/vomiting/diarrhea, fast breathing, hiccupping, and mottling of skin (Logan, Brown & Hayes, 2013).

NAS babies have difficulty with state regulation, maintaining a quiet alert state which is needed to interact with caregivers and to feed and grow. These babies have problems going smoothly from sleep to awake states, being irritable and crying frequently. Consequently, they have difficulties with reactivity to stimuli, atypical responses to touch, sound, movement or visual stimulation and can become either overstimulated and poorly reactive, or severely withdrawn in order to avoid stimulation (Behnke et al., 2013; Sutter, Leeman, & His, 2014).

As a result of these symptoms, NAS babies have difficulty connecting and attaching with the caregiver due to resistance to cuddling or soothing and decreased ability to respond normally to auditory or visual stimuli. Added complications of attachment result from placement after birth in foster care or orphanages (Burgos & Burke, 2009).

Hospital Stay and Treatment

The majority of babies experiencing NAS require Neonatal Intensive Care (NICU) for an average length of 25 days (Saiki et al., 2010). There is no gold standard hospital treatment of NAS. As a result, there variability depending on institution and philosophy of the physicians. Consequently, the National Institute of Health has earmarked $1 million for grants to identify practices toward a national standard for evidence-based treatment of NAS (Saiki, Lee et. al., 2010).

Diagnostic Testing

Typically, blood and urine drug screens from the mother and baby are collected. If drug exposure was not recent, tests show no sensitivity. Meconium in the embryotic sac will accumulate drugs in utero for approximately the last five months of pregnancy and is a good option for diagnostic testing, along with maternal urine testing and drug history. In addition, the Lipsitz Tool is utilized (77% sensitivity) using a value of four indicating significant withdrawal (Lipsitz,

1975). The Finnegan scoring system assesses neonatal withdrawal, with symptom ratings in four areas: CNS irritation; respiratory distress; gastrointestinal distress; and vegetative symptoms. A score higher than 8 is clinically significant, with testing every 8 hours recommended (Finnegan et al., 1975).

Pharmacologic Treatments for NAS

The American Academy of Pediatrics (AAP) recommends newborns with NAS initially receive treatment using non-pharmacologic means. According to AAP, pharmacologic treatment is indicated to relieve more severe symptoms of NAS when non-pharmacologic measures have been unsuccessful (Hudak, Tan, et al., 2012). However, NAS treatment using pharmacologic methods varies greatly (Sarkar & Donn, 2006) and non-pharmacologic means are often not tried initially. Approximately half of opioid-addicted infants will require some form of pharmacologic approach. Treatment options include: slowly tapering opioid doses, switching to longer-acting opioids, or specifically treating symptoms of opioid withdrawal. Once pharmacologic treatment is initiated, hospital stay will vary in the NICU. Medications, such as methadone, buprenorphine, morphine, phenobarbital and diluted tincture of opium are used (Logan, Brown & Hayes, 2013). The AAP (Hudak, Tan, et al., 2012) initially recommended tincture of opium as the preferred choice of treatment for infant opiate withdrawal. AAP guidelines now recommend oral morphine and methadone as first-line therapies. Clonidine is also suggested as first-line therapy or adjunctive therapy. The most commonly used medication is methadone (synthetic opiate). If an infant has two Finnegan scores above 8, they will be started on methadone therapy to reduce the score. If methadone therapy is insufficient, then phenobarbital therapy concurrently is added (for sedation more than managing symptoms). Use of clonidine has also been trialed (Logan, Brown & Hayes, 2013).

These medications have side effects not only in children and adults but in infants with NAS. Clonidine is used for high blood pressure, anxiety, Tourette's, ADHD, anxiety, insomnia and addiction-related withdrawal in children and adults. Side effects include drowsiness, dizziness, irritability, running or stuffy nose, sneezing, cough, hallucinations and depression. Phenobarbital is used for seizures, and short-term for insomnia. Side effects include excitement, irritability, dizziness, nausea, constipation, headache, memory/concentration loss, vomiting and loss of appetite (Logan, Brown & Hayes, 2013).

Complex Trauma and Impact of Cortisol

Infants born opioid-addicted not only have withdrawal trauma and subsequent hospitalization with probable removal from their bio-mother, but also are subjected to additional complex traumas and traumatic stress. The parent is often in a low socio-economic status, making it difficult to get adequate prenatal care, adequate food and clothing, and safe and adequate housing. Continued use of drugs by caregiver/s, poor parenting skills, possible domestic violence and parental stress during pregnancy (resulting in higher cortisol levels in utero impacting the developing infant's brain) further add stress on the infant. NAS babies are unable to regulate stress and reduce high cortisol levels impacting their developing brain (Lester et al., 2002; Logan, Brown & Hayes, 2013).

Opioid-addicted infants have a blunted cortisol response to chronic stress resulting in a dysregulated HPA axis. Heightened and chronic cortisol results in a compromised immune response, and overall disruption of the sleep/wake cycle (Bendersky, Ramsay & Lewis, 2006; Gunnar & Vazquez, 2015). Severe chronic stress can create a toxic level of cortisol and inhibit neural development in the hippocampus (Gunnar & Vazquez, 2015). Consequently, the infant is hyper-responsive to mild stressors (Gunnar & Vazquez, 2015) and slow to calm, with difficult recovery from upset (Bendersky, Ramsay & Lewis, 2006).

Early trauma and neglect results in a developmentally impaired and inefficient orbitofrontal regulatory system (Perry, 2009; Schore, 2003) along with poor emotional attachment. As a result, the most far-reaching effect of relational trauma is the loss of the ability to regulate the intensity of affect (Schore, 2003). The impairment of the orbitofrontal cortex and circuits connecting it with subcortical areas can diminish the child's sense of self, leading to disconnection from other people. This neurological impairment creates a hyperarousal response, leading to higher levels of cortisol and poor regulation of emotional responding. The sympathetic ANS is impacted serving the frontal cortex, the area involved in attachment and leads to problems picking up social cues and in creating emotional bonds (Perry, 2009).

The infant's brain develops from bottom to the top (brain stem to cortex), from the inside to the outside, with 50% of the brain neural connections forming in the first year, 25% more in the second year, and 25% remaining neural connections and brain formations in the third year. Therefore, the first three years of development are significant for brain growth which can be adversely impacted by negative environmental cues and connections. Thus, an intricate interactive sensory "dance" between the child and its environment occurs which creates internal, molecular responses that will organize and form the infant's developing brain and the information that it contains (Perry, 2009).

Attachment

Parents/caregivers of NAS infants have difficulty creating a secure attachment due to poor attention to the infant's cues, lack of opportunities for mutual regulation and repair (Rutherford, Potenza & Mayes, 2013) and providing a "secure base" (Bowlby, 1969). Dr. Stephen Porges' (2011, 2015) polyvagal theory deals with infant attachment. He posits two ways to help children with attachment: alter the caregiving environment so it will appear and be safer for children and less likely to evoke mobilization or immobilization responses; and intervene directly with the infant/child through exercising neural regulation of brainstem structures, stimulating neural regulation of the social engagement system and encouraging positive behavior (Porges, 2011). Under stress the CNS mobilizes the body and increases heart rate, while the ventral vagus inhibits the influence of the sympathetic nervous system on the heart, which Porges (2011) calls the vagal brake.

NAS children do not feel safe and have a compromised attachment with their caregiver. They cannot maintain attachment to help with emotional regulation, social engagement and a physiologically optimal arousal state. Often the caregiver has difficulty providing the infant with the required level of attunement and co-regulation due to their own anxiety, dysregulation and difficult life circumstances. Porges (2015) posits that "polyvagal" play should be done as a neural exercise which requires reciprocal interaction and constant awareness of the action of others. There needs to be reciprocal movement, proximity and touch, synchronous face-to face interactions, with play providing repeated practice opportunities for the social engagement system to efficiently down-regulate sympathetic activation. Through caregiver-led baby games, use of social cues to regulate physiological states helps form trusting relationships. The caregiver is taught to help the infant "rest and digest," resulting in immobilization without fear. The parent/caregiver and baby are in close body contact that inhibits movement without fear. Gentle face-to-face and vocal exchanges, rocking, singing and feeding stimulate the ventral vagus which results in oxytocin secretion. This in turn supports health, growth and restoration, optimizes the infant's ability to rest, relax and sleep, and enables feelings of trust, love and safety (Porges, 2015).

Long Range Impact of NAS

The Adverse Childhood Experiences Study (ACEs) is used generically to refer to overlapping sets of traumatic and adverse childhood experiences and home environment factors that substantially increase a child's risk for serious, lifelong medical and mental illnesses. As the number of ACEs increase, the negative outcome (e.g. mental, medical, social, fiscal) increases in graded fashion. A dose-dependent relationship exists between the number of traumatic experiences and development of adult illnesses, with clearly increased odds ratios for additional difficulties in those experiencing four or more traumas (Felitti et. al., 1998). Sixty-five per cent of traumatized children exhibit clinical levels of internalizing, externalizing or post-trauma stress symptoms (Hagan, Sulik, & Lieberman, 2016). Brazilay and colleagues (Brazilay, Calkins, Moore, et. al., 2018) report that greater exposure to traumatic events was associated with increased psychopathology across all assessed domains, including mood/anxiety symptoms, psychotic spectrum symptoms, externalizing behaviors and fear in youth up to 21 years of age.

Environmental risk factors often associated with opioid exposure include: chronic poverty, poor nutrition, inadequate or no prenatal health care, sexually transmitted diseases, domestic violence, child abuse or neglect, alcohol or other drug abuse (including one/both caregivers and extended family), homelessness, transient, inadequate or substandard living arrangements/housing, chaotic home, unemployment, incarceration history, low educational achievement, poor parenting skills, and discrimination based on race, gender or culture (Hagan, Sulik, & Lieberman, 2016). Children born opioid-addicted have many of the above, raising the likelihood of direct and future impact on development, and emotional and psychological well-being. Long-term consequences of ACEs for these children can lead to disease and disability such as major depression, suicide, PTSD, drug and alcohol abuse, heart disease, cancer, chronic lung disease, sexually transmitted diseases, and intergenerational transmission of abuse. Social problems are also more likely to occur, such as homelessness, prostitution, criminal behavior, unemployment, parenting problems, high utilization of health and social services, lower educational and occupational achievement, and shortened lifespan (Logan, Brown & Hayes, 2013). Child maltreatment victims have 2–7 times higher risk of being re-victimized in the future compared with non-victims.

There is also a synergistic effect of ACEs whereby two or more adverse experiences interact so that the risk of a psychological disturbance following in time is multiplied, often many times over. Thus, the interaction of two or more ACEs has a combined effect that is greater than the sum of their individual effects. Regardless of the exposure by infants and children and the extent of the effects posed on the child, it is critical to consider that living in a family with drug abusers, is in itself, a significant risk factor (Hagan, Sulik & Lieberman, 2016). Consequently, early prevention and intervention is critical in shifting the balance from vulnerability to resilience by decreasing exposure to risk factors or by increasing the number of available protective factors in the lives of these vulnerable infants and children (Logan, Brown, & Hayes, 2013; Rutherford, Potenza & Mayes, 2013).

Non-pharmacological Treatments

Environmental stimuli are important to consider for NAS babies who tend to go into withdrawal or hyperactive response with too much stimulation. Ideally the environment should be quiet (<50 dB), dark, with voices softly spoken, phones silenced, conversations outside the room, and TV and electronic items discouraged. Phototherapy can produce anti-inflammatory effects. Light therapy can help infants establish normal circadian rhythm. Avoidance of bright colors helps prevent visual overstimulation, with black-and-white shades being more soothing (Saiki, Hannam & Greenough, 2010).

Handling of the infant should be slow and gentle to reduce stimuli. If the infant begins to show distress, caretaking tasks should stop momentarily (Logan, Brown & Hayes, 2013; Saiki et al., 2010). Rather than holding the infant horizontally, NAS babies need to be held vertically, upright, with slow, gentle rocking. Positioning the NAS infant on their back or side helps mimic a fetal position, and pressure applied over the infant's head and body can have calming effects. Tight swaddling can be effective in containing hypertonic and erratic movements and help promote self-calming behaviors. Arching and extension need to be discouraged. Ideally the swaddling should allow hands to be free or arms flexed towards the face (Logan, Brown & Hayes, 2013).

Use of water beds and rocking chairs is effective for soothing; allow the child to sleep and wake gently, only when necessary. Implement a 5-second rule: caregiver speaks softly, then holds the infant for at least 5 seconds before trying to offer any other care. Utilize a two-person care strategy with one person supporting the infant and the other completing the necessary task, ideally the nurse and parent/caregiver working together (Logan, Brown & Hayes, 2013). Encourage the parent to be present in the room, rooming-in, holding and carrying the infant; using a kangaroo or sling pouch allows for bonding and soothing. NAS infants need frequent holding, along with singing and reading for physical and emotional contact (Logan, Brown & Hayes, 2013; Saiki, Hannam & Greenough, 2010).

Pacifiers help NAS infants to self-soothe; non-nutritive sucking helps decrease stress, resulting in less erratic, uncoordinated movements, facilitating flexion and neurobehavioral organization. Small frequent feedings help lessen gastrointestinal upset, especially with cues of hunger (i.e. rooting). High caloric formula helps facilitate weight gain. Rubbing instead of patting the infant, and frequent burping, can help decrease stimulation and avoid stress. Patting can cause more distress to an NAS baby, so holding, rocking or gentle rubbing works best.

Breastfeeding or breast milk is ideal for the NAS infant even if the mother is on methadone or taking buprenorphine. Methadone is transmitted by breast milk but in very low doses; buprenorphine has poor availability through the oral route and therefore is also compatible for breastfeeding. Breastfeeding helps with infant bonding, decreases risk of abuse (which is higher with this population), decreases stress response of the mother and leads to calm interactions with the infant. Further, maternal breast milk can decrease the length of stay for the infant, resulting in an earlier discharge. Yet, breastfeeding rates are still low among this population despite lack of contraindications (Abel-Latif et.al., 2006).

The use of music therapy with classical music played in the NICU helps decrease agitation and assists with sleep. Live singing, patting and rocking to match the baby's behavior state is beneficial. There are also special pressurized pacifiers that play music. The caregiver gradually adjusts the pressure level, forcing the infant to suck. The more and harder the sucking, the longer the music plays (Logan, Brown & Hayes, 2013; Saiki, Hannam & Greenough, 2010).

Aromatherapy can also help soothe, with oils such as lavender or the mother's scent decreasing crying, cortisol levels and amount of time to fall asleep. Use of lavender-scented bath water not only helps soothe the infant but also decreases the mother's own cortisol levels, and increases attentiveness to the infant. Use of vanillin, mimicking the scent of the mother, also decreases crying. The mother should be encouraged to leave personal articles of clothing with her scent on it, in the infant's bed, to decrease agitation and assist with bonding (Logan, Brown & Hayes, 2013; Saiki et al., 2010).

The Healing Power of Touch

Deprivation of sensory stimulation, especially touch, adversely effects the health and CNS development of the child (Bendersky, Ramsay & Lewis, 2006, Bendersky, Bennett & Lewis, 2006) and can lead to an increase in physical aggression (Bendersky, Ramsay & Lewis, 2006) and emotional disturbances (anxiety, depression, ADHD, sensory integration dysfunction, aggression). Touch helps with sensory integration and self-regulation of affect and behavior along with sustained attention (Morrow et al., 2006).

NAS babies need to be held more, have regular skin-to-skin contact, engage regularly in hugging, share close moments, be held close/carried for the first month until the baby "body-molds" to the caregiver, along with use of a rocking chair to rhythmically duplicate the pace of the heartbeat. Touch needs to be gently adjusted, with stroking and kinesthetic stimulation, to the infant's age and needs (Spielman et al., 2015). Infant massage has been shown to have many benefits for the infant in improving weight gain, sleep/wake cycle, decreasing pain/stress response, improving neurological, sensorimotor and behavioral development, improving muscle tone, bone density, circulation, immune function and temperature stability, and enhancing feeding outcomes, relieving constipation and gas and reducing length of hospital stay. With slow, rhymical movement the infant is able to have longer periods of quiet sleep, decreased irritability, fewer jittery movements, increased visual and auditory responses, and decreased frequency of apnea, bradycardia and hypoxia (Spielman et al., 2015).

By massaging the infant, it eases parental stress about separation, provides an active parenting role, decreases depression, increases the responsiveness of the infant, optimizes the mother–infant interaction and increases the sense of maternal competence (Renk et al., 2016).

Obtaining Parental Attachment Histories

Not all mothers seeking substance abuse treatment have difficulties parenting. But as a group, they are twice as likely to lose custody of their children because of child neglect. And most parents of NAS babies are at greater risk for maladaptive parenting. Before determining the best treatment approach it is important to obtain a thorough attachment history, as mothers with substance use disorders commonly have developmental histories involving their own insecure attachment (Morrow et al., 2006). Stored memories of psychological "representations" of their early caregiving experiences become the prototype for newly formed relationships. This in turn influences the new mother's expectations of herself and her child and strongly influences her parenting behavior (Logan, Brown & Hayes, 2013). Distortion and denial defenses may prevent the mother from recognizing and responding sensitively to her child's emotional signals (notably crying, clinging, hitting, running away) and results in parental aggression, neglect and poor limit setting. In addition, continued use of addictive substances drastically reduces dopaminergic responses to stress, leaving the mother vulnerable to negative emotions and absence of pleasure or reward ordinarily associated with caring for young children. Thus, parenting interventions may need to first address personal unmet attachment issues before targeting behavior management skills. Without improving the parent's capacity to recognize and respond sensitively to their child's emotional cues, there will be little improvement in the mother–child relationship (Logan, Brown & Hayes, 2013).

Symptoms in Preschoolers and School-Age Children and Treatment Options

Treatment options for NAS infants and children include use of the Neurosequential Model of Therapeutics (Perry, 2009); Developmental Play Therapy (Brody, 1997); Theraplay (Booth & Jernberg, 2010); FirstPlay Therapy (Courtney & Nolan, 2017; Courtney, Velasquez & Bakal Toth, 2017); Filial Therapy (Guerney & Ryan, 2013) and Child–Parent Relationship Therapy (Landreth & Bratton, 2006), along with use of the therapeutic powers of play therapy and play-based techniques (Schaefer & Drewes, 2014) which can enhance parent/caregiver and infant/child attachment. Toddler/preschool symptoms include mental and motor deficits, cognitive delays, hyperactivity, impulsivity, ADD, behavior disorders, aggressiveness, poor social engagement, and even short stature compared to peers (Behnke et al., 2013; Lester & Lagasse, 2010).

Brainstem activities for neuroenhancement include:

- Pacification: soothing activities in the child's preferred sensory modality; rocking, massage, brushing hair, painting nails, swinging, cuddling, singing, telling stories, feeding (Brazilay et al., 2018; Courtney, Velasquez & Bakal Toth, 2017; Perry, 2009).
- Sensory stimulation: touching sand and clay, finger painting, shaving cream play; making cookies or banana bread (touch and scent); smelling for fun – household smells (orange, onion, cinnamon, vanilla, lemon,

baby lotion, talc, etc.); touching textured items (rough, smooth, silky, hard, etc.); sounds: songs, identification of sounds (natural, household and everyday sounds); and tastes for identification (Perry, 2009).

- Use of Developmental Play, FirstPlay Therapy or Theraplay is useful for stimulation, achieving mutual attention and a sense of attunement. The interactions should be face-to-face, eye-to-eye, contact with mutual enjoyment, using songs, nursery rhymes, touching games, and nurturing activities (i.e. Slippery Hand Games, Hills and Valleys, The Little Piggy Went to Market).

School age symptoms include impaired verbal, reading, arithmetic skills; poor mental and motor development; memory and perception problems; ADHD with weak executive functioning, problems planning, organizing time and materials, shifting from one situation to another, and learning from past mistakes (Bendersky, Ramsay & Lewis, 2006; Brazilay et al., 2018). Additional symptoms include developmental delays, speech problems (producing correct sounds, fluency; voice or resonance), language disorders (understanding others or sharing thoughts, ideas, feelings), and impaired self-regulation (Bada et al., 2007). Furthermore, school absence or failure, behavioral problems, depressed respiration or hypoxia, poor response to stressful situations, poorly developed sense of confidence or efficacy in task performance, depressive disorder and substance use disorder may be evident (Behnke et al., 2013; Bendersky, Bennett & Lewis, 2006; Lester & Lagasse, 2010).

Teachers and therapists need to establish a relationship first, and be spontaneous and in contact with the child when giving instruction or relating. Sensory activities should be used before structured activities, avoiding overstimulation, allowing time to calm down and help self-regulate (Lester & Lagasse, 2010). Sensory activities should include play with soaps, lotions, shaving cream on plastic, carrying pots or bags of flour (for weight), and having a quiet place to get away from the environment (Bada et al., 2007; Bendersky, Bennett & Lewis, 2006; Lester & Lagasse, 2010; Kool & Lawver, 2010). Midbrain activities that help with limbic system integration should include narrative, movement, social skills, and expressive arts:

- Narrative activities include dramatic storytelling, books and poems with rhyme and rhythm (Dr. Seuss stories and nursery rhymes).
- Movement: music, singing, chanting, rhyming, rhythm, marching, complex dance movements, or movement activities (i.e. wave like a tree blown by the wind, pretend you are rain falling down, Ring Around the Rosy); use of jungle gyms, crawling tubes, cardboard box tunnels/mazes, balance beams, swings, merry-go-rounds, balls, hoops, waving ribbons of various sizes.
- Social skills games: sharing, cooperative, taking-turn games (Red Rover, Simon Says, Red Light, Green Light).

Animal-assisted therapy with a dog or cat helps the child to learn to touch softly, gently, and empathically. Walks or trips to discover the natural world helps with heightening the child's senses (Kool & Lawver, 2010; Perry, 2009).

Summary

Use of opioids and illicit drugs has reached epidemic levels. Consequently, use of illicit drugs by pregnant mothers has put unborn children at risk resulting in addiction in utero and Neonatal Abstinence Syndrome post-partum at unprecedented rates. NAS results in a constellation of signs and symptoms of infant neurobehavioral dysregulation that occurs in the immediate neonatal period, resulting in a central and autonomic nervous system regulatory dysfunction. As a result of these symptoms, NAS babies have a difficult time connecting and attaching, resistance to cuddling or soothing, and decreased ability to respond normally to auditory or visual stimuli. Added complications of attachment result from placement after birth in foster care or orphanages and continued exposure to trauma within the home environment.

A variety of pharmacological and non-pharmacological treatments are available post-partum. Of particular importance is use of attachment-based approaches through massage, physical contact, use of touch, Developmental Play, Theraplay, FirstPlay Therapy and other play-based approaches. NAS babies face long-term difficulties with affect regulation and learning difficulties into preschool and school age which will require developmentally sensitive and sequenced approaches including play therapy.

Discussion Questions

1 Discuss what NAS is and its impact on bonding and attachment with caregivers.
2 Discuss what non-pharmacological treatment approaches could be utilized with NAS infants while in the hospital.
3 Utilizing an integrative treatment approach, discuss how best to work with school-age children born opioid-addicted evidencing affect dysregulation.

References

Abel-Latif, M., Pinner, J., Clews, S., Cooke, F., Lui, K. & Oei, J. (2006). Effects of breast milk on the severity and outcome of neonatal abstinence syndrome among infants of drug-dependent mothers. *Pediatrics*, 117(6), 1163–1169. Retrieved July 27, 2019 from: https://pediatrics.aappublications.org/content/121/1/106?download=true

American College of Obstetricians and Gynecologists (ACOG) & American Society of Addiction Medicine (ASAM) (2012). Committee opinion: Opioid abuse, dependence, and addiction in pregnancy. Committee on Health Care for Underserved Women and the American Society of Addiction Medicine, 524, 1–7. Retrieved July 27, 2019 from: https://www.acog.org/Clinical-Guidance-and-Pu

blications/Committee-Opinions/Committee-on-Obstetric-Practice/Opioid-Use-a
nd-Opioid-Use-Disorder-in-Pregnancy?IsMobileSet=false

Bada, H. S., Das, A., Bauer, C. R., Shankaran, S., Lester, B., LaGasse, L., Hammond, L., Wright, L., & Higgins, R. (2007). Impact of prenatal cocaine exposure on child behavior problems through school age. *Pediatrics*, 119(2), 348–359. doi:10.1542/peds.2006–1404

Behnke, M., Smith, V. C., Committee on Substance Abuse, & Committee on Fetus and Newborn. (2013). Prenatal substance abuse: Short- and long-term effects on the exposed fetus (Technical Report). *Pediatrics*. Retrieved July 27, 2019 from: https://www.mofas.org/wp-content/uploads/2015/01/Prenatal-Substance-Abuse-Short-and-Long-term-Effects-on-the-ExposedFetus2.pdf

Bendersky, M., Bennett, D., & Lewis, M. (2006). Aggression at age 5 as a function of prenatal exposure to cocaine, gender, and environmental risk. *Journal of Pediatric Psychology*, 31(1), 71–84. Retrieved July 27, 2019 from: http://dx.doi.org/10.1093/jpepsy/jsj025

Bendersky, M., Ramsay, D., Lewis, M. (2006). Reactivity and regulation in children prenatally exposed to cocaine. *Developmental Psychology*, 42(4), 688–697. doi:10.1037/0012–1649. 42. 4. 688

Booth, P. B. & Jernberg, A. M. (2010). *Theraplay: Helping Parents and Child Build Better Relationships Though Attachment-Based Play* (3rd ed.). New York, NY: Wiley & Sons.

Bowlby, J. (1969). *Attachment and loss.* Vol. 1. New York, NY: Random House.

Brazilay, R., Calkins, M. E., Moore, T. M., Wolf, D. H., Satterthwaite, T. D., Scott, J. C., Gur, R. E. (2018). Association between traumatic stress load, psychopathology, and cognition in Philadelphia Neurodevelopmental Cohort. *Psychological Medicine*, 49(2), 325–334. doi:10. 1017/S0033291718000880

Brody, V. (1997). *Dialogue of touch: Developmental play therapy.* New York, NY: Rowman & Littlefield.

Burgos, A., & Burke, B. (2009). Neonatal abstinence syndrome. *NeoReviews*, 10(5), 222–229. Retrieved July 27, 2019 from: https://www.semanticscholar.org/paper/Neonatal-Resource-Services-Neonatal-Abstinence-(-)/47e713495979c0b6c46641c47b0a5d196ce54bc2

Centers for Disease Control and Prevention (CDC). (2016). *Injury prevention and control: Opioid overdose.* Atlanta, GA: Author. Retrieved from http://www.cdc.gov/drugoverdose/epidemic/index.html

Courtney, J. A., & Nolan, R. D. (2017). *Touch in child counseling and play therapy: An ethical and clinical guide.* New York, NY: Routledge.

Courtney, J. A., Velasquez, M., & Bakal Toth, V. (2017). FirstPlay infant massage storytelling: Facilitating corrective touch experiences with a teenage mother and her abused infant. In J. A. Courtney & R. D. Nolan (Eds.), *Touch in child counseling and play therapy: An ethical and clinical guide* (pp. 48–62). New York, NY: Routledge.

Felitti, V., Anda, R., Nordenberg, D., Williamson, D., Spitz, A., Edwards, V., & Marks, J. (1998). Relationship of childhood abuse and household dysfunction to many of the leading causes of death in adults. The Adverse Childhood Experiences (ACE) Study. *American Journal of Preventive Medicine*, 14(4), 245–258. Retrieved July 27, 2019 from: https://www.ncbi.nlm.nih.gov/pubmed/9635069

Finnegan, L. P., Kron, R. E., Connaughton, J. F., & Emich, J. P. (1975). Assessment and treatment of abstinence in the infant of the drug-dependent mother.

International Journal of Clinical Pharmacological Biopharmacology, 12, 19–32. Retrieved July 27, 2019 from: http://europepmc.org/abstract/MED/1100537

Guerney, L., & Ryan, V. (2013). *Group Filial Therapy: The Complete Guide to Teaching Parents to Play Therapeutically with Their Children*. London: Jessica Kingsley Publishers.

Gunnar, M., & Vazquez, D. (2015). Stress neurobiology and developmental psycho-pathology. In D. Cicchetti & D. Cohen (Eds.), *Developmental psychopathology*. Vol. 2: *Developmental neuroscience* (2nd ed., pp. 533–577). New York, NY: Wiley & Sons.

Hagan, M. J., Sulik, M. J., & Lieberman, A. F. (2016). Traumatic life events and psychopathology in a high risk, ethnically diverse sample of young children: A person-approach. *Abnormal Child Psychology*, 44(5), 833–844. doi:10. 1007/s1080 2–10015–0078–0078

Hudak, M. L., Tan, R. C., the Committee on Drugs, & the Committee on Fetus and Newborn. (2012). Clinical report: Neonatal drug withdrawal. *Pediatrics*, 129(2), 540–560. doi:10.1542/peds.2011–3212

Jansson, L. M., DiPietro, J. A., Elko, A., & Velez, M. (2010). Infant autonomic functioning and neonatal abstinence syndrome. *Drug & Alcohol Dependence*, 109 (1–3), 198–204. doi:10. 1016/j.drugalcdep.2010. 01. 004

Kool, R., & Lawver, T. (2010). Play therapy: Considerations and applications for the practitioner. *Psychiatry (Edgmont)*, 7(10), 19–24. Retrieved July 27, 2019 from: https://www.ncbi.nlm.nih.gov/pubmed/21103141

Landreth, G. L., & Bratton, S. C. (2006). *Child parent relationship therapy (CPRT). A 10-session filial therapy model*. New York, NY: Routledge.

Lester, B. M., & Lagasse, L. L. (2010). Children of addicted women. *Journal of Addictive Diseases*, 29(2), 259–276. Retrieved July 27, 2019 from: https://www. ncbi.nim.nih.gov/pubmed/20407981

Lester, B., Tronick, E., LaGasse, L., Seifer, R., Bauer, C., Shankaran, S., Bada, H., Wright, L., Smeriglio, V., Lu, J., Finnegan, L., & Maza, P. (2002). The Maternal Lifestyle Study: Effects of substance exposure during pregnancy on neurodevelop-mental outcome in 1-month-old infants. *Pediatrics*, 110(6), 1182–1192. doi:10. 1542/peds.110. 6. 1182

Lipsitz, P. J. A. (1975). A proposed narcotic withdrawal score for use with newborn infants. A pragmatic evaluation of its efficacy. *Clinical Pediatrics*, 14, 592–594. doi:10. 1177/0009922875014006 13

Logan, B. A., Brown, M. S., & Hayes, M. J. (2013). Neonatal abstinence syndrome: Treatment and pediatric outcomes. *Clinical Obstetrics and Gynecology*, 56(1), 186–192. Retrieved July 27, 2019 from: https://www.ncbi.nim.nih.gov/pmc/articles/ PMC3589586/

Morrow, C. E., Culbertson, J. L., Accornero, V. H., Xue, L., Anthony, J. C., & Bandstra, E. S. (2006). Learning disabilities and intellectual functioning in school-aged children with prenatal cocaine exposure. *Developmental Neuropsychology*, 30(3), 905–931. doi:10. 1207/s15326942dn3003_8

National Institute on Drug Abuse. (2015). *Dramatic increases in maternal opioid use and neonatal abstinence syndrome*. Bethesda, MD: Author. Retrieved July 27, 2019 from: https://www.drugabuse.gov/related-topics/trends-statistics/infographics/ dramaticincreases-in-maternal-opioid-use-neonatal-abstinence-*syndrome*?utm_sou rce=external&utm_medium=ap&utm_campaign=infographics-api

Patrick, S. W., Davis, M. M., Lehmann, C. U., & Cooper, W. O. (2015). Increasing incidence and geographic distribution of neonatal abstinence syndrome: United States 2009 to 2012. *Journal of Perinatology*, 35(8), 650–655. Retrieved July 27, 2019 from: https://www.ncbi.nlm.nih.gov/pubmed/25927272

Patrick, S. W., Schumacher, P. E., Benneyworth, B. D., Krans, E. E., McAllister, J. M., & Davis, M. M. (2012) Neonatal abstinence syndrome and associated health care expenditures: United States 2000–2009. *Journal of the American Medical Association*, 307(18), 1934–1940. doi:10. 1001/jama.2012. 3951

Perry, B. D. (2009). Examining child maltreatment through a neurodevelopmental lens: Clinical applications of the neurosequential model of therapeutics. *Journal of Loss and Trauma*, 14(4), 240–255. Retrieved July 27, 2019 from: https://childtrauma.org/wp-content/uploads/2013/09/TraumaLoss_BDP_Final_7_09.pdf

Porges, S. W. (2011). *The polyvagal theory: Neurophysiological foundations of emotions, attachment, communication and self-regulation.* New York, NY: W.W. Norton.

Porges, S. W. (2015). Play as neural exercise: Insights form the polyvagal theory. In D. Pearce McCall (Ed.), *The power of play for mind brain health* (pp. 3–7). Global Association for Interpersonal Neurobiology Studies (GAINS). Available from: https://mindgains.org/bonus/GAINS-The-Power-of-Play-for-Mind-Brain-Health.pdf

Renk, K., Boris, N. W., Kolomeyer, E., Lowell, A., Puff, J.Cunningham, A., Khan, M., & McSwiggan, M. (2016). The state of evidence-based parenting interventions for parents who are substance-involved. *Pediatric Research-Nature*, 79(1), 177–183. doi:10.1038/pr.2015.201

Rutherford, H., Potenza, M. & Mayes, L. (2013). The neurobiology of addiction and attachment. In N. E. Suchman, M. Pajulo, & L. M. Mayes (Eds.), *Parenting and substance abuse* (pp. 3–23). New York, NY: Oxford University Press.

Saiki, T., Lee, S., Hannam, S., & Greenough, A. (2010). Neonatal abstinence syndrome postnatal ward versus neonatal unit management. *European Journal of Pediatrics*, 169, 95–98.

Sarkar, S., & Donn, S. M. (2006). Management of neonatal abstinence syndrome in neonatal intensive care units: A national survey. *Journal of Perinatology*, 26, 15–17. doi:10.1038/sj.jp.7211427

Schaefer, C. E., & Drewes, A. (2014). *The therapeutic powers of play: 20 core agents of Change* (2nd ed.). New York, NY: Wiley & Sons.

Schore, D. (2003). Early relational trauma, disorganized attachment and the development of a predisposition to violence. In M. F. Solomon & D. J. Siegel (Eds.), *Healing trauma, attachment, mind, body and brain* (pp. 107–168). New York, NY: W. W. Norton.

Spielman, E., Herriott, A., Paris, R., & Sommer, A. (2015). Building a model program for substance exposed newborns and their families: From needs assessment to intervention, evaluation and consultation. *Zero to Three Journal*, 36(1), 47–56. Retrieved July 27, 2019 from: https://eric.ed.gov/?id=EJ1123853

Stahl, M. (2000). *Essential psychopharmacology. Neuroscientific basis and practical Applications* (2nd ed.). Cambridge, UK: Cambridge University Press.

Sutter, M. B., Leeman, L., & His, A. (2014). Neonatal opioid withdrawal syndrome. *Obstetrics and Gynecology Clinics of North America*, 41(2), 317–334. doi:10.1016/j.ogc.2014. 02. 010

Chapter 16

Hope After the Storm

Addressing the Impact of Perinatal grief on Attachment with Rainbow Babies Through an Embodied Grief Process

Renee Turner and Christina Villarreal-Davis

Pregnancy loss is a terrifying and complicated situation which impacts between 20% and 30% of women in their lifetime (Ordóñez, Díaz, Gil, & Manzanares, 2018). Although a common occurrence, a review of the literature suggests that follow-up care for women with pregnancy, or perinatal, loss is disproportionate (Ordóñez et al., 2018). Healthy babies born after a perinatal loss are colloquially referred to as rainbow babies, as they light up the sky and give hope after the storm. Minimal research exists regarding the impacts of perinatal loss on a woman's emotional and spiritual health, even less regarding the impacts on men and couples. For transparency purposes, we disclose that both authors experienced perinatal loss, in their second and first trimesters respectively. We write this chapter to further therapeutic knowledge and practice, with the hope that women will find additional treatment options during a time of devastation. In this chapter, we discuss the emotional reactions to perinatal loss, barriers to healthy prenatal and postpartum attachment, and post perinatal loss treatment options with an illustrative clinical case study.

Although attachment is widely discussed and examined in the literature, it has gained exponential interest in recent years as researchers examine how this construct affects all forms of human relationships and various aspects of human development throughout the lifespan (Brandon, Pitts, Denton, Stringer, & Evans, 2009). Maternal attachment, the process of emotional bonding and connecting between mother and infant, occurs long before the mother gives birth. This relational and emotional attachment between the mother and her unborn child in utero has been referred to in the literature as prenatal attachment. However, when a mother who has experienced a perinatal loss becomes pregnant again, she is faced with the daunting task of confronting new or old feelings of grief and loss while bonding with her unborn child (O'Leary, 2004).

For this chapter, we define pregnancy loss as any loss which occurs involuntarily regardless of gestational age. Losses may include miscarriage, stillbirth, premature or complicated birth, or early neonatal death (i.e., the death of neonate within 30 days). We chose to exclude voluntary abortions and terminations due to a fetal anomaly in this chapter based on the unique factors and healing trajectories associated with these types of losses (Maguire et al., 2015). We also make frequent reference to subsequent pregnancies which we operationally defined as any pregnancy which occurs directly after a perinatal loss. Finally, while fathers and couple relationships are of clear importance in infant mental health and impacted by perinatal loss, due to the brevity of this chapter, we focus on the experiences of pregnant women's post-perinatal loss. Therefore, while not mentioned here, we highly encourage treatment providers to include fathers and couples work when therapeutically appropriate.

Impacts of Pregnancy Loss

Pregnancy loss is a unique and individualized process; thus, determining the appropriate course of mental health treatment for women post perinatal loss can be difficult. The devastating effects of perinatal loss may lead to severe feelings of grief or complicated grief, anxiety, depression, post-traumatic stress disorder (PTSD), or other psychological disorders (for an extensive review, see Diamond & Diamond, 2016). Moreover, when a woman becomes pregnant after a perinatal loss, she is faced with a higher risk for feelings of grief, symptoms of depression, stress, and chronic anxiety over another possible loss (Gaudet, 2010; Ordóñez et al., 2018). A range of emotions is common including grief, confusion, depression, anxiety, shame, and fear (Markin, 2018; Ordóñez et al., 2018), with an increased potential for symptoms of specific phobias, PTSD, and hypochondria (Ordóñez et al., 2018). Recent findings suggest that gestational age at the time of loss and the time between perinatal loss and the subsequent pregnancy are the most influential factors in women developing mental health concerns including depression, anxiety, and PTSD (Ordóñez et al., 2018). In the following sections, we expand upon these mental health concerns.

Anxiety and Depression

It is not surprising that women in subsequent pregnancies experience heightened levels of anxiety as they approach the gestational age of loss (Hunter, Tussis, & MacBeth, 2017). Specific stressors include routine visits, fear of abnormal scans, and fear of their ability to successfully carry a child to term (Markin, 2018; Ordóñez et al., 2018). Providers may be encouraged to learn anxiety and specific fears of sudden loss decrease after receiving a "normal" ultrasound or passing the gestational age of previous loss (Hunter et al., 2017). Depression, on the other hand, may be more persistent due to identity loss, marital strain, and changes or losses in social standing/support (Jaffe & Diamond, 2011). One study found depression in one-third of mothers after a pregnancy loss which persisted months after a successful birth (Hunter et al., 2017). When further examining depression and anxiety, Blackmore et al. (2011) found that 15% of pregnant mothers experience these symptoms that extend up to 3 years postpartum. Furthermore, to validate these findings, a 2017 meta-analysis was conducted and confirmed elevated levels of anxiety and depression during pregnancy in subsequent pregnancies after a perinatal loss (Hunter et al., 2017). Thus, providers should screen for depression perinatal and postnatal if the mother has a history of perinatal loss and make mental health referrals as needed.

Post-traumatic Stress Disorder

Reactions to the loss may also include symptoms of post-traumatic stress, causing women to become hypervigilant about their health, fearing another loss. Turton, Hughes, Evans, and Fainman (2001) found a higher risk of PTSD-related symptoms and reported about 21% of the woman pregnant after stillbirth or miscarriage met the criteria for PTSD. Daugirdaitė, van den Akker, and Purewal (2015) reported two-thirds of mothers diagnosed with PTSD due to perinatal loss had persistent symptoms up to 12 months post subsequent birth. Findings suggest that a more extended gestational age at the time of loss (i.e., six vs. 27 weeks) further increases the likelihood of a PTSD diagnosis (Daugirdaitė et al., 2015). Another study reported an increase in PTSD symptoms for mothers who had less time between peri-natal loss and subsequent pregnancy (DeBackere, Hill, & Kavanaugh, 2008), which is consistent with increased symptoms of depression cited earlier. Providers should also screen for PTSD perinatal and postnatal if the mother has a history of perinatal loss and make mental health referrals as needed.

Grief

A period of grief is a normal and an expected reaction to perinatal loss. According to research findings, grief symptoms after a perinatal loss typi-cally abate within 12–18 months (Hutti, Armstrong, Myers, & Hall, 2015); however, some reports suggest up to 25–30% of women experience compli-cated grief (Kersting & Wagner, 2012; Ordóñez et al., 2018), which is per-sistent and longer lasting (Worden, 2009). Markin (2018) suggests grief after pregnancy loss "has been shown to extend for years, beyond the birth of a healthy baby" (p. 276). For pregnancy loss, complicated grief and disen-franchised grief seem to go hand in hand as avenues for support are often blocked (Worden, 2009).

Disenfranchised grief is a type of loss which is not openly acknowledged and processed (Doka, 1989). Perinatal loss, especially miscarriage (medically characterized as a loss before 20 weeks gestation), is not always viewed in the Western world as a legitimate form of grief (Markin, 2018). Family members and friends, pastoral support, and medical teams often unknow-ingly minimize perinatal loss, especially if the couple is young or had another child. Comments such as, "just try again" and "at least you already have a child" further reduce the likelihood that mourners will seek clinical support. Unlike typical grief patterns which lessen over time, disenfranchised grief and complicated grief may persist and increase feelings of guilt, shame, and anger or resentment.

It appears that grief is influenced by several factors, including a gestational age of 20 weeks or higher, infertility, living children, and marital satisfaction (Daugirdaitė et al., 2015). Clinicians should consider these key factors as they may indicate increased potential for complicated grief.

Maternal Attachment After Perinatal Loss

An understanding of prenatal attachment will lay the foundation for comprehending the emotional pain and grief that comes with perinatal loss. Women who experienced a perinatal loss are at a higher risk of compromised mother–infant attachment since postpartum attachment has been significantly correlated with prenatal attachment (Kinsey, Baptist-Roberts, Zhu, & Kjerulff, 2014). Kinsey and colleagues also identified several studies that investigated mother and child relationships after a perinatal loss and concluded that "these studies all indirectly describe a disruption in the emotional relationship between the parent and a child born subsequent to perinatal loss" (p. 84). To better understand postpartum attachment, a brief description of the foundations of prenatal attachment and bonding, as well as attachment styles, is explored.

The Beginnings of Prenatal Attachment

Reva Rubin, a nurse who conducted doctoral research on the prenatal process, has often been credited for formulating and introducing the concept of attachment during a mother's pregnancy (Brandon et al., 2009). In her research, Rubin (1975) discovered four maternal tasks women navigated through prior to giving birth: (1) pursuing safety for self and baby, (2) ensuring that others will fully accept the baby, (3) incorporating the baby into her sense of self, which was termed *binding-in*, and (4) providing of herself. Brandon et al. noted that Rubin did not use the term *attachment* when she described pregnancy as a psychological experience, but the women in her study, by the end of their second trimester, experienced significant pleasure and pride as they became more aware of the unborn child growing inside them, as well as, attached so much meaning to the unborn child.

Prenatal Bonding After Perinatal Loss

Research findings described have identified the impact of grief and highlighted the overwhelming task of prenatal bonding that pregnant woman encounter after perinatal loss, which can lead to prenatal attachment difficulties during pregnancy. Two research groups discovered that women with a history of perinatal loss reported lower attachment to their unborn child during pregnancy when compared to women who did not have a history of perinatal loss (Armstrong & Hutti, 1998; Gaudet, 2010). According to Côté-Arsenault and Donato (2011), pregnant women who have experienced a perinatal loss often express protecting their feelings by avoiding prenatal bonding out of fear of another loss. These researchers presented the coping mechanism of emotional cushioning, which is a conscious or subconscious method used by the mother to protect her emotions, level of anxiety, and possible pain of another loss. Furthermore, they emphasized that the effects of emotional cushioning may lead to delayed attachment (also known as *binding-in* according to Rubin, 1975), which can impact the future relationship between mother and infant.

Prenatal bonding and attachment can also be hindered by unresolved grief when old feelings associated with perinatal loss resurface. According to O'Leary (2004), the current pregnancy is being intertwined with the past loss, and therefore, prenatal attachment occurs within the context of these past experiences, feelings, and unresolved grief. Based on her clinical experience, new pregnancies reactivate feelings that trigger emotions associated with the loss. As such, O'Leary posited that attachment and loss are merged together in such a complicated way that the mother is faced with bonding and attaching to their unborn child while grieving the loss of another baby simultaneously. Similarly, Markin (2018) stated:

> the capacity to hold in mind both life and death, loss and love, and the fantasy of a deceased baby one never knew alongside the image of a future child one has yet to meet, without confusing these subjective experiences, is a challenging task to say the least.
>
> (p. 285)

However, in their review of the literature, Ordóñez et al. (2018) noted that even though the effects of perinatal losses can lead to a broad range of psychopathologies and impede on the quality of attachment between the mother and her unborn child, psychological support has shown positive results in overcoming the barriers to prenatal attachment.

Foundations of Attachment and Bonding

According to Broderick and Blewit (2015), attachment has been described as a system, not a set of behaviors, that serves three purposes: to nurture the emotional bond through proximity between infant and caregiver (termed as *proximity maintenance*), to provide the ability for continuing protection (termed as *secure base*), and to create a shelter for the infant when distraught (termed as *safe haven*). These authors also note that all infant behaviors, as diverse as smiling to crying, serve as attachment functions. Furthermore, when an infant is showing signs of distress by crying, clinging, or some other manner, his attachment system has been activated and he is looking for relief from his caregiver to deactivate his mounting discomfort (Broderick & Blewit, 2015). How the caregiver responds to the infant's behaviors and signs of discomfort will ultimately lead and impact his level of attachments (Bowlby, 1958; Ainsworth, Blehar, Walters, & Wall, 1978).

Attachment Styles

Bowlby (1958) was the first to discuss and advance the understanding of human development in infants by focusing on the emotional attachment and bonding between mother and infant. He believed that an infant's primary goal, which was based on fear, was to be in close physical proximity to their mother for the sole purpose of survival. Mary Ainsworth, a colleague of Bowlby, believed that an infant's attachment to his or her mother was more than biological and included the infant's appraisal of the mother's affective response and behaviors (Ainsworth et al., 1978). Her research was the initial attempt to scientifically portray the foundation of behaviors in attachment styles between mother and child, which included secure attachment, anxious-ambivalent insecure attachment, and avoidant insecure attachment. Main and Solomon (1990), based on Ainsworth's research, identified a fourth attachment style known as disorganized-disoriented insecure attachment.

In their research, Ainsworth and colleagues (1978) found that most infants were securely attached, which meant that when the infants experienced responsive and sensitive care from the mothers, the infants felt a sense of security and safety that lead to secure attachment and confidence to explore the world around them knowing their secure base was available. However, some infants in Ainsworth's study showed insecure patterns of attachment. The infants in the anxious-ambivalent insecure attachment category displayed a pattern that revealed high levels of anxiety as if the infants could not ascertain a sense of safety and security, even when the mother was present. In the next category, avoidant insecure attachment, infants failed to cry when separated from their mothers and when she returned, the infants avoided or ignored the mothers by moving or turning away. Unlike the infants in the other categories who displayed some emotional distress, these infants seemed emotionless during times of separation and reunification. Lastly, infants in the disorganized-disoriented insecure attachment category showed no organized pattern of behaviors and when under stress, these infant behaviors were simultaneous displays of inconsistent and ambivalent behaviors, awkward movements, disorientation, freezing in position for a considerable amount of time, and apprehension or anxiety of the mother (Main & Solomon, 1990).

Attachment Styles and Postpartum Attachment After Perinatal Loss

As previously discussed, unresolved grief, depression, anxiety, and PTSD symptoms associated with perinatal loss can have a profound impact on the mother–infant relationship in utero and after delivery. Markin (2018) noted several studies that indicate that the mother's mental wellbeing concerning the grief over a previous perinatal loss plays a significant part in her bonding and attachment behaviors to the subsequent baby. Additionally, some studies have suggested a relationship concern between the mother and child after examining the mother's interactions with their infant or how they perceived their child after a perinatal loss (Hunfeld, Taselaar-Kloos, Agterberg, Wladimiroff, & Passchier, 1997; Turton, Badenhorst, Pawlby, White, & Hughes; 2009). However, other studies examining mother–infant bonding did not find significant differences in the level of bonding after a perinatal loss (Kinsey et al., 2014; Price, 2008). Kinsey et al. (2014) suggested that it is "important for clinicians to recognize that even though some women may experience impaired bonding related to a history of miscarriage, the majority of women form a healthy bond with their infant despite this history" (p. 83). However, since some women may experience more severe symptoms of depression and anxiety, the next sections will briefly explore these topics.

Postpartum Depression and Attachment

According to Dubber, Reck, Müller, and Gawlik (2015), postpartum depression can have a negative impact on the mother–child relationship, bonding experiences, and interactions. Dubber et al. (2015) reviewed several studies on mother–infant interactions and reported that depressed mothers are frequently portrayed as being submissive, withdrawn, unresponsive, or invasive. Furthermore, a meta-analysis by Atkinson et al. (2000) discovered that maternal depression had a significant influence on the future child attachment safety and security. These findings suggest that postpartum depression plays a significant role in mother–infant attachment, thus highlighting the need for early intervention.

Postpartum Anxiety and Attachment

The adverse effects of postpartum anxiety are not as evident in the literature as the effects of postpartum depression (Dubber et al., 2015). In their study, Dubber and colleagues did not conclude that postpartum anxiety influenced mother's emotional bonding. However, these researchers noted an earlier study that indicated "increased anxiety … postnatally seemed to interfere with the mother's ability to bond and interact sensitively with the child" (p. 188).

Treatment

Scant research exists regarding complications arising from perinatal loss and psychological treatment for women grieving a perinatal loss. Similarly, there are no known evidence-based treatment modalities or protocols designed specifically for women grieving a perinatal loss or pregnant women with a prior perinatal loss. Generally, it is recommended to utilize interventions which are grounded in the here-and-now, normalize, and validate the client (Diamond & Diamond, 2017). A brief review of current treatment follows.

Exploring the Reproductive Story

Jaffe and Diamond (2011) describe an overall grief narrative they call the *reproductive story*. The purpose of the reproductive story is to "(a) understand that the reproductive story, although core to their identity, is but one facet of themselves; (b) work through their grief and sense of loss; and (c) accept that [the] story can be edited and rewritten" (Jaffe, 2017, p. 380). This mostly unconscious story begins in childhood and holds embedded beliefs about family, parenthood, relationships, and legacy, along with fantasies of future interactions with the unborn child. Before and during pregnancy, the reproductive story remains largely unconscious; however, pregnancy loss floods the material to the surface. From this flood may come a loss of identity if mothers have already shifted their identities to that of a mother. Because the reproductive story is influenced by culture, religion, family, and peer groups, it is critical for mental health providers to explore the client's unique meaning in being a parent and experiencing a loss (Jaffe & Diamond, 2011). Losses in the reproductive story may trigger additional losses in identity and self-concept (Diamond & Diamond, 2017), which could further impact grief and recovery. The reproductive story plays a vital role in the healing process and is discussed in the treatment section of this chapter.

Cognitive Behavioral Therapy

In one study, Cognitive Behavioral Therapy (CBT) was found helpful with grieving mothers in reframing negative beliefs about themselves and their bodies' ability to sustain a healthy pregnancy and promote acceptance of the loss (Wenzel, 2017). In a similar study, CBT demonstrated a reduction in symptoms of grief and post-traumatic stress (Kersting, Kroker, Schlicht, Baust, & Wagner, 2011). While encouraging, these results are not echoed elsewhere in the literature, and neither study demonstrated significant reductions in somatization or traits of anxiety. Thus, a more holistic approach which marries body and mind may be warranted.

Embodied Storytelling

Markin (2018) describes a cultural phenomenon in which pregnancy is viewed solely as a medical/biological event rather than a set of psychological, emotional, and spiritual experiences. It stands to reason the application of gestalt and somatic-based therapies may facilitate the integration of lost parts and increased somatic awareness to process the physical components of pregnancy loss (e.g., dilation and curettage (D&C), birthing late-term fetuses).

Embodiment refers to living with an integrated awareness of emotions, physical sensations, and experiences (Herbert & Pollatos, 2012; Piran & Teall, 2012). *Embodied storytelling* involves telling a story intentionally using the whole body as a language source. Norrmann-Vigil (2015) captures the importance of embodied storytelling by telling clients, "in the midst of understanding their own experiences sometimes cannot articulate those past traumas beyond representational gestures" (p. 74). After a traumatic perinatal loss, the mind may not be able to grasp the body's experience (Norrmann-Vigil, 2015); thus, symbolic and gestural therapies may be indicated. Embodiment of the loss can occur using gestalt-based techniques such as "show me" or "act it out" or the use of sand tray therapy to elicit unconscious or somatic material.

Establishing Continued Bonds

Maintaining continued bonds with the deceased is thought to improve long-term grief outcomes (Worden, 2009). Engaging in rituals and memorials is one method for enhancing a continued bond (Jaffe & Diamond, 2011; Worden, 2009). Unfortunately, as previously referenced, a perinatal loss is often minimized, creating fewer opportunities to establish or maintain continued bonds (Doka, 1989; Markin, 2018; Worden, 2009). Consequently, providers may explore if and how grieving mothers said "goodbye" to their child(ren). Incomplete goodbyes can create future attachment complications (Garcia, 2012), including future successful pregnancies. To reduce a sense of unfinished business, providers may find experiential interventions (e.g.; empty chair, guided imagery) or talk-based support groups useful (Ordóñez et al., 2018).

Expressive interventions such as the creation of memory boxes, collages, eulogies, or poetry and journaling provide a tangible representation of the child lost (Jaffe & Diamond, 2011). Other rituals that may help facilitate the grieving process include holding a funeral or memorial service, planting a commemorative tree, making a monetary donation in the baby's name, starting a foundation in honor of the baby (Diamond & Diamond, 2017). When the period for usual funerals or memorials have passed, I (first author) have encouraged clients to imagine the service they would have wished for had they been able to facilitate saying goodbye. Finally, we have also found it helpful to give a name to the baby, particularly in a perinatal loss in which a death certificate is not issued (20–24 weeks, varies by state or region).

Indeed, not all women who experience a pregnancy loss will need or require supportive therapy; however, research findings suggest that mothers without professional support are more likely to experience adverse and prolonged outcomes (Shear, 2012). Therefore, these authors provide anecdotal information which may be helpful in the process and acceptance of pregnancy loss. Individuals' factors such as culture, age, sexual orientation, marital satisfaction, and mental health history should be considered when establishing treatment for perinatal loss.

Case Illustration

Avery is a 30-year-old working class biracial female of German-Peruvian decent. She was referred to outpatient psychotherapy by her obstetrician/gynecologist for persistent symptoms of depression following the pre-term birth of her son at 27 weeks gestation four weeks prior. Her son, Alex, lived approximately four hours after birth but was too underdeveloped to survive. Doctors did not provide any conclusive reason for the pre-term labor as Avery was in good health and did not exhibit pregnancy complications. She had a diagnosis of Major Depressive Disorder pre-pregnancy and exhibited symptoms of PTSD after the birth of Alex. Avery has no other living children. She had to return to work soon and was not sure she could "face" her coworkers. She reported some coworkers reached out to her but said "they have no idea what I have gone through."

During the first session with Avery, it is apparent she has not told her *reproductive story*. She identified talking to her mother and husband about the birth experience but did not feel supported by either. Her mother was sympathetic but minimized her feelings by saying, "I know exactly how you feel, I had a miscarriage at eight weeks." Her husband is supportive but is ready to "try again." She felt pressured to become pregnant quickly and resentful toward her husband for not grieving the loss of Alex. In the first two sessions, the therapist offered emotional support with brief interludes of psychoeducation regarding the grief process and normalized the experience of sadness, anger, and longing for her son.

After the therapist normalized the process of grief and built rapport, Avery was invited to tell her reproductive story. This phase of therapy takes several sessions as Avery explored her family constellation and belief surround having a child. She identified as the oldest of five, wherein caregiving was a natural part of her identity. She further stated she had "always wanted children" and it took a "long time" to get pregnant with Alex.

During the next phase of therapy, we begin to explore the physical and psychological trauma associated with her pregnancy loss. Avery had difficulty expressing how she felt during the delivery with some inability to recall specific events. The therapist (first author) used embodied storytelling to facilitate a connection between her reproductive story and the feelings of loss in her body, using facilitative somatic questions (e.g., "as you tell me that story, where do you feel it in your body"). Avery connected with anger at the attending physician for forcing her to "push" before she was ready to deliver. And while she was able to hold Alex after delivery, she did not feel ready to "let go" of him and has a strong physical desire to "hold him once more."

In the next phase of treatment, we addressed her grief and establishing continued bonds. Using guided imagery and expressive arts, Avery said "goodbye" to Alex and created a memory box. During the next session, she brought sonogram photos and photos of her and Alex together, placing them in the box together. We did another guided imagery and anchored the image of Avery and Alex together in a special place she created using sand tray therapy. A few weeks later, Avery shared she was ten weeks pregnant. She was understandably fearful of another loss and experiencing guilt "how can I love this one, when I miss Alex so much. I don't want to forget him."

The next phase of therapy is focused on managing Avery's fear of having another perinatal loss and feelings of guilt for bonding to another baby, "I'm afraid to love this one too much because what if it happens again?" As her anxiety increased, Avery became obsessed with "seeing" the baby and requested bi-weekly scans and using a heart-beat detector. A combination of CBT, grounding, and stabilization exercises were utilized to address her fear and stay grounded in the present moment. It was also clear that Avery was struggling to attach to her new pregnancy, therefore, we engaged in several attachment-based therapy interventions to increase her bond. First, Avery created a series of sand trays which included both babies. She reported the visual representation of "having both my babies with me" gave her a physical sense of peace. Finally, using embodied storytelling, I (first author) taught Avery an attachment-based method to "tell" her baby a story by "drawing" on her belly. Avery was encouraged to "tell" her unborn child this "belly story" every night at bedtime to increase a ritualized bond. Avery had her final session six weeks postpartum and had continued to tell her belly story on her baby girl, Abigail. At the close of treatment, Avery sought referrals for couples counseling to address the issues in her marriage but appeared to have a secure attachment with Abigail.

Summary

The joy and excitement of pregnancy is quickly extinguished when a woman is faced with perinatal loss. The emotional aftermath of grief can lead to disenfranchised grief, complicated grief, unresolved grief, anxiety, depression, and/or PTSD while methods used to protect the emotional pain of another possible loss (i.e., emotional cushioning), levels of fear and anxiety, and unresolved grief can have a profound effect on prenatal bonding and hinder prenatal attachment. The impact of perinatal loss also influences postpartum attachment and can adversely affect the mother–infant bonding and relationship. While research indicates that postpartum depression plays a significant role on mother–infant attachment, researchers only suggest that postpartum anxiety interferes with mother–infant attachment. On a positive note, there is hope for women experiencing the impact of perinatal loss, and clinicians, as well as infant mental health providers, should be cognizant of the signs and symptoms of unresolved grief and attachment disturbances. Although there is no empirically validated modality and/or theory used to treat the symptoms related to perinatal loss, researchers have suggested interventions and methods that focus on the here and now, validate the woman's feelings and experiences, explore the *reproductive story*, utilize CBT, implement *embodied storytelling*, and establish continued bonds through verbal and expressive arts interventions.

Discussion Questions

1 What primary factors does research suggest are the most important influencers of emotional wellness after a perinatal loss?
2 Describe the importance of exploring the reproductive story as a therapeutic tool.
3 What are the four attachment styles and how do they influence maternal attachment?
4 What is emotional cushioning and how does it affect prenatal attachment after perinatal loss?

References

Ainsworth, M. D. S., Blehar, M. C., Walters, E., & Wall, S. (1978). *Patterns of attachment: A psychological study of the strange situation*. Hillsdale, NJ: Erlbaum.

Armstrong, D., & Hutti, M. (1998). Pregnancy after perinatal loss: The relationship between anxiety and prenatal attachment. *Journal of Obstetric, Gynecologic and Neonatal Nursing*, 27(2), 183–189. https://doi.org/10.1111/j.1552-6909.1998.tb02609.x

Atkinson, L., Paglia, A., Coolbear, J., Niccols, A., Parker, K. C. H., & Guger, S. (2000). Attachment security: A meta-analysis of maternal mental health correlates. *Clinical Psychology Review*, 20(8), 1019–1040. https://doi.org/10.1016/S0272-7358(99)00023-00029

Blackmore, E. R., Côté-Arsenault, D., Tang, W., Glover, V., Evans, J. G., Golding, J., & O'Conner, T. G. (2011). Previous prenatal loss as a predictor of perinatal depression and anxiety. *The British Journal of Psychiatry*, 198, 373–378. http://dx.doi.org/10.1192/blp.bp.110.083105

Bowlby, J. (1958). The nature of the child's tie to his mother. *International Journal of Psycho-Analysis*, 39, 350–373.

Brandon, A. R., Pitts, S., Denton, W. H., Stringer, A., & Evans, H. M. (2009). A history of the theory of prenatal attachment. *Journal of Prenatal and Perinatal Psychology and Health*, 23(4), 201–222.

Broderick, P. C., & Blewit, P. (2015). *The life span: Human development for helping professionals* (4th ed.). Boston, MA: Pearson Education.

Côté-Arsenault, D., & Donato, K. (2011). Emotional cushioning in pregnancy after perinatal loss. *Journal of Reproductive and Infant Psychology*, 29(1), 81–92. http://dx.doi.org/10.1080/02646838.2010.513115

Daugirdaitė, V., van den Akker, O., & Purewal, S. (2015). Posttraumatic stress and posttraumatic stress disorder after termination of pregnancy and reproductive loss: A systematic review. *Journal of Pregnancy*, 2015, 1–14. https://doi.org/10.1155/2015/646345

DeBackere, K. J., Hill, P. D., & Kavanaugh, K. L. (2008). The parental experience of pregnancy after perinatal loss. *Journal of Obstetric, Gynecologic & Neonatal Nursing*, 37(5), 525–537. https://doi.org/10.1111/j.1552-6909.2008.00275.x

Diamond, D. J., & Diamond, M. O. (2016). Understanding and treating the psychosocial consequences of pregnancy loss. In A. Wenzel (Ed.), *Oxford handbook of perinatal psychology* (pp. 487–523). New York, NY: Oxford University Press.

Diamond, D. J., & Diamond, M. O. (2017). Parenthood after reproductive loss: How psychotherapy can help with postpartum adjustment and parent–infant attachment. *Psychotherapy*, 54(4), 373–379. https://doi.org/10.1037/pst0000127

Doka, K. J. (1989). *Disenfranchised grief: Recognizing hidden sorrow*. Lexington, MA: Lexington Books.

Dubber, S., Reck, C., Müller, M., & Gawlik, S. (2015). Postpartum bonding: The role of perinatal depression, anxiety and maternal-fetal bonding during pregnancy. *Archives of Women's Mental Health*, 18(2), 187–195. http://dx.doi.org/10.1007/s00737-014-0445-4

Garcia, F. (2012). Healing good-byes and healthy hellos: Learning and growing from painful endings and transitions. *Transactional Analysis Journal*, 42(1), 53–61. http://dx.doi.org/10.1177%2F036215371204200107

Gaudet, C. (2010). Pregnancy after perinatal loss: Association of grief, anxiety and attachment. *Journal of Reproductive and Infant Psychology*, 28(3), 240–251. http://dx.doi.org/10.1080/02646830903487342

Herbert, B. M., & Pollatos, O. (2012). The body in the mind: On the relationship between introception and embodiment. *Topics in Cognitive Science*, 4, 692–704. doi:10.1111/j.1756-8765.2012.01189.x

Hunfeld, J. A. M., Taselaar-Kloos, A. K. G., Agterberg, G., Wladimiroff, J. W., & Passchier, J. (1997). Trait anxiety, negative emotions, and the mothers' adaption to an infant born subsequent to late pregnancy loss: A case-control study. *Prenatal Diagnosis*, 17(9), 843–851.

Hunter, A., Tussis, L., & MacBeth, A. (2017). The presence of anxiety, depression and stress in women and their partners during pregnancies following perinatal loss: A meta-analysis. *Journal of Affective Disorders*, 223, 153–164. http://dx.doi.org/10.1016/j.jad.2017.07.004

Hutti, M. H., Armstrong, D. S., Myers, J. A., & Hall, L. A. (2015). Grief intensity, psychological well-being, and the intimate partner relationship in the subsequent pregnancy after a perinatal loss. *Journal of Obstetrics and Gynecological Neonatal Nurses*, 44(1), 42–50. https://dx.doi.org/0.1111/1552-6909.125391

Jaffe, J. (2017). Reproductive trauma: Psychotherapy for pregnancy loss and infertility clients from a reproductive story perspective. *Psychotherapy*, 54(4), 380–385. https://dx.doi.org/10.1037/pst0000125

Jaffe, J., & Diamond, M. O. (2011). *Reproductive trauma: Psychotherapy with infertility and pregnancy loss clients*. Washington, DC: American Psychological Association.

Kersting, A., & Wagner, B. (2012). Complicated grief after perinatal loss. *Dialogues in Clinical Neuroscience*, 14(2), 187–194. Retrieved from https://www.ncbi.nlm.nih.gov/pmc/articles/PMC3384447/

Kersting, A., Kroker, K., Schlicht, S., Baust, K., & Wagner, B. (2011). Efficacy of cognitive behavioral internet-based therapy in parents after the loss of a child during pregnancy: Pilot data from a randomized controlled trial. *Archives of Women's Mental Health*, 14(6), 465–477. https://dx.doi.org/10.1007/s00737-011-0240-4

Kinsey, C. B., Baptiste-Roberts, K., Zhu, J., & Kjerulff, K. (2014). Effect of miscarriage history on maternal-infant bonding during the first year postpartum the first baby study: A longitudinal cohort study. *BMC Women's Health*, 14, 83–90. http://dx.doi.org/10.1186/1472-6874-14-83

Maguire M., Light A., Kuppermann M., Dalton V. K., Steinauer J. E., & Kerns J. L. (2015). Grief after second-trimester termination for fetal anomaly: A qualitative study. *Contraception*, 91(3), 234–239. https://dx.doi.org/10.1016/j.contraception.2014.11.015

Main, M., & Solomon, J. (1990). Procedures for identifying infants as disorganized/disoriented during the Ainsworth Strange Situation. In M. T. Greenberg, D. Cicchetti, & E. M. Cummings (Eds.), *Attachment in the preschool years* (pp. 121–160). Chicago, IL: University of Chicago Press.

Markin, R. D. (2018). "Ghosts" in the womb: A mentalizing approach to understanding and treating prenatal attachment disturbances during pregnancies after loss. *Psychotherapy*, 55(3), 275–288. http://dx.doi.org/10.1037/pst0000186

Norrmann-Vigil, I. H. (2015). Conceptualizing and articulating pregnancy loss through embodiment in peer interaction. *Language and Communication*, 45(1), 70–82. https://dx.doi.org/10.1016/j.langcom.2015.10.002

O'Leary, J. (2004). Grief and its impact on prenatal attachment in the subsequent pregnancy. *Archives of Women's Health*, 7, 7–18. http://dx.doi.org/10.1007/s00737-003-0037-1

Ordóñez, E. F., Díaz, C. R., Gil, I. M. M., & Manzanares, M. T. L. (2018). Posttraumatic stress and related symptoms in a gestation after a gestational loss: Narrative review. *Salud Mental*, 41(5), 237–243. http://dx.doi.org/10.17711/SM.0185-3325.2018.035

Piran N., & Teall, T. L. (2012). The developmental theory of embodiment. In G. McVey, M. P. Levine, N. Piran, & H. B. Ferguson (Eds.), *Preventing eating-related and weight-related disorders: Collaborative research, advocacy, and policy change* (pp. 171–199). Waterloo, ON: Wilfred Laurier.

Price, S. K. (2008). Stepping back to gain perspective: Pregnancy loss history, depression, and parenting capacity in the early childhood longitudinal study, birth cohort (ECLS-B). *Death Studies*, 32, 92–122. http://dx/doi.org/10.1080/07481180701801170

Rubin, R. (1975). Maternal tasks in pregnancy. *Maternal Child Nursing Journal*, 4, 143–153.

Shear, M. K. (2012). Grief and mourning gone awry: Pathway and course of complicated grief. *Dialogues in Clinical Neuroscience*, 14(2), 119–128. Retrieved from: https://www.ncbi.nlm.nih.gov/pmc/articles/PMC3384440/

Turton, P., Badenhorst, W., Pawlby, S., White, S., & Hughes, P. (2009). Psychological vulnerability in children next-born after stillbirth: A case-control follow-up study. *Journal of Child Psychology and Psychiatry*, 50(12), 1451–1458. http://dx/doi.org/10.1111/j.1469-7610.2009.02111.x

Turton, P., Hughes, P., Evans, C. D. H., & Fainman, D. (2001). Incidence, correlates and predictors of post-traumatic stress disorder in the pregnancy after stillbirth. *The British Journal of Psychiatry*, 178, 556–560. http://dx.doi.org/10.1192/bjp.178.6.556

Wenzel, A. (2017). Cognitive behavioral therapy for pregnancy loss. *Psychotherapy*, 54(4), 400–405. https://dx.doi.org/10.1037/pst0000132

Worden, J. W. (2009). *Grief counseling and grief therapy: A handbook for the mental health practitioner* (4th ed.). New York, NY: Springer Publishing Company.

Chapter 17

Healing Reactive Attachment Disorder with Young Children Through FirstPlay® Kinesthetic Storytelling

Janet A. Courtney, Viktoria Bakai Toth and Carmen Jimenez-Pride

The authors of this chapter have witnessed the powerful responses of children to the experience of FirstPlay® Kinesthetic Storytelling. Co-author, Jimenez-Pride, shares about her personal experience in the following account:

> As a parent I had always utilized evening story time as a method to introduce amazing children's literary works—introducing new words in hopes of building my child's vocabulary. After learning more about the power of therapeutic storytelling and (metaphoric Kinesthetic (Multi-Sensory) Storytelling, the evening time has become more valuable. When paying attention to the look on my children's face, when reading a therapeutic story, I notice the way my children maintain eye contact with the illustrations on the page, or the way they maintain eye contact with me. When my voice elevates to show excitement, I notice their eyes getting bigger and a smile on their faces. When I whisper a passage, they may position their bodies closer to me demonstrating what they are hearing by their body movements. Even bringing the written work alive with 'BACK Stories,' reveals the amazing power of touch combined with creative storytelling. These simple actions are demonstrations of attunement and attachment.

FirstPlay® Kinesthetic (Multi-sensory) Storytelling Foundations

(In order to reduce redundancy, please refer to Chapter 6 *for a complete summary of the underlying theories of FirstPlay® that are relevant to this chapter as noted in the following section.)*

The approach of FirstPlay Therapy® is designed for two different developmental levels, first for ages birth to two years, "FirstPlay® Infant Story-Massage" (see Chapter 6) and the other for ages two years and above, "FirstPlay® Kinesthetic Storytelling," which is the focus of this chapter (Baldwin, 2019; Courtney & Gray, 2019; Courtney & Nowakowski-Sims, 2019; Courtney,

Velasquez, & Bakai Toth, 2017). The foundations of FirstPlay® Kinesthetic Storytelling are the same as found in the infant model including Developmental Play Therapy, Ericksonian Play Therapy (StoryPlay®), Filial Play Therapy, Attachment Theory, mindfulness practice, and the research into touch (Courtney & Nolan, 2017; Courtney & Siu, 2018). The exception is that this model also adapts and incorporates the peer-to-peer massage in schools program concepts into practice with children and parents (Palmer & Barlow, 2017), whereas the FirstPlay® infant model draws upon the infant massage literature. Moreover, FirstPlay® Kinesthetic Storytelling draws more upon the Ericksonian-based storytelling foundations and the work of Joyce Mills (Courtney & Mills, 2016; Mills & Crowley, 2014). Because FirstPlay® is a touch-based intervention with its focus on the body, it naturally comes under the umbrella of somatic or body therapies (Courtney, 2020; Courtney & Nolan, 2017; Derapelian, 2019a, 2019b; Ogden & Fisher, 2015). Practitioner's utilize an adapted Filial Play Therapy approach (review in Chapter 6) to demonstrate the therapeutic story techniques to parents via Teddy Bear or Pillow cushion while the parent simultaneously draws the story-techniques on the child's back. With this in mind, children may know this approach not as Kinesthetic (multi-sensory) Storytelling but as a fun and relatable activity known as "BACK Stories" (Figure 17.1). Note, "BACK" is an acronym to remind about the benefits of multi-sensory storytelling to include the following:

"**B**" Be Focused
"**A**" Attachment
"**C**" Calming
"**K**" Kindness

FirstPlay® Kinesthetic Storytelling Parent–Child Manual

The *FirstPlay® Kinesthetic Parent–Child Manual* is a supplemental resource book to help guide practitioners, parents, and children in the storytelling process. This manual is divided into four modules: Module I includes "Getting Started" and introductory types of activities designed to include the younger child and to help a child get familiar with the new interactive experiences. Module II provides "ready-made" stories that have already been written, for example, *The Magic Rainbow Hug*© (Courtney, 2013). Module III outlines a step-by-step method where practitioners then create in-the-moment stories utilizing a FirstPlay® Child Interview Grid. And, in Module IV, children are guided to write or draw their own stories. (The implementation of Modules I–III are demonstrated in the case study in this chapter.)

Figure 17.1. Facilitating a FirstPlay® Kinesthetic Storytelling session: Mother, Stephanie Crowley is getting ready to tell a "BACK Story" to three-year-old Sophia. Used with permission from Stephanie and Sophia Crowley and Author.

FirstPlay® Kinesthetic Storytelling Guiding Principles

- Always ask permission first from the child prior to a kinesthetic First-Play® activity or a "BACK Story." You can do this by simply saying "Hey, would you like for me to tell you a BACK Story?" Or "Would you like for me to tell you *The Magic Rainbow Hug*© story?"
- Avoid areas that are bruised or with rash when completing the kinesthetic activities.
- The child is respected to guide a parent regarding the type of touch— such as a little firmer or lighter touch, or slower or faster movements.
- Follow the child's lead regarding when they have had enough of the kinesthetic activities. If a child is not in the mood for a FirstPlay® activity or BACK Story, then stop the activities and continue by telling the story without adding the activities.

Reactive Attachment Disorder

(The following review is intended to support understanding for the case study presenting problem in this chapter.)

Reactive Attachment Disorder (RAD) is a rare condition [according to the *Diagnostic and Statistical Manual of Mental Disorder,* 5th edition (*DSM-5*) (American Psychiatric Association [APA], 2013)] in infants and young children causing inappropriate attachment behaviors to parents and caregivers. Children experience symptoms prior to the age of five and after nine months old, and symptoms must be present for more than 12 months (APA, 2013). Children with RAD can appear irritable, sad, fearless with a limited positive affect when a parent or caregiver attempts to provide comfort; and when distressed, may not seek out comfort (APA, 2013). The *DSM-5* describes social neglect as the absence of adequate caregiving during childhood (APA, 2013). Inadequate caregiving can be described as lacking parent–child inter- action or early attunement and lack of positive stimulation from the care- giver. When a child experiences multiple changes with their primary caregiver this can lower the opportunity for the child to develop appropriate attachment (Levy & Orlans, 2014). This includes changes in foster care placements, or the child being placed in settings where there are fewer caregiver–child interactions.

Children diagnosed with RAD often do not like or respond well to being touched or held, making activities such as a hug difficult. Children may demonstrate a need of being in control, and defiant behaviors may emerge. Such behaviors may reflect Oppositional Defiant Disorder or Conduct Disorder. Children may also demonstrate inappropriate affection towards a non-caregiver. This can lead to challenges in parenting and the safety of the child. Reactive Attachment Disorder is placed under Trauma and Stressor Related Disorders in the *DSM-5* (APA, 2013). Children who were exposed to early trauma are at a higher risk to showing symptoms of RAD. Gil (2017) found that Type II traumas are complex, causing distress resulting from severe neglect, physical abuse, and fetal substance exposure, among others.

Treatment

Children who do not receive treatment may be withdrawn and lack interest in social interactions and play, and these behaviors are easily observed within the social environments such as child development centers and school settings. The symptoms of RAD can decrease or disappear with a combination of treatment and stability within a nurturing environment. Treatment goals will consist of building a level of trust with the parent or caregiver, engaging in parent–child interactions, and learning to express feelings and address aggressive or defiant behaviors. Goodyear-Brown (2019) found the importance of what she called the "play therapist's palette" which gives a visual metaphor to trauma treat- ment as a painter's palette. The palette consists of key points that can be viewed as: metaphor, kinesthetic grounding, humor, the attachment relation- ship, and touch. The key points in the play therapist's palette are concepts that can also be found in FirstPlay® Kinesthetic Storytelling.

The Case of Harper

Presenting Problem

The client, Harper was a three-year-old Caucasian girl who resided with her maternal grandmother and grandfather (who were also legally her adoptive mother and father). The grandmother stated that they were seeking treat- ment for "unusual family dynamics," as she described it. The initial assessment identified the following areas of concern, nocturnal enuresis, aggressive behaviors, irritability, hyperactivity, oppositional behavior, poor impulse control, and often odd behaviors, such as acting like a cat, "hissing and clawing others" when frustrated.

Brief Child Background and Assessment

The grandmother reported that Harper was exposed to drugs in utero and was born prematurely at 36 weeks via emergency C-section due to prenatal distress. Harper's birth weight was three pounds seven ounces, and she was diagnosed with *intrauterine growth restriction*. As the biological mother tested positive for methadone and oxycodone at birth, the Department of Children and Families were immediately notified. Harper was in NICU for five days. She was then placed in foster care. The grandmother fought in court for custody, but there was significant animosity surrounding the case, and when Harper was six months old law enforcement had to forcibly remove Harper from the foster home placement. The grandparents then were able to adopt Harper. The biological mother did not reside in the home at that time.

The grandmother advised that Harper did not hold her head up and gave no response to stimuli at age six months. It appeared she had not been provided with adequate care in her foster care setting. Mental health records of services provided from age two years and six months describe Harper as impulsive, controlling, dysregulated with disorganized thought patterns and play patterns, and obsessive thoughts leading to compulsive behaviors and rumination. She had low frustration tolerance and was aggressive towards peers and adults. At age three, the Occupational Therapy Assessment found significant deficits in tolerance, modulation, and processing of sensory information and noted developmental delays, slight low muscle tone, and Sensory Processing Disorder with sensory-avoiding behaviors across all sensory systems. This resulted in flight-or-fight response behaviors at times of dressing, grooming, and in response to "loud" noises, including common household noises, such as the hair-dryer or vacuum.

Eventually, the biological mother moved into the grandparent's household. The grandmother stated that the biological mother gave Harper only a minimum of attention. However, Harper desired more engagement with her biological mother, but the mother remained disconnected and at times avoidant, which may be attributed to her diagnosis of Schizoaffective Disorder, Bipolar Type and Post Traumatic Stress Disorder. The grandmother advised that the mother's ongoing psychiatric care and medication management made little difference in her functioning as she struggled with delusions, including the belief that Harper was not her child.

Assessment and Treatment Plan

The treatment plan consisted of goals for age appropriate social interactions and communication skills. FirstPlay® Kinesthetic Storytelling was deemed appropriate to address Harper's diagnosis of RAD. The biological mother was also invited to participate, but unfortunately, her mental health conditions worsened. After rapport was established with Harper via individual sessions, the grandmother was then included for family FirstPlay® sessions. Harper initially declined engaging in the introductory FirstPlay® interactions with the grandmother. This therapist then demonstrated the activities with the grandmother, such as the "Itsy Bitsy Love Bug" (adapted from the "Itsy Bitsy Spider"), "Row, Row, Row Your Boat," and "This Little Piggy," and Harper sat at a distance and curiously observed the activities. Nevertheless, Harper was inching closer during these activities and finally sat by the grandmother and initiated "peek-a-boo," using metacommunication that resembled a much younger developmental age. The grandmother was supported by the therapist to engage with Harper in this activity and was also encouraged to utilize these FirstPlay® interactions at home between sessions.

At the next session, the grandmother advised that the FirstPlay® activities were going well. She stated happily, "Harper just loves it. She seems she would love to be a baby! I love it also." In the next few sessions Harper and the grandmother engaged in FirstPlay® activities, and the grandmother advised that Harper was beginning to be more verbal and expressive for the first time. The grandmother shared that Harper stated to her that she wished her "Mommy would get well and give her love and talk to her." As well, during therapy sessions, Harper was also beginning to verbalize her internal feeling states and needs, as well as her feelings about her biological mother.

Over time, this therapist began to introduce the next module of FirstPlay® related to the incorporation of "Ready Made Stories," and *The Magic Rainbow Hug*©, a multi-sensory kinesthetic story, was introduced (Courtney, 2013; see also Derapelian, 2019a, 2019b; Jimenez-Pride, 2019; Van Hollander, 2018). Although Harper was initially hesitant, she agreed to engage and seemed to enjoy this interaction with her grandmother. This therapist demonstrated the story-massage techniques on a large stuffed animal, while the grandmother did the "BACK Story" with Harper. At the end of the story, Harper asked her grandmother to "turn around," so she could draw a story on her back. The therapist observed attuned, nurturing and joyful interactions between the dyad. During a subsequent appointment, the grandmother advised that they were using *The Magic Rainbow Hug*© at home and that Harper enjoyed and asked for the story daily.

Over time, Harper began showing improvement not only in increased verbalizations of internal feeling states including thoughts about her biological mother, but in increased representational play as well, with themes of nurturing and caretaking. Unfortunately, Harper's seeking for nurturing interactions with the biological mother evoked little response, and at times were even met with anger from the biological mother due to her mental health conditions. Eventually, this therapist introduced Module III (Creating Multi-Sensory Stories from Scratch) from the FirstPlay® Parent–Child Manual. During this session, the therapist used the *FirstPlay Multi-Sensory Interview Grid*© with Harper to elicit her inner resources. Contemplating the answers to her questions revealed during the story-interview session, this therapist wrote a metaphorical FirstPlay® kinesthetic story for Harper that paralleled some of her presenting issues. During the next session, this therapist shared the therapeutic story, "The Rainbow for Mama Cat," with Harper and the grandmother.

FirstPlay® Kinesthetic Story: "The Rainbow for Mama Cat" (Selected Excerpt)

(*The set-up for the implementation for the following story is that while the therapist read and demonstrated the story on a stuffed animal, the grandmother sat behind Harper and drew and played out some of the story firstplay activities on Harper's back. Prior to the story, the grandmother was guided by the therapist in a brief imagery called the "Rainbow Hug" to "calm, relax, and connect" with Harper. Next, the grandmother asked "permission" from Harper to do the "BACK Story" and Harper agreed. Note, the kinesthetic activities are highlighted in italics.*)

Once upon a time, in a magical place far, far away from here there lived a special cat family, Pete Cat, Penny Cat, and Mama Cat. Their house was the coziest and homiest place. It felt so special to be here, to be home. Pete Cat and Penny Cat loved coming home from school and would tell their Mama Cat everything that happened to them that day and Mama Cat loved to listen to their stories as they were all sitting in their favorite rocking chair. (*The therapist demonstrated a sweeping movement using both hands going from the right side of stuffed animal's back to the left side, to simulate a back and forth movement. The Therapist demonstrated rocking with the large stuffed animal, while the grandmother rocked Harper gently.*)

One day, when Pete, Penny Cat, and Mama Cat played in the backyard, an ice-cold wind started to blow. It got so cold that even the birds stopped chirping and the whole yard went silent. Mama Cat sent Pete Cat and Penny Cat inside and she quickly packed up all the toys in the yard.

The next morning, Penny Cat woke up and found Mama Cat in bed, still sleeping. Penny Cat grew worried as Mama Cat had never slept in. As she gently touched Mama Cat to wake up, she noticed Mama Cat felt hot. "Call grandma and tell her to come over right away," said Mama Cat.

Grandma Cat was there soon. "Mama has a fever, we need to call the doctor," exclaimed Grandma Cat.

Doctor Ollie, the Owl came quickly. "Mama Cat got sick from the cold winds. This will have to take its course," said Doctor Ollie. "What is wrong with Mama?" whispered Pete Cat. "Is she going to be okay?" sighed Penny Cat. They both got silent. As they sat, tears began to roll down their cheeks—all the way down to the end of their whiskers. Grandma Cat came in the room.

"Grandma Cat, is Mama alright?" asked Penny Cat with great concern. Grandma Cat sat next to Penny Cat and Pete Cat and hugged them as she said, "Doctor Ollie says Mama Cat is very sick." "Will she ever ask me about my day and giggle when I tell her my story? Will Mama Cat ever hug me and kiss me again?" Penny Cat asked as she buried her face in Grandma Cat's arm. Grandma Cat hugged her even tighter.

"I am not a doctor Penny Cat, but Doctor Ollie said a lot of love and a lot of care goes a long way to help someone use their inner strength and that I can do. I can give her a lot of love and care. And you can too. The rest is not up to us," said Grandma Cat caringly. Grandma Cat just finished that sentence, when all of a sudden, dark clouds came in the sky. (*The therapist demonstrated a sweeping movement using both hands going from the right side of stuffed animal's back to the left side, as if she was clearing the clouds. The therapist drew cloud shapes on the top of the stuffed animal's back. Grandmother did the same with Harper.*) The sun was covered by the clouds and it got darker in the house. Penny Cat and Pete Cat ran to the window. As they peeked out they noticed the leaves started to swirl play-fully around. (*Imitating falling leaves, the therapist drew small circles with both hands using at least a two-finger touch starting on the top of stuffed animal's back and ending about midway.*)

Drop, drop, drop (*Imitating raindrops, the therapist gently tapped on the stuffed animal's back starting from the top and then moving downwards*) the raindrops fell faster and faster (*Continuing with the same hand move-ments, the therapist began tapping faster*). Then suddenly it started to pour. (*Imitating heavy rain, the therapist drew lines on the stuffed animal down-wards starting at the top of the back and ended at the lower back. This was repeated a few times. Harper appeared to enjoy this activity.*)

The thunderstorm passed by quickly as a gentle warm breeze chased the dark clouds away like a shepherd dog would herd the sheep in the meadows. (*The therapist demonstrated a sweeping movement using both hands going from the right side of stuffed animal's back to the left side, as if she was clearing the clouds.*) With the rainclouds halfway across the skies, the sun returned (*The therapist drew a sun in the middle of stuffed animal's back*) and brought a beautiful, colorful rainbow. (*The therapist drew an arch with a loose fist with one hand, followed by open palm of other hand as if drawing a rainbow across stuffed animal's back. This motion was repeated with each color of the rainbow. At the same time, the grandmother drew all the rainbow motions on Harper's back.*)

"Pete Cat, this gives me an idea," said Penny Cat. "Let's draw a rainbow for Mama! I will also pick her some lavender and put it in vase." Penny Cat and Pete Cat brought the beautiful picture of a magnificent rainbow and a small bouquet of lavender to Mama Cat's room and she was sleeping. Putting the lavender near Mama Cat, they noticed her nose twitched a little. Then she inhaled deeply and smiled in her sleep. Grandma Cat said, "You see Mama is smelling the lavender and is loving it. Now, let her sleep, so she finds that inner strength and can get better. Now, who would like some yummy lollipops for a snack?"

Case Summary and Follow-up

The grandmother continued the "Rainbow for Mama Cat" story with Harper at home and shared that during one storytelling session, Harper interrupted her grandmother and said she would like for her to "rock" her. The grandmother then asked about her day at school and for the first time ever, Harper gave a detailed account of her school day. The grandmother and Harper used this kinesthetic story daily and embellished their interactions with the some of the FirstPlay® activities. The grandmother advised that Harper's behaviors were improving, including less confrontation, a decrease in inappropriate and aggressive behaviors, and an emergence of age appropriate social behaviors in school. According to her pre-school teacher, Harper was on task, worked hard, and followed instructions in class with no academic concerns. The grandmother continued to use Harper's Kinesthetic story as needed and reported that she felt the "story is fun, wonderful, and an intricate tool that was so helpful to Harper."

Discussion Questions

Together with a colleague or in a small group discuss the following questions:
   1 Reflecting on the case presentation, discuss your thoughts and feelings about the therapist's introduction and utilization of the different modules of FirstPlay® within the sessions and at home. Discuss some of your thoughts regarding the reactions of Harper and the grandmother to the interventions.
   2 Share your reactions to the kinesthetic story, "The Rainbow for Mama Cat." In what ways do you think this story might have helped Harper with any of the presenting case problems?
   3 Recall a childhood familiar nursery rhythm or young child's song. Next, think about how you can adapt that song or nursery rhythm to include a parent–child interactive FirstPlay® type activity. Finally, share your idea with a partner and then play out and practice the new interactive activity together.

References

American Psychiatric Association. (2013). *Diagnostic and statistical manual of mental disorders* (5th ed.). Washington, DC: American Psychiatric Association.

Baldwin, K. M. (2020). *An examination of adolescent maternal-infant attachment relationship outcomes following a FirstPlay® therapy infant storytelling-massage intervention: A pilot study* (IRB approved, doctoral dissertation). Boca Raton, FL: Florida Atlantic University.

Courtney, J. A. (2013). *The magic rainbow hug: Calm & relax.* Palm Beach Gardens, FL: Developmental Play & Attachment Therapies.

Courtney, J. A. (2017). *FirstPlay kinesthetic storytelling parent manual.* Boynton Beach, FL: Developmental Play & Attachment Therapies.

Courtney, J. A. (2020). *Healing child and family trauma through expressive and play therapies: Art, nature, storytelling, body and mindfulness.* New York, NY: Norton.

Courtney, J. A., & Gray, S. W. (2014). A phenomenological inquiry into practitioner experiences of developmental play therapy: Implications for training in touch. *International Journal of Play Therapy*, 23(2), 114–129. http://dx.doi.org/10.1037/a0036366

Courtney, J. A., & Mills, J. C. (2016). Utilizing the metaphor of nature as co-therapist in StoryPlay® Play Therapy. *Play Therapy*, 11(1), 18–21.

Courtney, J. A., & Nolan, R. D. (2017). *Touch in child counseling and play therapy: An ethical and clinical guide.* New York, NY: Routledge.

Courtney, J. A., & Nowakowski-Sims, E. (2019) Technology's impact on the parent-infant attachment relationship: Intervening through FirstPlay® therapy. *International Journal of Play Therapy*. 28(2), 57–68. http://dx.doi.org/10.1037/pla0000090

Courtney, J. A., & Siu, A. F. Y. (2018). Practitioner experiences of touch in working with children in play therapy. *International Journal of Play Therapy*, 27(2), 92–102. http://dx.doi.org/10.1037/pla0000064

Courtney, J. A., Velasquez, M., & Bakai Toth, V. (2017). FirstPlay® infant massage storytelling: Facilitating corrective touch experiences with a teenage mother and her abused infant. In J. A. Courtney & R. D. Nolan (Eds.), *Touch in child counseling and play therapy: An ethical and clinical guide* (pp. 48–62). New York, NY: Routledge.

Derapelian, D. (2019a). *Core attachment therapy: Secure attachment for the adopted child* (3rd Rev.). USA: Author.

Derapelian, D. (2019b). *Letting us into your heart.* USA: Author.

Gil, E. (2017). *Posttraumatic play in children.* New York, NY: The Guilford Press.

Goodyear-Brown, P. (2019). *Trauma and play therapy.* New York, NY: Routledge.

Jimenez-Pride, C. (2019). *Amir's brave adventure.* Augusta, GA: Play Therapy with Carmen Publishing.

Levy, T. M., & Orlans, M. (2014). *Attachment, trauma, and healing: Understanding and treating attachment disorder in children, families and adults* (2nd ed.). Philadelphia, PA: Jessica Kingsley Publishers.

Mills, J. C., & Crowley, R. J. (2014). *Therapeutic metaphors for children and the child within* (2nd ed.). New York, NY: Routledge.

Ogden, P., & Fisher, J. (2015). *Sensorimotor psychotherapy: Interventions for trauma and attachment.* New York, NY: W. W. Norton & Company.

Palmer, D., & Barlow, J. (2017). Teaching positive touch: A child-to-child massage model for the classroom. In J. A. Courtney & R. D. Nolan (Eds.), *Touch in Child Counseling and Play Therapy: An Ethical and Clinical Guide* (pp. 189–201). New York, NY: Routledge.

Van Hollander, T. (2018). *Casey's greatness wings: Teaching mindfulness, connection & courage to children.* Bryn Mawr, PA: Main Line Therapy.

Index

AAI *see* Adult Attachment Interview (AAI)
AAP *see* American Academy of Pediatrics (AAP)
ABI *see* Acquired Brain Injury (ABI)
ACEs *see* Adverse Childhood Experiences (ACEs)
acetylcholine 31
Acquired Brain Injury (ABI) 59
Adelson, E. 187
ADHD *see* Attention Deficit/ Hyperactivity Disorder (ADHD)
Adult Attachment Interview (AAI) 208
Adverse Childhood Experiences (ACEs) 3–4, 76, 89, 161, 220; survey 208; synergistic effect of 221
Affective Neuroscience: The Foundations of Human and Animal Emotions (Panksepp) 20
affective touch 26
Affect Regulation and the Origin of the Self: The Neurobiology of Emotional Development (Schore) 10
Ages and Stages Questionnaire, The 172
Ainsworth, M. 235
ALS *see* amyotrophic lateral sclerosis (ALS)
American Academy of Pediatrics (AAP) 102, 218
amyotrophic lateral sclerosis (ALS) 29
animal-assisted therapy 226
animal models: of neonatal decortication 29
animal's body surface: anesthetisation of 27
antagonists: opiate receptor 31
anxiety 231–2
anxiety, postpartum: adverse effects of 236; and attachment 236

aromatherapy 223
assessing pretend play ability 54
Atkinson, L. 236
attachment: approach 161; assessment 71, 73, 76; behaviors, 59, 185, 236, 247; disorganized 72, 160; disrupted 90; enhancing 117; figures, 130, 131, 138, 139; games, 131; healthy 12, 130, 136, 162; history(ies) 208, 223–4; insecure 25, 69, 76, 85, 159, 224, 235; interferences 41, 44; loss 43; mother-infant 233, 236, 241; parent-infant 68, 186, 189, 224; prenatal 230, 233, 240–1; primary 71, 84; postpartum anxiety and 236; postpartum depression and 236; reclaiming 160–1; play 112; primates 30; relationship(s) xxi, 25, 60, 86, 87, 89, 92, 97, 101, 159, 172–4, 178, 182, 186, 248; risk 143, 159–60; secure 24, 32, 43, 45, 68, 69, 83, 85, 97, 159, 165, 204, 219, 235; style(s) 25, 204, 210, 233, 234–5, 241
Attachment Theory 24, 25, 27, 68, 83, 84–5, 103, 159, 161, 199, 246; modern 68, 86; problems with 24–5
attention deficit disorder 28
Attention Deficit/Hyperactivity Disorder (ADHD) 29
attentive listeners 38
auditory system 27
autism 28; spectrum disorder 141, 143
autoradiography 30
Axline, V. 5, 55, 103, 188

Baby Doll Circle Time 129–30; beginning awareness 130–1; connection 131; Courtney (Lead Teacher, Toddler Classroom) 137–9; cuddling and soothing 131; Eli (20 Months Old) 136–7; ending and transition to next 131; group play 132–4; individual play 132; Nate (18 Months Old) 134–6; sample activity 131–2; transition to getting your baby 130

Baby Doll Circle Time: Strengthening Attunement, Attachment and Social Play (Bailey, 2012) 129

Baby Tree Hug© 86, 161, 163

"BACK Stories" 246, 247, 250

Basic Principles of Infant Rights 12

behavioral matching 199

behaviour: empathy-related caring 31; physically active 21; play-solicitation 27

Bell, M. A. 86

Bernard, K. 55, 102

Bernier, A. 86

Bipolar Type Disorder 249

Biringen, Z. 118

birth: preterm, complications from 158; preterm, epidemiology of 158; traumatic 159

Blackmore, E. R. 231

Blewit, P. 234

Booth, P. 84

Bowlby, J. 5, 10, 24, 68, 85, 117, 185, 235

Brahms's Lullaby 39

brain: abilities 28; development 43; injury, traumatic 59; maturation 28; opioids 31; play networks 28–30

Brandon, A. R. 233

Bratton, S. C. 102

Brazelton, T. B. 10

breastfeeding 222

breast milk 222

Broderick, P. C. 234

Brody, V. A. 84, 88, 117

buprenorphine 222

Calkins, S. 86

call out and respond games 42

caregiver 68, 86, 87, 141, 199, 200, 220

caregiver–infant interaction 141; disruptions in 68–9; disturbances in 68

caregiver–infant relationship 97

caring behaviour: empathy-related 31

caring touch: games 40; nurturing 42

Center on the Developing Child 11, 185

Centers for Disease Control and Prevention (CDC) 215

central nervous system (CNS) 37, 215, 220

Certified FirstPlay® Practitioner 85, 161

Certified FirstPlay® Supervisor 90

C-fibres 26

C-fos expression 29

child attachment interactions 68

child counselors 3

Child First® infant mental health professional 75

Child First® program, assessment process 71–5

childhood: domestic violence (DV) in early 189; experiences, impact 25

childhood play 19; adult support during 24

child (infant) maltreatment 4

child mental health 6

Child–Parent Psychotherapy (CPP) 10, 171–2, 186–7; advanced phases of treatment (sessions 14–20) 178; assessment and engagement phase 172–3, 190–1; assessments 208; case study 173–82, 190–4; core phase 192–3; final phase (sessions 20–38) 178–9; initial phase (sessions 1–6) 175, 175–7; intervention and termination phase 173; intervention and treatment phase 174–5; middle phase (sessions 7–13) 177–8; post-assessment intervention phase 191–2; presence and the therapeutic use of self 181–1; termination phase 193; treatment completion 179–80; treatment goals 191; utilization of play in 188

child–parent relationship 117; therapy 102

child protective services (CPS) 4

Children's Healing Institute 157

children's playfulness 24

children's play types 7–9

Child Trends 75–6

cholinergic activity 31

chronic stress 219

clonidine 218

Cognitive Behavioral Therapy (CBT) 237

cognitive effort 54

competent fathers 24

conduct disorder 248

congenital insensitivity to pain 27

constructive play 20

contact: eye 199; physical, innate desire for 24; skin-to-skin 160
Cornett, N. 102
cortisol: impact of 218–19
Côté-Arsenault, D. 234
Courtney, J. A. Dr. 83, 161
CPP see Child–Parent Psychotherapy (CPP)
CPS see child protective services (CPS)
Craig, J. W. 159
Cross, D. Dr. 198
Crowell Assessment, The 172
Crowley, S. 89
crying and laugher 29–30
C-tactile (CT) 27; afferents 18, 26; targeted touch 30

Daugirdaite, V. 232
demyelination: of motor neurons 29
depression 89, 231–2; case study 239–40; postpartum 89
depression, postpartum 89; and attachment 236; symptoms of 89
Des Lauriers, A. 84, 117
Developmental Play Therapy (DPT) 6, 83–4, 161
developmental therapy models 143
Diagnostic and Statistical Manual of Mental Disorder, 5th edition (DSM-5) 247
Diagnostic and Statistical Manual 5th Edition (DSM 5) 75
Diagnostic Classification of Mental Health and Developmental Disorders of Infancy and Early Childhood manual 9
Diamond, M. O. 237
DIR®/Floortime™ model 141, 142, 144; developmental framework 142; following the child's lead 144–5; individual, underlying, neurological processing differences 142–3; relationship and affect 143–4
DIR®/Floortime™ model, autistic toddler treatment 145, 147–50, 152–3; assessment 145–7; first year of treatment 147; parents 150–2
disciplines: professional 3
disenfranchised grief 232
doll play 55
domestic violence (DV): in early childhood 189; instances of 189

Donato, K. 234
dopamine receptors 31
DPT see Developmental Play Therapy (DPT)
drum beat game 39
drumming and action songs games 46
Dubber, S. 236
Dunbar, R. I. 30
DV see domestic violence (DV)
dyadic model 187
dyadic therapy 186

EA see Emotional Availability (EA)
early childhood: domestic violence (DV) in 189; trauma 185–6
early play development 53–4
Edinburg Postnatal Depression Scale (EPDS) 90
Educating Children with Autism report 143
Edwards, J. 12
embodiment 238
emotion: physiology of 44; preborns express 38
Emotional Availability (EA) 118
emotion-based parent–infant attachment communications 68
emotion regulation: internal schemas for 24
empathy-related caring behaviour 31
endogenous opioids 30
endorphins 30
enjoyment: pretend play 55, 61, 63; score 55
enthusiasm: for nurturing 23
environmental risk factors 221
environmental stimuli 221
EPDS see Edinburg Postnatal Depression Scale (EPDS)
Ericksonian-based storytelling (StoryPlay®) 83, 86
Escalona, S. 10
Evans, C. D. H. 232
exploratory play 8
expression: C-fos 29; of play 22
extension program skills: with descriptions 57
eye contact 199
eye–hand coordination skills 45

face-painting games 46
face-to-face interactions 129

Fainman, D. 232
family play observation (FPO) 105
fantasy play 8, 53
father: competent 24; father–toddler physical play 24; sensitive 24
feeding cycles 141
feet games 47
filial play therapy 161, 246
filial therapist 103; clinical considerations for 101
filial therapy 55, 101, 102–3; defined 102; interventions 101; parents' experiences of 102
finger-painting games 46
FirstPlay®: "Baby Tree Hug" story-massage 89; facilitating attunement and attachment in 88; model 161; practitioners 88; therapy 83, 84, 161
FirstPlay® Infant Story-Massage 83, 88, 90, 161
FirstPlay® Kinesthetic Parent–Child Manual 246
FirstPlay® Kinesthetic Storytelling 245, 247; assessment and treatment plan 250–1; case study 248–53; child background and assessment 249; foundations 245–6; guiding principles 247; "Rainbow for Mama Cat, The" 251–3
FirstPlay Multi-Sensory Interview Grid© 251
FirstPlay® sessions 92; implementation 92–6
Foley, Y. C. 102
FPO see family play observation (FPO)
Fraiberg, S. 10, 11, 187

game: call out and respond 42; caring touch 40; drum beat 39; drumming and action songs 46; face-painting 46; feet 47; finger-painting 46; hand-clapping 46; kick 39; knock-'em-down 47; look at me and voice 42; matching rhythm 46; music 39; nurturing touch 40; one, two, three drop it 46; peek-a-boo and where's baby 44; peek-a-boo, hiding, and all-gone 47; serve and return 42; slap the floor 46; slippery hands 47; slippery hands and feet 47; take a bike ride 45; touching and naming 44–5; toy ring 46; tummy time 44; visual 46; vocal 46
games-with-rules play 20

Gastrostomy Tube (GT) 119
Gawlik, S. 236
genesis of attachment: touch role in 25–7
gentle touch learning process 131
Gil, E. 248
Glazer, H. R. 102
Goodyear-Brown, P. 248
Greenspan, S. Dr. 141
grief 232–3; disenfranchised 232; period of 232
Group Filial Therapy 102
Guerney, L. 55, 85, 102

Handbook of Infant Mental Health (Zeanah) 10
hand-clapping games 46
Harlow's monkeys 25
healing power: of touch 223
healthy touch: TBRI 199
Higdon, L 102
homeostatic imbalances 30
Howard, H. 118
Hughes, P. 232
humanistic play therapy skills 105, 106
human laughter systems 29

IDEAL Response 200–1
imaginative play 8, 53
immature nervous systems 4–5
infant(s): development, parent–infant play 187–8; and families, intervention and prevention 5; preborn 38; rights of infants, World Association for Infant Mental Health (WAIMH) 12; societal myth of 3; and trauma 3–5, 43–4; traumatized 44
infant–father bonds 22–3
infant filial therapy, case study 103–5, 108–9; bio-psycho-social difficulties 105; clinical considerations 109; clinical setting 104; demographics 104; family assessment 109; family play observation (FPO) 105–6; naturalistic observation 106; outcomes 107–8; planning with parents 110, 111; sequence of filial therapy 107, 108; thematic tracking 107; therapeutic assessment 105, 106, 107; toy considerations and playful interaction ideas 112; transferring and integrating skills into family life 110, 113

infant massage: touch and 87
infant mental health 3, 6, 76, 198;
    defined 9; landscape 9; organizational
    framework 7; shapers of the field of
    9–11; trauma-informed assessment in
    69–71
infant neurosensory development
    (four to six months) 43
infant neurosensory play interaction
    mismatch 45
infant neurosensory play interventions:
    four to six months 44–5; seven to
    nine months 45–6; ten to twelve
    months 46–7
infant–parent dyad 43
infant–parent play interactions 43
infant–parent psychotherapy 187
infant play therapy: concept of 6; in
    context 6–7; defined 7; models 7
infant–primary caregiver relationship 24
interactions see also caregiver–infant
    interaction: child attachment 68;
    face-to-face 129; parent–child 117,
    119, 143; social 55, 141
internal working model (Bowlby) 5, 24
interpersonal neuroscience 86–7

Jaffe, J. 237
Jefferies, A. 160
Jernberg, A. 84, 117
Jimenez-Pride 245
Johnson, K. V. A. 30

"Kangaroo Care" 160
Kelly-Zion, S. 5
Keverne, E. B. 30
kick game 39
King, L. S. 3
Kinsey, C. B. 233, 236
knock-'em-down game 47

laugher and crying 29–30
"learn to play" 53
Learn to Play program 60–2
lesions 28, 29
Lieberman, A. 10
Life Stressor Checklist Index-Revised 172
light therapy 221
Lillas, C. 143
limbic brain 37
Linden, D. J. 87
listeners: attentive 38

locomotor-active play 8
look at me and voice games 42
low-threshold mechanoreceptors
    (LTMs) 26

MacDonald, K. 22
Magic Rainbow Hug© 246, 250
Main, M. 235
maltreatment: child (infant) 4
Markin, R. D. 234, 236, 238
Marschack Interaction method (MIM):
    assessment 119; observations
    from 121
Marschack, M. 119
mastery play 8
matching rhythm game 46
maternal attachment after perinatal loss
    233–9; attachment styles 235, 236;
    cognitive behavioral therapy 237;
    Embodied storytelling 238;
    establishing continued bonds 238–9;
    exploring the reproductive story 237;
    foundations of attachment and
    bonding 234–5; postpartum anxiety
    and attachment 236; postpartum
    attachment after perinatal loss 236;
    postpartum depression and attachment
    236; prenatal attachment 233; prenatal
    bonding after perinatal loss 233–4;
    treatment 237
McArdle, P. 24
McCormick, J. 5
mental disorders: in infancy 67
mental health, infant 3, 6, 76, 198;
    defined 9; landscape 9; organizational
    framework 7; perinatal 88–90;
    problems 68; shapers of the field of
    9–11; trauma-informed assessment in
    69–71
mental illness: parental 89
mental models 130
methadone 222
Michigan Association for Infant Mental
    Health (MIAIMH) 11
midbrain activities 225
MIM see Marschack Interaction method
    (MIM)
mindfulness 87–8; strategies, TBRI
    199–200
modern attachment theory
    68, 86
Moe, V. 86

mother: joyful mother and baby playing 8; mother–child relationship 224; mother–infant attachment 233; mother–offspring play 23
motor neurons: demyelination of 29
motor vehicle accident 59–60
Müller, M. 236
multi-cultural and diversity considerations 12–13
music: game 39; and movement 43; therapy 160, 222

naloxone-treated animals 31
NAS see Neonatal Abstinence Syndrome (NAS)
National Center for Infants 11
National Institute of Child Health and Human Development (NICHD) 158
National Registry for Evidence-based Programs and Practices 118
National Research Council of the National Academy of Sciences 143
natural opioids 215
neocortex brain system 37
Neonatal Abstinence Syndrome (NAS) 215–16; attachment 219–20; brainstem activities for neuroenhancement 224–5; complex trauma and impact of cortisol 218–19; diagnostic testing 217–18; healing power of touch 223; hospital stay and treatment 217; long range impact of 220–1; non-pharmacological treatments 221–3; obtaining parental attachment histories 223–4; parents/caregivers of 219; pharmacologic treatments for 218; signs and symptoms 216–17; symptoms in preschoolers and school-age children 224–5; treatment options for 224–6
Neonatal Behavioral Assessment Scale 10
neonatal decortication: animal models of 29
Neonatal Intensive Care Unit (NICU) 157; emotional impact of 159–60; music therapy 160
neonatal neurosensory play interventions 40
neonatal play interventions 39–40
nervous system: central nervous system (CNS) 37, 215, 220; immature 4–5; parasympathetic 37; sensory 38
neural play circuits 28

neural systems 28, 31–2
neuroanatomy of play 28–30
neuro-bio-psycho-social approach 103
neurochemical system 31, 43
neurochemistry of play 30–1
neurological system 37
neuroplasticity 185
neuroscience 5; interpersonal 86–7
neurosensory development: newborn 40–1; preborn 37–8
neurosensory play: activities 39; interaction mismatch 45; interactions 47; with newborns 42
neurosensory play interventions: four to six months 44–5; newborn 42–3; seven to nine months 45–6; ten to twelve months 46–7
neurotransmitters 31
newborns: neurosensory development, birth to three months 40–1; neurosensory play interventions 42–3; preemie 159; sleep 41; trauma 41–2
NICHD see National Institute of Child Health and Human Development (NICHD)
NICU see Neonatal Intensive Care Unit (NICU)
nociceptor (pain nerve) 27
Norrmann-Vigil, I. H. 238
nurturing caring touch 42
nurturing touch: games 40; role of 24

object play 8
object substitution 55
O'Brien, W. 12
Ohnogi, A. 5
O'Leary, J. 234
one, two, three drop it games 46
opiate-addicted babies 216
opiate receptor antagonists 31
opioid-addicted infants 219
opioids 31, 215, 216, 226; brain 31; endogenous 30; natural 215
Oppositional Defiant Disorder 248
orbitofrontal cortex: impairment of 219
Ordóñez, E. F. 234
Orobio de Castro, B. 22
Osofsky, J. D. 3, 11, 171
oxytocin 162

pain: congenital insensitivity to 27
Panksepp, J. 19–22, 28, 30, 31

parafascicular thalamic nucleus 29
parallel play 8
parasympathetic nervous system 37
parental mental illness 89
parent–child interaction 117, 119, 143, 248
parent–child relationship 102, 171
parent–child therapeutic approach 102
parent–infant play: in infant
    development 187–8
parent–infant relationship 186, 187–8
parent–infant sessions 186
Parent Learn to Play program 53, 54–5;
    individualized sessions 58; informa-
    tion session 56; small groups 56–7;
    theoretical underpinnings of 55–6
Parent Learn to Play therapeutic
    intervention 58, 63–4; assessment 60;
    attention to the stages of therapy 62;
    clinical considerations 64; family
    background 59; motor vehicle
    accident 59–60; post-assessment 62;
    setting for therapy 60–1; treatment
    plan 61–2
parents: balance stimulation 40; as
    "change agent" 85–6; mimic infant
    sounds 42; play and 22–4; skills 22
Parsons, J. 12
peek-a-boo and where's baby games 44
peek-a-boo, hiding, and all-gone
    games 47
perinatal loss 232; devastating effects of
    231; maternal attachment after 233–9;
    postpartum attachment after 236;
    prenatal bonding after 233–4;
    traumatic 238
perinatal mental health 88–90
perinatal mental health therapist 90–2;
    assessment and beginning of
    treatment 90–1; individual and family
    91; problem and family background
    90; rationale for Introducing
    FirstPlay® into treatment 92; session
    seven 91–2; treatment plan following
    assessment 91
phototherapy 221
physical contact: innate desire for 24
physically active behaviours 21
Piaget, J. 172
Pikler, E. 10
play see also specific types of play:
    actions, sequences 55; adaptive nature
    of 21; behaviours 22, 23; constructive

20; doll 55; early development 53–4;
    expression of 22; forms of 20;
    imaginative 8, 53; interventions,
    newborn neurosensory 42–3; "learn to
    play" 53; locomotor-active 8; mastery
    8; motivation 29; neuroanatomy of
    28–30; neurochemistry of 30–1; object
    8; parallel 8; and parents 22–4;
    perspectives on 23; pretend 53;
    purpose of 21–2; scripts 55; skills and
    descriptors 55; somatosensory control
    of 27–8; symbolic 6, 20; therapists 3, 7
play ability: pretend, assessing 54
playful engagement; TBRI 199
play-instigation signals 27
"play skin": somatosensory stimulation
    of 28
play-solicitation behaviours 27
"play therapist's palette" 248
play therapy 53; room 6; sensory issues
    and interventions in 209–10; themes
    in 107
Play Therapy for Very Young Children
    (Schaefer) 5
"play/tickle skin" 27–8
polyvagal play 220
Porges, S. W. 87, 220
postpartum anxiety: adverse effects of
    236; and attachment 236
postpartum attachment: after perinatal
    loss 236
postpartum depression 89; and attach-
    ment 236; symptoms of 89
post-traumatic stress disorder (PTSD)
    159, 232, 249
PPE-DC see Pretend Play Enjoyment –
    Developmental Checklist (PPE-DC)
preborn: express emotions 38; infants
    38; infant's brain 37; neurosensory
    development 37–8; sensory system of
    39; trauma 38–9
preemie babies 158
pregnancy loss 230, 232; impacts of
    231–3
prenatal bonding: after perinatal loss
    233–4
prenatal neurosensory play
    interventions 40
prenatal play interventions 39–40
pre-symbolic play 8
pretend play 53; ability, assessing 54;
    enjoyment 55, 61, 63

Pretend Play Enjoyment–Developmental Checklist (PPE-DC) 54, 57, 59, 60, 64
preterm birth: complications from 158; epidemiology of 158
prevailing sensory system 30
professional disciplines 3
program skills: with descriptions 57
psychiatric problems 28
psychopathology 129
psychosocial health: and well-being 59
psychosocial well-being 25
PTSD see post-traumatic stress disorder (PTSD)
puberty 28
Purdy, I. B. 159
Purewal, S. 232
Purvis, K. Dr. 198
pyramidal neurons: dendritic morphology of 19

RAD see Reactive Attachment Disorder (RAD)
rainbow babies 230
Rainbow Hug® 88
Reactive Attachment Disorder (RAD) 247–8
receptors: dopamine 31; sensory system 37
Reck, C. 236
relational play 20
rhesus macaque's neural opioid systems 30
risk factors 5; environmental 221
rodents 21; model 29
Roggman, L. A. 24
role play 55
rough-and-tumble play 20–2, 28, 32
rough play 8
Rubin, R. 233
Ryan, V. 102

Salo, S. 118
Schaefer, C. 5
Schizoaffective Disorder 249
Schore, A. N. 10, 68
scopolamine 30–1
Scott, E. 22
secure attachment 24
self-awareness 199–200
self-regulation 24
self-representation: in play 55
senses: in social play 27

sensitive fathers 24
sensorimotor play 20
sensory activities 225
sensory-based trauma 43
sensory nervous system 38
sensory/perceptual qualities 26
sensory stimulation 224–5
sensory stimuli 42
sensory system 27, 40; of preborn 39; prevailing 30; receptors 37
sequences of play actions 55
serve and return games 42
Shapiro, V. 187
Siqveland, T. S. 86
Siu, A. F. Y. 118
skills: and descriptors 55; eye–hand coordination 45; humanistic play therapy 105, 106; parenting 22; program, with descriptions 57; social 24
skin-to-skin contact 160
slap the floor games 46
sleep–wake rhythms 141
slippery hands games 47
social bonds 22
social interaction 55, 141
social isolation 21
social joy 20
socially contagious process 22
social play: senses in 27
social relating: internal schemas for 24
social skills 24
Social Touch Hypothesis 27
Solomon, J. 235
somatic well-being 25
somatosensory control: of play 27–8
somatosensory cortex 19
somatosensory stimulation: of "play skin" 28
sound emotional base 68
Stepka, P. T. 3
Stern 118
Stern, D. N. 10
"Still Face Experiment, The" 10
stimulation: parents balance 40; sensory 224–5; somatosensory 28
stimuli: sensory 42
StoryPlay® 83, 86
stress: chronic 219; toxic 69
stressors 231
symbolic play 6, 20
sympathetic ANS 219

synthetic fentanyl 215
systemic practice 103
systemic thinking 103

take a bike ride game 45
Tavistock Approach 106
TBRI see Trust-Based Relational
Intervention (TBRI)
TEACUP Preemie Program® 157,
161–2; case study 162–5
teddy play 55
thalamic nucleus: parafascicular 29
thalamus: parafascicular region of 29
therapeutic interventions: during
infancy 69
therapeutic powers of play 3
Theraplay 6; in action 119, 120;
development of 117; dimensions 118,
118; effectiveness of 118; goal of 119;
history 117–18; practitioners 119;
research 118; treatment 119
Theraplay with 12-month-old infant:
baby dance 123; checkup activity 122;
follow-up session at 19 months
124–5; nurture 123; observations from
the MIM 121; ongoing sessions
123–4; outcomes 124–5; reason for
referral 119–20; session 121–4, 122;
soap bubbles activity 123; swinging in
a blanket 123; welcome activity 121–2
TIC see trauma-informed care (TIC)
Toddlers 11
Too Scared to Cry (1990) (Terr) 4
touch 18; affective 26; caring 40, 42;
C-tactile (CT)-targeted 30; healing
power of 223; healthy, TBRI 199; and
infant massage 87; and naming games
44–5; nurturing 24, 40; nurturing
caring 42; power of 25–6; role in
genesis of attachment 25–7; social
significance of 32; Social Touch
Hypothesis 27; TBRI 199
Touchpoints 10
toxic stress 69
toy ring games 46
trauma 186; care 47; early childhood
185–6; harmful form of 189; healing
early trauma experiences 5–6; infants
and 3–5, 43–4; newborn 41–2;
preborn 38–9; screening and
assessment 71; sensory-based 43

trauma-informed assessment: choice and
collaboration 70; empowerment 71; in
infant mental health 69–71; safety
and trust 70; strategies 70
trauma-informed care (TIC) 69, 71
trauma-informed lens 76
trauma-informed programming 70
trauma-informed services 70
traumatic birth 159
traumatic brain injury 59
Traumatic Events Screening
Inventory-Parent Report Revised 172
traumatic perinatal loss 238
traumatized infants 44
Tronick, E. 10
Trust-Based Relational Intervention
(TBRI) 198–201; awareness of child
200; behavioral matching 199;
correcting principles 200–1; ecological
strategies 200; empowering principles
200; engagement strategies 199; eye
contact 199; flexible responding and
creative problem solving 200; healthy
touch 199; levels of response 201;
medical/mental health 202;
mindfulness strategies 199–200;
physiological strategies 200; playful
engagement 199; in play therapy
202–10; post-assessment considerations 208–9; proactive strategies 200;
responsive strategies 200–1;
self-awareness 199–200; sensory
issues and interventions in Play
Therapy 209–10; voice 199
tumble play 8
tummy time game 44
Turnball, J. 143
Turton, P. 232

UN Convention on the Rights of the
Child 12, 18
United States Centers for Disease
Control and Prevention 4
University of Massachusetts Boston 11
UN Rights of the Child Articles 12
U.S. child protection authorities
(2014) 67
US National Association for the
Education of Young Children 22
U.S. Substance abuse and Mental Health
Services Administration 118

vagal nerve 37
van den Akker, O. 232
VanFleet, R. 102
Van Horn, P. 10
visual and vocal games 46
visual games 46
vocal games 46
voice, TBRI 199
Vygotsky, L. 56

WAIMH *see* World Association for
    Infant Mental Health (WAIMH)
well-being: psychosocial health and 59

White, J. A. F. 102
Wieder, S. Dr. 141
Winnicott, D. W. 9, 53, 171
*Working Model of the Child
    Interview* 172
World Association for Infant Mental
    Health (WAIMH) 11; rights of
    infants 12

young children's play: types 7–9

Zeanah, C. H. 6, 10
Zeanah, P. D. 6, 9, 159